C!
PROGRAMMING
PRINCIPLES and PRA

C!
PROGRAMMING PRINCIPLES and PRACTICES

M. Tim Grady
Austin Peay State University

McGRAW-HILL BOOK COMPANY
New York St. Louis San Francisco Auckland Bogotá Caracas
Colorado Springs Hamburg London Lisbon Madrid Mexico Milan
Montreal New Delhi Oklahoma City Panama Paris
San Juan São Paulo Singapore Sydney Tokyo Toronto

C ! Programming principles and practices
INTERNATIONAL EDITION

1 2 3 4 5 6 7 8 9 0 SEP PMP 8 9 4 3 2 1 0 9

When ordering this title use ISBM 0-07-100516-1

Printed in Singapore

CONTENTS IN BRIEF

CONTENTS IN DETAIL

Preface

This work is a comprehensive text on the **C** language; a dynamic, changing language that enjoys a broad base of popularity. As the title suggests, this book describes standard programming practices, such as the accepted way of organizing a file and the variable naming conventions. The book also discusses **C** programming principles such as the efficient use of variable data types within functions

C! *Programming Principles and Practices* is a textbook written with pedagogy in mind. It is replete with example program segments and sample programs. It teaches **C**, but it also teaches about programming and algorithms. There are study questions, usage exercises, puzzles, thought-provoking questions, programming problems (most of which result in a useful tool or program for your personal **C** library), and projects. The usage exercises provide a vehicle for class discussion. The programming problems vary in difficulty: some are small extensions of the text material; some are quite difficult. The projects require a substantial investment of time.

This text is also a reference book. It contains extensive appendices, such as a complete alphabetical list of functions, their parameters, values returned, and error codes. A table of program listings and a detailed table of contents make it easy for the programmer to find information and relevant examples to assist with programming or syntax problems. The table of program listings also serves as a supplemental index, providing another means to locate important topics.

The **C** language is undergoing a standardization process which, as of this writing, has not been completed. A discussion of the proposed standards weaves its way through the text; differences and additions are discussed in the context of each chapter.

Intended Audience and Coverage

This text covers a wide range of topics. At one end of the spectrum it teaches elementary concepts such as data types and control structures. At the other end the book contains explanations of data structure topics and hardware related programming.

Topic coverage is sequential. A programmer new to **C** can begin on page 1 and proceed in order. An experienced programmer might skim Chapters 3 and 4 (variables; input and output), study the examples in Chapters 4 and 5 (control of program flow and loops), and begin careful study in Chapter 6 (functions). A programmer with some **C** experience might start in Chapter 8 or 9 (arrays, pointers and the preprocessor). These two chapters unlock some of **C**'s secrets, provide examples of accepted practices and discuss principles of **C** programming. The advanced topics in Chapters 10 through 13 give the experienced programmer a collection of software tools, some useful examples, and a review of basic topics. All users of this text can benefit from the reference materials found in the Appendices.

Principles of Organization

C is a language with no real starting point. Chapter 1 circles the language as if poising for attack by presenting a general overview via a sample program. This chapter illustrates several **C** concepts, such as variable declarations, and presents key words such as **main()** and **#include** but it does so at the intuitive level.

Chapters 2 through 9 provide the formal presentation of **C**. Programming topics begin, predictably, with simple data types and input and output. The middle chapters discuss concepts usually found in a programming text, such as control of program flow, loops, functions, arrays and files. The topics are developed carefully with attention to pedagogy. Standard practices, as suggested by the title, are the basis for many examples throughout the text. The emphasis pedagogy is brought forth by discussions on programming principles. The text uses interesting problems such as the ladder problem in Chapter 5 to illustrate important principles of **C** programming. The fun nature of such examples makes the text more interesting than a reference book and provides a teacher with good class discussion material.

Chapters 9, 10, 12, and 13 present topics sometimes found in advanced texts, such as data structures, random access files, sorting and searching, stacks, queues, linked lists, and video i/o concepts.

Programs and Program Listings

A helpful feature of this text is the large number of example programs. These provide you with a collection of useful tools such as file copy utilities; command line option parser; input functions, such as the function to read a single integer, not provided with the standard **C** library; data abstraction tools, such as the function to open a pair of files with error checking; and file filter programs, such as the program for converting a Wordstar document file to a straight ASCII file.

The program listings are provided on disk. This saves a teacher valuable time. Although most of the early programs are simple and instructional in nature, the bulk of the programs contain useful code. Many were taken from programmers' tool kits; For example, the Wordstar file filter program was originally written as a utility to clean up a file. The programs can be used and modified to suit your own needs. For example, the file printing program that dumps a file, such as a program source listing, to the printer while adding line numbers, page numbers, and page headers is invoked with a Unix style command line. A teacher might ask the students to modify the program so that it is invoked with an IBM PC style command line and option list.

Hardware and Software Requirements

C is a portable language. compilers are available for most computers. On Unix machines, it is the principal language. Many microcomputer programmers are using **C**and the VAX world makes extensive use of it. For the most part, this text is hardware and compiler–independent. Chapter 11 is the major exception, as it deals exclusively with hardware dependent topics.

The programs in this text, except for a few noted instances, run on any computer with a **C** compiler. Because of this independence, your compiler may include features and functions not discussed in this book. For example, some compilers for the IBM PC include color graphics routines that are not portable to Unix or VAX environments. This text is about principles and practices of programming in **C** not about any one computer or compiler. The examples presented here are portable. You may, of course, add to the programs to suit your own needs.

Supplementary Materials

C! *Programming Principles and Practices* comes with teaching support materials. A diskette containing all source listings is available to adopters of the text. The diskette also contains source code for selected exercises, including alternate solutions to some of the problems. The Instructor's Manual contains chapter tests, teaching tips, a discussion of the material in each Chapter, and solutions to the exercises.

Acknowledgments

I would like to thank many people for their contributions to this book. A special acknowledgment is due **Raleigh Wilson** of Mitchell Publishing . for his calm persistence. I owe an overdue thank you to **Dave Hein** of Texas Instruments for his reviews, program testing, program contibutions and general all-around support of this project. A special thanks to **Patricia Bomba** of Mid-America Remote Sensing Center, Murray, Kentucky for her herculean formatting effort and contributions to the completion of this work. I owe much to the many students and colleagues who worked with early versions of the manuscript and provided exercise solutions and text examples. These include, but are not limited to, **Ken Taylor**, **William Raiser**, **Mark Workman**, **Ken McReynolds**, **Wayne Smith**, **Pat Green**, **Chuck Kise**, **Barry Bugg**, **Kathy Stewart**, **Evan Noynaert**, **Stephanie Compton**, **Ben Brown**, **K.A. Arjani**, **Kathy Cupp**, **Beth Widick**, **Don Fama**,and **Gary Henaline**.

I wish to thank the following manuscript reviewers: **Walter Beck**, *University of Northern Iowa*; **David Green**, *Nashville State Technical Institute*; **Peter Herne**, *California State Technical Institute*; **Tim Holland-Davis**, *Orangeburg-Calhoun Technical College*; **Connie Lightfoot**, *Taylor University*; **Paul Ross**, *Lancaster Pennsylvania.*; **Susan Simons**, *Memphis State University*; and **Ken Taylor**, *Thomas-More College.*

1

Concepts, Style Conventions and Syntax

C is a powerful, flexible language that gained wide acceptance in recent years. C is concise, yet powerful in its scope. It is a high level language that also incorporates features of low level languages. It is becoming the standard for program development on small machines and microcomputers. For example, the operating system OS/2 for the latest generation of IBM microcomputers is written in C.

It is possible to apply C to most every application area. Modularity makes C ideal for projects involving several programmers. C permits nearly every programming technique. C is widely available of most brands and types of computers. It is portable in that it is one of the easiest languages with which to take your program to a different hardware environment.

This chapter introduces the reader to the ways of C. A simple program provides examples of what is involved in this language. Some syntax is not unusual at all. Some syntax is very different from other languages. This chapter also introduces you to style conventions that are unique to C. Later chapters provide detailed explanations of all the aspects of C programming.

Background: Where Did C Come From?

C has its origins in the early 1970's in BCPL, a project shared by AT&T's Bell Labs and others. Dennis Ritchie worked on that project and was influenced by that work as well as Ken Thompson's work on Unix. Ritchie is credited with defining and creating C. Many others also influenced the language's development. C is closely related to the Unix operating System. Most of Unix is now written in C. The basic goal was to create a language for writing operating systems. C was a mechanism for providing a portable assembly language. Hence, C was originally intended for system level programming. Now, C has been implemented on many different types of hardware and the language is used for any number of programming problems.

C is both a low level language and a high level language. It provides the low level features needed by the operating system implementers and compiler writers. It also provides the high level features of control structures and data structures characteristic of a procedural language. C is flexible as a low level language must be. C provides the tools for a structured program as a high level language must. C is modular, thus allowing large scale projects to be implemented in C. C is portable.

It is available on a wide range of computers from small MS-DOS personal computers to large scale IBM main frames.

C and Unix have grown together. Unix is available in many forms: System V, XENIX , and others. It is available on mini- computers, micros, and special purpose machines such as the RTPC. **C** itself, has enjoyed a defacto standard (Kernighan & Ritchie, The **C** Programming Language, Prentice-Hall, 1978, frequently referred to as K&R) and is undergoing an American National Standards Institute (ANSI) standardization process. AT&T's Unix version System V seems to be the standard for 1986–87. Much of Unix is written in **C**. Hence, Unix utilities, can be utilized in or by a programmer's own projects. The key word here is growth. **C** is growing in popularity and use. Small systems programmers are turning to **C** because of its portability, flexibility, and modularity. **C** code is typically fast and compact when compared to other languages. The low level features of **C** have allowed programmers to avoid assembly language and speed up the process of porting a program to a different architecture. **C** has become the language of choice for small systems applications programmers.

Style

C is unique in the style in which programs are written. It is a modern style language in that the line format is free and comments may be placed just about anywhere. It uses the `/*      */` style of comments, as do several other languages. The syntax of **C** is case sensitive. That is, it makes a difference whether one uses uppercase or lowercase. In fact, most of **C** uses lowercase. These are conventions, however. Only a few restrictions are imposed by the language itself. **C** makes use of a wide variety of operators. Some of these (e.g. `++`) are unfamiliar to programmers. The result is a source document that may, at first glance, appear to be rather cryptic. With practice, standard usage becomes quite identifiable. For example, the statement

```
while ((ch = getchar()) != '\n')
```

appears so frequently in **C** that programmers recognize it as a standard way of doing something. This chapter introduces the reader to the conventional ways of handling style and syntax.

Internal Documentation

C programs contain many comments. A comment is written

```
/* this is a comment */
```

Comments can appear anywhere except in another comment. Comments cannot be nested. There are a number of compilers that allow nested comments, but when writing programs that may need to be moved to another machine, avoid nesting comments. The value in nesting comments comes from the ability to "comment out" a section of a program for debugging purposes.

Most **C** programs begin with a comment.

```
/* Driver program for modem monitor */
```

and utilize a comment block near the top of a program to explain its function and history. For example

```
/* **********************************/
/*                                   */
/*    Program:      Modem Monitor    */
/*                                   */
/*    Function:     logs all calls to system */
/*                  from off site users */
/*                                   */
/*    Author:       M. Tim Grady     */
/*                                   */
/*    Date:         August, 1989     */
/*                                   */
/*    Located in file:  term.c       */
/*                                   */
/* **********************************/
```

This type of use of comments in a title block is important to good programming practice. The only line in this title block that may be unusual is the "located in file" line. **C** programs are often written in modules containing several functions each. Each module is stored in a file and that file name is used at compile and link time.

All **C** programs must contain a line consisting of **main()** which is the identifier for the main part of the program. Pascal programmers can equate it to the main block of program code surrounded by BEGIN ... END. appearing as the end of a Pascal program. The **main()** command must be in all lower case letters. Look at this sample program;

```
/* Sample C program */
  main()
{
printf("This is a test.");
}
```

This example contains a comment line, the **main()** command, an opening brace {, a strange looking statement that causes a message to be printed, and a closing brace }. The **printf** statement is an output command that prints the string. The statement ends in a semicolon. The **main()** command does not end in a semicolon. This statement must always be present and be in lower case letters. The opening and closing braces surround the actual statements in the program. A section of code surrounded by braces is called a block of code.

Statements in C

C uses the semicolon as a statement terminator. Some languages use the semicolon as a statement separator. Here, it is a terminator. All statements end in a semicolon. The line containing **main()** is not a statement but an identifying line. It signifies where the main program starts.

Examples of **C** statements follow:

```
diff = x - y;
y = 2 * x + 3 * y;
```

Functions: In our earlier example **main()** is a function name. All subroutines in **C** are considered functions as is function. The functions are usually grouped together, but may legally appear in any order. It is standard practice to place the **main()** function first, but it is not a requirement.

It is helpful to examine a sample program to begin to see how a **C** program is organized.

Listing 1.1

Sample Program

```
ref no.
/* 0 */    /* Sample C Program */
/* 1 */    #include <stdio.h>
/* 2 */    #define OFFSET 2
/* 3 */    main()
/* 4 */    {
               /* declaration section */
/* 5 */        int m,n;
/* 6 */
               /* read single values from keyboard */
/* 7 */        printf("Type a digit.");
/* 8 */        n = getchar();
/* 9 */        m = n + OFFSET;
/* 10 */       putchar('G');  /* print single value */
               /* print values with labels */
/* 11 */       printf("The first number is %2d",n);
/* 12 */       printf("\n and the other one is %d\n",m);
/* 13 */   }
```

note: the line numbers are comments only and are not required.

End of Listing

line 0 is a comment only

line 1 says to make the standard i/o library enhancements available.

line 2 defines a symbolic constant called OFFSET

line 3 is the **main()** function identifier

line 4 is the declaration section. It comes immediately after the open brace. m and n are declared as integers.

line 6 is a blank line. It is used to separate sections of a program to make it more readable. **C** ignores blank lines.

line 8 is a command to read a single value from the standard input device. The **getchar()** function reads a single character. If a 6 is typed, n is not six, but the ASCII value of 6, 54.

line 9 is an arithmetic assignment statement to add an integer and a constant.

line 10 prints a character on the standard output device.

lines 11 and 12 will print only one line of text and values. The special characters %2d,%d,and \n are formatting and control characters to be discussed in more detail in Chapter 4. The \n character is a linefeed and will cause the output pointer to be moved to the beginning of the nextline.

line 13 contains the closing brace which signifies the end of a block. In this case it is also the end of the program.

C Conventions

As mentioned earlier, **C** uses mostly lowercase letters. Line 1a of the example has the word OFFSET in all caps. It is common practice in **C** to use uppercase letters for constants. One can easily tell which name is a variable and avoid such errors as trying to assign a new value to a constant. Notice that lines 1 and 2 do not end in a semicolon. They are not statements. They begin with a # sign and are also outside of the **main()** function. The **C** compiler deals with them in a special way. Some of the comments in the example appear on separate lines and some are on the same line as the statement. It is a matter of taste and readability. Some programmers place comments on separate lines when a new section of code is to follow and also try to place short comments on the same line within a section of code. Extra lines and blanks (whitespace) are ignored.

A number of special symbols are used in **C**. These are partly responsible for the "strange" appearance of **C** programs. We have already mentioned the opening and closing braces, {}. In addition to their use with blocks, they are used in ways we will see later. When used to denote blocks of code, braces serve a purpose similar to the BEGIN-END keywords in Pascal. The `&` symbol and the backslash \ are also used. These special characters will be explained in detail as the text goes on. Some are used in punctuation while others have more than one purpose depending on the context.

The `%` sign is another symbol and one that is used in a couple of different ways (as an unary operator and as a binary operator) as is the asterisk * symbol. Parenthesis are used in functions and to surround argument lists. Square brackets `[]` are used in arrays. The semicolon is a statement terminator. As you learn **C**, the use of special symbols is salient to development of good **C** programming skills.

The Character Set is usually ASCII, but **C** has been implemented on IBM 370 type machines and hence, might use the EBCDIC character set. This book employes the ASCII character set.

Compiling a C Program

C has found its widest use on Unix based systems. Many microcomputer programmers also work in **C**. The two implementations are similar, but not exactly the same.

Under Unix, once the source file has been created with an editor and saved as the disk file `sample.c` it can be compiled. **C** programs usually end with the extension `.c` although some compilers allow one to specify other extensions. The command to compile the program is

```
cc sample.c
```

This command instructs the compiler to translate the source document into an executable object file. The object file is called `a.out` and serves as the temporary name of your program. To run the program type

```
a.out
```

and it will begin execution.

The name `a.out` may not suit you. Also, it will be replaced next time you compile another **C** program. It is a good temporary name during the testing and debugging phase of the project. At some point you will need to rename the executable version. One way is to "move" it to another name by typing

```
mv a.out newname
```

where `newname` is the name you wish to give to the working version of the program. To run this version simply type

```
newname
```

Another method of renaming the version is to specify the name of the object file on the command line. For example:

```
cc -o newname sample.c
```

This command specifies that the `o` option is to be used. It means that you wish to specify the name of the object file and finally the name of the file to be compiled. There are other compiler options or switches with which you will become familiar with as the text proceeds.

C provides the option of compiling more than one file and combining the overall result into one working object file. There are many advantages to this that will be discussed for the first time in Chapter 7. For now the method of compiling several files is

```
cc filename1.c, filename2.c, ..., lastfile.c
```

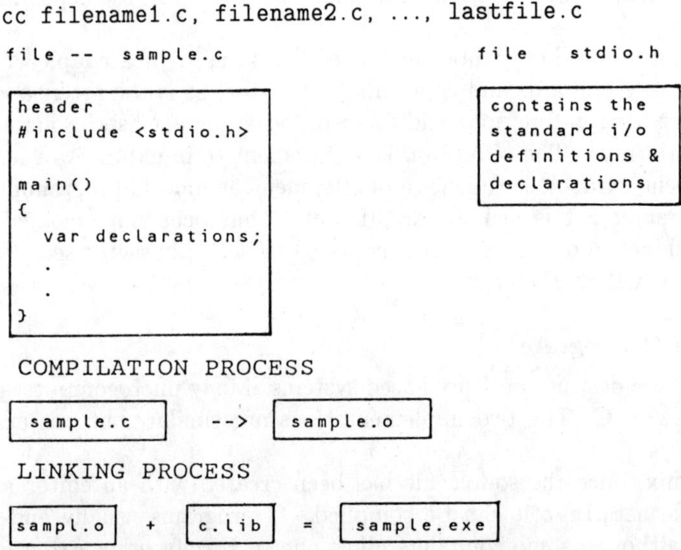

Figure 1.1: *Compiling a* **C** *program*

On most microcomputers, compilers work in one of two ways. The first is to compile the source file (e.g., `sample.c`) into a relocatable object module called `sample.o` or `sample.obj`. The second step is to use a linker that places the object files and necessary libraries into an executable file with the extension into an assembly language program. The system's assembler is then used to create the relocatable object module. The compilers vary so greatly in their specifics, that a programmer must become familiar with each individually.

Overview of a C Program

This section is not intended to provide a detailed picture of how a **C** program is developed, but to provide a sneak preview. The rest of the text provide the details.

C programs are composed of functions. We have already seen a simple use of the **main()** function. The parentheses () signify the use of a function. A **C** file consists of a collection of related functions. Each file may be compiled separately. The functions in a file can be related by type or related by purpose. The compiler works on a file. The linker combines the compiled files into a working program.

The **C** preprocessor is a program that accepts commands and information from the header section of the program and after processing that information, makes available the necessary information to the compiler. For example, the preprocessor may specify that a collection of definitions (which are themselves in a file), be included in the compiler process. A **C** program before it is compiled may look like the one in Figure 1.2.

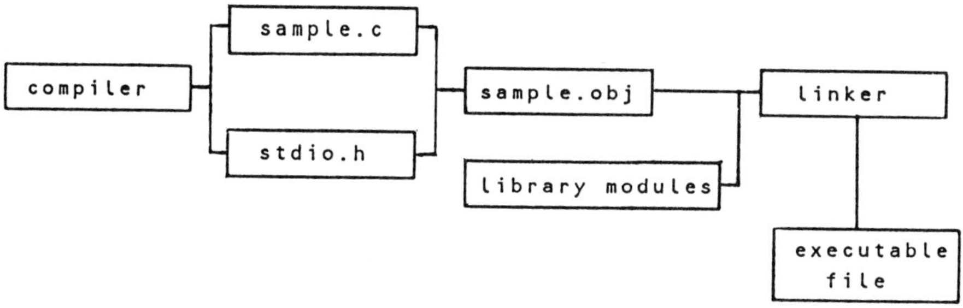

Figure 1.2: *A* **C** *program before and after compilation*

The file called `sample.c` contains the **main()** function and as such has to be considered the main file. It includes the preprocessor directives to include the standard i/o header. The compiler would compile the source file (`sample.c`) and follow the preprocessor directives to include certain header files. (**note**: header files are not programs, but definitions such as constant declarations). The linker would combine the resulting object module(s) into an executable program. These ideas will become more clear as you progress through the text.

Summary

A **C** program is a collection of functions. All **C** programs must have a function called **main()** which is the first to be executed. Comments are enclosed in `/*    */` symbols. The language is case sensitive. That is, uppercase and lowercase symbols are different. Variables are usually specified using lowercase letters while symbolic constants are represented with uppercase letters. **C** is a free form language so that blanks, tabs, newlines, and other whitespace are used for appearance, but do not influence the flow of control or program operation. All statements terminate with a semicolon.

The **C** preprocessor handles any definitions and file inclusion commands that appear prior to the first function definition. The most common preprocessor command is **#include** <stdio.h>. This is a file inclusion command that makes many of the system dependent i/o operations transparent to the user. Some i/o operations are defined in this file.

The typical sequence of events in writing a **C** program is to develop the source code in a file; compile the program, (possibly assemble the resulting asm file) and finally, linking the compiled files with other files such as the standard library. The resulting file is executable. Under Unix, the compile and link operations are handled by a simple `cc` command. With microcomputers, the compile operation is usually several steps.

EXERCISES

1. Write a short explanation of each or these terms:
   a. comment
   b. **main()**
   c. **C** program source file
   d. free format
   e. block of code
2. In **C** the semicolon is a statement terminator. True or false?
3. Which of the following are valid variable names?
   a. `sam` d. `9%d4`
   b. `SAM` e. `howdoyoudothis`
   c. `hi_cost`
4. Why is **C** considered both a high level language and a low level language?
5. What factors contribute to **C**'s cryptic appearance?
6. Write a **C** program that prints your name.

2

Input and Output: an Introduction

The **C** language is relatively small. The language itself excludes many of the features and keywords one usually finds in other languages. **C** makes use of a collection of libraries (i.e., functions and commands available to the **C** programmer, but not part of the language). Library members are only included in the program if actually needed. The result is fast, compact code. The standard input/ output library is embellished via a header file called `stdio.h`. The header is not actually the input output library, but a set of declarations and definitions that add features to the i/o library. Almost every **C** program begins with the statement

```
#include <stdio.h>
```

or

```
#include "stdio.h"
```

Both statements instruct the compiler to include the header file for compilation. The program may then make use of the enhancements to the standard input and output functions of **C**. The use of angle (i.e.,<>) brackets or double quotation marks means to either look for the header file in the root directory or to begin looking for the header file in the user's directory. On microcomputers, there is usually no difference in the meaning of the two styles. In this text, the angle brackets will be used for file inclusion. The reader may need to use double quotation marks with some compilers.

Input and output can be very complicated. This chapter deals only with introductory concepts. As one's experience with **C** grows, the more sophisticated i/o techniques will be learned.

Introduction to Data Types

You need to know a little about simple data types in **C** before studying input and output. Chapter 3 provides a more detailed discussion of this important topic. Only the very basics are presented at this time.

There are four elementary data types: (1) integers, (2) characters, (3) single precision floating point, and (4) **double** precision floating-point numbers. They are called **int**, **char**, **float**, and **double** respectively. Strings can be very complicated. For now, a string is a literal enclosed in double quotation marks.

Variables are declared in the following manner.

```
int n;
char ch;
float x;
double y;
```

In practice you whould declare them in the inverse order with the data type that occupies the most memory declared first. **Int** and **char** are both considered to be integral data types. **Float** and **double** are both floating-point objects.

Single Character Input: getchar()

C allows you to treat characters as integers and to accept a character as a value for a variable of type **int**. The **getchar**() function returns the single character from the standard input device (usually the keyboard). Hence, the code to read a keyboard character is

```
int ch;
ch = getchar();
```

Notice that there are no arguments to the **getchar** function. [**note**: the use of the term function is, at this time, used intuitively. A function is a subprogram or procedure that returns a value. Functions are discussed in detail in Chapter 6.] The **getchar** function returns the ASCII value of the key that was pressed. Hence, **if** an uppercase A was pressed, ch would have the value 65. (Some systems provide exceptions to this rule.) The ASCII value is an integer and the appropriate data type is **int**. These surely seems like a contradiction. We declare ch to be of type **char** and then understand that it is an integer. Actually, this proves to be of great benefit, not hindrance.

It is legal to declare ch to be type **char** but there are other reasons for declaring ch to be an **int**. The most often cited is that the **getchar**() function has to be able to return any valid character. One of these is the normal default of −1 for an end-of-file marker. If the **char** data type is used, the value of -1 may never be returned. Any checks for the occurrence of end-of-file would always fail.

Listing 2.1

Read One Character

```
#include <stdio.h >
main()
{
  int ch;
  ch = getchar();
}
```

End of Listing

Single Character Output: putchar()

The inverse of **getchar**() is **putchar**(ch) in which ch is the character to be output. The function **putchar**(x) displays the value of x on the standard output device. This function is more subtle than **getchar**(). The data object may be of several different types and sometimes involves indirection (to be discussed later.) For now, consider the simple program echo_one.

Listing 2.2

Echo One Character

```
#include <stdio.h>
main()
{
  int ch;
  putchar('?');      /* display a prompt */
  ch = getchar();    /* read a keyboard char */
  putchar(ch);       /* echo to screen */
}
```

End of Listing

The program is not very useful, but illustrates the simplest form of **putchar**(). The **printf**() function is much more useful in printing output with labels.

Note :**putchar**() and **getchar**() both require the inclusion of stdio.h.

Printing One Line: printf()

Most simple output requires labels. These are readily available via the **printf**() function. It allows you to display the contents of several variables in formatted output and to provide text labels. The simplest label is a prompt such as:

```
printf("Type any keyboard character.");
```

This prompt causes the message enclosed inside quotation marks to be printed. The quotation marks are delimiters and not printed. This message would leave the printer carriage or cursor at the end of the line. If one wishes to have the carriage returned to the beginning of the next line, a "newline" character must be placed inside the quotation marks. For example

```
printf("Type any keyboard character.\n");
```

The \n character looks like two characters but is, in fact, a single character. It is the newline character and forces the execution of a typewriterlike carriage return whenever it is found. The \n character is one of several "escape" or ESC characters used in **C**. The others appear in Table 2.1.

Table 2.1
Special C Character Constants

constant	ASCII name	hex value	meaning
`\n`	LF	0x0a	newline
`\t`	HT	0x09	tab
`\v`	VT	0x0b	vert tab
`\b`	BS	0x08	backspace
`\r`	CR	0x0d	return
`\f`	FF	0x0c	formfeed
`\\`		0x5c	backslash
`\"`		0x22	quotation marks
`\'`		0x27	apostrophe
`\0`	NUL	0x00	null

These escape characters can be used to provide formatting instructions to a line of printed output. The `\n` character is used quite often. On some systems, newline (or linefeed) behaves like a carriage return and a linefeed.

The simple echo program in listing 2.2 can be modified to provide a prompt and labels.

Listing 2.3

Labels and Special Print Characters

```
#include <stdio.h>
main()
{
  int ch;
  printf("Type any character.");  /* prompt */
  ch = getchar();                 /* read a keyboard char */
  printf("\n Your character is"); /* label + CRs */
  putchar(ch);                    /* echo to screen */
  printf("\n");                   /* return carriage */
}
```

End of Listing

The prompt line prints the message and leaves the cursor at the end of the message. The second **printf** statement returns the carriage before printing the new message. The **putchar** statement displays the character and the last **printf** statement returns the carriage. Actually, this is a good example to illustrate the consequences of using `\n` but is a poor example of programming style. In practice, the newline character, `\n`, is generally included in the conversion string in the **printf** command. For example, the **printf** function can also print the character.

```
printf("\nYour character is %c \n",ch);
```

This line contains a new wrinkle. The variable `ch` appears outside the quotation marks and is separated from the quotation marks by a comma. The %c character appears inside the quotes. The %c is called a conversion specifier. In this case it means to print a character. Other specifiers are discussed in the next section. The statement causes a newline to be executed that places the cursor at the beginning of the next line, a message is displayed and then the character is printed with a space inbetween. Finally another newline is executed. The %c also indicates where in the line of output the character `ch` should be printed.

Conversion Strings and Specifiers

The **printf** function is quite flexible. It allows variable number of arguments, labels, and sophisticated formatting of output. The general form of the **printf** function is:

```
printf("conversion string", variable list);
```

The conversion string includes all the text labels, escape characters, and conversion specifiers required for the desired output. The variable list includes all of the variables to be printed in the order they are to be printed. There must be a conversion specifier for each variable. The conversion specifiers are listed in Table 2.2.

Table 2.2
printf Conversion Specifiers

Specifier	meaning
%c	print a character
%d	print an integer
%e	print **float** value in exponential form
%f	print **float** value
%g	print using %e or %f whichever is smaller
%o	print octal value (unsigned)
%s	print a string
%x	print hexadecimal integer (unsigned)
%u	print an unsigned integer

note: To print a percent sign, specify %%

Additional modifiers may be added to specify field width, left justification, and **long** values. The modifiers in the form `% - n . p l` are:

- `-` left justify the argument
- `n` field width [optional]
- `.` separates field width from precision
- `p` number of places after decimal (precision)
- `l` indicates **long** type

For example

```
        if n is 256
           x is 129.546
       and ch is the letter R
```

the following specifiers would have these effects

printing n	%3d	prints as	256
printing n	%d	prints as	256
printing n	%10d	prints as	256
printing n	%f	prints as	256.000
printing n	%-8d	prints as	256 with 5 trailing blanks
printing n	%o	prints as	400
printing n	%x	prints as	100
printing n	%u	prints as	256
printing ch	%c	prints as	R
printing ch	%d	prints as	82
printing x	%e	prints as	1.29546 E2
printing x	%7.2f	prints as	129.55
printing x	%.3f	prints as	129.546

The field width is placed after the % symbol and before the type specifier. The **long** modifier is placed in front of the type specifier. In the example

```
printf("The average is %5.2f.\n",avg);
```

the value of `average` would appear in a field 5 characters wide with two places after the decimal. The period after the `f` is a sentence punctuation mark and not part of the field specifier.

When the argument is longer than the field width in the specifier, the printed value is truncated (and in some cases, rounded). For example, if `n` is 128764 and the specifier is %3d, only 128 is printed. The %7.2f in the example prints 129.546 as a rounded value of 129.55.

Type conversions can be interesting. Consider the following code:

```
char ch = '0';
int n = 50;
printf("%c %d %c %d %o %x \n", ch,ch,n,n,ch,n);
```

The code produces this output:

```
0 48 2 50 60 32
```

because

the character 0 prints as itself
zero has the ASCII value 48
the 50th character is 2
n prints as its value which is 50
the octal representation of 48 (base 10) is 60
the hex representation of 50 (base 10) is 32

These implicit type conversions can be useful but be very careful in their use. Differences in how some machines store data can result in unexpected results. Full and complete testing of a program is always appropriate. Some types simply do not convert.

Sending Output to the Printer

Unix users are familiar with the redirection commands of < and >. With these, the output of a program can be sent or "redirected" to a disk file or another system device such as the printer. The limitation of this practice is that a programmer may want part of the output to go to the standard output device (usually the screen) and other parts of the output to go to the printer. Microcomputer users frequently have total use of their system and would like to send output to the printer whenever they wish.

This example is an easy, albeit non-standard, way to send output to the line printer. Assuming that you are using MS-DOS or one of its derivatives the line printer is called `PRN` by the system. A VAX or Unix machine will create a disk file called `PRN` that can be sent to the printer with an operating system command. Formatted output can be created to the printer with this command.

```
PRINT(PRN," conversion string ", var list);
```

The words `PRINT` and `PRN` are specially defined and not part of standard **C**. A single character can be sent to the line printer with the command:

```
PUTCHAR( character,PRN);
```

Both of these special printer commands have `PRN` added within the parentheses. Otherwise the conversion control string and variable list are the same as for a **printf** or **putchar** command. There are a few other requirements as illustrated in Listing 2.4.

This program includes four special lines. The first two lines are mandatory. The `stdio.h` file must be included. The `print.h` file must also be included. It is not a standard file supplied with your system, but will be shown here. The two lines

```
open_prn();
```

and

```
clos_prn();
```

are required. The first makes a logical connection to the printer and once it has been established, you may use the printer all you like. The second terminates the logical relationship between your program and the printer. A programmer can open the printer; write something to it; close the printer; and later do the same thing again. Or, alternatively, one can open the printer in **main**, write to the printer whenever you wish, and close the printer at the end of the program.

Listing 2.4

Printer Output on IBM PC style Machine

```
#include <stdio.h>
#include "print.h"     /* created by the user */
main()
{
int n = 5;
char ch = 'G';
float x = 12.375;

/* print to the screen */
putchar(ch); putchar('\n');
printf("This is a normal output line.\n");

/* print to the lineprinter */
open_prn();               /* makes printer available */
PRINT(PRN,"Sample line of text.\n");
                          /* print a string on printer */
PUTCHAR(ch,PRN); PUTCHAR('\n',PRN);
                          /* print a character */
                          /* and a newline */

/* print to screen again */
printf("x is %f and n is %d\n",x,n);

/* print to printer again */
PRINT(PRN,"x is %f and n is %d\n",x,n);

/* break the connection between printer and program */
clos_prn();

}
```

End of Listing

The print.h file is a little bit of magic. The commands are all dealt with in later chapters. For now, you must simply create the file with an editor and save it in the directory that will contain the program source file or some other directory in which the compiler looks for requested files. Listing 2.5 shows how this is done.

Listing 2.5

print.h Header File

```
/* print.h */
/*          header file to be included with */
/*          programs that write to the lineprinter */
#define PRINT fprintf
#define PUTCHAR fputc
FILE *PRN;
static char stdlst[] = "prn";
open_prn()
{  if((PRN = fopen(stdlst,"w")) != NULL) ;
   else printf("Error --- printer not ready.\n");
}
clos_prn()
{  fclose(PRN); }
```

End of Listing

The print.h file is not a standard **C** library member. It is created to make the printer available without all of the confusion and work it usually takes to do that. A programmer can simply include **print.h** at the top of the program and then use the two printer commands, PRINT and PUTCHAR, as often as needed. These two keywords are written in all caps to remind us that they are not standard output commands. The PRINT command is much like the **printf** command with the exception of **PRN** which is inserted in front of the conversion control string. The **PUTCHAR** command is much like the **putchar** command with the exception that **PRN** is added inside the parentheses right after the variable to be printed. Finally, before using **PRINT** and **PUTCHAR** one must issue a **open_prn();** command and after completion of the printer output, one must use the **clos_prn();** command.

Once the file **print.h** has been created, it can be used by any program. This method of writing to the printer is simple, and not very flexible, yet it can be very useful. You will learn more about using the printer when files are discussed.

The following program prints a header at the top of a page.

Listing 2.6

Print header to line printer

```
#include <stdio.h>
#include "print.h"

main()
{  open_prn();     /* connect to lineprinter */
   PRINT(PRN,"\f\n\n\n\n \n\n");
   PRINT(PRN,"\t\t\t\t\t TITLE OF THIS DOCUMENT \n");

   PRINT(PRN,"\n\n\n\t The first line one tab in\n");
   PRINT(PRN,"%s\n","The second line with no tab\n");

   clos_prn();  /* disconnect from line printer */
}
```

End of Listing

Formatted Input: scanf()

The **scanf** function is the input counterpart of **printf**. The general form is

`scanf("conversion string",variable list);`

The conversion string contains the conversion specifiers and modifiers in much the same way that **printf** does. All the conversion specifiers are used except the %g. The %e and %f specifiers are identical. Another specifier, %h is available for reading **short** integers. Table 2.3 summarizes the **scanf** conversion specifiers:

Table 2.3
scanf Conversion Specifiers

Specifier	meaning
%c	reads a character
%d	reads an integer
%e	reads a **float** value
%f	reads a **float** value
%h	reads a **short** integer
%o	reads an octal value (**unsigned**)
%s	reads a string
%x	reads a hexadecimal integer (**unsigned**)
%u	reads an **unsigned** integer

The modifier `l` (el) may prefix a specifier to make it **long**.

The variable list is really a list of variable addresses. The & operator is the address operator. To read an integer into the variable m, you might use

```
scanf("%d",&n);
```

This convention of using the address operator is not the mirror image of using the **printf** function. The input function **scanf**() has some other potential problems which will be pointed out as other topics are discussed.

An example of a use of the **scanf**() function is:

```
scanf("%7.f,%3d",&average,&count);
```

The preceding results in a **float** value of field width 7 being read into `average` and an integer of field width 3 being read into the variable `count`.

The next example illustrates reading a string.

```
char name[20];
scanf("%20s",name);
```

Because strings are accessed via pointers and as such follow a different set of rules, there will be further discussion of this concept in Chapters 6,8, and 10. At first, it seems strange that integers, characters, and real numbers must be prefaced by the address operator, &, while strings are not. The mystery will go away as we learn more about strings.

Listing 2.7 illustrates the use of simple input and output.

Listing 2.7

Sample I/O Program

```
        #include <stdio.h>
        main()
        {
          int n;
          char first_nm[20],last_nm[20];
          float cost;
/* 1 */   printf ("Please Type in your first and last names.");
/* 2 */   scanf("%s %s",first_nm,last_nm);
/* 3 */   putchar('\n');
/* 4 */   printf("How many items are there?");
/* 5 */   scanf("%d",&n);
/* 6 */   putchar('\n');
/* 7 */   printf("What is the unit cost?");
/* 8 */   scanf("%f",&cost);
/* 9 */   printf("\n\nOk %s %s, \n There are %d items at $%4.2f\n",
                  first_nm,last_nm,n,cost);
        }
```

End of Listing

Suppose the name typed in is `Sammy White` and the number of items is 12 with a product code of Q and a cost of 4.29, the session would look like this:

Please type in your first and last names.*Sammy White*
How many items are there?*12*

What is the unit cost?*4.29*

Ok, Sammy White,
There are 12 items at $4.29.

Check this example closely. The dollar sign (line 9) and sentence punctuation (lines 4,7 and 9) are provided in the conversion string. The **putchar** (lines 3 and 6) is used to print a character constant (newline). Some lines (7 and 9) have a newline character at the beginning. Some of the prompts do not have a newline character at the end of the conversion string (lines 1, 4 and 7). **C** permits us to perform input and output in a variety of ways. We will come across other ways to do the same things illustrated by Listing 2.6 as we progress.

Skipping a data field: There are often instances where one wishes to read only some of the data items that appear on one line of input. The asterisk (*) is used to indicate that a field is to be ignored or skipped. Suppose you wish to read the data line

```
12 14.2 18 Smith 20
```

but wish to ignore the string "Smith". A correct input command would be

```
scanf("%2d %f %d %*s %d", &m,&x,&n,&i);
```

Even though the input line contains five data items, only four are actually read. The * or suppression specifier may be used with any conversion specifier.

White space in scanf(): White space that appears in the conversion string is ignored. Thus %d %c and %d %c are equivalent. Whitespace in the variable list is mostly ignored. However, if the conversion specifier %c is used, then a space is considered a valid character. Consider this code segment:

```
int n,m;
char ch;

scanf("%2d %c %d",&n,&ch,&m);
printf("%d %d %d \n",n,ch,m);
```

with this input:

```
14  5
```

The character ch has the space (decimal 32 (or 20h)) as its value.

> **Note:** Some compilers will wait for non-white space character and this example would not work.

Matching Characters: The **scanf** function allows the use of "matching" characters that must be present in the input stream to act as delimiters. Consider the use of a colon to separate two data items. The input stream is

```
12A:34
```

and the accompanying **scanf** is

```
scanf("%2d %s:%2d",&m,letter,&d);
```

The colon appears in the conversion string and must appear in the input stream. It acts as a field delimiter. One of the most common uses is to strip out commas from a data line. The data line may have been used by another program that required them.

Consider this data stream:

```
10, 15, 17
```

and the input command

```
scanf("%d, %d, %d",&m,&n,&o);
```

The commas in the conversion string match the commas in the input stream and hence will serve as delimiters.

> **Note:** Not all compilers support the matching characters features. Some only support the matching commas for use with data files that delimit fields with commas.

Error traps: The **scanf** function places the data into the appropriate memory locations. It also returns a value as do most functions. The value returned by **scanf** is the number of arguments it has passed. If a conversion string asks for three fields, the variable list includes three addresses, and the data stream passes three values, and the value of **scanf** is 3. If an error occurs, **scanf** returns −1. Thus, a programmer can trap errors by checking on the value of **scanf** after it has been used. Error checking will be taken up repeatedly in later chapters. For now the following pseudocode illustrates how the value of **scanf** can be used.

```
/* use scanf to read m and n */
numarg ← scanf("%d %d",&m,&n);
if numarg is not equal to 2 then
    display error message
    and exit program
otherwise continue processing.
```

Similarly, **printf** returns a −1 if an error occurs and a zero if no error occurs. **Getchar** and **putchar** return a −1 if an error occurs. Conditional statements and input loops will be taken up in Chapters 4 and 5 along with further discussion of error checking.

ANSI Standard and Conversion Specifiers

The proposed ANSI standard includes a new specifier of %i. It permits the reading of an integer in any of the three forms— decimal, octal, or hexadecimal. In **printf**, %i is a synonym for %d.

Reading a line of Data: gets()

Although not a part of the K&R standard, the two functions **gets**() and **puts**() are usually implemented by **C** compilers. If your compiler does not provide these two functions, you may do so yourself by adding them to one of your libraries. The code for these functions appears in Chapter 6. The **gets**() function allows one to read an entire string while the **puts** function allows one to print a string. **Gets**() is short for "get string" and **puts**() is short for "put string".

The **gets**() function accepts an entire line of input from the standard input device (assumed to be the keyboard), appends a null character '\0' and hands it to the program. The string is of any length. The newline character '\n' (created by pressing the return or enter key) signals the end of the string. Consider this line of data typed from the keyboard

```
This is a sample string input.<return>
```

and the code to read it:

```
char inbuff[81];     /* assume 80 col screen */
printf("What is the input?\n");
gets(inbuff);  /* read a line */
printf("You typed %s\n",inbuff);  /* echo */
```

The result is

What is the input?
This is a sample string input.
You typed This is a sample string input.

The newline character is required in the last line because the inbuff string looks like this:

```
This is a sample string input\0
```

The return key (newline or \n)is not part of the string. The function **gets**() appends the null character.

Errors and Returned Values: The **gets**() function can be used as in the above example. One simply writes

```
gets(name);
```

and the string name takes on the value of the typed string. However, it also returns a value. The value is a pointer (a subject of significant discussion in later chapters) and as such may be used for error checking. The sample code

```
char *result,inbuff[81];     /* result is a pointer to */
                             /* a memory address */
result = gets(inbuff);
```

causes the typed line to be placed in the string called `inbuff`. It also places the value of the pointer to the first character in the string in `result`. If `result` is printed it will be displayed just like the string. For example if the preceding code is modified to include

```
printf("%s\n and result is %s\n",inbuff,result);
```

The printed reults is

```
This is a sample string input.
and result is This is ...input.
```

If an error occurs in the input (such as an end of file) the **gets**() returns 0 (or **NULL**). The returned value can be used in an error check.

Many programmers use **gets**() and **getchar**() as their principal method of accepting input from the keyboard. Used in this way the functions facilitate error checking and help prevent program crashes.

Printing a String: puts()

The **puts**() function is the complement of **gets**(). It displays a string on the standard output device. The form of **puts**() can be any of several equivalent forms:

```
char name[] ;
gets(name);
puts("This is a sample string.");
puts(name);
puts(&name);
```

The **main** restriction is using **puts**() is that it must be on a newline each time it is used. must go on a newline. The **puts**() function always executes a newline character when it is used.

NOTE: The proposed ANSI standard includes both **gets**() and **puts**().

Buffered Input

Most systems buffer the input from the standard input device. That is, the keyboard characters are stored in a buffer until the return key is pressed. Then the program processes the buffer as the data stream. This makes a difference in how your program treats the input data stream. Look at this program segment:

```
int ch;
ch = getchar();
putchar(ch);
```

If you have buffered input and type

```
Hello <return>
```

```
     Hello <return>     /* what is typed */
```

the result is `H` `/* the first char */`

But if your input is not buffered you get

```
HHello <return>
```

because the `H` is handed to your program as soon as it is typed.

In many instances programmers prefer buffered input because the backspace key or delete key to back up and fix typing errors. Other programs (such as command processors and editors, need to process each character as it is typed. In most implementations of **C**, **getchar**() is used with buffered input and **getch**() is used with unbuffered. Kernighan and Ritchie (K&R, pp 79) provide an unbuffered character input **getch**().

The function **getch**() can be used to provide direct input when needed. It is simply the unbuffered version of **getchar**(). It also has a complementary function **ungetch**() that puts a character back onto the data stream. It allows one to get a character, examine it and if it meets certain conditions, to place it back so it can be read by the next input command. We will encounter this function again as we see examples of command handlers and character streams handed to editors and video display routines.

The general form of getch() is

```
result = getch();
```

The general form of **ungetch**() is

```
ungetch(result);
```

Some implementations of **C** include these two functions. The proposed ANSI standard does not.

Redirection

Unix and MS-DOS systems allow redirection of input and output. When redirection is specified, a program either sends its output to a file other than **stdout** or receives its input from a file other than **stdin**. For example, a program that had received all input from the keyboard, may instead receive input from a file called `test.dat`. The command that specifies the redirection is:

```
program <test.dat
```

This command uses a left angle bracket (less than sign) to indicate the direction of the data flow. On Unix systems, one may use spaces on either side of the bracket. On MS-DOS systems, there must be a space to the left of the bracket but may NOT have a space between the bracket and the name of the file. The redirection is handled by the operating system. The program knows nothing about it.

A program may send its output to a file.

```
program >results.dat
```

Any output created by the program is sent to the file `results.dat` instead of the stdout device. The file may then be listed out on the printer by using lp results.dat on a Unix machine or type results.dat on an MS-DOS machine.

Usually there are several ways to dump the contents of a file to the screen or printer. The choice is operating system dependent and is left to the user. This technique of redirecting output to a file is ok for programs that you know are working correctly. The problem is that all output goes to the file including error messages and prompts that were to be displayed on the screen.

Redirection may be nested. A program may get input from one file and send output to another.

```
program <test.dat >results.dat
```

The order of the two redirections is not important. They could have been written

```
program >results.dat <test.dat
```

The program will get input from test.dat and send the output to `results.dat`.

There are rules to remember. The first word on the command line must be a program name. The files to or from which i/o is redirected must be text files; not programs. When one wants the output of one program to serve as the input for another program, a pipe must be used.

Pipes

A pipe is similar to redirection except that the output is received from or sent to a program, not a file. Suppose a program to register a student in a course needs to send the output to another program that merges the new student into a database.

```
register | update
```

The pipe is signified by the symbol |. A pipe is an appropriate name because the output of one program can be sent to the next as input just as a physical pipe can feed a flow of materials from one place (operation) to another.

Redirection and pipes are useful tools. Yet, they have limitations. Suppose you have written an interactive program that produces a formatted table after a series of questions are answered on the terminal. You want the table to be sent to a file (or the printer) but redirection sends all output, including the questions the user must answer to the file. You write this code to achieve your goal.

```
program >table.dat
```

The file table.dat will contain the desired table. It will also contain the questions that were supposed to appear on the screen. We need more control over the input and output. We have seen one way to get around the pipe vs printer limitation (see Listing 2.6) and future examples will expand i/o concepts.

Summary

Input and output are not part of the **C** language itself. All i/o functions are in the standard library. Enhancements to the library as well as system dependent features are implemented via the stdio.h file. Most programs contain the statement

```
#include <stdio.h>
```

which causes the definitions and macros contained in this file to be available to the rest of the program.

Single character input is provided via the **getchar**() function. Single character output is done via the **putchar**(c) function. Formatted input is done through **scanf**() while **printf**() provides for formatted output. Both **scanf**() and **printf**() make use of conversion strings.

A conversion string is the first argument inside the function parentheses. It contains the labels and format specifiers to indicate the placement and field width of variables to be printed. The specifiers provide for characters, strings, integers, reals, hex values, octal values, and a variety of modifiers.

Most implementations of **C** provide puts and gets functions that print and read entire strings. Some also provide **getch**() and **ungetch**() that are ways of reading a character from a non buffered input while **ungetch** allows you to place a value back onto the input stream.

EXERCISES

UNDERSTANDINGS

1. What is meant by a conversion specifier?
2. Are the **scanf**() and **printf**() conversion specifiers exactly the same? Why or why not?
3. What is the difference between redirection and pipes?
4. What is the purpose of special symbols for newline, tab, and so on?

USAGE

5. What will the values of each variable be after the input command:

   data Tom 34678.2 AA4231

   scanf("%s %3d %f %c %*c %1d %x", name,&m,&x,&ch,&i,&j)
6. What output does each of these produce?
   a. **putchar**('a');
   b. **putchar**('007')
   c. **putchar**('\n')
   d. **putchar**('\t')
   e. n = 32; **putchar**(n);
   f. **putchar**('\"');
7. For the different values of n, what is the output?

   printf("%d %c %o %x",n,n,n,n);

   a. n = 67
   b. n = 20
   c. n = 128
   d. n = 255
   e. n = 100
8. What is wrong with each of these?
   a. **scanf**("%d",i);
   b. **#include** stdio.h
   c. **putchar**('/n')
9. How do you print a percent sign in the conversion string?

APPLICATIONS

10. Write a **scanf** command that reads a name, an integer, skips a name, and reads a floating point number.
11. Write a program to read and print your name, address, phone number, age, and social security number.

12. Find the error in each of these:
    a. **scanf("%d",n)**
    b. **putchar("%f",x)**
    c. **getchar(x);**
    d. **printf("%c","Tom")**
13. Write a program that accepts names typed at the keyboard and prints them on the printer. (PC only)
14. Write a program that accepts a sentence one word at a time. Each word is entered and then the return key is pressed. The program assembles the words into a sentence and prints it as a sentence on one line.
15. Write a program to read and echo the following passage.

Down by the **C** shore,
  by the **C**,
    by the **C**,
      by the beautiful **C**.

16. Write a program to produce this output:

123.45	$45.89	21.3
89.4	$54.21	9.8
329.65	$16.16	25.76

3

Variables, Data Types and Operators

All programming languages provide mechanisms for specifying variables and dealing with data. C provides ways of dealing with simple data types, such as integers, character data, and floating point numbers. In addition, it also provides many unusual methods of manipulating data that make it a particularly powerful language.

This chapter contains concepts and information that must be mastered by the **C** programmer. The flexibility and uniqueness of **C** are derived from the many operators and data types.

The power and flexibility of **C** can also be nemeses for students of the language. A programmer must learn equivalent methods of doing a task with **C**. The student of **C** must learn about many special cases and how to balance efficiency and readability.

Identifiers

Identifiers are names of things such as variables and functions. An identifier in C is made up of letters, numerals, and the underscore. An identifier may start with any of the three types of elements. The underscore is used to make the identifier easy to read and to mark functions or library members.

An identifier must be fewer that nine characters long. Many compilers allow much longer identifiers. Although the proposed ANSI standard permits longer identifiers, it is good practice to restrict identifiers to eight or less characters. You can port your program to a different machine without difficulty. It is not a hard and fast rule that an identifier must begin with a letter, but it is good practice to pretend that it is a rule. An identifier may begin with an underscore (e.g., `_salt`), but there is a good reason for not doing so. Some compilers and assemblers add an underscore to the beginning of library or function names. To eliminate a conflict between identifiers used by the programmer and symbols created by the assembler. Because the assembler might add an underscore of its own restrict names of external variables (such as filename), external functions, and library members to seven or less characters.

Identifiers can contain both uppercase and lowercase letters. **C** is case sensitive, that is, lowercase letters are not converted to uppercase letters when used in identifiers. The three names: `Boat`, `boat`, and `BOAT` have different meanings. It has become accepted practice to use only lowercase letters for variables, uppercase letters for symbolic constants, and the underscore for readability.

legal identifiers	illegal identifiers	legal but poor
far_out	Toms's	_do_it
TIME	whichamacallit	_help
age	%dollar	Cost
time	do-it	2by4
exponent		

Good programming practice dictates that the variable and constant names enhance understanding and readability. For example, a program in which a variable involving temperature was called `temp` would be easier to read than a program in which the variable was `t1`. A constant that specifies a character's color might be `CH_COLOR`. Note that the constant is named with all caps and that the underscore is used to make the identifier readable.

Keywords

The list of keywords (albeit, reserved words) is short and presented in Table 3.1. All keywords such as if and **for** are lowercase. A variable may contain a reserved word as part of its name (for example, `former`), but the identifier may not be exactly the same. The identifier FOR is legal, but is considered an example of poor programming practice.

Table 3.1
Keywords

int	**extern**	**else**
char	**register**	**for**
float	**typedef**	**do**
double	**static**	**while**
struct	**goto**	**switch**
union	**return**	**case**
long	**sizeof**	**default**
short	**break**	**auto**
unsigned	**continue**	**if**
asm	**fortran**	

In addition, the proposed ANSI standard includes these keywords: **void**, **enum**, **const**, **signed**, and **volatile**. Avoid using these five words unless the program will be used with the proposed standard.

Simple Data Types

Data types are things and rules about their use. More specifically, a data type consists of a set of values together with the operations that may be performed on those values. **C** includes simple or fundamental data types as well as derived types, which are defined or constructed from the simple types. This section deals only with the simple data types.

Objects are the name of an area of storage or memory. Objects are declared to be of a certain type and follow the storage allocation rules for that data type. The four simple data types are:

1. **int** which means that the object is an integer. It also means that the amount of storage reserved is system dependent. In most cases an integer is one word in length, but on some microcomputers it is 1 byte long. A programmer should become familiar with the restrictions imposed by the hardware.
2. **char** which means that the object is a character. **C** is not simplistic in its treatment of characters. Some programmers avoid using type **char** as much as possible, because objects of type **char** are treated as if they were of type **int**. Type **char** objects are stored as 1 byte. If **unsigned**, the values may be in the range 0 to 255. Treated as signed values they may be in the range −127 to 127.
3. **float** which means that the object is a real number. Again, the way the object is stored is system dependent. The typical method allots 32 bits with seven significant digits. This places the range of floating-point values between 10E−38 and 10E+38. Some microcomputer systems use a 16 bit floating-point type.
4. **double** which means that the object is a **double** precision **float** type. In most cases this is a 64 bit value.

Most floating point arithmetic in **C** is performed in **double** precision. Objects of type **float** must be converted to **double** before the operation can take place.

Modifiers

C allows you to modify the object type by affixing a modifier. The modifiers are **short**, **long**, and **unsigned**.

short int which means that the integer is no bigger than an **int**. The size is highly machine dependent. On some machines **short int** is half as big as **int**, but on others, they are the same size.

long int which means that the integer may be twice as **long** as an **int** (but not necessarily). Again, the memory allocated for a **long int** is machine dependent. Most of the time it is two words.

long float which means that the object is twice as **long** as a **float** object. In effect, it creates a **double** type and is therefore redundant.

unsigned int which means that it is stored without a sign. All **unsigned** integers are positive. An **unsigned int** can be 1 bit larger than an ordinary **int**. Use an **unsigned int** to manipulate the bits in a byte, create bit masks, and manipulate register values.

A typical storage allocation is summarized in Table 3.2.

Table 3.2
Data Type Storage Allocation

data type	bytes	bits
char	1	8
int	2	16
short	2	16
long	4	32
unsigned	2	16
float	4	32
double	8	64

note: On larger machines, **int** may be 32 bits.

The modifiers **short**, **long**, and **unsigned** refer to integers. Although, **long float** is legal, it is not needed. **C** treats **short int** and **short** as synonyms. Similarly **long int** is a synonym for **long** and **unsigned int** a synonym for **unsigned**.

Objects and Memory Addresses

Objects may be referred to by their memory address. In some cases this is required. Consider the variable named `cost`. It may be declared as

```
int cost;
```

In most instances the variable `cost` is stored in 2 or sometimes 4 bytes. The individual computer system determines exactly how the variable's value is stored and how the address is specified. **C** provides a convenient way to refer to the address of the object: the unary operator `&`. For example, the address of `cost` is `&cost`. The programmer uses the address in an expression such as

```
place = &cost;
```

or as seen in Chapter 2, with the formatted input function **scanf**.

```
scanf("%d",&cost);
```

lvalues and rvalues

C manuals frequently refer to lvalue and occassionally to rvalue which are **short** names for left value and right value. Both are identifiers, but not all identifiers are eligible to be lvalues. The identifier must be a variable. Figure 3.1 shows the relationship of an identifer, lvalue, and rvalue.

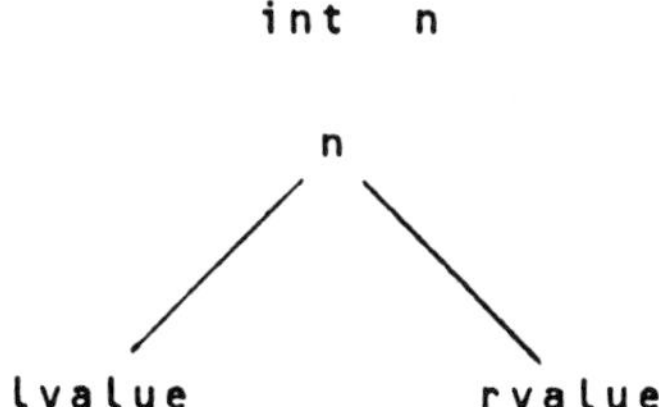

Figure 3.1: *Relationship of lvalue to identifier*

The lvalue is the address of the data object. The rvalue is the value stored in that address. The identifier is the symbol associated with the lvalue.

sizeof and Storage Allocation

C provides an unusual operator that returns the number of bytes used to store an object. For example, if k is of type **int**, the expression

```
sizeof(k)
```

has as its value the number of bytes used to store k. **Sizeof** may appear in **C** expressions and statements.

```
x = s / sizeof(k);   /*  x is an int */
```

In the preceding statement, s will be divided by the number of bytes needed to store the variable k.

Most programmers use **sizeof** in the manner shown, that is, **sizeof**(expression), but the parentheses are not always necessary because **sizeof** is an operator, not a function. The two statements

```
a = sizeof(cost);
a = sizeof cost;
```

are equivalent. A few compilers insist on the parentheses so, always use them to guarantee portability. When **sizeof** is used to determine the storage requirements of a data object, the parentheses are required. For example:

```
n = sizeof(int);
```

As a **C** programmer, you should write a utility program to display the storage requirements of the system. You could use the program each time the system environment changed.

An ANSI modifer: signed

The type **unsigned** is extended to **long**, **short**, and **char**, so users of the proposed ANSI standard should always declare an **unsigned** type with both terms (for example, **unsigned char** ch;). The ANSI standard includes the modifier signed so that the programmer does not have to depend on the compiler to treat an **int** or **char** as signed or **unsigned**. Use of the modifier signed places control with the programmer and not with the compiler. Most compilers treat a **char** within the range 0 to 255.

Some treat **char** as within the range −127 to 127. The signed modifier may be added to **char** to eliminate the guesswork and make programs portable. The ANSI standard will make more use of **float** arithmetic and **float** arguments.

Variables

A variable is an object that may take on values of the specified type. Variables must be declared by specifying the data type and the identifier. For example:

```
char     ch;
short    i,j;
int      x;
long     y,z,temp;
unsignedlimit;
float    average, length;
double   percent, acid, humidity;
```

An object is declared when its properties have been specified. An object is defined when it has been declared and the object has been initialized. When a debugging tool says a variable is undefined and the programmer has declared its type, it means that the variable has never been initialized with a value.

C provides a default type declaration. If the variable is not declared, it is assumed to be of type **int**. Good practice requires that you always declare all variables.

Initializing Variables: A variable is considered undefined until it has a value. There are two ways to initialize a variable. The first is to do so when the object is declared:

```
int last = 32767;
char capc = 'C';
float pi = 3.141593
double expo = 1.0e6;
```

This method works only for certain variables, depending on their storage class. (You will learn about the topic of storage classes a later.)

The second way to initialize a variable is to use an assignment statement:

```
main()
  {
    int last;
    char capc;
    float pi;
    double expo;
      last = 32767;
      capc = 'C';
      pi = 3.141593;
      expo = 1.0e6;
  }
```

C provides for values that depend upon storage class. For now, suffice it to say that variables should be initialized; you will read about special cases in context as you continue.

Constants

Constants are data objects that have fixed values throughout the life of the program. In **C** a constant is called a symbolic constant and the identifier is usually written in uppercase letters. For example, TRUE might be a symbollic constant with the value 1. Any expression using TRUE would use 1 as the value.

The term **#define** is used to define symbolic constants. The statements that follow show the form of the term. Notice that there is no semicolon after a define statement.

```
#define TRUE 1     /* TRUE HAS THE VALUE 1  */
#define EOF -1     /* end of file is -1  */
```

The **#define** statements are placed outside the body of the **main**() function.

```
#include  <stdio.h>

#define   TRUE  1
#define   FALSE 0

main()
{

}
```

Integer constants: Integer constants are simply the value of the integer. A constant may be made **long** by affixing an L to the end of the number. For example, 1989L is a **long** integer. Some examples of integer constants are

```
#define YES    1
#define NO     0
#define LIMIT  100000L
```

One of the important features of **C** is the ability to define one constant in terms of a previously defined constant. For example:

```
#define TOP      1000
#define PEN_ULT  TOP-1
```

When a change is made to TOP no change need be made to PEN_ULT This helps a programmer maintain the program and enhances readability.

Integer constants can be in any one of three numeration systems: decimal, octal, and hexadecimal. Decimal constants may consist of the digits 0–9 and an optional sign. Decimal constants may not begin with a 0.

Octal constants are made up of the digits 0–7 and are prefixed by the numeral 0. The 0 (zero) indicates that the number that follows is expressed in octal form; The indicator 0 is not part of the number. Examples of octal constants follow.

07 is octal 7, the ASCII character that represents the bell.
015 is octal 15 or decimal 13, which is the ASCII value for the carriage return.
012 is octal 12 or decimal 10, which is the ASCII value of the line feed.
0 is octal 0, or decimal 0.

Hex or **hexadecimal constants** are made up of the digits 0–9 plus the letters a–f and or A–F. Hex constants are prefixed by the symbols 0x. For example:

0xd	is hex d	or decimal 13.
0x20	is hex 20	or decimal 32,which is the ASCII character 'space'.
0x100	is hex 100,	or decimal 256.

Symbolic constants are frequently defined in terms of octal or hex values such as shown in the following examples.

```
#define  CR         0x0d   /*  hex d = dec 13  */
#define  LINE_FEED  012    /*  octal 12 = dec 10  */
#define  NULL       0      /*  octal zero  */
#define  SPACE      0x20   /*  hex 20 = dec 32  */
#define  BELL       07     /*  octal 7 = dec 7  */
```

An **int** constant can be either an **int** or a **long int** (For example, 465L) and may or may not have a sign. Problems arise when constants are used as memory addresses. Addresses do not have signs and should not be used in variables that contain an address. To avoid the possibility of creating a signed address, add the suffix u or U to an integer constant to force the object to be **unsigned**. For example:

```
#define  OFF_SET  12u
#define  PORT     16U
#define  KEY_BUF  1028u
```

By using these suffixes, you can be sure that **int** constants used as memory addresses are acceptable.

Character Constants: Most **C** implementations use the ASCII character set in which values range from 0 to 127. Many implementations extend the set by another 128 values. These extensions are highly implementation dependent.

A character constant is a literal surrounded by an apostrophe. Usually, the literal is a single character. For example, the first letter of the alphabet is 'a' or 'A'. Character constants can be used in assignment statements or in symbolic constant definitions as this example shows.

```
ch = 'd';
#define PERIOD '.'
```

A character constant is usually a single character. However, **C** contains a few special characters that look like two characters but are treated as one character. These are listed in Table 3.3.

Table 3.3
Special C Character Constants

constant	ASCII name	hex value	meaning
`\n`	LF	0x0a	linefeed
`\t`	HT	0x09	tab
`\v`	VT	0x0b	vertical tab
`\b`	BS	0x08	backspace
`\r`	CR	0x0d	return
`\f`	FF	0x0c	formfeed
`\\`		0x5c	backslash
`\"`		0x22	double quotation marks
`\'`		0x27	single apostrophe
`\0`	NUL	0x00	null

The special constants in Table 3.3 appear often in **C**. They may be used in expressions with single apostrophes around them. For example:

```
ch = '\f';
```

They may appear in symbolic constant definitions:

```
#define CR '\r'
```

A character constant can also be expressed as 1 byte in octal form using the general form

```
'\xxx'
```

where `xxx` is a three digit octal number. For example, the space bar and bell can be defined as

```
#define  SPACE  '\040'
#define  BELL   '\007'
```

String constants: Character constants are surrounded by single apostrophes. String constants are surrounded by double quotation marks. For example:

```
"This is a fine time to say so."
```

is a string constant. The double quotation marks are not part of the string. The compiler places a null character '\0' as the last element in the string. Strings will be discussed again in Chapter 8. For now, most string constants will be used as labels in input and output commands.

A string constant can contain one or more of the special character constants. For example:

```
"The carriage will return after this.\n"
```

This string contains the character \n. In an output statement, a line feed is executed when `\n` is encountered.

String constants can be defined as symbolic constants. For example:

```
#define  TELL_EM  "The jig is up boys."
#define  FIGURE   "Triangle"
```

Be careful not to confuse character constants and string constants that contain only one character. Strings always contain the null character as the last element. Hence, the string "A" consists of two characters. The character constant 'A' is only one character with a unique ASCII value.

ANSI Standard Addition - type const: **C** makes use of symbolic constants in a major way. The addition of a data type const allows a programmer to specify an object within a function that is either not to be modified or is resident in ROM. Consider this program fragment:

```
main()
{
  int i,j;
  const max_num = 1000;
```

This code provides a mechanism for the compiler to check on the validity of the use of a constant in an expression. In addition, it can often improve the size and speed of the object code. The const data type is functionally equivalent to constants in other languages such as Pascal and it aides in the conversion of routines in these languages to **C**. The term `max_num` is in lowercase because the proposed **const** will be a real constant. The current symbolic constant in **C** is a definition, and the value of the constant is substituted in the code for the constant name.

The ANSI standard permits use of **long double**. To specify a **long double** constant, append an L to the end of the number. For example, **const** delta 0.00001L

Storage Classes

C provides a variety of storage classes. A storage class is an explicit definition of the scope and lifetime of an object. In many languages only scope is defined, that is, an identifier or object is known to certain routines and not to others. In , the notion of life time is important. Life of a variable refers to the existence of the definition of the object as a function of flow of control. For example, if a variable exists within a function and does not exist when control is passed from the function to another module, it is said to have a life equal to the time within which control is within the function. If a variable continues to be defined even when control is passed away from the function, its life is longer than the time control is within the function. Storage classes define both scope and life.

This topic will be taken up again in later chapters. For now, remember that storage classes modifiers are added to variable declarations as in the following example.

```
storage_class   data_type   identifier;
```

Storage class is another modifier like **long** or **unsigned**. When omitted, the **default** storage class is **auto**. The classes are introduced in Table 3.4.

When a variable is declared, the storage class modifier is affixed. When no storage class modifier is present, the default is **auto**. For example,

```
auto int i;
register ch char;
extern short int year;
```

Static and external variables are initialized to 0. Automatic (**auto**) variables do not exist until control is passed to the function in which they are known.

Table 3.4
Storage Classes

storage class	meaning
auto	The default storage class which is a local variable known only to the function in which it is declared. Its life is equal to the time control is passed to a function.
static	A local variable like **auto** except that it exists and retains its value after control passes from a function to the calling function.
register	A local variable like **auto** except that the contents are stored in a **register**. Some compilers treat **register** objects exactly like **auto**.
extern	A global variable known to the functions in the file.

Type Conversions

C can perform conversions between different data types, but a programmer should take care with these conversions. For example, some **int**s are out of the range of possible **char**(s), so results are unpredictable. When objects of different types appear in expressions, the following rules apply:

float oper **int** converts **int** to **float** and returns **float**.

char oper **int** treats both as **int** and returns **int**. This is a dangerous procedure.

float oper **double** converts **float** to **double** and returns **double**. An assignment may change the result back to **float**. For example, **float** = **float** oper **double**;

int oper **short** converts **short** to **int**.

int oper **long** converts **int** to **long**.

unsigned oper **int** converts **int** to **unsigned** if no sign is present.

Other conversions occur in assignment statements.

float = **int**;	converts **int** to **float**
int = **float**;	truncates the fractional part of **float**
int = **char**;	assigns the ASCII value of **char** to **int**
char = **int**;	depends on the value of **int**. If it is within the values allowed for **char**, the assignment is as expected. If not, it is compiler independent. Most compilers will assign 0 to **char**, others drop the high order bits.
double = **float**	converts **float** to **double**.
float = **double**	rounds off **double** as needed.

Explicit Conversions: Casting

Objects may be converted explicitly by type casting. The general form is

```
(datatype) expression
```

In the example that follows the variable x is converted from integer to **float**.

```
int x;
...
(float) x;
```

Type casting can be done within the assignment statement

```
int sum;
float avg;
...
avg = (float) sum / avg;
```

This assignment statement causes sum to be converted to type **float** before the division takes place. Casting is frequently used when integers are passed as arguments to mathematical functions. All the math functions expect **double** to be the type of the object passed. If x is an **int** type and you wish to find the **sin** use this expression.

```
answer = sin( (double) x);
```

This expression converts x to **double** and then passes it to the **sin** function. Note, however, that the type of x is not permanently changed. A copy of x is made, converted to **double**, passed to the **sin** function, and then discarded. After the execution of the assignment statement, x is still of type **int**.

Conversion Quicksand

The fact that characters are operated on as **int** can cause problems. For example, the program segment that follows is legal, but may not be useful.

```
char ch;
int x;
{
   x = 24;
   ch = 'a'
   x = x + ch;
}
```

Another problem often develops in connection with an input function called **getchar**. The **getchar** function gets a single character from the standard input device (Usually this is the keyboard) and always returns an integer. To get a character ch from the keyboard you write:

```
{
   int ch;
   ch = getchar();
}
```

The function's name implies that you are expecting a character, but actually, you pick off an integer. Consider what happens when you use the symbolic constant **EOF** to test for the end of a file:

```
#include <stdio.h>
#define EOF -1
main()
{
   int ch;
   ch = getchar();
   /*  test to see if ch is equal to EOF  */
   ...
}
```

The error would be to declare `ch` as a type **char**

```
char ch;
```

The declaration is legal, but the **char** type is usually restricted to positive values; the type can never be equal to -1. So the test for end of file will always fail. To avoid this problem remember this rule: Declare the input variable to be used with **getchar** to be of type **int**.

Also remember the exception to the rule: Characters in a text file should be stored as characters to save space. When an individual character is extracted to be used in an expression, it should be explicitly converted to type **int** using the cast operator.

Data Overflow

The problem of data overflow occurs when the value of a variable is too big or too small for the object to hold. On most systems **double** can hold very large values, but **int** cannot. The consequences of overflow vary from system to system.

In general, an integer overflow just starts over at the smallest possible value. For example if MAXINT contains the value of the biggest possible integer, then

```
int x;
x = MAXINT + 1;
```

results in x having the value of the smallest possible integer. **C** compilers do does not provide an error message in cases of integer overflow. It is the programmer's responsibility to handle such errors in the program code..

Floating-point overflow typically results in the largest possible real value being assigned to the answer. Underflow typically results in the assignment 0.

An ANSI Standard Data Type: enum

The ANSI standard provides a data type called **enum**; many existing compilers support it. The **enum** data type allows you to use identifiers as values in a set or list of possible values. In general the form of a statement that contains **enum** is

```
enum identifier {element1, element2,...,elementn};
```

In this statement the elements are themselves identifiers. in the example that follows, the days of the week are variables of type day.

```
enum day {Sun, Mon, Tue, Weds, Thur, Fri, Sat};
```

Other variables can be declared of type day:

```
day week_day;
day holiday;
```

The values that represent weekdays and holiays can take on any value from the set of possible values of type day. For example:

```
week_day = Mon;
```

is valid and so is

```
holiday = week_day;
```

Remember, however, that the values of a variable of type **enum** can be only one of the elements in the set. For example week_day cannot be assigned the value week_end because it is not in the list.

C assigns an ordinal position (beginning with 0) to each element in the value list. In the list of days, Sun has the value 0, Mon has the value 1, and Sat has the value 6. The programmer can force the ordinal values to be different than the default 0–n by specifying the values in the **enum** statement.

```
enum month {Jan = 1, Feb = 2,/* etc */..,Dec = 12};
```

Or, alternately, the first element can be assigned an integer value and the remainder will assume the next values in the sequence. Thus, the example can be rewritten to

```
enum month {Jan = 1, Feb,Mar,/* etc */..,Dec};
```

The values of an **enum** type may be used in assignment statements and integer arithmetic. For example:

```
month first_mo,last_mo;
int num_mo;
...
first_mo = Feb;
last_mo = July;
num_mo = (int) (last_mo - first_mo);
```

This segment is interesting because `last_mo - first_mo` yields May (not 5) but the cast operator (**int**) converts May to its **int** equivalent and `num_mo` becomes 5.

There is no automatic type conversion between **enum** and other types. For this reason the statement

```
num_mo = last_mo - first_mo;
```

would have been illegal. The cast operator solves the problem. The statement may have also been written as

```
num_mo = (int)last_mo - (int) first_mo;
```

This method is probably less risky than using the cast operator because if there is no existing value to represent the result of the expression, then an error may result. For example, given that

```
last_mo = Mar;
first_mo = Jun;
```

the expression

```
last_mo - first_mo
```

results in an underflow.. If written as

```
num_mo = (int)last_mo - (int) first_mo;
```

the error can be trapped and handled with appropriate program logic and code.

Synonyms for Data Types: typedef

C provides the capability to define synonyms for data types. To define a synonym, use this form:

```
typedef exp1...expn identifier;
```

everything between **typedef** and the identifier can now be referred to by the identifier alone. For example, the statement

```
typedef register short int reg;
```

defines new type `reg` and variables may now be declared of that type. The statement that follows declares the variable address.

```
reg address;
```

Some programmers prefer to use all caps for user-defined types:

```
typedef float REAL;
```

After declaring the type this way, these programmers declare reals as

```
REAL x,y;
```

A major advantage of **typedef** is to enhance portability. Some computers store an **int** as 16 bits; others as 32 bits. Similarly, storage alloted to **long int** and **short int** is not always the same. A programmer can define a new type integer by stating

typedef int integer;

which appears in the version for one computer and the type integer

typedef short int integer;

which appears in the version for the other computer. This allows the user to modify only the **typedef** line to make the program portable with the other computer. All variables used in the program are declared the same way:

```
integer i,j;
```

The use of **typedef** also enhances a program's readability and so makes it easier to maintain. For example, suppose your program includes units of measure, such as ohms, volts, and amps. You could define the type measure or MEASURE as a synonym for **double**:

```
typedef double MEASURE;
...
MEASURE volts,amps, ohms;
```

The use of **typedef** also affects portability, by affecting scope, header files, and conditional compilation. Appendix E discusses these relationships at length.

Operators

One feature in **C** is its large set of operators. This section discusses "standard" operators and a few of the special operators. Additional operators appear in other chapters. The unusually rich set of operators helps give **C** its flexibility and power.

Arithmetic Operators

The common operators (+, -, /, and *) appear in **C** as expected. Missing from this list is an exponent operator. The reason is that a programmer can easily provide it as a function without cluttering up the language. The operators that **C** includes are designed to save time and effort. Four of these operators are binary operators. **C** also provides the unary minus (-) operator (an operator that requires only one expression). The unary minus simply evaluates to the negative value of the expression. The proposed ANSI standard includes the unary + although K& R C does not.

Expressions

An expression is a collection of data objects and operators that can be evaluated to a single value. An object is a constant, variable, or another expression. The most general form is

```
object1 operation object2
```

The result is a new data object. For example:

```
2 + 4  evaluates to 6
3*5    evaluates to 15
64 / 8 evaluates to 8
12 - 3 evaluates to 9
17.2 - 4  evaluates to 13.2
```

Note that the use of whitespace (that is, blanks) has no effect on the evaluation of the expression.

```
3 + ((2 * x)(y) * (2*x/-b) + 13.2
```

The use of parentheses also improves the readability and guarantees the order of evaluation according to precedence rules.

Precedence of Arithmetic Operators

The fundamental operators follow a predictable set of precedence rules as Table 3.5 illustrates.

Table 3.5
Precedence of Simple Arithmetic Operators

operators	associativityhfil		
( )	left	to	righthfil
- "unary"	left	to	righthfil
* /	left	to	righthfil
+ -	left	to	righthfil

Each succeeding line represents a lower level of precedence.
The expression below shows the order of evaluation.

```
- (-3 * (5 + 2*6)) + (3 *4 +4)/2
- (-3 * (5 + 12 )) + (3 *4 +4)/2
- (-3 * 17) + ( 3 *4 + 4)/2
- -51 +(3 *4 + 4)/2
- -51 +(12 + 4)/2
- -51 + 16/2
  51 + 16/2
  51 + 8
  59
```

Notice that the unary operator is evaluated before the division operator. When the level of precedence is the same for two or more operators, the order of evaluation is not guaranteed. It is considered poor programming practice to write code that depends on the order of precedence to ensure results. The programmer should write the statements so that there is no ambiguity; do not leave the results of an evaluation to the individual compiler.

The Assignment Operator

The symbol = is also an operator, and it but is evaluated last. In this statement all the fundamental operators are evaluated before =, the assignment operator.

```
a = 2 + 3 * 4;
```

The result is a = 14.

The assignment operator allows you to create familiar mathematical sentences such as the previous example. Remember, however, that = is in fact an operator and not an equation maker, so it can appear anywhere another operator might. The following are legal **C** statements.

```
a = b = c + 4;
c = 3 * ( d = 12.0/x);
```

Incrementation Operators

The operators that most quickly jump out at the new **C** programmer are the increment and decrement operators, `++` and `--`, respectively. These are substitutes for some very common expressions. For example, the assignment statement

```
i = i + 1;
```

can be replaced by

```
i++;
```

The increment operator `++` causes the operand to be incremented by 1. This is a particularly useful operator, but a programmer may require some practice in their use. You must keep the order of evaluation in mind when using them. In the expression

```
c + i++
```

the value of `i` before the evaluation begins is first added to `c` and then the value of `i` is increased by 1. The two sets of statements

```
b = c + i++;   and   b = c + i;
                     i = i + 1;
```

are equivalent in that both produce the same result.

The `++` operator can also appear in front of the operand.

```
c = ++i
```

The position of `++` before `i` causes the value of `i` to be increased before `i` is assigned to `c`. Again, the two sets of statements

```
b = c + ++i;   smfont and   i = i + 1;
                            b = c + i;
```

produce the same result.

The decrement operator `--` works similarly. The two operators appear higher than the four fundamental types in the order of precedence and on the same level as the unary type. Table 3.5a shows the increment and decrement operators position in the precedence table.

Table 3.5a
Order of Precedence II

Operators
()
++ -- -"unary"
/ *
+ -
=

Keep in mind though, that the operand to which the incrementation operator is affixed is evaluated according to whether the operator is used in prefix or postfix syntax.

Most **C** operators can accept expressions as operands. The increment operator may only use simple variables; not expressions. The code

```
(2*x + y)++
```

is illegal because there is no way to know which of the variables, x or y, to increment.

Be careful with the incrementation operators; they can lead to unexpected results. Various **C** compilers evaluate individual terms of an expression in an indeterminate order. For example, the statements

```
c = 2;
b = 2 * c + 3 - c++;
```

may or may not work out the way you intend. It is possible that the leftmost term on the right side of the assignment will be evaluated first so that b becomes 5 and then c becomes 3. Some compilers however, will evaluate the c++ first. In this case, when the leftmost term (2*c) is evaluated, c is 3; the result is that b becomes 6. To avoid the variability that using different compilers could introduce never place an increment or decrement operator on a variable that appears more than once in an expression.

The incrementation operator is intended for use with integral data types. It works with real values, but with restrictions. For example, the expression

```
float f,g;
...
f = g++;
```

is illegal. However, you could write

```
f = g, g++;
```

and get the intended result. But it would be better practice to write expressions that do not depend on implicit type coercion. The expressions that follow avoid the possibility of type conflict.

```
f = g;
g += 1.0;
```

The operator += provides an alternate way to express incrementing by amounts other than 1. For example:

the statement `smfont is equivalent to`

```
i += 2; i = i + 2;
i -= j; i = i - j;
i *= 3; i = i *3;
j /= i; j = j/i;
```

The incrementation and assignment operators can be combined in interesting ways. For example:

`i += j++;` means to assign `i` the value of `(i + j)` and then increment `j`.

`answer *= 2*i++;` means to multiply `i` times two, and then multiple that times `answer`. Then increment i.

The Modulus Operator

The operator % is the modulus operator. When applied to integers, it returns the remainder of the division. Consider the following:

```
y = 5;
z = x % y;
```

The % specifies that `z` take on the value 2, which is the remainder after 12 is divided by 5. The modulus operator does not work with **float** or **double** operands. Operands must be of type **int** or **char**. There are many uses for the modulus operator. For example:

```
dq#define ONE 60
  int minutes,hours,min_left;
  minutes = 135;
  hours = minutes / ONE; q/*  find hours as int  */
  min_left = minutes % ONEcomment find num mins in
                          /*  fraction of hour  */
```

This program segment divides the number of minutes by 60 to yield the number of hours. Suppose `minutes` is 135 — `hours` would be 2. The variable `hours` is truncated because the right side of the assignment statement has an integer divided by an integer constant. The number of minutes left over after the division by 60 is calculated by the modulus operator in the last line of code. In the example, `min_left` is 15.

C does not include `DIV`, the quotient operator, as do other languages. The next-to-the-last statement in the previous example illustrates why. In that statement the number of minutes (an integer) is divided by 60 (an integer constant), which automatically results in an integer. The fractional part is truncated. Similarly, **C** does not include a round-off function. Rounding may be accomplished by adding 0.5 to the operand before using the truncating result. For example:

```
#define HALF 0.5
float x;
int m;
m = x + HALF;
```

The result of these steps is that m is the nearest whole number to x (with the restriction that x is positive.)

These additional operators are now added to the precedence table as shown on Table 3.5b.

Table 3.5b
Order of Precedence III

Operators
()
++ -- - "unary"
/ * %
+ -
= += -= *= /= %=

For now, make sure that you have a firm grasp of the order of precedence of the operators discussed to this point. Remember that the incrementation operators (unary) are at a higher level than the arithmetic operators (binary) which are higher than the assignment operators.

Type Conversions and the Assignment Statement

The cast operator is frequently used to convert an object from one data type to another. For example, if you wish to use a floating-point variable in an expression involving the modulus operator, you might write:

```
float x;
int m,n;
...
m = (int)x % n;
```

This code successfully presents the modulus operator with the correct data type. Another way to cause type conversion is through the assignment operator. The expression on the right side of = is evaluated, and the resulting value is assigned to the variable on the left side. If the receiving variable is of a different type than the result of the expression evaluation, the data object (result) is converted to the same type as the receiving variable. When the conversion is to a higher type, there is seldom a problem. For example, an **int** can be converted to a **float** with no difficulty. Also, a **float** can be converted to a **double** without difficulty. When the conversion is down to a lower type, for example, converting a **float** to an **int**, problems may occur.

In some downward conversions the result is simply the truncating of the fractional part. For example, the **float** value 15.27 converts to the **int** 15 without difficulty. However, if the number of significant places is too large to convert to an integer, the result is unpredictable.

Make a practice of using an implicit type conversion with a temporary value to safeguard against side effects. Consider this example:

```
float x,y;
int m,n;
...
x = 14.23567;
n = x;            /*  convert float to int   */
m = n % 3;        /*  use integer operands   */
y = x * m;        /*  use float in expression  */
```

The temporary variable n is used to hold the integer version of `x` (`n = 14`) and to supply the modulus operator with the proper type of operand (`m = 14 % 3` which yields 2). The last line contains another implicit type conversion. A **float** type (`x = 14.23567`) is multiplied by an **int** type (`m = 2`), which yields a **float** type (`y = 28.47134`). If `y` had been of type **int**, still another conversion would have taken place: `y = 28`.

The relationship between **int** and **char** is not as simple as it seems at first glance. In expressions **char** and **int** may be freely intermixed. When an **int** is converted to a **char**, however, the outcome is predictable only as **long** as the integer is within the ordinal range of the character set. The ordinal range of the character set is system dependent. On some machines the ASCII set is used and the range of values is 0 to 127. On others the range is 0–255. Still others use −127 to 127. Standard **C** does not specify that variables of type **char** be **signed** or **unsigned**. On some machines a variable of type **char** whose leftmost bit is 1 converts to a negative **int**; On others it does not. The proposed ANSI standard specifies that the keyword **unsigned** be applicable to type **char**. So that the programmer can be certain of the conversion results.

A summary of the assignment conversions follows:

int = **char**;	conversion of **char** to **int**. Sign extension is system dependent.
char = **int**;	Conversion of **int** to **char**. Usually, excess high-order bits are discarded.
float = **int**;	Straight promotion to **float**.
int = **float**;	Truncation of fractional part.
double = **float**;	Straight promotion.
float = **double**;	Possiblity of round off error.

In general, when two operands of different types are evaluated via an arithmetic operator, the lower type is converted to the higher type. The rules that govern multitype conversion follow:

dq**short** converts to **int**, then is evaluated.
char converts to **int**, then is evaluated.
float converts to **double**, then is evaluated.

```
dqif one operator is double, the other is converted to
    double, then is evaluated.
  if one operand is long and the other is char,
    int, or short, the latter is converted to long.
  if one operand is unsigned, the other is converted
    to unsigned, then is evaluated.
```

C includes a number of functions to perform complicated conversions, such as changing an integer to a string. These will be discussed in later chapters.

Mathematical Functions in Expressions

C makes use of a number of mathematical functions. Strictly speaking, these are not part of the C language but part of a mathematical library. The math library can be used once an **include** statement is placed near the top of the file. The math library is set up for the user by the math.h file. The usual way of invoking the file is

```
#include <math.h>
```

or, on some systems

```
#include "math.h"
```

The difference in access methods is system dependent. The angle brackets are used when the header file is located in the root or default directory. The quotation marks are used when the header file is in the user's directory or the root directory. Remember, the header file is not the math library. On micros the math library should be included at link time. The exact command is system dependent. For example, Unix systems typically require a `-lm` option be included in the compile command line. The statement **#include** `"math.h"` must be placed in your program to ensure proper operation of the math library.

The mathematics library usually contains the functions listed in Table 3.6. Since this library varies from compiler to compiler, other functions may be included in your system. For example, some math libraries include **log** base 10. Appendix C lists functions typically found in C libraries.

Table 3.6
Mathematical Functions usually in math.h

function identifier	description	function identifier	description
abs	absolute value	**exp**	exponential value
acos	arc cosine	**fabs**	floating-point absolute value
asin	arc sine	**floor**	integer = x or (**ceil**-1)
atan	arc tangent	**log**	**log** base e
atan2	arc tangent of two numbers	**pow**	raise a to the b power
atof	ASCII to **float**	**sin**	sine
atoi	ASCII to integer	**sinh**	hyperbolic sine
atol	ASCII to **long**	sqr	square of number
ceil	greatest integer	**sqrt**	square root
cos	cosine	**tan**	tangent
cosh	hyperbolic cosine	**tanh**	hyperbolic tangent

The math functions are called by passing an argument to the function: **sin**(x). The argument type must be **double**. If it is not **double**, the function converts it to **double** (except with ANSI versions which may report a computer warning or error.) Consider the simple case of finding the square root of a number:

```
#include "math.h"
double x,y;
y = sqrt(x);
```

The value of y becomes the square root of x. Type conversion can be explicit:

```
float x; double y;
y = sqrt((double)x);
```

or implicit:

```
float x,y;
y = sqrt(x);
```

The last example seems innocent enough. The variable x is converted to **double**, and the result of the square root function is a **double**. Then the **double** is converted to **float** via the assignment operator. In some instances,however, round off error occurs on the last conversion from **double** to **float**. Moreover, some ANSI standard compilers generate an error on implicit type conversions for math functions.

Mathematical functions may appear anywhere a valid **C** expression may appear such as in an expression like this:

```
y = 4 * x + sin(alpha);
```

Sometimes the correct placement of math functions may seem strange:

```
y = printf("%f",sqrt(x));
```

In this case the **sqrt** function returns a **double**, which is printed by the **printf** function.

Using Variables, Data Types, and Operators in the ANSI Standard

The proposed ANSI standard includes several recommendations relevant to this chapter.

First, the standard allows you to force the order of evaluation of the terms of an expression. Second, the **signed** keyword allows you to force a **char** or **int** to be **signed**. This eliminates problems with reading **char** as **int** on input and a host of other problems. Third, math functions allow the passing of **float** types and get a result of type **float**. This allows one to choose between speed and accuracy. The proposed new standard also allows you to use a **long double** which makes high-precision arithmetic possible.

Summary

An identifier is a name of a variable, symbolic constant, function, or other object that can appear in an expression. The identifier may be composed of letters and numerals and the underscore. The length of an identifier is 8 or less characters although many compilers allow longer names.

By convention, variables are written in lowercase notation, and symbolic constants are written in uppercase letters. **C** is case sensitive, so most programmers follow the conventions carefully.

The four simple data types are **char**, **int**, **float**, and **double**. Each type may be modified. Integer modifiers are **short**, **long**, and **unsigned**. Floats may be modified to **long**. In a declaration statement the modifier precedes the type. The operator **sizeof** is used to **return** the number of bytes used to store a data type or data object.

Data types may be converted to another type. Promoting a type is usually done without difficulty, but demoting can be risky. The cast operator is used to explicitly convert a type to another type.

Symbolic constants are created with the **#define** command. In this command **#define** `MAX 100`, where the symbolic constant `MAX` represents the number 100, `MAX` may then be used in expressions such as `m = i + MAX`.

Character constants are surrounded by single quotation marks. String constants are surrounded by double quotation marks and end with a null character.

Variables may be one of the storage classes: **auto**, **register**, **static**, **extern**, and **extern static**.

The storage class defines the scope and lifetime of a variable. **Auto** and **register** variables are created each time a function is called and cease to exist when the function terminates. Variables that are **static** are global to the functions defined below them but are persistent past the end of the function's life. **Extern** variables are global to the program and last for the length of the program. **Static** and **extern** variables are always initialized to 0. Strings must be **static** before they can be initialized; Auto strings cannot be initialized.

The keyword **typedef** is used to provide synonyms for data types. This helps make a program readable and portable.

C includes many operators. The arithmetic operators `+`,`-`, `*`, and `/` behave as expected, that is multiplication and division are higher in precedence than addition and subtraction. Expressions are created by combining variables or other expressions with operators. The assignment operator, =, is low in priority and assigns the result of an expression to the variable on the left of the =.

Unary minus and parentheses are higher in precedence than multiplication and division. Parentheses are used for clarity and in some cases to force the desired order of operations.

The incremention operators, `++` and `--` are a shorthand way for adding or subtracting 1 from a variable. If the variable `i` is incremented as `i++` then `i` is increased by 1. The `++` or `--` may appear in front of a variable or after a variable. In an expression, if the `++` is a prefix for example (`++i`), the value of `i` is increased, then the new value of `i` is used in the expression. If the `++` is a suffix (`i++`), the old value of `i` is used in the expression, and then `i` is increased by 1.

The modulus operator, %, yields the remainder when an integer is divided by another integer. For example, 12 % 5 yields 2.

The arithmetic operators and the modulus operator can be combined with the assignment operator. For example `j += i;` means to add `i` to `j` and assign the result to `j` and is the same as `j = j + 1;`. Similar operators are `-=`, `*=`, `/=`, and `%=`.

Mathematical functions are provided via the standard library or the math library. A header file, `math.h`, is required so that the math functions are properly defined. The arguments for the math functions are always of the double type. The result is always a double.

EXERCISES

UNDERSTANDINGS

1. Define each of the terms that follow in your own words.
   a. data type
   b. object
   c. declaring an object
   d. defining an object
   e. symbolic constant
   f. type conversion
   g. keyword
   h. modifier
   i. variable
   j. variable initialization
2. What does the cast operator do? Why is it useful?

3. When using the **getchar**() function to read a single character from the keyboard, what should be the character's type? Why?
4. What is an lvalue?
5. Write a **short** definition of each of these terms:
   a. operator
   b. operand
   c. precedence
   d. associativity
   e. evaluation
   f. type conversion

USAGE

6. Write a symbolic constant to define each of the following:
   a. yes is a 1
   b. question mark ?
   c. taxrate of 6.5%
   d. starting value of hex 100
   e. color is octal 15
   f. next to last number is last-1
   g. the flag is "no more names"
   h. upper limit of 100000 as a **long int**
   i. **NULL** is octal zero
7. Write declarations that include the initializations described:
   a. set i to 1
   b. set pi to 3.14159
   c. set lastletter to Z
   d. set a limit of 1000.0
   e. set 16 bit flag to 127
8. Write the expression to round a real number to the nearest integer when cast from **float** to **int**?
9. What is the value of k at the end of the segment that follows?

```
dqint i,j,k;
  i = 4; j = -3;
  k = 5 - j + i % 3 -6/4;
```

10. Use a **typedef** to create the type lfloat that is a **double** precision **float**.
11. Write a program to determine the number of bytes of each of the data types in your system environment.

APPLICATIONS

12. Write a program to read two integers from the keyboard and perform the operations that follow. Print each result.
    a. add the numbers, subtract the numbers
    b. multiply the numbers, divide the numbers
    c. find the result of first modulo second

13. Read a character of type **char** from the keyboard and find out what happens when it is used in expressions of this type:

    int = **int** + **char**;
    float = **float** + **char**;
    float = **int** / **char**;

    Determine the value and storage class of each result.
14. Write a program to discover the type conversion rules of your system.
15. Suppose electricity costs 6.72 cents per kwh and a state tax of 8% is added as is a city tax of 3.5%. Write a program that accepts the number of hours and calculates a bill. Print the bill rounded to two decimal places.
16. Write a program that calculates the area of a circle. Use a π value of 3.1416. Make π a defined constant.

4

Control of Program Flow

All languages contain mechanisms for controlling the program's flow. There are keywords and control structures that allow you to transfer control to another function, to repeat a process a number of times, and to make decisions about program flow. C has a full complement of such mechanisms. Each of these is explored in detail in this chapter. Because of their importance and the frequency of their use in all programs, the concepts in this chapter are especially important.

The Relational Operators

C has a very rich set of operators. Earlier, arithmetic and other elementary operators were discussed. For program flow you need relational operators as well as logical operators. The relational operators are shown in Table 4.1

Table 4.1
Relational Operators

operator	meaning
==	equal
!=	not equal
<	less than
>	greater than
<=	less than or equal
>=	greater than or equal

In terms of precedence, think of relational operators as being on two levels. The high level relational operators are

```
<    >    <=    >=
```

The low level relational operators are

```
==    !=
```

In other words, == (equal) and != (not equal) are evaluated after the other four, which are evaluated at the same level. For example, where `x = 5`, `y = 2`, and `z = 0`:

```
a. x > y + z;              evaluates to 1 (true).
b. x + z <= y;             evaluates to 0 (false).
c. z < x == y + z >= x;    evaluates to 0 (false).
```

In **a**, the addition is first so `5 > 2` is true. In **b**, the addition is also first, so 5 <= 2 is false. In **c**, the addition is done first, followed by the < and >=, and finally by the ==:

```
0 < 5 ==  2 >= 5
    1   ==    0
        0
```

Good programming practice suggests you use parentheses whenever clarity is needed or to ensure the desired order of precedence.

The if Statement

The **if**, the simplest of conditional statements, takes the general form

```
if (expression)
    statement;
```

where the expression is any valid **C** expression. For example:

```
if (weight > 1000)
    printf ("Allowable weight exceeded.\n" );
```

This expression causes the message to be printed only when the variable `weight` has a value greater than 1000. **C** does allow you to take advantage of the fact that the expression is evaluated as a number. If the expression evaluates to 0, it is false and if non-zero, the expression is evaluated as true. Consider the following segment:

```
#define
...
done = TRUE;
...
if (done)
    stmnt;
```

Since `done` is not zero the `stmnt` is executed. In other words, `stmnt` is executed if

```
if (done == TRUE)  or   if (done != 0).
```

The `stmnt` may be a simple **C** statement or a block of statements enclosed in braces.

```
if (expression)
  {
    stmnt1;
    stmnt2;
    stmnt3;
  }
```

The expression that follows is common statement in **C** but is not usually found in other languages.

```
if ((ch = getchar()) == '\n')
  stmnt;
```

Consider the complicated-looking expression following the **if**.

```
(ch = getchar()) == '\n')
```

First the expression calls the function **getchar()**, then the result is assigned to `ch`. Finally the value of `ch` is examined to see if it is equal to a newline character (a carriage return). The parentheses are required because == has a higher precedence than = and you want the assignment operator to take effect before the relational operator. The power of **C** is evident in this statement. Most languages would require that the programmer write

```
read a character;
if (character is equal to c/r) then
  stmnt;
```

or some equivalent pair of statements.

The if-else statement

The general form of the **if-else** is

```
if (expression)
  stmnt1;
else
  stmnt2;
```

The **if-else** statement allows two alternates. When the expression is false, control is transferred to the statement or block following the keyword else. For example, suppose you want to find the real roots of a quadratic equation:

```
discrim=b*b-4*a*c;
if (discrim)>=0)
  {
    x1=(-b+sqrt(discrim))/(2*a);
    x2=(-b-sqrt(discrim))/(2*a);
    printf("The roots are %f and %f \n",x1,x2);
  }
else
    printf("There are no real roots.  \n");
```

In this example **else** provides an alternative action if there are no real roots.

Nested ifs

The **if** statement may be nested as deeply as you need to nest it. One block of code will only be executed if two conditions are true. First `expression1` is tested and then `expression2` is tested.

```
if (expression1)
  if (expression2)
    stmnt;
```

Consider a text-analysis program that counts words. A sentence ends with a period or a question mark; a word ends with either a blank or a sentence-ending character. Clearly there are other possibilities, but for now consider only these. If ch is the character under consideration and prev is the previous character, you can say that a word ends when the previous character was a letter and the current character is one of the word or sentence ending characters.

```
if (prev is a letter)
  if (ch is a word ending character)
    number_of_words++;
```

In this case if the current character is a sentence-ending character, then the word count should be increased. In this program there are two cases that will bump the word count.

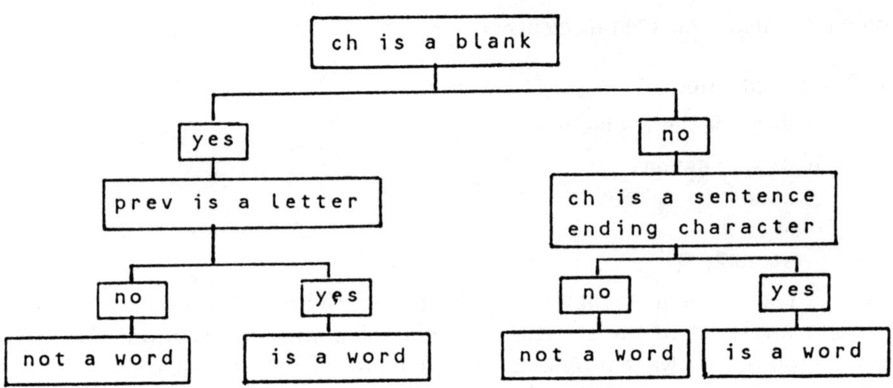

Figure 4.1: *Decision tree for text analysis*

The fragment that follows translates Figure 4.1 into inelegant but effective **C**.

```
if (ch == ' ')
  {
    if ( letter (prev) )      /* 1 */
      num_words++
  }
else
  {
    if ( end_sent (ch) )      /* 2 */
      if ( letter (prev) )
        num_words++
  }
```

Note: Lines 1 and 2 will be discussed in detail later. For now, just remember that letter(prev) evaluates to true if previous is a letter. There are several ways to provide this evaluation.

The careful use of braces is necessary because of the possible mispairing of **ifs** and **elses**. For example, the segment

```
if (exp1)
  if (expr2)
    stmnt1;
  else
    stmnt2;
```

looks as if it is perfectly clear. If both `exp1` and `exp2` are true, then `stmnt1` is executed and if `exp1` is true and `exp2` is false then `stmnt2` is executed. Looking again, the preceding segment presents a classic programming error, the case of the lost else. Rewritten, the segment is

```
if (exp1)
  if (exp2)
    stmnt1;
else
  stmnt2;
```

It looks as if this version executes stmnt2 when `exp1` is false. Which is correct?. The **C** compiler doesn't care about spaces and indentation. There are two ways to clarify the example:

```
if (exp1)
  {
    if (exp2)
      stmnt1;
    else
      stmnt2;
  }
```

or

```
if (exp1)
  if (exp2)
    stmnt1;
  else
    ;
else
    stmnt2;
```

The first of these two segments assigns the **else** to the nested **if**; the second assigns the **else** to the first **if**. Note the use of the null statement (;) following the first **else**. The null statement is often used to provide the correct **C** syntax and improve readability. As a rule, **C** pairs an **else** with the nearest previous **if**, provided the **if** does not already have an **else** assigned.

It is considered good practice to use braces whenever they help clarify the situation. Comments help too. For example, in the above example you could have written

```
if(ch == ' ')               /* char is a blank */
  {
    if( letter(prev) )      /* and prev is a letter */
      num_words++
  }
else                        /* check for end of sentence */
  {
if( end_sent(ch) )
    if( letter (prev) )     /* 2 */
      num_words++
  }
```

Look at the quadratic formula to see another example of using an **if-else** to solve a problem. In the familiar quadratic formula

$$ax^2 + bx + c = 0$$

the solution depends on the discriminant

$$d = b^2 - 4ac$$

If the discriminant is positive, there are two real roots. If d is negative, there are no real roots, and if d is 0, there is exactly one real root. The code segment that follows uses two **if-else** statements to allow for any of the three situations.

```
d = b * b - 4 * a * c;
if(d<0) nroots = 0;       /* there are no roots */
  else
  if(d == 0)
    {
      nroots = 1;
      x1 = -b/(2 * a);   /* calculate real root */
    }
  else
    {
      nroots = 2;
      x1 = (-b + sqrt(d))/(s * a);
      x2 = (-b - sqrt(d))/(2 * a);
    }
```

The Ternary Operator ?:

C includes a very special operator called the ternary or conditional operator. It is called ternary because it uses three expressions. It is sometimes called the conditional operator. The ternary operator acts like a shorthand version of the **if-else** construct. In general the structure in which it is used is

```
exp1 ? exp2 : exp3
```

which results in either `exp2` or `exp3` being evaluated. If `exp1` is true then `exp2` is evaluated; otherwise, `exp3` is evaluated. The conditional operator is used in place of a simple **if-else** to make an assignment. Consider the situation in which you want to assign TRUE to the variable even if the number is divisible by 2 and FALSE otherwise. One way to make the assignment is

```
if (number % 2 == 0)
  even = TRUE;
else
  even = FALSE;
```

which can also be written

```
even = (number % 2 == 0) ?  TRUE : FALSE;
```

Of course 1 and 0 may be used instead of true and false.

```
even = (number % 2 == 0) ?  1 :  0;
```

C can appear cryptic at times because it allows programmers choices and simplified notation. In the above example the first expression is not really evaluated as true or false. It is evaluated to see if it is not zero (or true). with this in mind you can rewrite the code as

```
even = (number % 2 ) ?  0 :  1;
```

which means that if `number` is not divisible by 2, then the expression immediately following the question mark is used. If `number` is divisible by 2, then the expression following the colon is used. Be careful that your program does not become too cryptic; Debugging cryptic (albeit clever) code is difficult. Some experienced programmers would write

```
even = !(number % 2 );
```

This code works because even is either 1 or 0, as before. It is both clever and cryptic. It may also be confusing.

Another example would be to find the smaller of two numbers:

```
min = (first <= second) ?  first :  second;
```

In this case minimum takes on the value of `first` if the first number is the same or smaller than the second number, but `min` is assigned the value of the second number if `second` is the larger.

Logical Operators

Nested ifs are seldom the best way to write a block of **C** code; you can frequently employ logical operators instead. **C** includes the logical operators `&&(AND)` and `||` `(OR)`.

Logical Operator Summary

The effect of the logical operators on the two operands (expressions) is shown in Table 4.2.

Table 4.2
Results of Logical Operators

situation	results
true && true	true
true && false	false
false && true	false
false && false	false
true || true	true
true || false	true
false || true	true
false || false	false

The logical operators && and || are lower in precedence than the relational operators < and > which are lower than + and -. The operator && is higher than the operator ||. Some other languages place the logical operators higher than the relational operators, which require parentheses. For example, in Pascal, in a case where a, b, c, and d are integers, the expression

```
a < b OR c > d
```

fails because OR is evaluated first and the result is a type conflict between the integer a and the expected boolean. In **C**, the expression is legal when written as

```
a < b || c > d
```

A Debugging Aid

When hunting for logical errors in a program, it is frequently useful to place temporary write statements in a program. After all the errors are repaired, the temporary lines can be removed. An effective way to place debugging code in your program is shown in this example:

```
#define DEBUG FALSE
...
if (DEBUG) printf("The value of i is %d\n";
```

To invoke your debugging write statements, simply modify the **#define** statement so that DEBUG has the value TRUE. Later, the DEBUG value can be changed to FALSE so that the program runs without the temporary write statements. Finally, remove the statements using a search function in the editor. Similar debugging strategies including conditional compilation, will be discussed in Chapter 7.

The Logical And &&

A compound expression is true when when two conditions (expressions) are true. To write both conditions, use the operator && in this manner:

```
exp1 && exp2
```

The two expressions in a conjuction must be either integers or pointers (pointers are explained later in chapter 8). Char data are converted to integer and are thus allowed in the expression.

The preceding fragment evaluates to true only when **exp1** is true and **exp2** is true. You can see that the logical operator **&&** provides the means to improve the text-analysis fragment presented earlier in this chapter.

```
if ( (ch == ' ') && (letter (prev) ) )
     numwords ++
else
   {
    if (end_sent(ch) && ( letter(prev) ) )
     num_words ++
   }
```

In the text-analysis fragment, the parentheses are not required. The compound expression

```
if ( (ch == ' ') && (letter(prev) ) )
```

can be written as

```
if ( ch == ' ' && letter(prev) )
```

and still work correctly. Remember, however, that good practice suggests that a programmer use parentheses and braces to improve readability.

The Logical Or ||

Similar to the logical AND is the logical OR which has the form

```
exp1 || exp2
```

and evaluates to true if either exp1 is true or exp2 is true.
For example:

```
(6 < 9) || (5 > 7)
```

evaluates to true even thought 5 is not greater than 7. Since the first expression, $6 < 9$, is true the entire compound expression is true.

The logical OR can be use in a compound expression to reduce the size of the code. In the text-analysis example, the logical OR can eliminate the **if** after the outside **else**:

```
if( (ch == ' ' &&letter(prev) ) ||  (end_sent(ch) && letter(prev) )
     num_words++;
```

With this revision the code is shorter, but harder to read and follow. The same **if** statement can be written without as many parentheses:

```
if( ch == ' ' &&letter(prev) || end_sent(ch)  &&letter(prev) )
  num_words++
```

The Logical Negation Operator

A logical expression can be changed from false to true or from true to false with the negation operator, !. For example:

```
!(5 < 7)
```

evaluates to false. The negation operator only applies to the expression that follows it.

```
!(5 < 7 ) || (3 > 2)
```

evaluates to true for example, but

```
!( 5 < 7 || 3 > 2)
```

evaluates to false.

The negation operator has a higher precedence level than && and ||. Parentheses are usually necessary to reduce unwanted or unexpected results.

Precedence Summary

A partial summary of the level of precedence of the operators used thus far is shown in Table 4.3

Table 4.3
Operator Precedence

name of operator	symbols
parentheses	()
negation	!
arithmetic	+ - * / %
relational	< > <= >=
	== !=
logical	&&
	||
incremental	++ --

Side Effects

Since the operator && is higher in precedence than ||, be careful to use parentheses when needed. For example:

```
exp1 || exp2 && exp3 || exp 4
```

is evaluated as

```
exp1 || ( exp2 &&exp3 ) || exp4
```

In other words, exp2 and exp3 are ANDed and the result is ORed with exp1. This second result is ORed with exp4. If the programmer meant

```
OR exp1 with exp2
then
OR exp3 with exp4
then
AND the two results
```

the compound expression should have been written as

```
(exp1 || exp2) &&(exp3 || exp4)
```

Usage of Logical and Relational Operators in C

C allows the terms of an expression to be any valid **C** expression. This can be both an advantage and a disadvantage. Consider the situation where the desired outcome is the assignment of the value of sum plus 1 provided answer is less than product or sum is greater than product.

```
if(answer < product || product < sum++)
  {
    answer = sum;
    printf(%d\n,answer);
  }
```

The intent of the preceding code is that **sum** be incremented during the evaluation of the compound expression every time the if statement is executed. However, the evaluation of an OR stops as soon as the left side of the OR is known to be true. Consequently, if answer is less than product, the right side is not evaluated and sum is not incremented. The intent of the above code is that sum be incremented every time the **if** statement is executed. The resulting side effect is very hard to detect.

Another problem often arises when the programmer means to write == ,but writes = instead. For example:

```
if( temp = 1000)
printf("Temperature is too high!\n");
```

is a valid **C** statement but, might not cause the intended message to appear on cue. Since the expression inside the parentheses is greater than 0 (or true), the message appears every time this sentence is encountered. **Temp** is also set to 1000 which is probably not intended.

The switch Statement

C provides an easy-to-read control mechanism in the form of the **switch** statement. The form of code that includes **switch** is

```
switch(expr1)
  {
    case value1:stmnt1;
                break;
    case value2:stmnt2;
                break;
    :
    case valuen:stmntn;
                break;
    default   : stmntn;
                break;
  }
```

The expression **expr1** is evaluated, and its value determines what statements are to be executed. If **expr1** has a value of **value1**, then **stmnt1** is executed. If **expr1** has the value of **value2**, then **stmnt2** is executed and so on. If the expression's value is not in the **case** list, then the default value is assumed and **stmntn** is executed.

There are variations on the general form. The **break** statements are not mandatory, the **default** value clause is optional, and the **stmnts** may be compound statements. The **default** clause does not have to be last and the last **break** is not required.

One rule to follow is that the expression must be of type **int**. Of course, since characters are treated like integers, the expression may be a character. Another rule is that all the cases must be different values.

When a value is matched, the statement(s) following the **case** are executed. Unlike some other languages, control does not leave the **switch** construct after a matching value is found and the statements executed. Consider this simple situation:

```
a = 2;
switch (a)
  {
    case  1:printf("value is one \n");
            break;
    case  2:printf("value is two \n");
    case  3:printf("value is three \n");
            break;
  }
```

In this example the output is

```
value is two
value is three
```

because there is no break after **printf** (”value is two“n”). Consequently, control flows on to the next **printf**, regardless of the match. Once a match has been found, each executable statement in the **switch** construct is executed in order until either a **break** statement is encountered or the end of the **switch** is reached. The **break** statement transfers control to the first executable statement after the **switch** construct.

The need for **break** statements is different in the **C switch** than in the Pascal CASE statement or the PL/1 SELECT statement. The other languages do not require the **break** statements. After a value match is found in Pascal and PL/1, the statement for that particular value is executed and control is transferred outside the structure. In **C** the **cases** are merely labels and do not influence control. Consequently, the **breaks** are required to transfer control from the **switch** statement construct. The **breaks** do provide the programmer with a bit of flexibility not found in other languages. For example, multiple values can be followed by the same statements. In the example that follows, the message is displayed when **x** is an even number less than 10.

```
switch (x)
  {
    case 2:
    case 4:
    case 6:
    case 8:printf ("even number\n");
           break;
    ...
  }
```

The switch can be used as a keyboard-character filter

```
ch = getchar();
switch (ch)
  {
    case 'a':
    case 'e':
    case 'i':
    case 'o':
    case 'u':   break
    default :  printf ("Error - not a vowel\n");
               break;
  }
```

When used with loop mechanisms explained later in this book, an interrogation of characters provides an easy-to-understand filter. Note that the only action taken when the character is a vowel is that control breaks out of the loop. This program segment simply examines the character to see if it is what is expected. If it is, then nothing happens. If it is not, then an error message is produced.

Following one hint about programming style will help prevent errors: Always use a **break** after the default action. This prevents the introduction of a logical error when the program is modified at a later date and other cases are added at the end of the **switch** structure.

When **break** is used properly, the **switch** statement is a clean alternative to nested **if** statements. It contributes to readable code and makes multiway selections in an orderly manner.

Comparison of Nested Ifs and Switch

Consider the case where a student's grade is based on the value of a test score.

```
if(score >= 90) grade = 'A';
  else if(score >= 80) grade = 'B';
    else if(score >= 70) grade = 'C';
      else if(score >= 60) grade = 'D';
        else grade = 'F';
```

The preceding code could be rewritten using a switch.

```
int n;
...
n = score /  10;      /* divide score by 10 and
                         convert to type int */
switch (n)
  {
    case 10:
    case 9:  grade = 'A';break;
    case 8:  grade = 'B';break;
    case 7:  grade = 'C';break;
    case 6:  grade = 'D';break;
    default:  grade = 'F';break;
  }
```

Both program segments work, but the code with the **switch** is easier to read and therefore should be easier to maintain. Note that this example places two statements on the same line. This is perfectly legal, even though some programmers consider it poor practice. In situations like this, the **break** belongs on the same line.

Bitwise Operators

A powerful set of bitwise operators helps set **C** apart from other high-level languages. The inclusion of bitwise operators give **C** features of low-level languages such as assembly. They are useful for controlling and interacting with hardware, other devices, and in performing some mathematical tasks. Bitwise operators allow you to perform logical AND,OR,and XOR and to shift left and shift right. One may create flags and masks to be used in comparison and machine-level control. The bitwise operators are shown in Table 4.4.

Table 4.4
Bitwise Operators

operator	meaning
&	bitwise AND
|	bitwise inclusive OR
^	bitwise exclusive OR
<<	shift left
>>	shift right
~	one's complement

Bitwise operators may only be applied to integers. They may not be used with **float** or **double**. All are binary operations except , ~ , which is unary. The shift operators are higher in precedence than the relational operators <=, >, >=, and the rest. The bitwise AND and OR operators are higher in precedence than the logical AND and OR.

The bitwise, or binary, operator AND, &, yields a 1 if the corresponding bits in both values are both 1. Otherwise, it yields 0.

```
  1010
& 0110
------
  0010
```

The operator `&` is very useful for "masking off" selected bits. Suppose a byte contains several flags. The 4th and 5th bits from the right contain the number of disk drives present in the system. The flag byte might look like this:

```
11010110
   ↑↑
```

the arrows point to the 4th and 5th bits. We can make sure that these 2 bits are the only bits in our variable by stripping off all the other bits. The mask would have a 1 in the 4th and 5th position and 0s everywhere else:

```
00011000
```

When `AND`ed with the first variable, it would yield a value that can be examined:

```
  11010110
& 00011000
----------
  00010000
```

Because the 4th and 5th digits represent the 8s place and the 16s place, the only possible resulting values are

```
00000     0
01000     8
10000    16
11000    24
```

No disk drives are represented by 0, one disk drive is represented by 8, two drives by 16, and three drives by 24.

Since you cannot represent the binary number 11000 conveniently, use any of the other three available forms: 24 decimal, 0x18 hexadecimal, or 030 octal. The resulting values when you use the flag this way are

binary	decimal	hexadecimal	octal
00000	0	0x00	000
01000	8	0x08	010
10000	16	0x10	020
11000	24	0x18	030

The orderliness of the octal representation might tempt you to use it in examination of the flag bits, but any of the numeration systems will do.

In **C** the representation of the flag problem is in binary form, however. Let `e_flag` be the byte that carries the equipment information. The mask is called `mask` and has the value 18 hex. Call the resulting value `test`.

```
short int e_flag, mask, value, n;
mask = 0x18;
value = e_flag & mask;
if(value == 0) n = 0;
else if(value == 8) n = 1;
  else if(value == 16) n = 2;
    else n = 3;
```

The inclusive OR, |, is used to make sure a value is 1. That is, OR turns bits on. The result of an inclusive OR is a 1 if either of the corresponding bits (or both) is a 1. The following example shows the result of an OR operation.

```
  1010
| 0110
------
  1110
```

The only bit not set to 0 is the last because neither of the two operands contained a 1 in that position. Suppose you want to tell the **e_flag** in the previous example that there are three disk drives present. You could OR the flag with 24 decimal or 11000 binary. The result would necessarily be two 1s in the 4th and 5th bits.

```
  e_flag        nnn10nnn
|   mask      | 00011000
--------      ----------
  e_flag        nnn11nnn
```

The **C** statement is

```
e_flag = e_flag | 0x18;
```

This problem is more complicated than shown. If the **e_flag** contained a 1 in the 4th and 5th bits already and you try to set them to the value for only 1 drive, the result is incorrect.

```
  nnn11nnn
| 00001000
----------
  nnn11nnn
```

The solution is to set the 2 bits to 0 and then OR in the desired bits.

```
   nnn11nnn
&  11100111
-----------
   nnn00nnn

   nnn00nnn
 | 00001000
-----------
   nnn01nnn
```

The corresponding **C** code is

```
flag = 0x10;           / * flag is 00010000 */
reset = 0xE7;          / * reset is 11100111 */
e_flag = e_flag &reset;
e_flag = e_flag | flag;
```

The last two statements can be combined as

```
e_flag = (e_flag &reset) | flag;
```

The parentheses are not really necessary since the operator & is higher in precedence than the operator |. Parentheses do improve readability, however.

The bitwise AND, &, is used to read the value of selected bits. The inclusive OR, |, is used to set selected bits. The exclusive OR, ^ , is used to set bits also, however, the result of an exclusive OR is 1 only if exactly one of the corresponding bits is 1.

```
 1010
^0110
-----
 1100
```

Shift Operators

The shift left and shift right operators, << and >>, rotate bits or move the bits to the left or right. For example, if the binary number 1010 is shifted left one place, the result is 0100. The leftmost bit is lost and the trailing bits, in this case the rightmost bit, are set to 0. The general form of code that includes the shift operators is

```
exp1 >> n;
```

or

```
exp2 << m;
```

In the first case **exp1** is shifted right **n** places. In the second case **exp2** is shifted left **m** places. For example:

```
exp1 = 13;           / * 1101 in binary */
ans = exp1 << 2
```

The value of **ans** is 0100. The two leftmost bits are shifted out of the picture. The rightmost bit is moved to the left two places. The right 2 bits are filled in as 0.

When the shift operators are applied to unsigned integers, the trailing bits are always set to 0. When the integer is signed, the result of a shift right operation is unpredictable. On some machines the trailing bits are always 0, on others they might be 1 if the sign bit had been set. The point to remember is that the shift right operator, when applied to signed integers produces a machine dependent outcome.

The shift operators can simplify some operations. Recall the earlier example of examining the 4th and 5th bits of one byte.

```
          short int e_flag, mask, value, n;
          mask = 0x18;
/ * 1 */  value = e_flag & mask;
          if(value == 0) n = 0;
            else if(value == 8) n = 1;
              else if(value == 16) n = 2;
                else n = 3;
```

The value variable in line 1 looks like this:

```
nnnNNnnn
```

NN are the 2 bits in question. In decimal form their possible values are 0, 8, 16, and 24. If the bits are shifted to the right three places, they occupy the rightmost two positions.

```
nnnnnnNN
```

Their possible values (decimal) are now 0,1,2, and 3. There is no need for the complicated if structure necessary to make these changes:

```
unsigned short int e_flag, mask, value, n;
mask = 0x18;
value = e_flag &mask;
n = value >> 3;
```

The last two steps can be combined as

```
n = (e_flag &mask) >> 3;
```

to further simplify the code and eliminates the need for the variable value.

The bitwise operators can be combined with the assignment operator to modify a variable:

```
exp &= mask;     is same as     exp = exp &mask;
exp |= mask;     is same as     exp = exp | mask;
exp ^= mask;     is same as     exp = exp ^ mask;
```

The IBM PC character display operations illustrate how the bitwise operators can be used. Consider a 16 bit unsigned integer that will eventually be copied into a 16 bit register. The word is divided into 2 bytes. The leftmost byte contains the ASCII character from an extended set of 256 characters. The 8 least significant bits are used to represent the character. The rightmost byte is used to store two 4-bit attribute flags. The leftmost 4 bits are the background attribute (the range is 0 to 15) and the rightmost 4 bits contain the foreground attribute. Suppose You wish to place the letter A (ASCII 65) in the leftmost byte, the number 7 in the background attribute flag, and the number 10 in the foreground attribute flag. The resulting 16 bit word is

```
0100000101111010
```

because 65 decimal is 1000001 in binary. Seven is 0111 in binary, while ten is 1010 in binary.

The character can be loaded by `ORing` the value with 65 decimal and then shifting the bits 8 places to the left.

```
ch = 0x41;       / * set character to "A" */
value = 0;       / * reset value to all zeros */
value = (value | ch) << 8;
```

The value variable now contains the character in the leftmost 8 bits.

```
0100000100000000
```

The background flag can be set to the leftmost four places in the righthand byte by setting a variable equal to the background value and shifting the value 4 bits to the left.

```
back = 7;           / * set background value */
temp |= back;       / * temp is 00000111 */
temp <<= 4;         / * shift left 4 places */
                    / * temp is 01110000 */
```

The foreground value can be added by `ORing` it with the temp variable.

```
fore = 10;          / * fore is 00001010 */
                    temp |= fore;/ * temp OR fore is */
                                        01110000
                                      | 00001010
                                      ----------
                                        01111010
```

These last three binary values are actually 16 bit values. The leftmost 8 bits are all zeros so they have been left off to simplify things. You now have two variables

```
value == 0100000100000000     / * A in left byte */
temp == 0000000001111010      / * flags in right */
                              / * byte */
```

The only thing left to do is `OR` them together. The complete code necessary to copy the unsigned integer into `value` is

```
unsigned value, temp;
int fore, back;
ch = 0x41;          / * set character to "A" */
back = 7;
fore = 10;
value = 0;          / * reset value to all zeros */
value = (value | ch) << 8;  / * load char */
temp = back << 4;           / * load back */
value |= (temp | fore);     / * merge all */
```

The contents of `value` must be passed to the operating system. You will learn how to do that in Chapter 11.

The inverse operation of pulling the foreground and background attributes can be done using bitwise operators. Consider just the right-hand or attribute byte. The foreground attribute can be pulled off using

```
value & 0x0f is    nnnnnnnnnnnnNNNN
                 &   0000000000001111
resulting in       000000000000NNNN
```

The NNNN bits represent the foreground attribute. The background attribute can be pulled out by shifting the bits 4 places to the right and ANDing the rightmost 4 bits again.

```
value &0xf0 is   nnnnnnnnNNNNnnnn
               & 0000000011110000
resulting in     00000000NNNN0000
```

If the result of the preceding AND operation is shifted right 4 places, the new result is `000000000000NNNN`, the value of the background attribute.

The bitwise operators can be used to shift the binary point much as you shift the decimal point in base ten. In base ten, you multiply by some power of ten by moving the decimal point `n` places to the right; you divide by ten by moving the decimal point to the left. Multiplying and dividing by two can be done by using the shift right and shift left operators. For example 7 multipiled by 4 is the same as

```
n = 7 << 2;
```

The binary representation is

```
00000111    / * seven */
00011100    / * shifted left 2 places */
```

The binary value `00011100` is twenty-eight in base ten.

A final bitwise operator is the unary one's complement. It reverses the values of all the bits.

```
~(1010) == 0101
```

It can be very useful in freeing you from machine dependence with regard to setting flags. For example, if you wanted to set all bits to 1s, you could AND the variable x with a flag of all 1s. But, if the size of **int** is not 16 bits, the number of 1s to be set is unknown. To get around that, simply apply the ~ operator to 0.

```
value = ~0 & value
```

The one's complement of 0 is all 1s, regardless of the size of **int**.

Another use is to set the rightmost n bits to 0. Suppose you want to set the rightmost 4 bits to 0 ain a way that ensures portability. A value of all 1s shifted left 4 places does the trick.

```
value = (~0 & value) << 4;
```

A flag with all 0s in the 8 rightmost bits could be created by using the 1's complement shifted left 8 places:

```
flag = ~0 << 8;
```

The same thing could be done by complementing the number created by eight 1s: 11111111, 377 (octal), or ff (hex) or 255 (decimal).

```
flag = ~0xff;
```

A portable program containing a mask with all 1s in the rightmost n places can be created by first creating a mask with all 0s in the rightmost n places and then complementing it. Consider a flag with all 1s in the rightmost five places:

```
flag = ~(~0 << 5);
```

This might cause you to ask why the flag had not simply been set equal to 0x1f? To discover what happens if you use a variable instead of 5. Suppose a program needs a flag of all 1s in the rightmost n places. The code is

```
flag = ~(~0 << n);
```

This works only as long as n does not exceed the length of an unsigned integer.

Summary

C uses a typical **if** statement. The statement is executed only if the expression inside the parentheses is non-zero. If the expression can be evaluated to zero (or false), the statement is not executed. The language also uses an **else** clause, which provides for action when the **if** expression evaluates to zero.

```
The relational operators are
  == equal
  < less than
  > greater than
  <= less than or equal
  >= greater than or equal
```

and the logical operators are

```
&&  and (conjunction)
||  or (disjunction)
```

The **switch** statement provides for case type branching. It also allows value-by-value comparison and a sequence of action to follow an equality. The **break** statement is used to exit from a **switch** statement.

The ternary or conditional operator has three arguments. The first is an expression much like the expression within the parentheses in an if statement. The second is the value to be returned if the expression is true, and the third is the value to be returned if the expression is false. The ternary operator is a convenient substitute for a simple **if-else** sequence.

C provides a set of bitwise operators to manipulate the individual bits of an integer value. These operators can be used to perform fast mathematical operations and to created important flags.

EXERCISES

UNDERSTANDINGS

1. What is the numerical equivalent to true? To false?
2. What restrictions are placed on the expression inside the parentheses of an if statement?
3. What restrictions are placed on the expression used in a switch statement?
4. What are the advantages of the ternary operator in lieu of the **if-else** construction?

USAGE

5. Consider the code fragment that follows, then determine if the statements are true or false.

```
ch = 'g';
i = 100;
j = 0;

    a.  i < 3;
    b.  !(j < i);
    c.  't' > ch;
    d.  i > 0 || ch > 50;
    e.  j < i &&'c' < ch;
```

6. What is the value of i and j at the end of the segment that follows?

```
i = 5; j = 1;
if(k = j < 1)
  if(j == 1)
    i = 3;
else i = 7;
```

7. What, if anything, is wrong with this statement?

```
if( x = 100) printf ("century mark achieved \n");
```

8. Write two **define** statements to set TRUE to 1 and FALSE to 0.
9. Write an **if** statement that prints your name if the variable i is equal to 10.
10. Write the binary version of the following:

```
a.  ~1
b.  12 &'a'
c.  5 | 8
d.  9 << 4
```

11. Which of these performs the operation before performing the equality check? Why?

```
a.  if(a*b == 0)
b.  if(a&b == 0)
```

APPLICATIONS

12. Write a statement that causes `n` to be incremented if a single character read from the keyboard is not equal to the newline character.
13. Write a program fragment that will print a 1 if an integer is odd or a 0 if even. Write it two ways: first use an **if**, then use the ternary operator.
14. Write one **if** statement that evaluates to true if `x >= 5` and `i` is equal to 10.
15. Write a program fragment that checks to see if a character is an uppercase vowel.
16. Write a program fragment that reads a line one character at a time and then counts the number of characters that are either a letter or a numeral.
17. Write a program fragment that pulls two 4 digit codes from the rightmost 8 digits of a 16-bit unsigned integer. Print the original 16 bit value and each of the two codes.
18. Write a program that reads a line of text until a newline is encountered. The program echos the line to the screen but strips out all blanks.
19. Write a program that calculates the payroll amounts for one person. It accepts the hourly rate and number of hours worked. It calculates gross pay, net pay and lists all deductions. Overtime pay is based on time-and-a-half. Income tax is simply based on gross annual amounts(0—$6000 = 0%; $6000—9000 = 15%; $9000—12000 = 18%; $18000—21000 = 21%; $21000—25000 = 24%; $25000—30000 = 26%; >$30000 = 28%) Social security tax is 8.9% of gross pay.
20. Write a program that calculates a product's wholesale price given the percentage of markup, the tax rate and the amount paid.

5

Control Structures

Control structures provide a systematic means of block-style programming. **C** has the usual variety of control, or loop, structures. As usual, the flexibility of **C** allows the programmer some freedom for creativeness (and trouble) not found in other languages. Since loops are so often used with arrays, this chapter begins with an introduction to arrays.

This chapter contains concepts that are familiar to most programmers, but **C** applies the concepts differently. Pay close attention to these topics. **C** provides flexibility and power in what appear to be familiar control structures. This chapter develops these topics and their special cases in detail.

A Preview of Arrays

An array is an arrangement of data objects of the same type. Mathematicians think of arrays as matrices with rows and columns. The point to be emphasized is that the data items in the array are homoegeneous or all of the same type.(**C** has another way of dealing with heterogeneous data.)

Consider a list of integers: 2,6,8,12,5,7,9. Suppose you want to place the integers in an array called x. The array can be declared in this way.

```
int x[7];
```

The array contains seven numbers. Any declaration of this kind should specify at least seven elements; of course, it may specify more numbers. Most languages require a declaration of this type. However, in **C** the programmer can also assign the values to the array by initializing it at declaration:

```
int x[] = {2,6,8,12,5,7,9};
```

The preceding declaration fills the array with the seven elements. Notice that the brackets are empty; the compiler assumes `x[7]`. You may also write `x[7] = {2,6,8,12,5,7,9};` (A character array can be filled in the same way, but there are other alternatives for doing so that are discussed in Chapter 8.)

If an array is declared by specifying the number of elements in the array, as in `x[n]`, the ordinal value (position) of the elements begins with 0 and ends with n−1. In the array x, 2 is in the zeroth position and 9 is in the sixth position. symbolically:

```
x[0] is 2 and x[6] is 9
```

Character arrays (or arrays of characters) are a way of looking at strings. In **C** a string is a character array with the null character (\0) in the last position. For example the declaration that follows establishes a string that holds 20 characters in positions 0–19 and allows room for \0 in the 21st position.

```
char name[21];
```

Strings of storage class **static** can be initialized in this manner:

```
char name[] = "San Francisco"
```

To the preceding initialization the compiler adds \0.

Character arrays can be used as normal arrays

```
char x[];
  :
x[i] = 'a';
```

or in this manner:

```
if(x[i] == '$') flag = TRUE;
```

Character arrays can be treated just like integer arrays, unless they are considered strings. In that case, the null character is the last character in the array.

Loops

The incrementation operators, ++ and --, were introduced in Chapter 3. These two operators are very important to loops and are worth a second look. The statement

```
i = i + 1;
```

can be rewritten as

```
i++;
```

In either case the result is to increment i by 1.

In the code fragment **exp1++**, **C** first evaluates the expression **exp1** and then increments it. In the fragment, **++exp2** **C** first increments the expression **exp2** and then evaluates it. Hence the two fragments

```
i = 10;            i =10;
j = i++;           j = ++i;
```

produce different results. In the first example j is assigned the value of 10 and then i becomes 11. In the second example i is incremented to 11 and then j is assigned a value of 11. For the purpose of examining similar operations, suppose that i = 1 and j = 1. In this case:

`j = ++i;`	increments i to 2 then assigns 2 to j.
`j = i++;`	assigns 2 to j then increments i to 3.
`j = --i;`	decrements i to 2 then assigns 2 to j
`j = i--;`	assigns 2 to j then decrements i to 1

An alternate way to express incrementing by amounts other than 1 is to use the operator +=. For example:

The expression	is equivalent to
`i += 2;`	`i = i + 2;`
`i -= j;`	`i = i - j;`
`i *= 3;`	`i = i * 3;`
`j /= i;`	`j = j / i;`
`m %= 7;`	`m = m % 7;`

The incrementation and assignment operators can be combined in interesting ways and are important in the use of loops.

The for Loop

In **C** the general form of the **for** loop is

```
for( initialization ; test condition ; incrementation )
    stmnt;
```

This structure is compact. It can be very complicated, because any of the three expressions in the parentheses can be any valid **C** expression. The `stmnt` can be either a simple statement or a block of statements enclosed by braces. The **for** statement requires both semicolons shown. It does not require that the expressions between the semicolons be present.

The order of tasks in the loop is execution of the initialization statement, a check to a check to see if the exit condition is true, performance of the body of the loop, and then to execute the incrementation step. On the second and subsequent passes, the loop starts with the test. Figure 5.1 shows the usual for loop sequence.

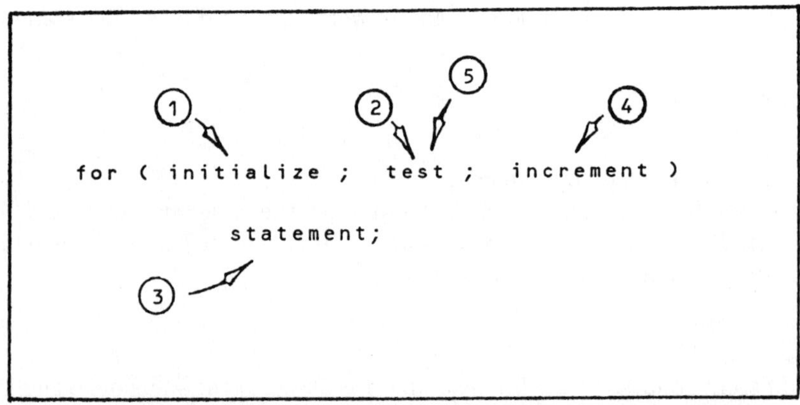

Figure 5.1: *The Usual Sequence of Tasks in a* **for** *Loop*

The process of summing n numbers provides an example of a **for** loop.

```
sum = 0;
for(i = 1; i <= n; i++)
  sum += i;
```

This loop begins at `i = 1` and ends at `i` equal `n`. The control variable, `i` , is incremented at the end of the loop.

A word of caution here! The code

```
for ( i =1; i = n; i++)
```

is legal, but will not produce the desired result. In this case `i = n` causes `i` to take on the value of `n` but is not a valid test condition. The expression `i = n` will always be true and the result is an infinite loop.

The incrementation could also be done with either `i++` in the **for** statement or at the end of the loop though this structure is infrequently used:

```
for ( i = 1;i <= n;)
   { sum += i;
     i++;
   }
```

All loops do not contain all the components of a typical loop. For example, a loop that is empty, that is, has no work to perform and which is one way of creating a time delay loop, follows:

```
for ( i = 1;i <= n;i++);
```

The following example shows a loop with no work section.

```
for( i = 1; (x[i] = getchar()) != ' '; i++);
```

A **for** loop may be used to accept a character from the keyboard and echo it to the screen (or standard output device) until return is pressed.

```
for (;(c = getchar()) != '\n';)
    printf("%d",c);
```

Loops can be used to solve familiar mathematics problems. Consider the case of checking to see if a number **n** is prime. Recalling that a prime number is divisible by only 1 and itself and that the largest divisor of a composite number is less than the square root of that number.

```
prime = TRUE;                    /* initialize value  */
if( (n % 2) == 0) prime = FALSE;/* is 2 a divisor?   */
else
   for (i = 3;i <= (int)sqrt ((double)n);i += 2;)
     if((n % i) == 0) prime = FALSE;
```

This loop is initialized to 3 because 2 is defined as prime. The test point is the square root of `n`, and `i` is incremented by 2 so that only odd numbers are used in the test. If any of the numbers between 3 and **sqrt**(n) divide into `n`, then the remainder is 0 which causes the prime flag to be set to false. Note that **sqrt** is not a part of **C**; but it is found in the math library so remember to include the math library header file (`math.h`). In lieu of using the math library, you could change the logic in the **for** statement to

```
for(i = 3; i * i < n ; i += 2)
```

which would achieve the same result and result in less complicated code. Another alternative is to have the body of the loop read

```
if(~n & 1) prime = FALSE;
```

Listing 5.1 uses a for loop to calculate straight-line depreciation for each year in the depreciation term. This program can be used to calculate the values for inventory, taxes, profit and loss statements, and so forth.

Listing 5.1

Business Asset Depreciation Schedule

```
/*  Business Depreciation Schedule
    Given initial cost, salvage value, and expected life,
    a depreciation schedule is generated.

    programmer is Barry Bugg

    file:    deprec.c

*/

#include <stdio.h>
main()
{
    char    asset[20];        /*  name of asset  */
    float   orig_cost,        /*  original cost  */
            sal_value,        /*  salvage value  */
            dep_value,        /*  depreciated value  */
            ann_dep.          /*  annual depreciation  */
            book_val,         /*  book value  */
            accum_dep;        /*  accumulated depreciation */
    int     life,             /*  expected life of asset  */
            i;

    /*  accept data from keyboard  */

    printf("Enter the asset name:  ");
      scanf("%s",asset);
    printf("\n\nEnter the original cost of asset:  ");
      scanf("%f",&orig_cost);
    printf("\n\nEnter estimated residual value of the asset:  ");
      scanf("%f",&sal_value);
    printf("\n\nEnter estimated useful life of asset:  ");
      scanf("%d",&life);
    putchar('\n');
```

```
/*  initial computations  */

dep_value = orig_cost - sal_value;
ann_dep = dep_value / (float) life;

/*  print headers  */

printf("STRAIGHT LINE DEPRECIATION SCHEDULE \n");
printf("Asset name                   :  %s",asset);
printf("\nOriginal Cost              :  $%8.2f",orig_cost);
printf("\nSalvage Value              :  $%8.2f",sal_value);
printf("\nLife of Asset              :  %2d",life);
printf("\nAmount to depreciate       :  $%8.2f",dep_value);
printf("\n\n\nYear     Annual Deprec.     Accum.  Depre.");
printf("    Book Value\n\n");
printf("-------     ------------     -----------     ");
printf("----------\n");

/*  Loop to print depreciation schedule  */

for(i = 0; i <= life; i++)
{  accum_dep += ann_dep;
   book_val = orig_cost - accum_dep;
   printf("%2d      $%8.2f          $%8.2f         $%8.2\n",
          i,ann_dep,accum_dep,book_val);
}
}
```

End of Listing

When a For is not a For: The **for** loop is found in most languages such as Pascal, PL/1, BASIC, and FORTRAN (where it is called the do loop). Thus far, we have treated the **C for** loop the same as its counterpart in other languages. The **C for** loop is not really a typical **for** loop, however . In other languages, the **exit** condition is in fact an **exit** condition. In **C**, the second expression is actually a stay-in-the-loop condition. Instead of specifying when the loop will end, **C** specifies the condition(s) for repeating the loop. Consider the simple task of counting to `n`:

a. `for(i = 1;i <= n;i++);`

b. `for(i = 1;i == n;i++);`

Fragment a is how the loop is expressed in **C**. In other languages, fragment b is correct. The **C** language will allows you to write fragment b, but the loop will not execute unless `n` is 1 and in that case will only execute 1 pass because b only executes when `i` is equal to `n`. In other languages, the programmer one expects the **for** loop to be executed at least once; in **C** this may not be the case.

While Loop

The second type of loop, the **while** structure, is used when you are not certain that the loop will be executed or when the number of passes through the loop is not predictable as a function of some value. The general form of the **while** loop is

```
while(exp1)
  stmnt;
```

where exp1 is any valid **C** statement and stmnt is a single statement or a block of statements enclosed in braces. The expression is actually the test condition. The **while** loop does not explicitly contain the initialization or incrementation parts of the loop. It is up to the programmer to provide these two steps. The **while** loop is frequently used to input data. For example:

```
while((ch = getchar()) != '\n')
  putchar(ch);
```

This routine accepts characters typed on the keyboard (or standard input device) and echoes them to the screen (or standard output device. The loop repeats until a newline (return key) is encountered; then the loop stops. A return key is not echoed.

Since placing a specific value in the expression is considered poor programming practice, we can modify the above segment to the following:

```
#define  NL  0x0D    /*  NL is newline  */
:
int ch
:
while((ch = getchar()) != NL)
  putchar(ch);
putchar(NL);
```

This version defines the symbolic constant NL so that if used in several places in the program, you need to change only the define statement and not each occurrence in the code. This version also prints a carriage return (NL) after exiting the loop. Again, note the use of parentheses around the assignment part of the expression. They are used because you want the assignment to happen before the relational comparison. (Remember that assignment operators are lower in precedence than relational operators.)

A **while** loop is repeated as long as the expression in the parentheses is true. Consequently, you frequently have to write the negation of the desired test condition. In the preceding example ! = served this purpose. In addition, consider the simple case of checking to see ifa flag called done is true. The loop in this example is repeated until done is equal to true. The code that follows shows the use of a negative condition.

```
done = 0;
while(!done)
  {
  stmnt1;
  stmnt2;
  :
  if(exp1)
    done = 1;
}
```

A good example of an effective use of a **while** loop is in the binary search problem. In this problem, we are trying to locate a particular value in an ordered list. The algorithm specifies that the search begin in the middle of the list and, based on what is found there, reduce the size of the list and repeat the process until the list consists of two elements. The left member of the two elements on the left is the desired element (provided it is in the list.)

Listing 5.2

Binary Search

```
#include <stdio.h>
#define MAX_LIST 10      /*  max number of elements   */

main()
{
int list[MAX_LIST];
int left,right,mid,x,i;

                         /*  left is leftmost position  */
                         /*  right is rightmost pos   */
                         /*  mid is middle position   */
                         /*  x is number we are looking for  */

   /*  fill up ordered list  */

   for(i=0;i < MAX_LIST -1;i++)
       list[i] = 2*i+3;

   /*  read in number to be found  */

   printf("Type a number.");
   scanf("%2d",&x);

   /*  initialize  */

   left = 0; right = MAX_LIST + 1;
```

```
        /*  begin search loop  */

        while( right != left+1)
            {  mid = (left + right)/2;
               if(list[mid] <= x)
                 left = mid;
               else
                 right = mid;
            }

        /*  output result  */

        if(list[left]==x)
            printf("Item is in position %d \n",left);
        else
            printf("Item is not in the list.\n");

    }   /*  end of main  */
```

End of Listing

The **while** loop is the appropriate structure to use in Listing 5.2 because the number of passes through the list is not a function of the length of the list. And, the list may be empty or only of length 1, in which case the loop would not be executed at all.

There are other variations of **while** loop use. For example, the **while** loop does not have to contain the incrementation part of the loop, but, **C** permits it. For example,

```
sum = 0;
i = 0;
while(i++ < 10)
  sum += i;
```

In this case `i` begins at 0 and 1 is added to sum on each pass through the loop. What is the value of `i` at the end of the loop? Recall the rule for the incrementation operator `++`. The value of `i` is evaluated before it is incremented. Thus, on the first pass `i` is evaluated to 0 and the test is true. After `i` is evaluated and compared to 10, it is incremented. So, during the first pass the value of `i` is 1 when it is added to sum. When `i` is 9 the **while** statement evaluates `i++` to 9 for the comparison to 10. Then `i` is incremented to 10 and 10 is added to sum. After exiting the loop `i` is 11 because after `i = 10` and the loop test evaluates to false, `i` is incremented. The same result could be achieved with

```
sum = 0;
i = 0;
while( ++i <= 10)
  sum += i;
```

Because the value of `i` is incremented before the test, the comparison must include the equals sign to allow the value 10 to be included in the summation. Two other nearly equivalent loops are

```
sum = 0;                sum = 0;
i = 1;                  i = 0;
while(i <= 10)          while(i < 10)
  sum += i++;             sum += ++i;
```

Both compute the same sum, but the first example exits with `i = 11` and the second example exits with `i = 10`.

It is easy to be off-by-one using the incrementation operator. Consider another example

```
sum = 0;
i = 1;
while(i < 100)
  {
    sum = i++;
    quiz = ++i;
  }
```

At the end `sum` is 99, `i` is 101 and `quiz` 101. Convince yourself that this is so to ensure that you understand how this code works.

The **while** loop is a commonly used method of reading data and processing it until the end-of-the-data is found. In some other higher level languages the problem is approached as follows.

```
read one value
while( value is not the end)
  process data
  read another value
end-while
```

In **C** the read statement is included within the parentheses of the **while** as in the next code fragment

```
while( (ch = getchar() ) != EOF)
  {
    :
    /*  process data  */
  }
```

The difference between **C** and other languages is that in **C** there is only one read statement. This technique can produce a hard to locate error. Consider the situation where a value is read and also compared within the bounds of a compound expression.

```
while ( (ch = getchar()) != '\n' && ch != ' ')
  {
    /*  process data  */
  }
```

Some compilers will evaluate the rightmost expression (`ch != ' '`) before they evaluate the leftmost expression (`( ch = getchar()) != '\n'`). The result may be an error because the variable `ch` will not have been read at the time `ch` is compared to `' '` in the rightmost expression. In that case, it is good practice to use two read statements, one outside the **while** loop and another at the end of the **while** loop.

The relationship of the for and while loops: In many other languages the **for** loop and the **while** loop are very different constructs that are used for different purposes. In **C** the two loops are simply two ways of doing the same thing. Because the middle expression in a **for** loop is really a stay-in-the-loop condition, the segment

```
for(;(ch=getchar())!= '\n';)
```

is equivalent to

```
while((ch=getchar()) != '\n')
```

The **while** structure can be used to increment through a loop much like a **for** loop. For example, instead of

```
for(i=1; i <= n; i++)
  print i;
```

you could write

```
i=1;
while(i++ <= n)
  print i;
```

The decision to use a **for** loop or a **while** loop is not dictated by **C** but by conventional usage, readability, and consistency.

The do-while Loop

The **do-while** construct is used in place of the **for** loop when the number of passes through the loop cannot be expressed as a function of the control variable. The **do-while** loop is always executed once. The general form of the **do-while** loop is

```
do
  stmnt1;
  stmnt2;
  ...
while(exp1);
```

The loop is repeated while the expression, exp1, is true. Like the **while** loop, the **do-while** does not explicitly contain the initialization and incrementation parts of the loop. The programmer is responsible for those segments.

The **do-while** loop (on most compilers) does not require the use of braces. It is good practice, however, to make use of braces for clarity and readability. For example:

```
do
  { stmnt1;
      ...
  }
while(exp1);
```

The expression is usually initialized to true and the loop continues until the condition becomes false.

```
flag = 1;
do
  {
    stmnts;
    if(exp2)
      flag = 0;
  }
while(flag);
```

The following example prints the even numbers less than 501.

```
i = 2;
do
  { if ((i % 2) == 0)
       printf("%3d",i);
    i +=2;
  }
while(i <= 500);
```

While not particularly useful, this example, contains several **C** constructs. The **if**, **do-while**, and increment operators are unique to **C**, but are used in nearly all programs.

Nested Loops

For statements may be nested to the needed level. Careful use of braces together with good indenting style help a programmer avoid debugging problems associated with nested constructs. Listing 5.3 combines these features in a program that performs the familiar selection and exchange sort. Listing 5.3 sorts a list of integers in ascending order by comparing the first element in the list to every other element. The smallest number in the remainder of the list is exchanged with the first number. The first element now contains the smallest number in the list. The sort continues by examining the second element as the start of a new list and it repeats the process.

Listing 5.3

Selection and Exchange Sort

```
int x[] ={12,15,5,9,4,7,3,19,4,20 };
main()
{
  int i,j,n,t,min;

  n = 10;  /*  normally set to constant in define */
  for (i=0;i<=(n-2);i++)
  { min = i;  /*  set pointer to i  */
```

```
        /*  begin inner loop  */

        for (j=i+1; j <= (n-1);j++)
          /*  check each number for min value  */
          if(x[j] < x[min])
            min = j;  /*  reassign pntr  */
        /*  end of inner loop  */

        /*  swap x[i] and min value  */
        t = x[i];x[i]=x[min];x[min]=t;
      } /*  end of outside loop  */

    } /*  end of main  */
```

End of Listing

This program also illustrates a potential problem with array indices. In **C**, the first element is identified by subscript 0. One would normally think to increment `i` between the first element and the next to last element while incrementing `j` from the second element to the last element. Thus `i` goes from 1 to n−1 and `j` goes from `i+1` to n. In this case, `i` goes from 0 to n−2 and `j` goes from `i+1` to `n - 1`. Such is **C**.

Counting lines in a file: Nested loops are also necessary in the next program that counts the number of lines in a file that you create by typing on the keyboard. The program continually looks for the end-of-file marker and the end-of-line marker.

```
#define EOF -1
#define EOL 0x0A

int ch, no_of_lines;
 :
 :
ch = getchar();
while(ch != EOF)
  {
    while(ch != EOL)
      ch = getchar();

    /*  end of line located  */
    no_of_lines++;
    ch = getchar();
}
```

This nesting causes the inside loop to read characters and look for the end-of-line marker. When found, the outside loop increments the number of lines and the outside loop repeats. This goes on until the end-of-file marker is located. This fragment can be rewritten as

```
while((ch = getchar()) != EOF)
  while( (ch = getchar() != EOL)
    no_of_lines++;
```

Another good example of nested loops is the familiar insertion sort. The insertion sort works the way you might put a hand of cards in order. The hand is scanned for the first card that is lower than the one to the left. When such a case is found, the smaller card is picked out and moved to or inserted at the correct location.

In the insertion sort, the first two numbers are compared. If the one on the right is larger than the one on the left, the second number is inserted in front of the first number. The first number slides over and takes the place of the second number. The process goes on by scanning to the right until a number is found that is smaller than the number to the left. The algorithm scans to the left and finds the correct spot for the smaller number. It is inserted at the correct location, and the rest of the numbers slide to the right one position.

This process is repeated until the end of the list is reached. The list is then sorted. This problem requires that the first element be placed in the ordinal position 1 and not 0. because the algorithm always looks one place to the left of each number. When looking to the left of the number in ordinal position 1, there must be a valid index for the number to the left. An insertion sort program is shown in Listing 5.4.

Listing 5.4

Insertion Sort

```
/* assume a list of size n stored
   in an array of size n + 1
   the first element is list[1] */

int i,j,t,n,ptr;
 :
 :
for( i = 2; i <= n ;i++)             /*  line 1  */
   { x[0] = x[i];
   ptr = i;
   j =i-1;                    /*  line 2  */
   while(x[i] < x[j])         /*  line 3  */
     ptr = j--;               /*  line 4  */
   t = x[i];
   if(i != ptr)
     { for(j= i-1; j >= ptr; j--)  /* 5 */
          x[j+1] = x[j];
        x[ptr] = t;                /* 6 */
     }
   }
```

End of Listing

Listing 5.4 illustrates several of the constructs explored so far. Line 1 is the standard for construct incrementing `i` from 2 to `n`. Line 2 initializes `j` to the number just to the left of `i`. At the very beginning `j` is 1. When `i` is `n`, `j` is `n`−1. Beginning in line 3, a **while** loop is used to find the first occurrence of `x[j]` that is smaller than the minimum value (`t`). As long as the elements in the list are larger than `t` they are moved to the right one position. When the correct position is found, the **while** loop is exited and line 6 places the `i`th element in the correct spot (`ptr`). Line 4 contains a bit of **C** code not usually found in most languages. In it `x[j+1]` is assigned the value of `x[j]`, and then `j` is decremented. In most languages, this requires two statements and braces following the **while** expression. Line 5 shows a loop using the decrement operator `j--` . It is used because the loop goes from right to left in the list.

The ladder problem: Some mathematics problems are difficult to solve by using equations, calculus, graphs, and the like. Some present formidable mathematical challenges. The problem that follows is one of these hard-to-solve problems. In it you arrive at a system of two equations in three variables. A computer can deal with this problem by simply reducing the two equations in three variables to one equation in two variables and then varying the second variable until an acceptable solution is found.

Consider two ladders, one 25 feet long and one 35 feet long. Both are placed at the base of a building in an alley so that they lean across the alley and touch the building across the alley. The two ladders are on opposite sides of the alley and cross each other at a point 8 feet from the ground. What is the width of the alley? Figure 5.2 shows the problem.

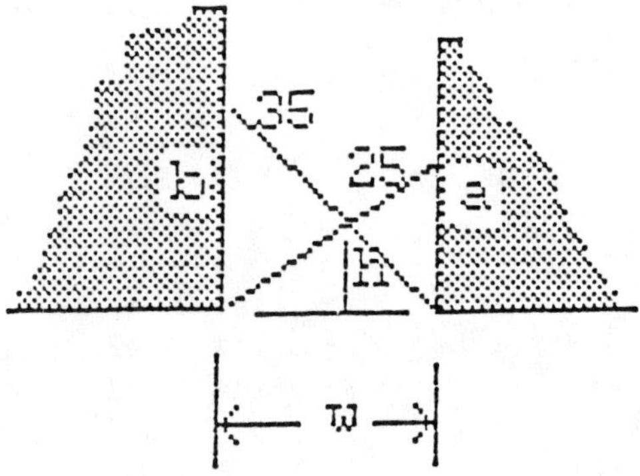

Figure 5.2: *The Graphic Representation of the Ladder Problem*

To solve the problem place an x-y coordinate system on the picture with the origin at the lower left corner. Relative to the coordinates the equation of one line is

$$Y = (a/w)X$$

and the other is

$$Y = -(b/w)X + b$$

Solving the system of equations by eliminating X yields

$$bY = (ab/w)X$$

$$aY = -(ab/w)X + ab$$

which, when added result in

$$(a+b)Y = ab$$

$$Y = ab/(a+b)$$

When Y is equal to 8, the intersection of the ladders has been found. If you recall that

$$a = \sqrt{(625 - w^2)} \quad and \quad b = \sqrt{(1225 - w^2)}$$

we can substitute for a and b.

$$Y = (\sqrt{(625 - w^2)})(\sqrt{(1225 - w^2)})/(\sqrt{(625 - w^2)} + \sqrt{(1225 - w^2)})$$

which is an equation in Y and w (the width of the alley).

Obviously, w is less than 25, so the search for w begins at 25/3 and is iterated until Y is 8. Because of round-off error and machine differences, the arbitrary criteria for finding w is **abs**(*Y-8*) < *0.001*. The code for this problem is found in Listing 5.5

Listing 5.5

Ladders in the Alley Problem

```
#include <stdio.h>
#include <math.h>

#define L1 25            /*  len of ladder 1  */
#define L2 35            /*  len of ladder 2  */
#define H 8              /*  height above ground  */

main()
{
  double a,b,w,f_of_w,diff;

  /*  initialize w and f(w) and old_w  */

  w = L1/3.0; f_of_w = H+1.0;diff = L1/6.0;

          /* L1/3 selected because w must be
             sig less than the ladder length
             diff is half of w because it must
             be smaller. */
```

```
/*  begin loop to find w  */

while( fabs(f_of_w - H) > 0.001)
  {
  if(f_of_w > H)
    w += diff;
  else
    {  diff /= 2.0;
       w -= diff;
    }

  /*  check to see if a solution exits  */

  if((diff < 0.001) || (w > L1) || (w > L2))
    {  printf(" There is no solution.\n");
       exit();
    }

  /*  calculate f(w)  */
  a = sqrt(L1*L1 - w * w);
  b = sqrt(L2*L2 - w * w);
  f_of_w = (a*b)/(a+b);
}

printf("The width of the alley is %f\n",w);
}
```

End of Listing

The ladder problem presents an example of using a computer to solve an otherwise difficult problem. The **while** construct is used because the number of iterations is unknown and there is not a counter type variable. The initial values for the ladders and crossing point are constants, and w and f(w) are initialized in terms of the constant so that the parameters of the problem may change.

The Comma Operator:

C uses the comma , two ways. The first uses the comma as a separator such as in **printf**`("%5d %7d\n",i,j)`. Another use is as an operator in an expression. You will frequently see the comma operator used in this way in **for** loops but its use is not restricted to that construct. The general form of the comma operator is

```
for( exp1,exp2 ; exp3; exp4,exp5)
```

Earlier you saw that the **for** loop allowed for three operands or expressions. With the use of the comma operator, the initialization and incrementation "expressions" can actually be two or more expressions. The comma operator guarantees that the expressions will be evaluated left to right. For example, the code that follows

```
sum = 0;
for(i=1;i<=10;i++)
  sum += i;
```

can be rewritten as

```
for(sum=0,i=1;i<=10;i++)
  sum += i;
```

The sum is initialized inside the **for** loop. Recall that the initialization part of a **for** loop occurs only once; therefore, using the comma operator makes good sense here.

The comma operator can be placed in the incrementation section too. which reduces the original loop to a single, rather complicated line of code.

```
for(sum=0,i=1;i <= 10; sum += i,i++);
```

Notice that the expression `sum += i` is placed before the term `i++`. If it were the other way around:

```
for(sum=0,i=1;i <= 10; i++,sum += i);
```

`i` would be 2 by the first time it were added to `sum`. If the desired result is the addition of the first ten integers, you could actually add 2 through 11 (`sum = 65`, not 55). Of course, you could initialize `i` to 0 and change the test condition to achieve the desired result:

```
for(sum=0,i=0;i < 10; i++,sum += i);
```

The comma operator can also be used to build a table of values. For example, suppose you want to show the first `n` integers and their squares.

```
printf("  n     n squared\n");
for(i = 1,s=1;i <= n; i++,s = i*i)
  printf("%3d %10d\n",i,s);
```

The values of `s` and `i` are both incremented inside the parentheses, and the only statement in the loop is the print statement. (Problems of this type, where the second value in a table is a function of the first value in the table, are often treated in this manner.)

The sample output from this program is:

```
n        n squared

1        1
2        4
3        9
...      ...
n        n²
```

The comma operator can be used in the middle or test condition, but it seldom is. For example

```
count = 10;
answer = 5;
for ( ;count < answer,answer <= 6; )
```

would be valid but not useful because only the rightmost expression in the series of expressions is used in the test. In other words, `answer <= 6` would be the test condition used.

The calculation of a factorial is a straight forward looping problem that you can use the comma operator to solve. The normal iteration method is to make sure that the number is positive. Then the special cases of 0 and 1 (one) are handled and finally, a loop is used to determine the value of the factorial. Listing 5.6 shows how loops can be used in finding n factorial.

Listing 5.6

N Factorial

```
/*  assume n exists  */
/*  fact is the variable to hold the result  */

if(n < 0) fact =-1;  /*  error condition  */
else
  {  fact = 1;
     if(n>1)
       for(i=2;i<=n;i++)
         fact *= i;
  }
```

End of Listing

Listing 5.6 could be simplified by using a comma operator:

```
if(n<0) fact = -1;
else for(fact=1,i=2;i<=n;fact *= i,i++);
```

In this code `fact` is initialized and the work of the loop is included inside the parentheses. The special cases of 0 and 1 are taken care of by the test condition `i <= n`.

The comma operator may be used as a statement separator to simplify some code. For example, a block of code using braces can be simplified by employing the comma operator. Consider the case of swapping two values `a` and `b`. The standard block of code is shown in the following example.

```
{
  temp = a;
  a = b;
  b = temp;
}
```

The block may be replaced by the following code.

```
temp = a, a = b, b = temp;
```

The use of the comma operator eliminates the need for the braces. It is commonly used after an **if** or an **else** to eliminate the braces as in this example.

```
if( a < b) t = a, a = b, b = t;
```

Breaking Out of Loops

The **break** Statement. You have encountered the **break** statement before; it is usually used in conjunction with the **switch** statement to cause control to leave the **switch** block after the desired action (case) has been executed. It may also be used with the **while**, **do**, and **for** loops to transfer control from the loop to the statement immediately following that same loop. Control exits the innermost loop only. If a **break** is found in nested loops, the **break** only transfers control to the outside of the loop actually containing the **break**. The general form of the **break** statement is

```
while(..)
  {
    ...
    if(..)  break;
    ...
  }
```

Be cautious in the use of **break** statements. Avoid their use if possible by careful use of error checks at the beginning of loops and **if** structures, which check for special cases. When a **break** statement is used in a loop, it should transfer control clearly and be accompanied by comments about its use. Never nest breaks to transfer control outside the present block of code.

The **continue** Statement. The **continue** statement is used to transfer control back to the top of a loop to begin another pass. It is just the opposite of the **break** statement, which transfers control out of the loop to the next statement. The **continue** statement simply skips the rest of the loop for the current pass and starts again at the top. More specifically, it transfers control to the test condition of the **while** and **do** loops and transfers control to the incrementation (reinitialization) part of the **for** loop. The general form of the **continue** is

```
while (..)
  {
    ...
    if( ..  )
      continue;
    ...
  }
```

The **continue** statement is not used with the **switch** statement.

The **goto** statement. The **goto** statement has a bad reputation and like **break** and **continue**, its use should be avoided. Programmers who use **goto**s are like people who associate with unsavory characters. They too get bad reputations. Yet, a **goto** that transfers control from a loop to a section of code within the same block can be a big help. A carefully used **goto** can result in a well-structured program that is clearer than the alternative code that uses only **while** and **if** statements.

```
while(..)
  {
    ...
    if( error == true) goto err_flg;
    ...
  }
err_flg:...
```

The **goto** statement says to transfer control to the label **err_flg** which must be in the same function. Therefore, it is impossible to use a **goto** to transfer control outside the current function. (Functions will be discussed in detail in Chapter 6.)

An example of a program that uses **goto** effectively is the Shell-Metzner sort routine. It is a modification of the Shell sort that uses a divide-and-conquer technique to break a list into smaller groups and then sort each one. The advantage of the Shell-Metzner sort over the quicksort is the lack of the need for recursion. Recursion as you will learn later, requires a good deal of processor overhead that many programmers feel is not worth the benefits received. In addition, the Shell-Metzner sort is robust; it does not break down when the data are nearly sorted or some other worst-case situation. The logic for the Shell- Metzner sort is shown in Figure 5.3. The code is in Listing 5.7.

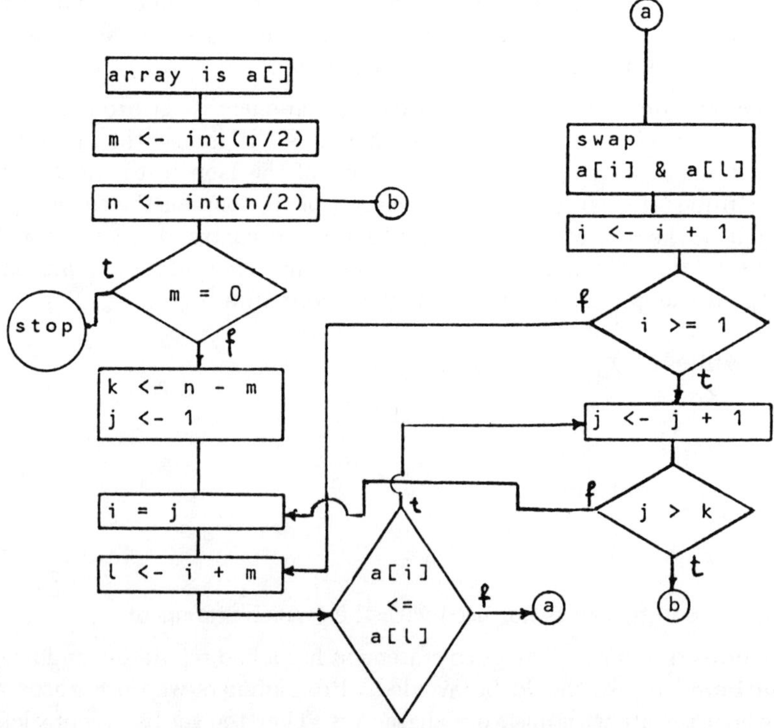

Figure 5.3: *Shell-Metzner sort algorithm*

Listing 5.7

Shell-Metzner Sort

```
      int x[] = {9,12,45,7,53,12,78,90,10,65,3,19,47 };
      main()
      {
      int i,j,k,l,m,n,t;
      n = 12;    /*  this will change later to an argument
                     passed to a function */
      m = n;     /*  m is the number of elements in a
                     partition.  n+1 is the number of elements
                     in the array x[]. */
                 /*  k is the number of partitions */
top:  m /= 2;
      while( m != 0)
        {
          k = n - m;
          j = 0;
   part:  i = j;
          while( i >= 0)
            {
              l = i + m;
              if(x[i] <= x[l])
                { j++;
                  goto bottom;
                }
              else
                { t = x[i];x[i] =x[l];x[l] = t;
                  i -= m;
                }
            }
 bottom:  if(j > k)
            goto top;
          else
            goto part;
        }
      }
```

End of Listing

The Shell-Metzner sort uses **goto** statements effectively because they transfer control only to a nearby segment of code. Control stays within the same block, and the resulting speed of the sort together with the robustness are two worthwhile reasons for using the **goto**.

The **goto** is sometimes used in place of a **break** or **continue** statement when you wishe to get out of a deeply nested loop. The **goto** statement can transfer control completely out of the nested structure, but the **break** and **continue** statements can transfer control only out of the immediate loop.

The **exit** statement. The **exit**() statement is actually a function call and can be used with integer arguments. It will be discussed in more detail later. The use of **exit**() to **break** out of a loop is generally restricted to handling an error. The **exit**() statement terminates the program entirely. The **exit**() statement is used to avoid a more complicated **if-else** structure to handle an error that would result in a more complicated algorithm.

Summary

C provides three loops: **for**, **while**, and **do-while**. The loops are executed until the **exit** condition is reached. The **while** loop is executed as long as the expression inside the parentheses is non-zero (true). The **do-while** loop is executed until the expression inside the parentheses evaluates to false. The **while** loop is tested at the beginning of the loop. The **do-while** loop is tested at the end of the loop. The **for** loop provides for a control variable to be initialized and incremented.

The **for** loop is a close cousin of the **while** loop. If the initialization and incrementation expressions are left out, the **for** loop is equivalent to a **while** loop. A comma operator may be used within the initialization and incrementation sections of the **for** loop to allow for a sophisticated, multi-step expression.

C provides three statements for getting out of loops: **break**, **continue**, and **goto**. The **break** statement terminates execution of the innermost loop and goes on with the program. The **continue** statement does not teminate loop execution but rather it goes on to the next iteration. The **goto** statement transfers control unconditionally to a label which must be located within the same block of code.

Control structures are most important to programs in general and **C** programs in particular. The three structures discussed in this chapter must be mastered. They offer flexibility that puts control of program flow squarely in the hands of the programmer.

EXERCISES

UNDERSTANDINGS

1. When are a **for** loop and a **while** loop the same?
2. Which of the three types of loop structures is always executed at least once?
3. What is wrong with this code? Assume all variables are valid.

```
for( i = 1; i <= (nspace - (col % nspace)) ;i++)
  { putchar(' ');
    col++;
  }
```

4. What does the program that follows do?

```
#include <stdio.h>
#define N 21
main()
  {
    int list[N],k,x,y,z;
    k = x = 0; y= 1; z = 6;
    while(k != N)
      {
        list[k] = x;
        x += y;
        y += z;
        z += 6;
        printf("%7d %10d\n",k,list[k]);
        k++;
      }
  }
```

USAGE

5. Test these two loops and explain the results.

```
a.  for(sum=0,i=0;i<=10;i++,sum += i);
b.  for(sum=0,i=1;i<=10;sum += i,i++);
```

6. What is the value of `i` after each of these fragments? In part e tell the values of `sum` and `i`.

```
a.  while(i++ <=10);
b.  while(++i <=10);
c.  for(i=0,x = i++;i<10; ++i);
d.  i = 0;
    do
      ++i;
    while(i++ < 10);
e.  note:  what are sum and i
    for(sum=0,i=1;i<=10;sum += i++);
```

7. What is the value of `i` and `j` (and sometimes `k`) after each of these fragments? Assume i = j = k = 0 at the start of each exercise.

```
a.  while( i < 5)
      ++i;
    j *= i;
b.  while (i < 5)
      i++;
    j = ++i;
c.  while ( i <= 20)
    j = ++i;
    k = i++;
d.  for( i += i++; i < 16 ; j += i++);
e.  for(++j,i +=j ; i < 100; ++i) k *= j++;
f.  do
      i *= j++;
    while( j < 6);
```

8. Rewrite this code segment to eliminate the use of the **continue** statement.

```
while( (ch = getchar()) != '\n')
  {
    if(ch == ' ')
      continue;
    putchar(ch);
  }
```

APPLICATIONS

9. Write a program to print a table of costs of 20 cases of soda. A single case costs $10.00. Each additional case costs $8.79. The program should contain a single **for** loop with only one print statement in the body of the loop. Use the comma operator in the **for** loop.
10. Consider a square table of side S. Four ants are positioned with one at each corner. Simultaneously, all four ants take one ant step of length X toward the ant to its "right" (i.e., counterclockwise). This process is repeated until the ants meet at some point. Write a program which generates all of the x,y coordinates of each ant from the start to the end. Make stepsize and table size symbollic constants.
11. Use loops and **if** statements to count the number of days, weeks, months, and years between two dates.
12 . Write a program to read a line of text and count the number of vowels in the line.
13. Write a program segment which prints the factorials for the numbers 0 through 15.
14. Write a program that places the first 100 numbers into one of two columns—prime or composite.
15. Write a program to calculate compound interest and accumulated principal plus interset for a period of n days. The interest is expressed in annual rates. Interest is compounded daily.

16. Write a number guessing program but where you know the secret number and the computer makes guesses until it finds the correct number.
17. Write a program to find the mean, standard deviation, minimum value, and maximum value of a set of numbers typed from the keyboard. Use −1 as the flag to end the input. Store the numbers in an array and print all the numbers and statistics at the end of data entry.
18. Use an array of 100 characters to create a "buffer" that holds one line of text. The text, when displayed, will fit in 60 columns, right-justified with word wrap. That is, if there are more than 60 characters in the buffer, any word that does not fit on the first line is moved to the second line. The first line is right justified by the following rules: beginning in the middle of the line, a white space is inserted. Alternating left and right and toward either end of the line, a white space is added before each word until enough spaces have been added to line the last character up in the 60th column.
19. Statistics books usually contain a set of tables for the cumulative probabilities of the binomial distribution. The tables usually look like this:

		p					
n	x	.05	.10	.15	...	...	.45
2	0						
	1						
	2						
3	0	.729					
	1	.972					
	2	.999					
	3	1.000					

Each set of entries is composed of cumulative probabilities for the values p,x,and n.

$$\texttt{cumulative prob} = \sum_{i=0}^{i=n} p(X = i)$$

where

$$p(X = i) = C_i^n \; p^i (1 - p)^{n-i}$$

Write a program to create this table for n = 2 to 10.

19. Write a checkbook balancing program. It starts by asking the previous ending balance. Each check has the standard inputs: date, payee, amount, & purpose (description). A record of the check is printed on the printer. The program must provide a method of adding deposits and subtracting service charges. The program stays in a loop until a sentinel is provided by the user.

6

Functions

Functions are the building blocks of the **C** language. All **C** programs are a collection of functions together with selected definitions, and global variable declarations. The selection of functions, scope of variables, and organization of functions into files makes up a good part of **C** program design. The use of functions affects a program's efficiency, readability, and maintainability.

Because the function is so important to creating a **C** program, this chapter is lengthy. A number of examples are used to illustrate variable scope, variable life, argument passing, and a range of standard practices. The heavy use of simple examples helps illustrate the many points to to made about **C** functions.

Functions: The Basic Form

A function takes the general form

```
datatype identifier(argument list)      /*  1  */
declaration of arguments                /*  2  */
{                                       /*  3  */
  declaration of
  local variables;                      /*  4  */

  statements;                           /*  5  */

  return(lvalue);                       /*  6  */
}
```

Line 1 is the header line. It includes the data type of the function. Actually, the data type is of the value returned by the function. The identifier is the name of the function and follows the naming rules of other identifiers. The argument list is enclosed in parentheses. There is no semicolon after the closing parenthesis. When a function name is used with a semicolon, it means that it is a function call. When it is used without the semicolon, as it is here, it is part of the function definition. Line 2 is the first line of the type declarations of the arguments. These appear above the opening brace (line 3) which signifies the body of the function.

Within the body of the function, the variable declarations and statements appear in typical **C** style. The exception is the **return** statement, which specifies the value to be returned to the calling routine. The value returned must be of the type specified in the header line. The parentheses are not required, but most programmers use them for clarity.

Here is a very simple function:

```
/*  example of a function  */
print_it(n)
int n;
{
  printf(" the number is %d\n",n);
  return;
}
```

This example has only one argument (n), which is an integer that is subsequently printed.

A function may have no arguments. Consider the function that prints a message:

```
notice()
{
  printf("Please wait while file is processed!\n");
}
```

This function has parentheses after its name, they are always required. Of course, there are no arguments to be declared so { appears immediately after the function header line. The function returns no values so, the **return** statement is missing and the data type is omitted from in front of the function name.

Some functions have all the components. Consider this function, which returns true (non-zero) if the number is even and false (0) if the number is odd.

```
even(n)
int n;
{
  int result;
  if( (n % 2) == 0)
    result = 1;
  else
    result = 0;
  return(result);
}
```

This function is not an example of efficient code, but it serves as a example of the form of a function. (You will revisit this function.) Because it returns an integer,the data type is omitted from the header line. The argument n is declared outside the body of the function, and the value of `result` is returned to the calling program.

The function may be called by the simple statement:

```
even(n);
```

or used in an expression

```
if(even(n) != 0)
  statement;
```

The argument can be any integer

```
main()
{
  int i,j;
  if(even(i) != 1)
    statement;
  else
    if(even(j) != 0)
      statement;
}
```

Listing 6.1 illustrates a function that counts the number of characters in a line of input.

Listing 6.1

Counting Characters

```
#include <stdio.h>
#define EOLN '\n'
main()
{
  int num_chars,count_ch();

  num_chars = count_ch();      /*  1  */
  printf("The number of characters is %d.\n",
         num_chars);
}

/*  function to count characters  */
count_ch()
{
  int ch,count = 0;
  while((ch=getchar()) != EOLN)
    count++;
  return(count);
}
```

End of Listing

The function `count_ch()` reads characters from the input stream until the the end of the line (EOLN) is read. The count is increased by 1 for each character found. This function is somewhat primitive because it counts blanks and any white space as a character. It can be improved to exclude blanks with the addition of a check for blanks inside the **while** statement:

```
while(/*  condition  */)
  if(ch != '\040') count++;
```

where the octal value of a blank is 40. Notice that the function is declared in the calling program's declaration section.

```
int num_chars,count_ch();
```

This is important to good programming practice. Any identifier of type **int** does not have to be declared, but it is good to declare all variables and functions.

Declaring Function Types

All the examples so far have used the **int** data type. A function may also return a **char**, **float**, **double** and so on. When a function returns a noninteger, the function and type must be declared as Listing 6.2 shows.

Listing 6.2

Round to N Places

```
/*  calling program  */
float round_n();       /*  declaration statement  */

round_n(123.6789,2); /*  calling statement  */

/*  function definition  */
/*  round off x to n places  */
float round_n(x,n)
float x;
int n;
{
  float factor = 1.0;
  int i;
  for(i = 1; i <= n ; i++)
    factor *= 10.0;
  return((float)(((int)(factor * x + 0.5))/factor));
}
```

End of Listing

The `round` function accepts arguments of the number to be rounded off (`x`) and the number of decimal places to be used (`n`). The factor is the power of 10 corresponding to the number of decimal places.

Consider the example of rounding 54.6789 to two decimal places. The factor is 10 * 10, or 100.0, and the steps for rounding are

> `Factor * x` yields 5467.89.
> Adding 0.5 yields 5468.39.
> The cast operator yields 5468.
> The division by `factor` yields
> 54.68, which is of type **float** and
> is returned to the calling routine.

The function can be called by any of several statements:

```
a.  x = round_n(y,2);

b.  m = 3;
    z = round_n(x,m);

c.  if(round_n(cost,2) > 100.0)
      statement;
```

The **return** statement uses an expression rather than a single value. You could have used a variable such as y and returned it:

```
y =(float)(((int)(factor * x + 0.5))/factor);
return(y);
```

In general, a function call can be placed in any valid expression. The function type should always be explicit, that is, do not use implicit type conversions when a result is returned. For example, suppose the function called **power** returns an integer. The function call should be

```
float x;
x = (float) power(a,b);
```

not

```
x = power(a,b);
```

Note that Listing 6.2 is equivalent to a Pascal or FORTRAN function to perform the same task. In **C** the same result can be achieved via the format conversion specifiers.

```
printf("x is %5.2f \n",x);
```

If x were 54.6789, it would be printed 54.68. The **printf**() function rounds it for you. The function is still useful, however, because you may wish to round off some values without printing.

If the name of the function is not preceded by a data type, the default data type is **int**. When the function does not return a value, it is also of type **int**. Clearly this can be confusing. How can a function be of type **int** and return nothing? This type of function is void. **C** as defined in K&R does not have a **void** function type; many compilers as well as the proposed ANSI standard do. Data type **void** could have been used in this case.

```
void print_it(n)
```

The data type **void** signifies a function which does not return a value. Its principle value is to reduce the confusion between a function declaration and a function call. Suppose you are using a function named wizard(). The calling routine could read

```
int i,j;
wizard();
```

You could interpret this use of wizard as a function declaration or as a function call. Since wizard() does not return a value, no data type is specified in the declaration. If it were declared as **void**, it would be

```
{ int i,j;
  void wizard();
```

The statement is now clearly a declaration.

The **return** statement in the function itself has no arguments. One way to write it is **return**(); or to exclude the return statement altogether. The important point is that the **void** type reduces ambiguity and possible declaration errors involving functions that return nothing.

Function Arguments: Formal and Actual

The function definition contains an argument list. Items in the list are known as the formal arguments. The list may be empty or contain any number of arguments. The calling routine also specifies an argument list to be passed to the function. The arguments in the calling routine are called actual arguments. In general, the number of actual arguments is equal to the number of formal arguments, but K&R **C** does not require it. This is a feature unique to K&R **C**. Most other high-level languages require a one-to-one match between the actual and formal argument lists. There are instances illustrated in later chapters where you may want to pass fewer actual arguments than formal arguments. The ANSI standard insists on an equal number of arguments in the calling statement and the function definition. Variable number of arguments depend on the file `varargs.h` and supporting macros.

When there are fewer actual arguments than formal, the "extra" arguments are initialized to garbage. It is up to the programmer to deal with the absence of an actual argument. Some of the standard **C** functions such as **printf**() deal with a variable number of arguments by utilizing the first argument to explain what is in the rest of the list.

Type Checking: C is not a strongly typed language. The types of the actual arguments do not have to match the types of the formal arguments. It is the programmer's responsibility check types. This is not all bad. Suppose you wish to have a function that returns the maximum of two numbers. In some cases, the numbers are reals and in others they are integers. In another case, some may be of type **int** and the other of type **float**. In a strongly typed language such as Pascal you would need a different function for each case. Consider the following example which includes different argument types:

```
main()
{
  int i,j,m,n;
  float x,y,z,w,max();

  i =5; j = 7; m = 2;
  x = 12.2; y = 32.7;

  n = (int) max((float)i,(float)j);      /* 1 */
  z = max(x,y);
```

```
    printf("%d %f\",n,z);
    w = max((float)i,x);
    m = (int) max(y,(float)j);
    printf("%f %d\n",w,m);
}
float max(a,b)
float a,b;
{
    if(a > b) return(a);
    else return(b);
}
```

Inside the function, the variables are treated as **float**. The value returned is always **float**. The calling program must deal with the type conversion as in the assignment statements for m and n. The cast operator is used inside the parentheses as in 1 to convert the argument list to all **float** types. Some compilers perform the type conversion on the fly; some ANSI standard compilers flag argument mismatches as errors. To guarantee that the program works on different machines, use the cast operator.

Notice the use of the **return** statements in the preceding function. With two returns and the actual arguments, there is no need for another variable. An alternate way of writing the function is

```
{  float x;
   if(a > b) x = a;
   else x = b;
   return(x);
}
```

You will see more efficient ways of writing this function in later sections.

It is not good programming practice to ignore data type conflicts. Sometimes they produce undesirable results. The math function **sqrt**() expects a **double** argument. The call

```
int n;
double x;
n=7;
x = sqrt(n);
```

may produce the wrong result. The argument n is the wrong data type. There are several possible fixes. Each ensures that the function argument is a **double**.

```
a.  y = (double) n;        b.  x = sqrt( (double)n);
    x = sqrt(y);
```

It is the programmer's responsibility to see that argument types are matched. Since K&R **C** is not a strongly typed language, some errors of this type will get by. The ANSI standard moves toward a more strongly typed language.

Some Useful Functions

Over a period of time, **C** programmers collect a variety of functions that can be placed in a library. The details of building a library are discussed in later chapters. Some of these useful functions are included here and discussed as both learning tools and as potential members of the reader's library. In Chapter 7 some of these functions will be converted to macros in a header file.

The function that follows in Listing 6.3 for example, can be very useful. It prints n blanks on the standard output device.

Listing 6.3

Tab N Spaces

```
tab(n)    /*  tab n spaces  */
int n;
{  int i;
   for(i = 0; i < n; i++)
     putchar('\040');
}
```

End of Listing

The function can be made more readable writing it in this form:

```
        {  int i;
        char c = ' ';
        for(i = 0;i < n; i++)
          putchar(c);
}
```

This rewrite has the added advantage of not depending on the ASCII character set. The character constant ' ' would be handled by the compiler of the host machine and as such is not machine character set dependent.

Skipping n Blank lines

A handy function in creating formatted output skips n lines on the standard output. Listing 6.4 shows such function.

Listing 6.4

Skip n Blank Lines

```
skip(n)
unsigned n;
{
  int i;
  for(i = 0; i <= n; i++) printf("\n");
}
```

End of Listing

Floating point mod function

Many languages include a modulus function for integers. A handy function is to find the remainder when a real is divided by an integer.

Listing 6.5

*Floating Point Mod... real/***int**

```
double mod( x, m)
double x;
int m;
{
  long int quotnt;
  double r, whole;
  quotnt = x/m;      /*  find integer quotient   */
  whole = quotnt * m;/*  whole number part  */
  r = x - whole;     /*  remainder is fractional   */
  return(r);         /*  part  */
}
```

End of Listing

The similar function in Listing 6.6 finds a modulus when a real number is divided by a real number.

Listing 6.6

Floating Point Mod...real/real

```
double modr(x,m)
double x,m;
{
  long int quotnt;
  quotnt = x/m;
  return(x - quotient * m);
}
```

End of Listing

The calling program must contain a declaration of the functions. Functions of type **int** are declared by default. **Double** type functions must be declared along with other variables in the calling program.

Math functions: absolute value and square root

The math library provides a full range of double-precision mathematics functions. However, for smaller, fast code, it is sometimes advantageous to write some of the math functions and avoid the math library provided with your compiler. Two of these are the absolute value and the square root function.

Listing 6.7

Square Root & Absolute Value

```
double abs_val(x)
double x;
{  return((x<0)?-x:x);}

/*  square root function  */
double sqr_rt(x)
double x;
{  double eps = 0.0001; /*  convergence criteria  */
   double guess = 1.0;
   while(abs_val(guess*guess - x) >= eps)
     guess = (x/guess + guess)/2.0;
   return(guess);
}
```

End of Listing

The square root function uses the absolute value function, so both must be present to use the square root function. Each of these math functions are of type **float**. This means that the double requirements of the normal math functions can be avoided. On older compilers the mathematics are still double precision; On newer compilers the mathematics may be carried out in single precision.

Functions that read a single real number

Suppose you need to read a single real number from the keyboard. The function that follows, `getnum`, avoids the overhead associated with the **scanf** function. It uses only the **getchar**() function, which results in increased efficiency. The function must be declared in the calling program and then may be used in normal expressions.

```
{  float x,getnum();
   ...
   x = getnum();
```

The code is shown in Listing 6.8.

As you will see, `getnum()` calls two more functions: One reads the integer part and another reads the decimal part. The two are combined in `getnum()`. These routines can be useful in a variety of programs that read numbers typed at the keyboard.

Listing 6.8

Get Single Number from Keyboard

```
/**************************************************
 *                                                *
 *  file:  getnum.c                               *
 *                                                *
 *   Task/function:  read a real number from      *
 *                   keyboard                     *
 *                                                *
 *   Returns:  a signed real number               *
 *                                                *
 *   Programmer:  Wayne D.Smith                   *
 *                                                *
 **************************************************
#include <stdio.h>

float getnum()
{
  int c;
  int intpart();
     /*  function to find integer part of number  */
  float decpart();
     /*  function to find decimal part  */

    int n;      /*  integer part  */
    float x;      /*  decimal part  */

    x = 0.0;

    printf("Enter number and press return \n");
    n = intpart();

    /*  check to see if there is a decimal part and read it  */
    if(c == '.')
      x = decpart();

    /*  merge integer and real parts  */
    x += n;

    if(n == 0)  /*  no integer part  */
      x *= sign;

    return(x);
}
```

```
int intpart()
{
  int val, digt;
    /*  val is the current value of integer part  */
    /*  digt is the current place in number  */

  val = 0;
  sign = 1;
  while(( (c =getchar()) != '\n') &&(c != '.'))
  /*  loop to read thru characters to left of decimal  */
    {
    /*  check for existence of a sign  */
    if(c == '-')
      {  sign = -1;
         c = getchar();
      }
    if(c == '+')
    c = getchar();
    /*  calculate place value and total value  */
    digt = c - '0';
    val = val*10 + digt;
    }
  val *= sign;    /*  affix the sign  */
  return(val);
}

float decpart()          /*  grab decimal part of number  */
{
  int digt;
  float val, divsr;
  divsr = 10;
  val = 0;
  while( (c = getchar()) != '\n')  /*  read to end of line  */
    {
      digt = c - '0';
      val += digt/divsr;
      divsr *= 10;
    }
  return(val);
}
```

End of Listing

A simpler function than the function shown in Listing 6.8 is **get_dec()** in Listing 6.9 which also can be used to read a single integer from the keyboard. Since it does not contain a fractional part, it can be as a string, and then the string is converted to a number.

Listing 6.9

Get a Single Integer From Keyboard

```
get_dec()
{  char s[80];
   int n;
   gets(s);      /*  grab string  */
   n = atoi(s); /*  convert string to integer  */
   return(n);
}
```

End of Listing

The functions `getnum()` and `get_dec()` improve the efficiency of reading single values from the keyboard. They avoid the use of **scanf** and its associated overhead.

K&R includes a function to read a line of text and place it in an array. This is extremely useful as a buffering technique and as a tool in any text analysis situation. The function is shown in Listing 6.10.

Listing 6.10

getline Function

```
getline(s,lim)
char s[];
int lim;
{
  int c,i;

  i = 0;
  while(--lim > 0 &&(c=getchar()) != EOF &&c != '\n')
    s[i++] = c;
  if (c == '\n')
    s[i++] = c;
  s[i] = '\0';
  return(i);
}
```

End of Listing

Reading and Writing a String

The standard i/o library does not provide a function as read string or a write string. However, many compilers support the two functions **gets**() and **puts**(), as mentioned in Chapter 4. The two functions can be implemented as shown in Listing 6.11.

Listing 6.11

Get String Function

```
gets(s)
char s[];
{
  int c,i=0;

  while((c=getchar()) != '\n')
    s[i++] = c;
  s[i] = '\0';
  return;
}
```

End of Listing

A calling program might include the segment

```
char name[];
...
gets(name);
```

which places the contents of a string found at the standard input device into the array `name`.

The complementary function, **puts**(), is shown in Listing 6.12.

Listing 6.12

Put String Function

```
puts(s);
char s[];
{
  int i = 0;
  while(s[i] != '\0')
    putchar(s[i++]);
  putchar('\n');
  return;
}
```

End of Listing

This function includes a linefeed, so the programmer need not provide it in the calling program.

Both string functions **gets**() and **puts**() include an empty **return** statement. The reason is that **s** is an array and when an array is passed to a function, only a pointer to the first element of the array is passed. Hence, the argument is similar to a var type argument in Pascal. The actual parameter or argument will be modified so there is no need to pass a value back via the **return** statement.

String Length

Strings can be of any length. A function that returns the number of characters in a string up to but not including the end of-string marker (null) is shown in Listing 6.13.

Listing 6.13

String Length

```
len(s)
char s[];
{  int count = 0;

   while(s[count] != '\0') ++count;
   return(count);
}
```

End of Listing

A null string would return a length of 0.

String Concatenation

Frequently, you needs to concatenate two strings. A function to do so is shown in Listing 6.14.

This function creates s3, which is the "addition" of s1 and s2. It calls the string length function so the string length function must be present to use this routine. Line 1 calls the length function for both s1 and s2. Line 2 fills the first part of s3 with a copy of s1. Line 3 fills in s3 with a copy of s2, beginning with the element immediately following the last element from s1. Note that i is incremented in line 2 so, it is left at the n1+1 position. Line 4 fills in the string with the required null value. A different version of this and other string functions will be discussed in Chapter 8.

Listing 6.14

String Concatenation

```
          concat(s1,s2,s3)
          char s1[],s2[],s3[];
          {
            int n1,n2,i,j;
/*  1  */   n1 = len(s1);n2 = len(s2);

/*  2  */   for(i=0;i< n1;i++)
              s3[i] = s1[i];
/*  3  */   for(j=0;j < n2; j++)
              s3[i++] = s2[j];
/*  4  */   s3[i] = '\0';
            return;
          }
```

End of Listing

Printing Binary Values

C provides conversion specifiers for hex and octal representations of integers. A handy function as shown in Listing 6.15 prints a binary representation of an integer. There are several ways to do this, and the Listing shows two methods. The first is to create an array containing the bits of the number and then display the array.

This function is machine independent because it calculates the maximum number of bits in an integer. If a machine uses a 16-bit integer, then it is possible to display all 16 bits. If it uses a 32-bit integer, all 32 bits can be displayed. The **for** loop prints only the bits that were calculated beginning at `m+1` and continue to the rightmost bit. As a result, there is no need to pad the binary representation with 0s or to initialize the array to 0.

Listing 6.15

Binary Print

```
bin_prt(n)
int n;
{
  unsigned int b[32];
  int i,length,m;
  length = sizeof(int) * 8;  /*  max no of bits  */
  m = length;
  while(n != 0 )             /*  standard conversion  */
  {  b[m--] = n % 2;         /*  from dec to binary  */
                             n /= 2;
  }
  for(i = ++m; i <= length; i++)
  printf("%1u",b[i]);        /*  output n  */

  return;
}
```

End of Listing

Error Handling

Because **C** is liberal in its type checking, the programmer must take into account the errors a user might make. For example, suppose no argument is given or an invalid (out-of- range) value is passed; the programmer must take care of the problem.

Consider the problem of raising a number to a power. The easiest case is that in which the number is a positive integer and the power is an integer. If x is the number in question and exponent is the actual exponent, then the body of the function could be

```
result = 1.0;
for(i = 1; i <= exponent ; i++)
   result *= x;
return(result);
```

However, this example does not take into account 0 exponents or negative exponents or fractional exponents. First consider a way to handle negative exponents.

```
if(exponent < 0.0)
  exponent = (-1.0) * exponent;
  result = 1;
  for(i = 1; i <= exponent; i++);
    result *= x;
  result = 1.0/result;
  return(result);
else
...
```

A quick observation shows too many duplicate statements. One statement can be moved outside the present set of statements, and conditional statement eliminates the last three duplicate lines.

```
result = 1.0; flag = 0;
ifexponent < 0.0)
{  exponent = (-1.0) * exponent; flag = 1;}
   for(i = 1; i <= exponent; i++);
   if(flag) t *= x;
     result = 1.0/result;
return(result);
```

Now add the check for a 0 exponent:

```
result = 1.0;
if(exponent == 0)
  ;
else
{ if(exponent < 0.0)
  {  exponent = (-1.0) * exponent;flag = 1;}
     for(i = 1; i <= exponent; i++);
     if(flag)
       result = 1.0/result;
}
return(result);
```

The empty statement after the check for 0 is placed on a separate line for readability. Since `result` had already been initialized to 1, there is nothing to be done in this case.

Now consider what to do when the exponent is fractional. One way to treat it is to pass back an error message.

```
if( (exponent > 0.0) &&(exponent < 1.0)
  printf("Invalid exponent \n");
```

The previous solution is probably inadequate however, because the program is probably not intended to crash when it receives this type of input.

Another special case with this function is when the value of `x` is 1.0 , 0, or negative. The following code deals with the first two cases.

```
if( x == 0) result = 0.0;
else if(x == 1.0) result = 1;
```

The code to take care of a negative exponent is shown next.

```
if(x == 0.0) result = 0.0;
  else
  {  result = 1.0;
     if((exponent == 0) || ( x == 1.0))
       ;
     else
     { if(exponent < 0.0)
       {  exponent = (-1.0) * exponent;flag=1;}
          for(i = 1; i <= exponent; i++);
            result *= x;
          if(flag) result = 1.0/result;
       }
  }
return(result);
```

If the value of x is negative you could set a flag and change the value of x to positive.

```
if( x < 0.0 ){x = -x; flag = 1;}
if(x == 0.0) result = 0.0;
...
if(flag1) result = -result;
return(result);
```

At the end of the function, the flag is used to change the sign of x again. This function now deals with the expected values of a positive x and an integer n. It accomodates x values of 1 and 0 as well as negative values of x. It also handles 0, 1 and negative exponents. Its completed form is shown in listing 6.16. This function will now work with any reasonable arguments except a fractional exponent. A fractional exponent or **float** type exponent presents a special problem.

Listing 6.16

Raising a to the b Power

```
/*  Function to return the nth power of x  */
double pwr(x,exponent)
double x,exponent;
{
int i;
int flag=0,flag2=0;
double result = 1.0;

/*  trap fractional exponent  */
  if(exponent > 0 &&exponent < 1)
  {  printf("Invalid exponent.\n");
     exit();
  }
/*  trap zero base  */
  if(x == 0.0) result = 0.0;

  else
  {  /*  trap base of 1 or expon of 0  */
     if(( x == 0.00) || ( x == 1.0))
       ;
     else
     { /*  trap negative exponent  */
       if(exponent < 0.0)
       {  exponent = -exponent;flag = 1;}

       /*  trap negative base value  */
       if(x < 0.0) {x = -x; flag2 = 1;}
       /*  calculate the raised power  */
       for(i = 1; i <= (int)exponent; i++)
         result *= x;
       /*  convert special cases  */
       if(flag) result = 1.0/result;
       if(flag2 &&((int)exponent &1) ) result = -result;
     }
  }
  return(result);
}
```

End of Listing

Returning Values via Arguments

As shown so far, all arguments have been copied into the function, that is, arguments have been "called by value". A copy of the argument from the calling program is used by the subroutine, but the values of the variables (arguments) in the calling program are not altered. With this arrangement only one value can be returned by the function.

A call-by-address process allows you to alter the values of the variables in the calling function. Instead of passing the variable itself, the address is passed. One reason for this approach is to encapsulate the inners workings of a process inside a function so as to make the calling program understandable. For example, a function to check the value of a parameter follows.

```
ck_limits(color)
int *color;
{
   color = (color > 15) ?  color :  15;
   *color( in each case ) = (*color < 0 ) :  color :  0;
}
```

The calling routine contains the statement:

```
ck_limits(&color);
```

The address of the variable `color` is passed to the function. If the value of `color` is out of range, it is changed by the `ck_limits()` function so as to be within limits.

A second reason to pass an address instead of a value is to reduce the amount of memory needed for a program. Another is to return more than one value to the calling program. For example, if you want to interchange two integers, you could use the function that follows.

```
/*  swap two integers  */
swap(m,n)
int *m,*n;
{  int temp;
   temp = *m;
   *m = *n;
   *n = temp;
   return;
}
```

The proper calling statement is `swap(&m,&n)`; in which the addresses are passed to the function. In this example, `m` and `n` contain addresses. To use the values stored in the address, one applies the indirection operator, `&`.

The preceding example is the classic method of using a temporary variable to hold one value while the original two are interchanged. It also introduces the indirection operator *. The indirection operator is used as a pointer to the address of an object. The address operator, `&`, is used to pass the address of `m` and `n` to the function. The parameter declaration section uses the indirection operator to show that `m` and `n` are now addresses, not the values those addresses contain. The temporary variable temp is a normal variable. The three lines in the body of function work as follows:

```
temp = *m;   /* put the contents of the address
                specified by m in temp */
*m = *n;     /* put the contents of the address
                specified by n into the address
                specified by n */
*n = temp;   /* put the value of temp into
                the address specified by n */
```

The parameter declaration section also merits another look. The statement **int** `*m,*n;` means that `m` and `n` are pointers to integers. The variables are, of course, integers. If the statement were **char** `*ch;`, then `ch` is a pointer to a **char** variable. The pointer itself is an address and has to be an integer.

The indirection operator makes it possible to declare pointers. A pointer is a variable that contains the address of a variable. Suppose `x` is a **float** variable and `ptr` is a pointer to `x`. They would be declared

```
float x,y, *ptr;
...
x = 213.45;
ptr = &x;
/*  now ptr contains the address of x  */
printf("%u\n",ptr);            /*  1  */
/*  print out the address of x  */
y = *ptr;
/* y takes on the value contained in
   the address contained in ptr */
printf("%g %g %g\n",x,y,*ptr);
/*  all three values are the same  */
```

In this case, `x` contains a real number and `ptr` contains the address (an unsigned integer) of `x`. The expression `*ptr` means the value stored in memory location `ptr`. The `ptr` itself is an unsigned integer. Line 1 shows the %u format used to display the pointer.

C allows pointer arithmetic which is both good and bad. It is good because you can increment pointers and perform calculations with pointers. The bad news is that you had better be careful. When a pointer such as `ptr` is incremented with a command like `++ptr`, the result is not the simple addition of 1 to the integer `ptr`. Instead, the value of `ptr` is increased by the number of bytes it takes to go to the next data object address of the same type. If the `ptr` is of type **int** (for example, **int** `*ptr;`) and your machine uses 2 bytes for the integer, `++ptr` adds 2 to the value of `ptr`. If your machine uses 4 bytes for an integer, `++ptr` adds 4 to the value of `ptr`. Pointer arithmetic is often hardware dependent. The effect of adding 1 to a pointer depends on how many bytes are used to store a data type.

Storage Classes and Scope

Data type declarations were first discussed in Chapter 3. The general form is

```
modifier type identifier;
```

Another prefix can be added which specifies the storage class:

```
storage_class modifier type identifier;
```

A storage class describes both scope and lifetime. You may specify that a variable in a function retain its value between calls.

The terminology applied to **C** tend to be a little confusing in the use of adjectives when referring to storage class. To say "automatic variable" is to mean a variable with a storage class of **automatic**. Similarly, a static variable has a storage class of **static**.

The default storage class is **automatic**. An automatic variable is local. That is, it is known only to the function in which it is declared. Its lifetime is temporary; an automatic variable lasts only during the lifetime of the function. When the function terminates, the variable ceases to exist.

A storage class with a persistent duration is **static**. A static variable is declared inside a function but retains its value after the function terminates.

A function may also be declared **extern** or **static**. A function is declared **extern** when its definition is found in another file. A function is declared **static** when you do not want functions in other files to be able to access it.

C also offers the storage class **register**. A register variable is usually stored in an actual register. Its use requires that the programmer be familiar with how the hardware works and how the operating system makes use of the registers. Register variables are used most frequently in bit fiddling. A second popular use is in loop control variables inside a function. Some compilers allow you to declare a storage class of **register**, but treat it as automatic. Register variables are always local in scope and have a temporary life.

The storage class **external** is used for global variables. You can use an external storage class (which is global to all files) or an external **static** (which is global to the functions in one file). External variables are always declared outside a function; local variables are declared inside a function. An ordinary external function can be used by functions in any file. An **external static** variable can be used only by functions in the same file and after the variable definition. Table 6.1 illustrates how storage classes and scope are used.

Table 6.1
Storage Classes, Scope, and Lifetime

storage class	keyword	scope	lifetime
automatic	**auto**	local*	temporary life of function
static	**static**	local	life of function
register	**register**	local	life of function
external	**extern**	all files	permanent
external static	**extern** **static**	one file	permanent

*local means variable is known only to to the function in which it is declared.

External and **static** arrays can be initialized outside a function. **Automatic** arrays cannot be initialized.

correct

```
int x[] = {2,4,6};
dothis()
{
...
```

incorrect

```
dothis()
{
int x[] = {2,4,6}
...
```

Using Storage Classes

The problem of creating a random-number generator can help you understand storage classes.

The random-number generator uses three values to get started. On 16-bit machines, the choices are commonly set at:

```
multiplier = 3373
increment = 6925
modulus = 32768
```

These choices produce acceptable results without overflowing the word size of the machine.

A simple random number generator is implemented in the following segment:

```
float random()
{ unsigned m = 3373 inc = 6925, mod = 32768;
  static float seed = 543.12347;

  seed = (seed - (int) (seed)) * 963;
  return ((int) seed % 10);
}
```

In this example seed is a **static** variable. It needs an initial value, so the arbitrary value of 1.0 is used. The value of seed is retained between calls to the function so that a different number is generated each time the function is called. However, if the program is run a second time, the same set of random numbers appears. The problem is to find a way to initialize the seed differently each time the program runs.

One possible solution is to make the seed variable global to all functions in the program.

```
static float seed;
main()
  seed = 2.1;

random()
{
  unsigned m = 3373; ...
    seed = (( seed * m + c ...

}
```

Making seed global does not really solve the problem because seed must still be initialized. Furthermore, it places a burden on the programmer to supply an appropriate seed. Of course, the program could ask the user to type in a seed.

Another method of varying seed at initialization consists of passing a seed as an argument in the function call.

```
main()
x = random(12);
float random(seed)
float seed;
{ unsigned m = 3373 inc = 6925, mod = 32768;

  seed = (seed -(int) (seed)) * 963;
  return ((int) seed % 10);
}
```

This method works better than the first except that any time the same number is used, seed is altered. A better method is to buffer the choice of seed and make use of only the first value passed to random(). This routine is shown in Listing 6.17.

Listing 6.17

Random-Number Generator

```
float random(temp)
float temp;
{  unsigned m = 3373 inc = 6925, mod = 32768;
   static int flag = 0;
   static float seed = 543.12347;
   if(!flag)
     {  flag++;
        seed = (temp < 0)?  -seed:  seed;
     }
   else
        seed = (seed -(int) (seed)) * 963;
   return ((int) seed % 10);
}
```

On the first call to random, the flag is 0, so `!flag` evaluates to true and the inner block of code is used. On all subsequent calls to random, the value of `flag` is non zero so `!flag` evaluates to false and the inner block is not evaluated. The inner block makes sure `seed` is positive and non-zero.

This method is an improvement over the first because the programmer or user cannot force a particular sequence of numbers by the choice of seeds in the second and subsequent calls. The static variable flag is used to make sure that a particular block of code is executed on only the first call to the function.

The user can take the initial value of `seed` out of the hands of the user by using some system constant, such as the minutes portion of the system clock. Such tricks really improve the randomness of the generator but are very system dependent and reduce the portability of the program.

Listing 6.17 is not only an effective example of a random- number function. It also illustrates the choices you must make in program design and shows the use of static variables. In this case static variables are used both as a way of retaining values between calls to a function and as a way of using a flag so a routine is used only once during program execution.

Typedef and scope. Recall that **typedef** is used to create synonyms for data types. For example, **typedef long int** BIGNUM; would make BIGNUM a synonym for a **long** integer. The scope of a **typedef** is dependent on where it is declared. A **typedef** made within a function is local to that function or a **long** integer. The scope of a **typedef** is dependent on where it is declared. A **typedef** made within a function is local to that function; if made outside a function, its scope is global. For example:

```
typedef float real;     /*  global definition  */
void f()
{  typedef short int integer; /*  local def   */ }
```

Block structure and Scope. Variables that are **automatic**, **register**, or

static variables are local in scope. You can also declare variables in a block of code within a function. These variables are local to the block because **C** does not allow functions to be declared within functions. The code that follows presents one way around that restriction, however.

```
type example(arg1,arg2)
int arg1;
int arg2;
{  int i,n;
   float x;
   ...
   {
     int i,temp;
     for(i=1;i< n;i++)
       temp += i;
   }
   ...
   return;
}
```

The i and temp in the inner block are not known outside the block. The i declared as a local variable in the function is a different object than the i inside the block.

A programmer should be careful of this type of code. It can lead to confusion and be hard to debug. Its most appropriate use is to hide a routine within an existing function that uses many variable names. Used in this way the routine's variables can avoid conflict with the variables in the function proper. Another use of new variables within a block is the handling of a special case. That is, suppose you want to use an **if** to check for the existence of an unusual value; one which will usually not occur. A block of code may be needed to provide an error message.

```
if( value < 0)  /*  and it never should be  */
  {  int i;
     for(i = 1; i < 6; i++)
       puts("Error in data - out of range");
  }
```

Boolean Functions

C does not provide a boolean type. One is not needed since an expression evaluates to false (0) or true (non-zero) for use in relational expressions. For example, `ch != '\n'` evaluates to true (in this case, 1) if the character is a newline otherwise it is 0.

Functions can be written that return boolean values (1 or 0) as they are returning integers. Listing 6.18 contains several boolean functions.

Listing 6.18

Boolean Functions

```
#include <stdio.h>

main()
{
  int n;
  printf("Please press one key ?");
  n = getchar();

  if(number(n))
    {  if(even(n)) printf("\n%3d is even.\n",n-48);
       else printf("\n%3d is odd.\n",n-48);
    }
  else if(letter(n))
       printf("\n%c is a letter.\n",n);
    else
       printf("\nNeither letter nor number!\n");
}
even(n)
int n;
{
  return(~n&1);
}
letter(n)
char n;
{
  return( (('A' <= n) &&(n <= 'Z'))
          || (('a' <= n) &&( n <= 'z')));
}
number(n)
int n;
{
  return( ('0' <= n) &&(n <= '9'));
}
```

Listing 6.18 provides an opportunity to illustrate how a problem can be solved in many different ways. Consider the case of the **even** function. Another way to use it is as a test of equality.

```
even(n)
int n;
{
  return((n % 2 == 0) ?  1 :  0 );
}
```

Used as a test, **even** reverses the values in the ternary operator. Another solution method is to define the values TRUE and FALSE

```
#define TRUE 1
#define FALSE 0

even(n)
int n;
{
  return((n % 2 == 0) ?  TRUE : FALSE );
}
```

Still another way is to define a new type called BOOLEAN and assign that type to the function.

```
#define BOOLEAN int
#define TRUE 1
#define FALSE 0

BOOLEAN even(n)
int n;
{
  return((n % 2 == 0) ?  TRUE : FALSE );
}
```

You could even define the type BOOLEAN by using the keyword **typedef** instead of the keyword **#define**.

```
typedef int BOOLEAN;
```

Readability in programs

Functions can be used to make a program readable. Consider the case of scanning a paragraph entered at the standard input device. The problem is to read the text one character at a time and count the number of words, the number of letters, and the number of sentences and print out certain statistics. These include the counts already mentioned, the average number of words per sentence, and the average number of letters per word.

Each function used to solve this problem must perform a specific task. Using some of the functions from Listing 6.18,you can determine if the character is a letter or a number. Your program must also be able to distinguish symbols that end a sentence and symbols that end a word, the period,the question mark, and the exclamation point. The following function checks for these symbols:

```
end_sent(n)
int n;
{
  return((n == '.')  || (n =='?')  || (n == '!'));
}
```

The end of word is any of the above plus the blank and the comma. The end-of-word function can use end-of-sentence logic to check for the blank and the comma and let the main program check for these cases where a symbol marks an end-of-word as well as an end-of-sentence. The end-of-word function is shown here

```
end_word(n)
int n;
{
  return((n == ' ') || (n == ','));
}
```

The program now accommodate the fact that after an end of word or end of sentence, the next character can be anything including another blank, another period as in an ellipsis or even a newline. Logically, the thing to do after an end of word or sentence is reached is to scan to the next occurrence of either a number or a letter. The function to do this is called move_next().

```
move_next( num_let)
int *num_let;
{
  int c;
  do
    {  c = getchar();
       putchar(c);
    }
  while( !letter(c) &&!number(c) &&(c !=EOF));
  if(c != EOF) (*num_let)++;
}
```

The function `move_next()` modifies `num_let`, which is originally declared in another function. You are faced with a choice about how to treat variable `num_let`. You can pass its address as a parameter or you can use an external (global) variable and allow the function to modify it. Suppose you decide to pass its address.

In natural language, the program progresses in this fashion:

as **long** as end of file not reached,
 as **long** as newline not found
  read a character.
  if it is end of word, bump word count and move
   on to next letter or number
  else if it is end of sentence bump both the
   end of word and end of sentence counts and
   move on to the next letter or number.
  else the **char** must be a letter or number so
   bump the letter count.
 perform statistics and display results.

Listing 6.19 shows the main program used to solve the text- analysis problem.

Listing 6.19

Text Analysis Program

```
#include <stdio.h>

static int num_let,num_sent,num_words,ch;

main()
{
float avg_word,avg_let;
num_sent = num_word = num_let = 0;

while((ch = getchar()) != EOF)
  {  putchar(ch);
     if(end_sent(ch))
       {  num_word++;
          num_sent++;
          move_next(&num_let);
       }
     else
       {
          if(end_word(ch) )
            {  num_word++;
               move_next(&num_let);
            }
          else
               num_let++;
          if(ch == EOF) break;
       }    /*  end else  */
  }    /*  end while  */
do_stats();
out_stats();
}
```

The functions do_stats and out_stats perform the calculations and print the results respectively. The heart of do_stats is

```
avg_let = (float) num_let / (float) num_words;
avg_word = (float) num_word / (float) num_sent;
```

The out_stats routine is a series of **printf** commands to display the results.

Recursion

C permits recursion, that is, a function may call itself. There are any number of typical examples of recursion. The most common is a factorial in which

$$n! = n(n-1)(n-2)\dots 2 * 1$$

or

$n! = n(n-1)(n-2)\ldots 2 * 1$

A recursive function is defined in terms of a previous term.

Not all programming examples of recursion are mathematical functions. Consider a program that places a menu on the screen by means of a function called `menu`. The menu contains 11 choices. The function called `choices` contains the call to the `menu` function. If the choice made is out of range, that is not between 1 and 11, then an error message is printed and the function calls itself. This is a simple but effective use of recursion, because the call to `menu` clears the screen and provides the user with a fresh start. A recursive call returns control to the next statement after it returns. In Listing 6.0, the call to `choices()` is followed by an exit from the function.

Listing 6.20

Menu of Choices

```
/*  sample recursive call  */
choices()

{
int n,td;
menu();      /*  call to display menu  */
scanf("%d",&n);
if(n > 0 &&n < 12) sendcode();
else
  { printf("\nPlease type a number between 1 &11.\n");
    for(td=1;td<4000;td++);      /*  time delay  */
    choices();      /*  recursive call  */
  }
return;
}
```

End of Listing

Perhaps the best-known use of recursion is with the quicksort. The idea behind the quicksort is to partition a list into two sublists. One sublist contains elements less than a pivot value. The other sublist contains elements greater than the pivot value. If each sublist is treated as a brand-new list (in other words, a recursive function) and itself subdivided, the entire list is sorted when the smallest sublist has only two members. Given a list of numbers to be placed in ascending order, the psuedocode goes like this:

```
as long as list has more than 2 elements,
  select a pivot value and then
  partition list into two sublists where
    all elements of one list > pivot
    and all elements of second list < pivot.
  place the pivot in between the lists.
quicksort the first partition
```

```
        quicksort the second partition
```

The code to implement this sort is shown in Listing 6.21.

Listing 6.21

Quicksort Program

```
static int x[] = {5,2,4,7,1,4,3,8,9,4,6,7,10,12,2,15,4};
left = 0; right = 16;

quick(x,left,right)
int x[], left,right;
{
int i,j,pivot,t;

if(right > left)
{  pivot = x[left];
   i = left + 1;
   j = right;
   do
   {
     while(x[i] <= pivot &&i < right)) i++;
     while(x[j] >= pivot &&j>left) j--;
     if(i<j)
       {  t = x[i];x[i] = x[j]; x[j] = t;}
   }
   while( i < j);
   t = x[left]; x[left] = x[j]; x[j] = t;
}

if( j > left + 1) quick(x,left,j-1);
if(j < right - 1) quick(x,j+1,right);
return;
}
```

End of Listing

The function `quicksort` uses a **do-while** construct because there will always be at least one pass through that section of the code. The last two **if** statements are not usually found in quicksort codings; they are there to avoid sorting partitions of size 2 or less.

Mathematical Recursion

Computer programmers make use of functions which call themselves and say it is recursion. The mathematical meaning is that one term of a sequence of terms is defined as a function of a previous term. When solving mathematical problems a recursive equation is frequently employed. The next program uses mathematical recursion to solve a fun puzzle type of problem.

A piece of railroad track is supposed to be exactly 1 mile long to fit into a 1 mile section of track. The rail is one foot too long. If the track is forced into the 1 mile section by bowing it up, how high above the ground will the track bow? Figure 6.1 illustrates the problem.

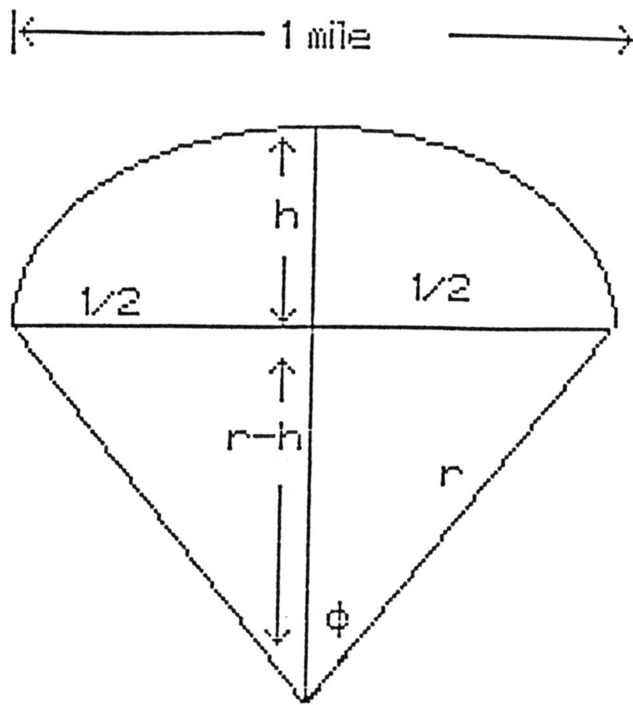

Figure 6.1: *The Railroad track problem*

The bowed track makes an an arc with radius r and h is the height you are looking for. The angle formed by the radius and angle bisector is theta (θ). The length of the arc is 1 mile plus 1 foot, which can be generalized to 1 plus e where e is the error (in this case $e = 1/5280$). The Pythagorean theorem can be used to find h as a function of r.

$$(r - h)^2 + \frac{1}{4} = r^2$$

$$\dots$$

$$h = \frac{(2r - \sqrt{(4r^2 - 1)})}{2}$$

Using some properties of geometry we know that

$$\frac{(1 + e)}{2} = r\theta$$

which leads to

$$\frac{\theta}{(1+e)} = \frac{1}{2r}$$

and from simple trigonometry we know

$$\sin\theta = \frac{1}{2r}$$

so by substitution

$$\sin\theta = \frac{\theta}{(1+e)}$$

and

$$\theta = (1+e)\sin\theta$$

By using the earlier equation, you know that r is a function of θ.

$$r = \frac{(1+e)}{2\theta}$$

The problem is to find θ. Find it by using recursion, then use θ to find r. and finally use r to find h. The core of the solution is finding θ.

You can find successive values for θ by guessing a value of θ and then revising the second guess based on the difference between the guess and the calculated value. If you initialize θ to a small value, (such as 0.034) the new value of θ is

$$\theta_2 = (1+e)\sin\theta_1$$

When the difference between the two thetas is very small, you have found it. The mathematical recursive code is

```
double eps = 1.0e-12;
double theta1 = 0.034;
double diff = 1.0;

while(fabs(diff) > eps)
  { theta2 = (1+e)*sin(theta1);
    diff = theta2 - theta1;
    theta1 = theta2;
  }
```

The mathematical recursion code does not use a function that calls itself, but it is a an implementation of a recursive equation nevertheless. It can be turned into a recursive function call be replacing the **while** loop with a function call to `angle()`.

```
    double eps = 1.0e-12;
    double theta1 = 0.034;
double diff = 1.0;

    angle(theta1);          /*  function call  */
    ...
    /*  end of main function  */

    double angle(theta1)     /*  function to determine angle */
    double theta1;
    {
      double theta2, diff;
      theta2 = (1+e)*sin(theta1);  /*  e is global  */
      diff = theta2 - theta1;
      theta1 = theta2;
      if(diff < eps)
        return(theta1)
      else
        angle(theta1);      /*  recursive call  */
    }
```

This is only a segment of the entire program. The entire program is in Listing 6.22. Although this problem is couched in terms of a railroad track, it can be generalized to determine the height in any arc- chord problem.

One inportant note: This program converges slowly because it employs a straight iteration method. On a small computer it takes awhile to solve the problem. You can speed it up by using the Newton- Raphson algorithm. It is based on the recursive equation

$$\frac{x_{i+1} = x_i - f(x_i)}{f'(x_i)}$$

In your railroad track program

$$f(\theta) = (1+e)sin\theta - \theta$$
$$f'(\theta) = (1+e)\cos(\theta) - 1$$

so the equation for **theta2** can be replaced by

```
            theta2 = theta1-((1+E)*sin(theta1)-theta1)/
                     ((1+E)*cos(theta1)-1);
```

Listing 6.22

Railroad Track Problem

```
/*  by Ken Taylor  */
#include<stdio.h>
#include<math.h>
#define E 1./5280.
#define EPS 1.0e-12
main()
{
  double theta1,theta2,diff,radius,h;

/*  Initialize theta1 and diff  */
  diff = 1.;
  theta1 = .034;
/*  recursive equation to find angle theta  */
  while(fabs(diff) > EPS)
    {
      theta2 = (1 + E)*sin(theta1);
      diff = theta2 - theta1;
      theta1 = theta2;
    } /*  end of while  */

/*  Find radius of bowed track  */

  radius = (1 + E)/(2 * theta1);

/*  Find height of arc and convert to feet  */
  h = ((2 * radius) - sqrt(4*radius*radius - 1))/2;
  h = h*5280;
/*  Print results  */
  printf("Height is %7.4f feet \n",h);

} /*  end of main  */
```

End of Listing

Command Line Arguments

A **C** program is a collection of functions. One of these is **main**(). All functions can accept arguments, but **main**() has a special way of using arguments. Since **main**() is always the first function called in a program, arguments can be passed to **main** when the program is executed. For example, the program call

```
edit sample.doc
```

executes the program `edit` and passes the name of the file `sample.doc` as an argument to the program. The arguments for **main** are **argc** (argument count) and **argv** (argument vector).

The argumnent **argc** is an integer that contains the number of arguments being passed to **main**; **argv** is an array of strings. Each string is an argument. The normal way of expressing **main**() with arguments is

```
main(argc,argv)
int argc;
char *argv[];
{
```

What is unusual is that **argc** is never actually passed as a value. It would be incorrect to say **main**(1,sample.doc).

The compiler is able to count the number of arguments and assign the value to **argc**. The array **argv**[1] contains the first argument, **argv**[2] contains the second argument and so on. The program's name is stored in **argv**[0]. See how these elements work in a simple example, Listing 6.23, which counts the number of letters in a word.

Listing 6.23

Using Arguments on the Command Line

```
/*  sample program to use a command line argument  */
main(argc,argv)
int argc;
char *argv[];
{  int n;
   n = 0;
/*  find out if any word passed to program  */
if(argc == 1)
   {  printf("No word to examine.\n");
      exit();
   }

/*  loop thru string and count characters  */
while(argv[1][n++] != '\0');

/*  print results  */
printf("The word %s has %d characters.\n",argv[1],n);
}
```

End of Listing

If the program is named count and it is used as follows:

```
count whatisthis
```

the program returns

```
The word whatisthis has 10 characters.
```

Passing Program Options via Command Line

The command line can be used to pass options to a program. Suppose the program is to perform some work with a file. The command may take either of two forms:

```
program -lnp filename
```

```
program filename
```

The options can be any combination of l, n, or p and can be in any order and in either uppercase or lowercase. The options can appear on the command line or may be omitted. The following code checks to see if the options are on the line:

```
    char *choices;
char flags[3];
...
if(argv[1][0] == '-')
{
  strcpy(choices,argv[1]);
  set_ops(&flags[0],choices);      /*  set flag values  */
  i = 2;                           /* use second command line
                                      parameter as file */
}
else
  i = 1; /*  use first command line parm as file  */
```

The program name is considered the 0th element of argv. that is, **argv[0]** is equal to program. The string **arg[1]** is the second to appear on the line. If the options are used, the file must be the third command line string (**argv[2]**). When no options are selected, the second command line string must be the file name.

Whenever options have been selected, a function is called to see which options were selected and set the proper flag values. The function which is shown in Listing 6.24. accepts either uppercase or lowercase values. The order of the command line options is not important because the **switch** statement examines each option in the order it was entered. The number of options can vary from 1 to 3. If extra, duplicate, or extraneous options are specified, they are ignored. The calling program is now free to do whatever it wants to with the flags that have been set.

Listing 6.24

Command Line Option Parser

```
void set_ops(flags,choices)
char flags[3];
char *choices;
{
  int i,n;
  n = strlen(choices)  /*  find out the length of the string  */
  i = 1;               /*  start at the second char in choices  */
    while(i<n)
      {  switch(choices[i])
           {  case 'l':
              case 'L': flags[0] = 1; break;
              case 'p':
              case 'P': flags[1] = 1; break;
              case 'n':
              case 'N': flags[2] = 1; break;
               default : break;
           }
         i++;  /*  repeat for next option in the list.   */
      }
}
```

End of Listing

Using the power of C in Functions

The extensive operator set of **C** allows you to create functions not possible in most other languages. Consider the problem of converting a decimal number into binary representation. If you use an array to hold a binary number in bit representation, the number 13 can be written as

```
13 (base 10) == 1101 (base 2)
```

An array to hold the binary representation must be of indeterminate length. The rightmost place value is bit 0, the position to its left is bit 1, and so on. As an array, the right-most value can be placed in the leftmost position in the array

1	0	1	1
↑	↑	↑	↑
0	1	2	3

Realize that 1011 stands for 1101 when written out in the standard place-value form. You can now declare an array to hold the binary representation and perform the standard conversion algorithm. The algorithm performs repeated division by 2 until the quotient is 0. The remainders are always 1 or 0. Each remainder is placed in the array. Figure 6.2 illustrates this algorithm.

$$2\overline{)13} \quad q = 6, \quad r = 1 \rightarrow \text{bit 0 is 1}$$
$$2\overline{)6} \quad q = 3, \quad r = 0 \rightarrow \text{bit 1 is 0}$$
$$2\overline{)3} \quad q = 1, \quad r = 1 \rightarrow \text{bit 2 is 1}$$
$$2\overline{)1} \quad q = 0, \quad r = 0 \rightarrow \text{bit 3 is 1}$$

Figure 6.2: *Conversion of decimal to binary*

A program segment to perform the conversion is:

```
unsigned short int bin_num[];
int n, q, i = 0;

n = 13;
q = n;
while( q != 0)
  { bin_num[i++] = q % 2;
      q /= 2;
  }
```

The **while** loop can be replaced by a **for** loop to produce a simpler code

```
unsigned short int bin_num[];
int n, q, i = 0;

n = 13;
q = n;
for(;q != 0; q /= 2)
  bin_num[i++] = q % 2;
```

The binary representation can be printed by using a simple loop.

```
i = 0;
while(i >= 0)
  printf("%1u",bin_num[i--]);
printf("\n");
```

The same operations can be performed more efficiently by using bitwise operators. The number q can be divided by 2 via the shift right operator. The remainder is the result of ANDing q with 1. When q is odd, the AND result is 1. When q is even, the AND result is 0.

```
unsigned short int bin_num[];
int n, q, i = 0;
n = 13;
q = n;
while( (q | 0) != 0)
  { bin_num[i++] = q &1;
    q >>= 1;
  }
bin_num[i] = 2;  /*  affix a terminator  */
```

The print routine is even simpler because there is no need for the number to be converted to an array. First, find the number of digits to print. The bits are shifted right n places and ANDed with all 1s. The process is repeated until the AND process yields 0. Now n is equal to the number of digits in the binary representation of the number.

```
t = q;
for(n= 0;(t & ~0) != 0; t>>1,n++);
```

To print q, use a loop that repeatedly shifts q right n-1 places and then ANDs the shifted value with 1 to print only one digit.

```
while( n >= 0)
  printf("%1u",((q >> --n) &1));
printf("\n");
```

The test in the **for** loop uses t &0 to make the program machine independent. You want to AND the number t with a binary number containing all 1s. The unary complement of 0 guarantees you will do that regardless of the size of an integer on your machine. You do not really care about the internal representation of a number. You want only to be able to input the number and display it, there is no real need in **C** for the array bin_num. The preceding routine can be used to display a binary representation. To read a number in binary form, you want to read a string of 1s and 0s until the Return key is pressed.

```
n = 0;
while (ch = getchar()) != '\n')
  { n <<= 1;
    n != (ch-48);
  }
```

The preceding routine reads either a 1 or a 0, shifts the bits to the left one place, then ORs n with ch-48. For example, if the bits 110101 ¡CR¿ were typed, the value of n would be

```
     0     /*  initial value  */
     0     /*  shifted left one place  */
     1     /*  value of first ch  */
     1     /*  n ORed with ch  */
     1     /*  second value of ch  */
    10     /*  n shifted left one place  */
    11     /*  n ORed with ch  */
                ...
110101     /*  final value of n  */
```

The final versions of the two functions bin_print and bin_read are shown in Listing 6.25.

Listing 6.25

Binary Read and Print Functions

```
void bin_print(q)
unsigned q;
{
  unsigned t, n;

  t = q;
  for(n = 0;(t & ~0) != 0; t>>1,n++);
  while( n >=0)
    printf("%1u",((q >> --n) & 1));

  printf("\n");
}

void bin_read(n)
unsigned *n;
{ int ch;
  *n = 0;
  while((ch = getchar()) != '\n')
    {  *n <<= 1;
       *n |= (ch-48);
    }
}
```

End of Listing

Many other languages do not have bitwise operators. The typical representation of a binary value is through an array of 1s and 0s. In **C** the existence of a binary read and a binary print function allow you to make full use of a number represented in base 2.

Prototyping

The ANSI standard has includes function prototyping. This has the effect of making **C** a much more strongly typed language. The data type and number of of arguments is specified in the function definition (prototype). The form of the prototyping changes the way a function is specified.

```
/*  old function declaration  */
int widget( ch,x, s)
char ch;
double x;
char *s;
{

/*  new style  */
int widget(char ch, double x, char *s)
{
```

Newer **C** compilers allow the old style to be used as well as the new prototyping style. In most cases the compiler generates error messages for type mismatches. In cases where a type coercion is possible, most compilers will force the coercion with a warning message. The function definition may be copied using a text editor and used as a declaration by simply adding a semicolon to the first line of the definition.

There are other new function definition styles. The two ways to declare a function with no arguments are

```
/*  old  */   f1()
/*  new  */   f1(void)
```

The new way to declare a variable number of arguments is

```
/*  new  */  f1( char *,...)
```

The ellipses indicate that a variable number of arguments are specified. New macros in the file `stdarg.h` provide access to the arguments.

C compilers are not obligated to check function prototyping across modules compiled separately. The ANSI standard proposes that every function be declared in a specific header file, which includes the appropriate type specifications. The appropriate header files are then included in the file. This guarantees that you get consistent function prototyping on each compilation. Under ANSI standards all library members (functions) are associated with a specific header file.

Prototyping introduces a potential problem when pointers are used as arguments. Since a pointer to a data type must be consistent, there are data type conflicts when the pointer references a different data type. For example, some functions contain arguments that are **char** pointers (**char** *) but are passed pointers to arrays, structures, unions, and the like. To avoid the need for a cast in almost every call, the generic data pointer, **void** *, was invented. It is is a pointer data type that is assignment compatible in either direction. The old function that was specified with a character pointer (**char** *) should be replaced with the generic data pointer, **void** *. To avoid going thru the old code looking for these character pointers, introduce a conditional **typedef** that uses **char** * for old compilers and **void** * for ANSI compilers.

Summary

C programs are a collection of functions. They are the building blocks of **C** programs. **C** functions can be of any valid data type: **int**, **char**, **float**, **double**, and **void**. A function's data type is the data type of the returned value.

The arguments to a function can be values (which are copied and used in the function as local variables) or they may be pointers to a data object through which a value may be returned. A call to a function that accepts a pointer as its argument must be made with the address of the variable.

A local variable in a function may be declared **static**. It then retains its value between calls to a function. This is a helpful feature in such functions as random-number generators since a different returned value is expected on each call to the function.

Recursion is permitted, so a function may call itself. Many familiar functions use recursion and, of course, can be implemented in **C**.

The **main**() function is always the first function called in any program. It accepts command line arguments `argc` and `argv`. The argument `argc` is the number of arguments on the command line; `argv` is an array of strings that are the actual arguments. The argument `argv[1]` is the first argument and `argv[argc-1]` is the last argument.

C functions have many, many uses. They are flexible in the number and type of arguments to be passed. Arguments may be values or pointers to an object. The function name may be used in an expression to return a single value, or pointer arguments may be used to pass back multiple values. A function may have no arguments and it may not return a value at all.

EXERCISES

UNDERSTANDINGS

1. Explain each of these terms:
   a. scope
   b. storage class
   c. formal arguments
   d. actual arguments
   e. type checking
   f. call by value
   g. call by address
   h. **static** data type
2. Determine what this program does:

```
main()     /* recursion madness */
{ doit();
}
doit()
{
  int ch;
  ch = getchar();
  switch(ch)
  {
     case ' ': doit();
    case '\n': break;
     default : putchar(ch);
               doit();
  }
  return;
}
```

3. What is the purpose of the **void** data type?
4. Explain the meaning of recursion
   a. as it applies to functions
   b. as a mathematical term.
5. Explain what this function does:

```
char *dothis(x)
int x;
{
  int i;
  char y[15];
  for(i=0;x>0;x>>=1,i++)
    y[i] = (x&1) + '0';
  return(y);
}
```

APPLICATIONS

6. Write a function to determine if the character set in use is ASCII or EBCDIC. The calling function expects a 1 if the character set is ASCII and a 0 if it is EBCDIC.
7. Write the two functions `putdec(n)` and `putnum(x)` which are the complements to the functions `getdec()` and `getnum()`.
8. Modify `swap()` to interchange two **float** values.
9. Write a function to return the rightmost `n` characters of a string, another to return the leftmost `n` characters of a string, and another to return a substring of length `n` beginning with the `m`th position in the string. Use character arrays to represent the strings.

10. Write a function to right-justify a line of text.
11. Complete this function. The purpose is to create a time delay of `n` seconds. The value of SEC will change from machine to machine. Conduct an experiment to determine the correct value of SEC for your system.

```
#define SEC 500
...
void delay(n)
int n;
  {
  register i;
  while( n-- >0)
    for( i = SEC; i >0; i--)
```

12. Write a program to accept a number in binary form, convert it to decimal form, and display the result. Provide the capability of inputting two numbers in binary form and performing the logical operations of AND, OR, XOR, shift right and shift left. Display the result in binary form.
13. Modify the function and calling program in the text analysis program so that `move_next` modifies the global variable `num_let`.
14. Write a function `bin_val(n,i,j)` that returns the value of the `j` bits from integer `n`, beginning with the `i`th bit. For example, if `n` is 51 then `bin_val(n,3,2)` returns 1. The binary representation of 51 is 110011. If the rightmost bit is considered bit 1, then 011 are bits 3, 2, and 1. Beginning with the 3rd bit, the two bits are 01 which is 1 in base ten. The assumption in this case is that the rightmost bit is bit one. Make your function independent of the size of the bit. Return −1 if `i` or `j` is an unreasonable value.
15. Write a function, `rightrot(n,i)` that rotates the integer `n` to the right `i` places.

⋆ Problems for Experts

⋆16. Write a program using functions to simulate a rpn calculator with the basic functions `+ - * / square root` and `reciprocal`.

⋆17. A well-known FORTRAN random-number generator is listed below. Figure out how it works and write an equivalent function in **C**.

```
  SUBROUTINE RANDU(IX,IY,YFL)
  IY = IX * 65539
  IF(IY)5,6,6
5 IY = IY + 2147483647 +1
6 YFL = YFL * 0.4656613E-9
  RETURN
  END
```

⋆18. Collect all the functions to the text-analysis program, add the `do_stats()` and `out_stats()` routines,and make the program work.

⋆19. Rewrite the quicksort example, Listing 6.21, and sort an array of real numbers.

★20. Create a function that recursively calculates the determinant of a matrix by using the expansion of cofactors method. The determinant of any matrix of at least 2 by 2 can be determined by this method. The function calls itself to calculate the determinant of each submatrix as needed. For example:

$$\begin{vmatrix} 12 & 2 \\ 6 & 5 \end{vmatrix} = 48$$

and

$$\begin{vmatrix} 2 & 9 & 4 \\ 7 & 6 & 2 \\ 5 & 3 & 1 \end{vmatrix} = \sum a(i,j) * A(i,j)$$

$A(i,j)$ = determinant of cofactor found by crossing off the ith row and jth column. Each term is multiplied by (-1) raised to the $i+j$ power. In the second row the results are

$$A(2,1) = (-1)\begin{vmatrix} 9 & 4 \\ 3 & 1 \end{vmatrix}$$

$$A(2,2) = \begin{vmatrix} 2 & 4 \\ 5 & 1 \end{vmatrix}$$

$$A(2,3) = (-1)\begin{vmatrix} 2 & 9 \\ 5 & 3 \end{vmatrix}$$

so

$$\begin{vmatrix} 2 & 9 & 4 \\ 7 & 6 & 2 \\ 5 & 3 & 1 \end{vmatrix} = 7 * (-1) * (-3) + 6 * (-18) + 2 * (-1) * (-39)$$

$$= 21 - 108 + 78$$

$$= -9$$

This method may be applied to larger matrices. Write your function so that it will work for square matrices up to 10 by 10.

★21. Rewrite the code fragment from Exercise 4, Chapter 5, so that it becomes a function called `cube(n)`.

7

Macros, Header Files and the Preprocessor

C uses a preprocessor to provide information and definitions to a program. It aids the portability, readability, and maintainability of C programs greatly. preprocessor accepts macro definitions via the keyword **#define**. Files containing functions needed by the current file may be included via the keyword **#include**. Several other preprocessor directives provide compilation and definition control. C gains much of its power from the preprocessor.

A preprocessor is a program that interprets a set of directives and creates or allows language extensions by substituting valid C code in place of the synonyms defined via preprocessor directives. The C compiler then translates the program. A macro is simply a substitution string that is placed in the program in lieu of the synonym that the programmer writes. For example: If the word BEGIN is defined as a synonym for the symbol `{`, when the programmer writes BEGIN the preprocessor changes the word BEGIN to the symbol `{`. The compiler sees `{` instead of BEGIN, which it would not recognized.

Macro Definitions and the #define Keyword

You have already used the keyword **#define** to create symbolic constants. For example you might have used:

```
#define EOF -1
#define TRUE 1
#define FALSE 0
```

These and other symbolic constants help to make code more readable.

Consider the statement that follows, which would appear in a function that returns `TRUE` if `a` is less than `b`.

```
if(a < b) return(TRUE);
```

Contrast the form of the next program line. Note that the **#define** line does not end with a semicolon. The general form of the **#define** statement is

```
#define M_NAME string to be substituted
```

The keyword **#define** creates a straight substitution of one string for another. Everything after the first space following the `M_NAME` is a synonym for the macro name `M_NAME`. No spaces are allowed in the macro name.

Since an entire string can be put in the place of a single macro name, all sorts of possibilities exist. Consider this example:

```
#define UOFC University of California
```

When UOFC is used in a program, the string substitution takes place. The code

```
printf("%s.  \n",UOFC);
```

results in this output:

```
University of California.
```

A macro may have an argument. Consider this equation definition:

```
#define fcn(x) (2*(x)*(x) + 3*(x) -4)
```

When used in a program, the value of x is used.

```
x = 3;
y = fcn(x);
printf(" The value of fcn(x) is %d.\n",y);
```

The output is

```
The value of fcn(x) is 23.
```

Take another look. The second line of code causes the substitution `y = 2*3*3 + 3*3 -4` which evaluates to 23. However, inside the double quotation marks of the control string, the substitution is not made. You can take advantage of this "trick" to create formatted output.

```
#define SQR(x) x*x
#define PRINT(x) printf(" x squared is %d\n",SQR(x));

PRINT(4);
```

The preceding produces

```
4 squared is 16
```

but

```
y = 3;
PRINT(y);
```

yields

```
y squared is 9
```

The substitution is quite literal. For example, the following code

```
x = 3; y = 5;
PRINT(x+y);
```

yields

```
x+y squared is 23
```

If you expected the answer to be 64, you must remember that a macro definition performs no arithmetic. The substitutions are exact and literal. Hence the statement PRINT(x+y) is replaced in the program by

```
printf("x+y squared %d\n",x+y*x+y);
```

When expanded like this see that 3+5*3+5 evaluates to 23. A macro definition is not the same thing as a function. The preprocessor does not perform any calculations; it merely replaces the code in the program with the replacement string in the **#define** statement.

Macros can be nested. In this program:

```
#define FORMAT printf("The answer is %d.\n"
#define fcn(x) (3*(x) - 2)
#define PRINT(x) FORMAT,fcn(x))

x = 5;
PRINT(x);
```

the PRINT(x) statement is replaced by

```
FORMAT,fcn(x);
```

which is then replaced by

```
printf("The answer is %d.\n",3*x-2);
```

so that the output is

```
The answer is 13.
```

Careful nesting of macro definitions can help create useful formatting. Suppose you want to show the value of the variable that is used by a function. If **x** is 3 and f(x) is 7, then you want the output to be

```
The f(x) value for x = 3 is 7.
```

The solution is in the creation of **#define** statements.

```
#define PRINT(item) printf("f(x) for x = item is %d.\n",
                    fcn(item)
#define fcn(x) 3*x + 2
```

If you use these values:

```
item = 5;
PRINT(item);
```

The PRINT macro is replaced by

```
printf("f(x) for x = item is %d.\n",fcn(item));
```

and the output is

```
f(x) for x = 5 is 13.
```

The preceding formatting takes advantage of two facts: A macro name inside a string is not expandedand a macro argument appearing inside a string is replaced. As a result, the item inside the string is replaced by 5. If the macro reads

```
("fcn(x) for x = ...
```

the result is the same

```
fcn(x) for x = 5 is 13.
```

because macros inside a string are not expanded further.

Definitions that are too long for one line on the screen may be continued by making a backslash (\ ) the last character on the line. The backslash used in this way is a continuation mark. It is not used in functions, only in definitions and macros.

Macro "Functions"

Macro definitions can be used to create simple functions. Consider this code which decides if a number is even:

```
#define EVEN(n) ((n)%2 == 0 ? 1 : 0)
```

A program that uses the macro simply includes the statement EVEN(x); as in this example:

```
while( EVEN(a)) ...
```

The preceding statement executes the loop as long as **a** is an even number. Another method to determine if a number is even is to perform a bitwise AND and compare the result to 0. In this case the macro would be The following macro definitions appear often in programs.

```
#define max(x,y)  ((x)>(y)?(x):(y))          /* 1 */
#define min(x,y)  ((x)<(y)?(x):(y))          /* 2 */
#PRINT(fmt,n)     printf("%fmt",n)           /* 3 */
#define square(x) ((x) * (x))                /* 4 */
#define cube(x)   ((x) * (x) * (x))          /* 5 */
#define abs(x)    ( (x) < 0 ?  -(x) :(x))    /* 6 */
#define recip(x)  ( (float)(x) = 1.0 /(float) (x) )
#define odd(x)    ( (x) &1 ? 1 : 0 )         /* 8 */
#define even(x)   ( (x) &1 ? 0 : 1 )         /* 9 */
#define tof()     (putchar('\014'))
```

Macros 1 and 2 yield the larger and smaller of two numbers respectively. Macro 3 prints a number with any desired specifier. Macros 4 and 5 calculate the square and cube of a number, respectively. Macro 6 finds the absolute values and macro 7 finds the reciprocal. Macro 8 returns true if a number is odd while macro 7 returns true if a number is even. The last macro causes a top-of-form character to be printed. Notice the use of parentheses. This is because the argument provided to a macro may not be a single value. The macro does not evaluate an expression, it simply provides a string substitution. For example, `odd(m+n)`, needs the parentheses to guarantee the correct interpretation.

As is frequently the case, there are alternate ways of doing things in **C**. A macro to identify odd numbers might be

```
#define odd(n) ((n)&1)
```

which could be followed by a macro for even

```
#define even(n) (!odd(n))
```

When deciding whether to use code like the preceding, you have to take into account readability and ease of maintenance.

Macros vs Functions

Since some macros seem to perform the same task as functions, how do you know which to use? It depends! A macro performs string substitution. If a macro call is used many times, the code substitution occurs in every case. The result is that the code might be increased by too much to justify its use. The function call does not increase the size of the code, but it does contribute the increased overhead of transferring control to the function and back. You must consider the space and efficiency trade offs in making the decision. In general, if the function call occurs repeatedly, a regular function is in order. If the function is quite short and is used sparingly, use a macro..

Macros do not require their arguments to be of a certain data type. As a result, use a macro to perform a task for which the data type is not certain. For example, the macros `max` and `min` work equally well with **char**, **int**, or **float** types.

Some compilers require that a macro not exceed one line. When a function is longer than one line, it is best, for portability considerations, to use the function. Limit macros to one line and you will also avoid portability problems.

Macros may also cause trouble if your code contains increment operators. The effect of a call such as `x = min( a++,b++)` is often unpredictable. This problem arises because the macro does not perform arithmetic. If you wish to use incrementation operators in the argument list, use a function, not a macro.

Header Files

You used **#include** in earlier sections. Most, notably, **#include** `<stdio.h>` was used to indicate to the preprocessor to include the `stdio` header file at compile time.The statement told the preprocessor to look for the header file in the main or root directory. The header file `stdio.h` contains macro definitions and function declarations needed by the program input and output statements. if a programmer writes the statement as

```
#include "stdio.h"
```

The preprocessor looks for the header file to begin looking in the user's directory. Most programmers use the quotation method for programmer created header files. You use the angle brackets for predefined header files like `stdio.h` and `math.h`. A programmer probably creates a header file for every serious applications program.

A header file contains the definitions, global variable declarations, and initializations used by all the files in a program. If a programmer is building a program called magic.c, an appropriate header file to contain the definitions might be called `magic.h`. The first line of the program would be **#include** `"magic.h"`. Every file in the program must contain the same **#include** command. If the file `magic.h` is modified, all files that include it, must be recompiled. Header files are not compiled separately.

An **#include** command can be used to merge two files. Suppose a set of geometry functions is contained in a file called `geom.c`. It would be ok to include it with the command

```
#include "geom.c"
```

but is not considered good practice. A better way would be to compile `geom.c` separately and link it in later.

Header Files Provided by C

Now that you have a general idea of how header files work, examine two important files: `ctype.h` and `math.h`. A header file provides the definitions and global variable declarations needed by the program. Most compilers include the file `ctype.h`. It allows a number of useful conversions and checks character types.

In Chapter 6 you studied a function that checked if a character was alphanumeric. The file `ctype.h` includes a macro called **isalnum**`(ch)`, which does the same thing. This and other macros are so widely used in examining text that they are always placed in `ctype.h`. The programmer does not need to write the functions as you did in Chapter 6. Table 7.1 lists many of the common macros found in `ctype.h`.

Table 7.1
ctype.h macros

macro	purpose
isalpha`(c)`	returns true if c is a letter
isdigit`(c)`	returns true if c is a numeral
isxdigit`(c)`	returns true if c is a hexadecimal digit
islower`(c)`	returns true if c is lowercase
isupper`(c)`	returns true if c is uppercase
iscntrl`(c)`	returns true if c is control char
isprint`(c)`	returns true if c is printable
isalnum`(c)`	returns true if c is letter or number
ispunct`(c)`	returns true if c is a punctuation character . It includes all printable characters except controls and letters and numbers.
isspace`(c)`	returns true if c is whitespace
toupper`(c)`	converts c to uppercase if not already
tolower`(c)`	converts c to lowercase if not already

Some compilers provide additional definitions such as **isgraph**(c) which returns true if the character is a graphics character. The argument `c` must be of type **char** or an **int** that represents a **char**.

Different implementations of `ctype.h` operate differently. For example, one version creates `isascii(c)` with a macro.

```
#define isascii(c) (( (c) &0x80) == 0)
```

Another uses a function.

```
#define TRUE 1
#define FALSE 0

isascii(c)
char c;
{ return (( 0 <= c &&c <=127 )? TRUE :FALSE);
}
```

Both versions do about the same thing. An ASCII character has the ordinal position 0 through 127. If the character is not in that range, it is not an ASCII value. The macro ANDs the character with 80 hex which is 128. The rightmost 7 bits are zeros. Any ascii character has ones in only the rightmost 7 positions. Hence, the AND of an ASCII character and 128 is always be 0. The second method simply checks to see if the character is in the range 0 to 127.

The text analysis program (Listing 6.19) can be modified to use several of these macros. To do so you need to include the file `ctype.h` and define a few more macros. The top of the revised program might look like this:

```
#include "ctype.h"
#define end_sent(c) ( (c)== '.' || (c)== '?' || (c)== '!')
#define end_word(c) ( (c) == ' ' || (c) == ',' )
```

The functions end_sent and end_word can be discarded and move_next can incorporate the macro **isalnum**() macro to check if a character is a letter or a number. The program becomes shorter and easier to read. The use of header files and macros can frequently provide the same benefits to other programs.

Math.h

The math functions are part of the standard **C** libraries. However, you need to be sure that the functions have been declared in the proper position in the file and that any special definitions about maximum and minimum values on the system are included. The file `math.h` performs this service. Whenever the program uses mathematical functions, include the file `math.h`. The typical math functions provided are listed in Table 7.2.

Table 7.2
Math.h Functions

function	description
sin(x)	sine of x
cos(x)	cosine of x
tan(x)	tangent of x
cotan(x)	cotangent of x
asin(x)	arc sine of x
acos(x)	arc cosine of x
atan(x)	arc tangent of x
atan2(x,y)	arc tangent of x and y
modf(x,y)	floating-point modulus
floor(x)	largest number <= x
ceil(x)	smallest number >= x
abs(x)	absolute value
fabs(x)	floating-point absolute value
log(x)	natural **log** of x
log10(x)	**log** base ten of x
exp(x)	exponential function
sqr(x)	square of x
sqrt(x)	square root of x
pow(x,n)	raise x to n power, n >= 1
sinh(x)	hyperbolic sine of x
cosh(x)	hyperbolic cosine
tanh(x)	hyperbolic tangent

Some libraries include more functions than those in Table 7.2. For example, **abs**(x) is frequently left to the programmer to code as a macro.

```
#define abs(x) ( (x) < 0 ?  -(x) :  (x) )
```

User-Created Header Files

You will probably find that you use the same **#defines** over and over again. A common header file can be used with most of your programs. It guarantees that the definitions are always the same and protects you from typing errors that you might make if you had to recreate them.

Listing 7.1 is an example of a common user-defined header file, `stddef.h`. (The extension h is a connection, not a requirement.) Each of your programs that uses `stddef.h`, must include it at the top of the program.

Listing 7.1

User-Defined Header File

```
/*  header file called stddef.h  */

#include <stdio.h>
#define NL '\n'
#define TAB '\t'
#define BACKSPC '\b'
#define TOF '\014'

#define TRUE 1
#define FALSE 0
#define NULL '\0'
#define YES 1
#define NO 0
#define COLS 80
#define ROWS 24
#define PGLEN 66

#define void int
#define bits unsigned int
#define boolean char

#define max(x,y) ( (x) < (y) ?  (y) :  (x) )
#define min(x,y) ( (x) < (y) ?  (x) :  (y) )
#define even(n) ( (n) &1 ?  0 :  1 )
#define odd(n) ( (n) &1 ?  1 :  0 )
```

End of Listing

Programmers are likely to develop a number of other header files. For example, you could have a header file of definitions for screen i/o. Another header might be for string handling. Header files provide tools for efficient programming and portability.

Typedef vs #define

At first glance **typedef** and **#define** seem to do the same thing. In some cases the programmer could use either to create a synonym for a data type. There are differences, however, and you should be aware of them.

The **typedef** is evaluated by the compiler, not the preprocessor. **Typedef** is not implementation dependent, but **typedef** is used whan portability is a consideration. The **#define** statements are evaluated by the preprocessor.

The **typedef** works only with data types, but **#define** works with strings, and pseudofunctions. In this instance **#define** is more flexible than **typedef**. Both can be used to establish data type synonyms.

```
#define float REAL
typedef float REAL;
```

but only **#define** can be used for a function call.

```
#define even(x) ((x) |1 ? 0 : 1)
```

The **typedef** can be used for control of scope. Any data type created with **typedef** has the same scope as any variable declared in the same place. A **typedef** may be local in scope or global depending on where it is used. The **#define** directive is always global to the file in which it is used.

ANSI Standard and the Preprocessor

The ANSI committee added two preprocessor directives: **#elif** and **#pragma**. The **#elif** directive may appear between an **#if** and its **#endif** or **#else** (if present). The **#pragma** is a compiler directive that allows compiler-dependent switches to be set.

The **#elif** has the form

```
#elif constant-expression
```

Any number of **#elif** lines may now appear between the **#if** and **#endif** directives.

The **#pragma** directive is actually a means of providing a system-dependent compiler **switch**. The directive aides portability because a compiler that does not recognize the **#pragma**, can simply ignore it. The **#pragma** also provides a standard method of specifying compiler options.

A new ANSI preprocessor operator definedidentifier is provided. It may only be used in the constant part of a **#if** or **#elif** directive. The result is 1 if the identifier is currently defined as a macro name and 0 if the identifier is not defined. The overall result is that **C** programmers must be aware of equivalent forms — the old style and the new style as illustrated in Table 7.3.

Table 7.3
Preprocessor Equivalent Forms

old	new
#ifdef identifier	**#if** definedidentifier
#ifndef identifier	**#if** !definedidentifier

The ANSI preprocessor allows for the concatenation of tokens thus forming new ones. This is done with the symbol ##. The following is the general form:

```
#define  merge(symbol, suffix)   symbol ## suffix
```

Which combines the symbol and the suffix into one token. For example:

```
merge (sales, amt)
```

results in salesamt. The new token salesamt is rescanned as a macro.

A final preprocessor change has to do with the K&R rule that strings in macro definitions are not scanned for tokens to be substituted. In ANSI **C** the symbol # is used to allow token substitution within strings. For example:

```
#define pr1(d) printf(# d " = %d\n",d)
```

The use of pr1(n * n) results in

```
printf("n * n" " = %d\n",n*n)
```

The proposed ANSI standard includes a list of header files. Table 7.4 summarizes the header files one can expect to be present for an ANSI standard compiler. The individual functions, macros, and usage are summarized in appendix B.

Table 7.4
Header Files in ANSI standard

header	purpose
assert.h	program diagnostics
ctype.h	character testing
float.h	floating type characteristics
limits.h	integral type sizes
math.h	math functions
setjump.h	nonlocal jump facility
signal.h	signal handling
stdarg.h	variable argument support
stddef.h	miscellaneous definitions
stdio.h	i/o definitions and macros
stdlib.h	utilities
string.h	string functions
time.h	data and time utilities

Compiler Directives

The preprocessor provides a gateway to debugging and portability through its compiler directives. They provide for conditional compilation, conditional definitions and cancelling a previous definition.

Conditional Compilation

It is frequently convenient to place debugging code into a program that is not to be used when the program is finally in production form. The **#if** and **#endif** directives provide this mechanism. Consider this example:

```
#define DEBUG_ON 1
...
#if DEBUG_ON
  debug print statements go here
#endif
```

The **#endif** statement is needed because the preprocessor does not recognize the { } braces. If DEBUG evaluates to true, then the statements between the **#if** and the **#endif** are executed. When the DEBUG flag is on, that is DEBUG is true, the programmer is free to make the debug statements as complicated as is helpful.

For example, a window of variables and values may be opened on the screen and displayed. Since the code for such debugging can be complicated, a simple way of including it or not including it is very helpful. The compiler only includes the statements in question if the expression is true. Consequently, the final program containing the statement

```
#define DEBUG 0
```

which causes the **#if** DEBUG to evaluate to false and the statements between **#if** and **#endif** are ignored by the compiler.

The preprocessor supports an **if-else-endif** structure. The statements following **#if** are executed if the expression following the **#if** is true. Otherwise, the statements following the **#else** are executed.

Conditional definition: A related directive is the keyword **#ifdef**. It is similar to **#if** but works with constants as opposed to expressions. The statements following **#ifdef** are included only if the constant has been defined. Consider this example:

```
#define LAST_ONE 999
...
#ifdef LAST_ONE
  statements
#endif
```

The statements following **#ifdef** are included ifLAST_ONE has been defined via the keyword **#define**. If it has not, the statements are ignored. The structure **#ifdef-#else-#endif** works as expected. Suppose a program on the IBM PC should work differently on a monochrome vs a color interface. You could define a constant COLOR.

```
#define COLOR
...
#ifdef COLOR
  #include "color.h"
#else
  #include "mono.h"
#endif
```

The program would include either the color or the monochrome header file depending on whether the constant COLOR had been defined.

Conditional compilation directives can be used to make a program portable. Suppose a programmer wants to use a 16-bit integer for a certain segment of code. If it is to be ported to a VAX from an IBM PC, the following statements work:

```
#define IBMPC 1
...
#if IBMPC
  typedef int integer;
#else
  typedef short int integer;
#endif
```

You could cause the second **typedef** to be executed by changing the constant IBMPC to 0.

A programmer can provide for the use of a conditional definition in a portable program. Suppose you wanted to define **EOF** but only if it does not exist.

```
#ifndef EOF
  #define EOF -1
#endif
```

These three lines provide a way of avoiding an error that states the constant **EOF** is already defined. Some systems define **EOF** in stdio.h; others do not. In a program that is to be portable, conditional compilation of this kind creates a safeguard against duplicate definitions.

A constant can be undefined if not needed by the **#undef** directive. In the following sequence, MASK is defined and then discarded:

```
#define MASK 0x20
...
#undef MASK
```

This directive produces an error if the identifier specified has not already been defined. In a complicated program, it is sometimes good (and cautious) practice to use the **#undef** conditionally as shown here:

```
#ifdef SIZE
  #undef SIZE
#endif
```

The preceding code checks first to see if the constant SIZE has been defined. If so, the code undefines it.

The compiler directives can be useful to the programmer as debugging aids and as the means to portability.

Frequently, a bug is local, yet persistent. Rather than use the conditional compilation technique to smoke out the critter, many programmers put temporary lines in the code. Two types of statements are typically used: one that prints a variables value and one that prints a message about where you are in a program. To print these kinds of statements, use these two helpful preprocessor macros:

```
#define show(i) (printf("value of i is %d",i))
#define testpoint(x) (printf("program is at point %d \n",i))
```

The program can call these macros as in the following examples:

a.
```
float f1(x)
float x;
{  float a,b;
testpoint(1);
   ...
}
```

b.
```
for(i=0;i<n;++i)
{  show(i);
   ...
}
```

These macros can be placed in your file **stddefs.h** and become available as debugging tools whenever needed.

PROGRAM ORGANIZATION

C programs are written in a modular style. Functions are grouped together by purpose and relationships. As you look at principles and practices, remember that not all are facts or rules. Rather, they are guidelines to help the programmer manage the development and maintenance of large programs.

Some well known **C** programmers claim that functions should be no longer that 100 lines of code and that most functions should fit on one page. Also, no file should contain more that 10 functions and no file should be longer than 500 lines of code. These are practical guidelines, but not strict rules. In addition to helping you organize your programs they give insight into the thinking of professional programmers. When programs of files get too long, they become unwieldy. The modularity of **C** helps with debugging, testing, maintenance, and efficiency. Big, cumbersome program modules are a bad idea.

Several Files: One Programs

The basic building block of a **C** program is the function. Functions that perform related tasks and depend on each other are grouped into one file. The files are compiled separately and then linked together into an executable program file. There are several points to keep in mind when creating programs in this way.

Global Definitions

Files frequently use the same set of global definitions. For example, a program may use a collection of **#defines** for such symbolic constants as COLOR, SIZE, TRUE, FALSE, and the like. Rather than retype the same definitions for every file, create one header file for the entire program. This header file contains all of the constants, functions, global typedefs, and global variable declarations and initializations needed by the files in the program. If the program is to bear a final name, such as **score.c**, it is common practice to name the common header file with the same name as the program; in this case the header is **score.h**. Each file includes the line

```
#include score.h
```

near the top of the file. There are several benefits to this approach. First, it is easier to maintain one header file than to maintain the same definition in several different files. When a change is made to the header file, you have only to recompile the appropriate files to ensure that all files are up to date. If each file has its own set of definitions, it is easy to forget to make a needed change to every file. It also reduces typing errors. Another benefit is that the header file provides all programmers, some of who are working on different aspects of the program, with a common set of global definitions and declarations. Large programs are easier to manage when there is one master header file used by everyone.

External Functions

A program may contain several files. Some files may make use of functions written and compiled in another file. Because each file is compiled separately, any file that needs to use the function must declare it. For example:

```
extern int func1();
```

The rule to follow is that you must define a global function in one file and declare it as **extern** in any other file that uses it.

file containing f	file using f

`int func1(m,n)`
`int m,n;`
`{ /* body */`
`}`
	`extern func1();`
	`...`
	`q = funct(a,b);`

In the preceding example the file containing the function definition may also use **extern**

```
extern int funct1();
```

but it is not necessary. Some programmers believe that by declaring the function as **extern** in the same file as the function definition, they are stating that funct1() is global in scope. Other programmers believe that it should only be declared **extern** in the files that use it, but do not define it.

The modifier **static** when applied to a function, limits its scope to a particular file. Sometimes you want to create a local function that has the same name as some other global function, such as a library function name. The function is declared as **static** within a file; defined in the same file, and called only from functions contained in that same file. Other files are free to use the same function name in a different context. An example of this usage follows.

Consider the case of using an external **static** variable to hold the value of the seed in the random number generator. (See Listing 6.17). A second function could be introduced to call the random number function to initialize the seed. The external **static** variable seed is known to both functions. Listing 7.2 shows how the function works.

The variable `seed` is external **static** as it is permanent in life but is known only to the functions in the file. The file would be compiled separately from the file containing the calling function. It would then be linked in as part of the total program. This separate compilation protects the variable seed from other functions. Yet seed is known to both functions in this file. The main program must have some mechanism for calling `int_rand()` one time to initialize the random-number generator. Any function called by a function from a different file must be declared **static** in the original file and **extern** in the file containing the calling program.

Listing 7.2

Random Number Generator..External Function

```
/*  random number generator file  */
static float seed ;
float random()
{  unsigned m = 3373 inc= 6925, mod= 32768;

   seed = (seed-(int)(seed))* 963;
   return ((int) (seed)% 10);
}

int_rand(int_seed)
float int_seed;
{  seed = int_seed;
}
```

End of Listing

Using files that contain several global functions used by several other files is a practical way to create a mini-library. You can then create a header file declaring all the external functions so that you must include only the header if a file needs any of the external functions. Figure 7.1 illustrates the concept.

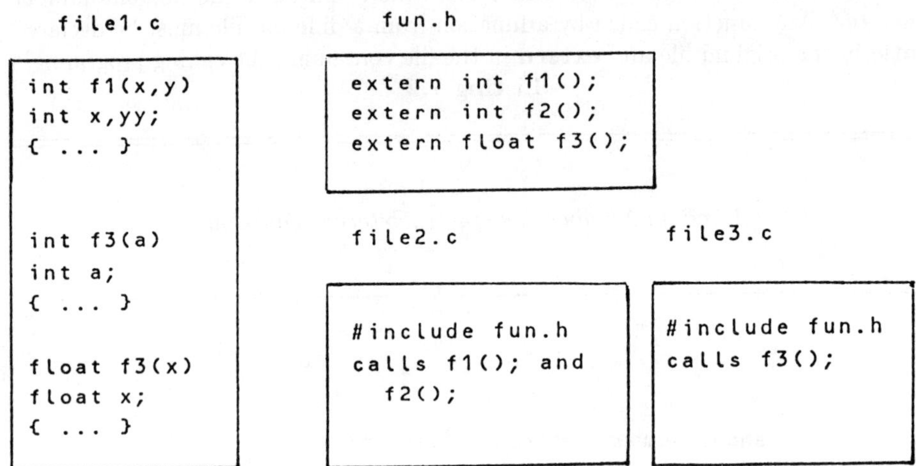

Figure 7.1: *Relationship of Program File to External File*

If external functions are used by almost every file,add the statement **#include** `fun.h` statement to the global header file, for example `score.h`. The software designer must then decide whether to use a separate header for global functions or to include it in the global header file for the whole program.

Libraries

C makes use of functions contained in precompiled libraries. The most common libraries are the standard library and the math library. Some implementations includespecial libraries such as string libraries or i/o interface libraries. Many programmers create their own libraries.

A library is basically a collection of functions. Since the calling functions are always in a different file from the library, each library function is external to the calling file. The function declarations and any special definitions needed by the library functions are included in a header file. Two of the most common are `stdio.h` and `math.h`. These header files contain such declarations as

```
extern double sin();
```

and such definitions as

```
#define EOF -1
```

Consequently, any file that uses a math function must also contain a line near the top to include the math header

```
        #include <math.h>
or      #include "math.h"
```

A programmer-created library must also be accompanied by an appropriate header file.

When using a function from the standard library that is not declared via `stdio.h`, the programmer must always declare the function prior to its use. Consider for example,a function that you will read about in detail later, **malloc**(). If it is to be used, the programmer must declare it as

```
extern char *malloc();
```

It is important to be familiar with the various header files, what definitions are specified, and which external functions are declared. Any other functions included in the library must be declared before they can be used. Appendix D summarizes all the ANSI standard header files and their contents.

Organizing Program Files

Look at a model of a large program. It is a database program that uses menus, windows, and provides built-in help. Figure 7.2 shows the block diagram of the program's main files. It makes use of the standard library, the math library, and related header files.

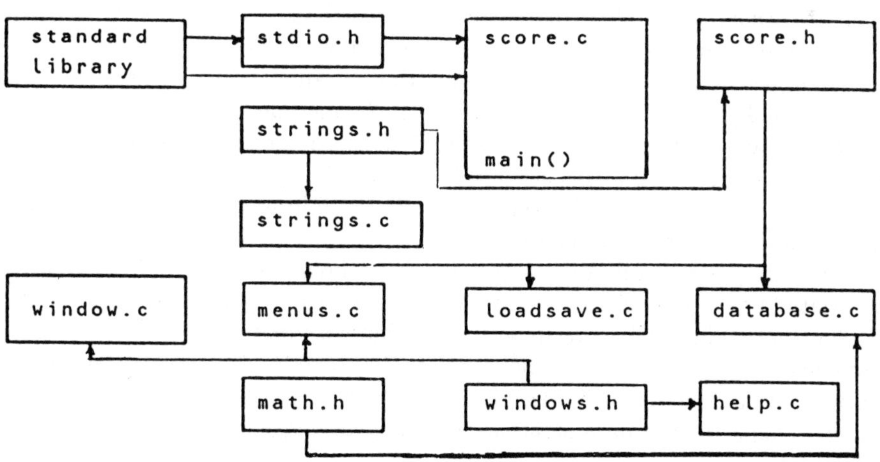

Figure 7.2: *A model of a large database program*

The program is score. So, the main module is called score.c and the header file is score.h. The file score.h contains all the global definitions, **typedefs**, and **extern** function declarations needed by the various files. File score.h contains **#include** <stdio.h> as its first line. The second line of score.h is **#include** <strings.h> because the string functions in strings.c are accessed via strings.h.

The program score.c uses the standard library and strings.c which is a collection of special string-handling routines. The module menu.c provides all the menus for the programs. The menus use window routines located in windows.c, so menu.c specifies **#include** windows.h in order to connect windows.c and menu.c. The file help.c uses windows.h in a similar way. The file database.c makes use of the math library, so it contains the line **#include** <math.h>.

When all of the modules are compiled and linked together, the executable file is called score. The naming conventions are to give the files names that are descriptive of the broad task the functions perform (such as, menu, loadsave, help, windows, and so forth). the functions are grouped together in files according to the task to be performed. Header files bear the names of the files they support (for example, score.h and windows.h), and the main module bears the same name as the final program.

Modularity and Information Hiding

Hiding information in modules is a way of black-box programming. A file may contain a function with the same name as the file. All definitions , and functions in the file support the main function with the module. The word main in this sense is not the same as **main**() in the first function in a program. The details of how a task is performed are hidden from the programmer that uses the file. This section looks at some of the principles that guide information hiding via modules.

A module consists of a function visible (to programmers) called an entry point. The name of this function is synonymous with the module (file). A module may or may not contain hidden routines. These functions are not available to other files in the program and are usually declared to be **static**. The job of the module is to hide the way a particular task is implemented. This facilitates program maintenance and helps in the design of other routines.

The entry point and its supporting functions should not be allowed to alter any global data. Only those data objects passed to the entry point may be altered. If you allow global data values to be altered by hidden functions, the debugging and maintenance of the larger program would be impossible. It is best to make each important data structure a hidden data structure in exactly one module. In this way any changes to the data structure can only be made via the the single entry point (function).

Do not overdo the information hiding. Modularity is a tool to be used by designers to facilitate program development, protect against side effects, and hide details of an implementation from other programmers. Many simple routines should be global; others are of minor importance and do not warrant a special file. A programmer must, at the design phase, decide what modules to use and how data should be passed between modules. Some cases are best handled via modules, others are not.

Using Register Variables

Register variables are not to be ignored. The best way to use a **register** variable is as a local variable within a function. With function arguments, some overhead is unavoidable. However, local variables, especially those used as loop counters, are excellent candidates for the **register** storage class. Such use can save hardware overhead and result in improved program efficiency.

Consider the example of a typical function call shown in Listing 7.3.

Listing 7.3

Register Variable Usage

```
f(x)
int x;          /*  this should not be a register */
{
  register int i;          /*  1  */
  register char *cp;       /*  good idea  */

  cp = &x;
  for( i= 0;i < 500; i ++)
                           { /*  some action with x  */
                             cp++;
                           }
}
```

End of Listing

You may declare x as **register int** x, but the declaration may result in larger code that may even be slower because of the way many implementations use the stack for parameters. Line 1 is a toss-up. Because a register may not be big enough to hold an integer, there may be some overhead involved with trying to store an integer as a **register**. On many microcomputers, however, line 1 works well.

Pointers are great candidates for **register** variables. If a pointer is stored in a register, a full move instruction will be saved in the assembly language translation. In a big loop the savings are noticeable; the compiled code is smaller and faster. Within functions, pointers are always candidates for **register** variables. If the **int** fits into a register, then **ints** are also candidates for **register** variables. Global variables and arguments are not good candidates for **register** variables. Pointers used in far calls are not good candidates for **register** variables because they usually involve more bytes than a register has available.

Programmers' Tools

Lint

The Unix program `lint` provides usage checks, type checking, and portability checking for **C** programs. It is very useful for avoiding those hard-to-find bugs that result from global variable misuse and type mismatches. It checks for loops that do not end, unreachable statements, and consistency in the use of function- returned values. It is good practice to run `lint` on all programs.

`Lint` has the general form:

```
lint [-optionslist] file1.c file2.c ... filen.c
```

The files in the list are the files that make up your program that lint will check for compatibility. The lint options are listed in Table 7.5.

Table 7.5
lint Options

option	meaning
h	do not apply heuristic to detect bugs, improve style, and improve efficiency.
b	do not report **break** statements that cannot be reached.
v	suppress complaints about unused arguments in functions.
x	do not report variables referred to by unused **extern** declarations.
a	do not report assignments of **long** to variables of type **int**.
c	report casts that might not be portable
u	Do not report functions or variables used but not defined. (to be able to run `lint` on only part of a file list.)
n	do not check compatibility with the standard library.

C programs can influence the operation of lint by placing selected comments in the program files. These comments and their meanings are listed in Table 7.6.

Table 7.6
Lint Comment Options

comment	meaning
`/* NOTREACHED */`	inhibit lint reports on unreachable code.
`/* VARARGSn */`	suppress check for variable number of arguments in the next function. Only check the first n arguments.
`/* NOSTRICT */`	turn off strict type checking for the next expression.
`/* ARGSUSED */`	turn off `-v` option as applies to next function.
`/* LINTLIBRARY */`	inhibits reporting of unused functions after this comment.

Grep

The Unix utility **grep** should be named find. It stands for generalized regular expression parser which is a formal way of saying that the program looks through text and finds strings that match a given string. The utility can be tremendously useful.

For example, suppose a multiple-file program contains several references to a function and then a change is made to the argument list of that function. It is helpful to be able to find all the files and all the instances of a reference to that function. The utility **grep** does that.

The general form of grep is

```
grep [-optionslist] string-to-find [files to look in]
```

Usually, each matching line is echoed to the standard output. A number of grep options are available and are listed in Table 7.7.

Table 7.7
grep Options

option	meaning
`-v`	all lines except the matching ones are printed.
`-c`	only a count of matching lines is printed.
`-i`	ignore u/l case distinction.
`-l`	list only the file names that contain matching lines.
`-n`	include line numbers when line is echoed to **stdout**.
`-s`	suppress error messages.

The `grep` options are useful in many instances. Say you are looking for an identifier and want to know all the files in which it appears. Suppose the identifier is `thingamajig`. The command to look for it might be:

```
grep [l] thingamajig *.c
```

In response, `grep` lists only the **C** source file names that have the identifier `thingamajig` in them.

Make

The Unix program `make` provides a way to create a script for conditionally compiling and linking programs that are made up of several files. When a programmer makes a change in one file, it may affect other files. For example, if a user-created header file is used by three other files, then any change to that header file means each of the three program files must be recompiled. These dependencies can be specified in a `make` file so that the programmers do not have to remember to recompile all the appropriate files when a change is made. Nor do they have to remember the order of compilation.

The utility `make` reduces errors and improves the efficiency of the development process. A `make` file is a script based on the dates of creation of the respective dependent files. The program `make` is called by the command

```
make [-f makefile] [-option1] [-option2]...[-last option]
```

The `make` file is created by the user with an editor. It specifies the dependencies and compilation conditions. The program options are extensive and complicated.

Understanding `make` is difficult. Consult the manual for your installation and try the examples. Once mastered, `make` can save you considerable effort.

Summary

The preprocessor provides several mechanisms to make **C** programs readable, efficient, and portable. The **#include** allows you to merge two files at compile time. **C** also permits header files, some provided with the compiler and some created by the programmer. These header files contain definitions and declarations needed by the programs.

The **#define** directive allows you to create symbolic constants and macros which are substituted for in the actual program. **C** macros are independent of datatype and can be used in place of functions. A macro is used when speed is important. A regular function adds overhead and a loss of speed but results in smaller code.

Several header files, `stdio.h`, `ctype.h`, and `math.h` are commonly used in all implementations of **C**. These headers help provide system independence. They provide mechanisms for using different word sizes, file characteristics, character sets and other system-dependent features. The programmer's code remains the same.

The preprocessor also provides for several conditional compilation directives. The directives allow debugging code that is compiled conditionally according to whether a flag is set, to conditionally define constants, and to increase portability by conditionally defining and compiling **typedefs** and **#defines**.

EXERCISES

UNDERSTANDINGS

1. Explain the difference between a macro and a function.
2. Does the preprocessor know ? What can you not do outside a function?
3. What are the substitution rules for inside and outside of strings?
4. Explain the meaning and differences between the use of **static** and **extern** as applied to variables and functions within the same file and in different files.

USAGE

5. Fix these statements:

```
#define BLUE = 1
#DEFINE YES 1;
```

6. Where `n` is 7 and `y` is 12, what will be the output of the macro `fcn(x)` in the text when called as `fcn(n+2*y)`?

APPLICATIONS

7. Write a macro to find the smallest of three integers.
8. Write a macro to swap two data objects.
9. Write a macro `PROMPT` which instructs the user to type in the test data.
10. Write a macro to print two integers with labels: Suppose `m` is 12 and `n` is 14, the macro should yield

```
m is 12, n is 14
```

11. Write a macro to find the cube of a number.
12. Write a macro called `BELL` which causes the terminal "bell" to beep.
13. Rewrite the text-analysis program from Chapter 6 by changing the **`end_sent`**, **`end_word`**, **`letter`**, and **`number`** functions to macros.
14. Write a macro to compute **`n`** factorial.
15. Write macros to replace the functions **`skip(n)`** and **`tab(n)`** found in Chapter 6.
16. Write a macro called `PR(i)` to print a single integer.
17. A stanine bivariate graph is a 9 by 9 cell array. An element of a cell is determined by the stanine of a person's IQ (on the x axis) and the stanine of the person's achievement score (y axis).

IQ Stanine

	1	2	3	4	5	6	7	8	9
9									
8									
7									
6									
5									
4									
3									
2									
1									

A person is an overachiever if his achievement score is more than one stanine higher than his IQ stanine. A person is an underachiever if his stanine is more than one stanine lower then his IQ stanine.
A stanine is 1/2 standard deviation wide. Stanine 5 is 1/4 stanine above and below the mean. The mean and standard deviation of the achievement score are 500 and 100 respectively. The mean and standard deviation of the IQ score are 100 and 15.
Write a program which places each child in the stanine bivariate table. Print the table showing the numebr of students falling in each cell. Calculate and print the number and percentage of overachievers and underachievers.
Use macros to calculate the stanines.

DATA

student	iq	achievement
1	107	510
2	110	750
3	80	490
4	92	650
5	120	800
6	118	640
7	105	700
8	124	900
9	112	350
10	110	720
11	98	650
12	105	580
13	120	600
14	134	720
15	147	700
16	102	440
17	90	400
18	80	460
19	130	580
20	128	710
21	109	650
22	102	480
23	116	550
24	110	690
35	118	610
end of data	0	0

8

Arrays, Pointers and Strings

This chapter explores **C**'s unique way of dealing with arrays and pointers. The two concepts are closely intertwined. You begin by reviewing simple arrays in terms of how they are used in **C** and in several other languages. From there you look at the relationship of arrays and pointers. Next strings are explained as indexed arrays and as pointers.

The material in this chapter applies to most programs. Some of these topics have cropped up before out of necessity; this chapter pulls the ideas together in preparation for the rest of the text. There are many special cases and typical uses to learn. The examples in this chapter illustrate the principles and practices of using arrays in **C**. Pointers are introduced, but you will see many new uses in later chapters.

Simple Arrays Reviewed

Arrays are a common item in programming. You have been using versions of arrays since Chapter 5. In **C**, arrays are different from arrays in other languages. An array name in **C**, is actually a pointer. In most languages, an array is an aggregate data type such as a collection of integers. In **C** an array of integers is declared by identifying the data type of the elements and giving the array a name. The example that follows sets up `x` as an array of integers.

```
int x[];
```

An alternate method would be to declare the array to have `n` (in this case six) elements.

```
int x[6];
```

The indices for this array would be 0 through 5. That is, `x[0]` is the first element and `x[5]` is the sixth element.

Some arrays can be initialized. A rule to remember is:

```
Only external and static arrays can be initialized.
Auto arrays cannot be initialized.
```

Hence the following is correct:

```
int x[] = {2,6,4,5,2 };
main()
...
```

The code that follows is incorrect:

```
main()
{  int x[] = {2,6,4,5,2 };
```

```
main()
```

This code, however is legal:

```
{  static x[] = {2,6,4,5,2};
```

Arrays can be of any data type and any storage class except **register**. The following are legal array declarations:

```
int x[];
char ch[];
float y[20];
static a[100];
extern static name[20];
```

Since **auto** arrays cannot be initialized when they are declared, you may elect to use a collection of assignment statements to perform the task.

```
main()
{int a[];

a[0] = 2;
a[1] = 5;
a[2] = 14;
a[3] = 20;
```

If not explicitly initialized, the elements of an **auto** array are set to whatever the memory contents happen to hold. In **int**[x], for example, x[4] might be just about anything. If not explicitly set, **external** and **static** arrays are initialized to 0. Consider this example:

```
static int x[];
main()
{  int y[];
   printf("%d %d\n",x[2],y[2]);
}
```

The output would be 0 nnnn, where nnnn is whatever happened to be in the memory location for y[2].

The Shell Sort

Sorting a list of objects provides a good example of using a single-dimension array.Consider an array of integers to be sorted using the Shell sort, a divide-and-conquer technique invented by Donald Shell. The list is divided into sublists by taking every ith element beginning with the first one. The "gap" is the size of i. Suppose we had a 12 item list

```
4 7 2 9 10 5 7 3 9 5 10 3
```

which was broken into three sublists using a gap of 4.

```
list 1  4  9  7  5
list 2   7  10 3  10
list 3    2  5  9  3
```

Each sublist is sorted and then a smaller gap size is selected.

```
list 1   4  5  7  9
list 2    3  7  10 10
list 3     2  3  5  9
```

The entire list after one gap size has been used is

```
4 3 2 5 7 3 7 10 5 9 10 9
```

A new gap size of 2 yields 2 sublists

```
list 1  4  2  7  7  5  10
list 2   3  5  3  10 9  9
```

These two lists are sorted individually

```
list 1  2  4  5  7  7  10
list 2   3  3  5  9  9  10
```

Finally, the gap size is cut to 1. Since it is almost sorted already, it does not take long to finish.

```
2 3 4 3 5 5 7 9 7 9 10 10

2 3 3 4 5 5 7 7 9 9 10 10
```

A crucial step in the shell sort is the size of the gap. In Listing 8.1 the gap is based on the sequence `( 3 * i + 1) modulus 4`, where `i` goes from 1 to `n`.

Listing 8.1

Shell Sort

```
int list[];
int n, i,j,t,gap;

{
/*  find gap size  */
gap = 1;
do {
       gap = 3 * gap + 1;  }
while( gap <= n);
gap /= 3;

/*  begin gap loops  */
for(;gap>0;gap /= 2)  /*  loop thru all gap sizes  */
      for(i=gap;i<n;i++)
        /*  sort sublists  */
        for(j=i-1;j>=0;j -= gap)
          if((list[j] > list[j+gap]) &&(j+gap < n))
            /*  swap two elements  */
            {  t = list[j];
               list[j] = list[j+gap];
               list[j+gap] = t;
            }
} /*  end sort  */
```

The program segment shown in Listing 8.1 will always use a gap size from the list 1,4,13,40, 121, and so on, for the first pass. This sequence effectively deals with lists of various sizes.

Using Arrays to Evaluate and Translate Character Types

An important use of arrays is to speed up the evaluations of characters as they are typed from the keyboard. Many modern applications packages such as word processors evaluate every keystroke "on the fly." Clearly, the goal is to do this as quickly as possible. We have already seen functions and macros that can perform the task.

```
#define isletter(n) ( (c > 64) && c < 91)?  1 :0 )
```

and

```
isletter(c)
char c;
{return( (c > 64 && c < 91) ?  1 :  0);  }
```

Each of these involves at least two comparisons, and a logical AND. The function adds the overhead of a function call. There must be a way that requires fewer steps.

To arrive at a better solution think of creating an array that is the same size as the character set. For example, if the ASCII character set of 128 elements is used, then another array of 128 elements is established. The new array is called a translation array (and in some cases a transition array). Its elements are "codes" to be used in the evaluation of the character type. Table 8.1 shows how ASCII characters and the translation array defined as **char** `c_type[128]` correspond.

Table 8.1

ASCII char set		Translation Array /* **char** `c_type[128];` */
value	character	code
0	NUL	0
⋮		
34	"	16
⋮		
51	3	4
52	4	4
⋮		
66	B	1
67	C	1

A code is found by using the ASCII value as the subscript of the array. For example, **if** c is a B then c_type[c] has the value 1. If the code for all letters is 1, then the application program has to check only **if** the code is 1 to determine if the character is a letter. The easiest way to do this is with a binary or bitwise AND. For example, the statement

```
isletter(c) = c_type[c] & 1;
```

will result in "isletter()" returning a true or false after only 1 bitwise operation. Compared to the multi-step comparisons shown earlier, this is a much faster procedure.

The characters can be evaluated for codes that represent valid keystrokes, invalid characters, or edit keys. The application program will accept only certain keys: letters, numbers, and punctuation marks. Most control characters and special characters such as the tilde and back slash are to be ignored (in other words they are invalid characters). An edit key is something like the @ symbol, control-h, and the tilde.

The program to evaluate keystrokes on the fly requires the creation of the translation array. The ASCII character set is shown in a corresponding array in the fragment that follows.

```
         NUL,^A,^B,^,^D,^E,^F,^G,^H,TAB   /*  0 - 9  */
         LF,^K,FF,CR,^N,^O,^P,^Q,^R,^S    /*  10-19  */
         ^T,^U,^V,^W,^X,^Y,^Z,ESC,^\,^]   /*  20-29  */
         ^^,^_,SPACE,!,",#,$,%,&,'        /*  30-39  */
         (,),*,+, , , -, .  , /, 0, 1     /*  40-49  */
ASCII    2 , 3, 4, 5, 6, 7, 8, 9, :, ;    /*  50-59  */
         <, =, >, ?  , @, A, B, , D, E,   /*  60-69  */
         F, G, H, I, J, K, L, M, N, O     /*  70-79  */
         P, Q, R, S, T, U, V, W, X, Y     /*  80-89  */
         Z, [. \. ]. ^, _, ` , a, b , c /*  90-99  */
         d , e , f , g , h , i , j ,k , l , m  /*  100-109  */
         n , o , p , q , r , s , t , u , v , w  /*  110-119  */
         x , y , z , {, |, }, ~, DEL      /*  120-127  */
```

The character translation array can be defined as

```
static short c_type[] = {
        0,0,0,0,0,0,0,0,2,2,       /*  0 - 9  */
        2,0,0,0,0,0,0,0,0,0,       /*  10-19  */
        0,0,0,0,0,0,0,2,0,0,       /*  20-29  */
        0,0,1,1,1,0,1,1,0,0,       /*  30-39  */
        1,1,0,0,1,1,1,0,1,1,       /*  40-49  */
        1,1,1,1,1,1,1,1,1,1,       /*  50-59  */
        0,0,0,1,2,1,1,1,1,1,       /*  60-69  */
        1,1,1,1,1,1,1,1,1,1,       /*  70-79  */
        1,1,1,1,1,1,1,1,1,1,       /*  80-89  */
        1,0,0,0,0,0,0,1,1,1,       /*  90-99  */
        1,1,1,1,1,1,1,1,1,1,       /*  100-109  */
        1,1,1,1,1,1,1,1,1,1,       /*  110-119  */
        1,1,1,0,0,0,0,0 };         /*  120-127  */
```

The 1s in the array correspond to valid characters, the 2s to edit characters, and the 0s to invalid characters that are to be ignored. The program needs these definitions:

```
#define VALID 1
#define INVALID 0
#define EDIT_TYPE 2
```

The program processes each character in the following manner

```
switch (c_type[ch])
{  case INVALID:  break;  /*  ignore it  */
   case VALID   :         /* call functions to process
                          the character*/;
                 break;
   case EDIT_TYPE         /*  call edit handler  */
                :  break;
}
```

The evaluation of each character is very fast because there are only three possible values to evaluate the ASCII value of each character. The keyboard character is simply an array **index**. The **switch** statement provides the branching needed by the application program.

Using code values to find character types

When a **switch** statement does not fit the program's logic, functions can be defined that return true or false according to the character type. The heart of the problem is to decide the codes' values. To some extent, the code choices are left to the programmer. If there are only a few codes, then they should correspond to the binary bits in one char or **int**. The codes should be 1,2,4,8,16,32,64 and so forth. The bit values are displayed here.

bit position

7	6	5	4	3	2	1	0
↑	↑	↑	↑	↑	↑	↑	↑
128	64	32	16	8	4	2	1

value

Each of these codes can be evaluated with a simple & operator. For example, **if** some characters all have the code 32, then they can all be evaluated to true or false with the statement

```
is_this_char_type(c) = c_type[c] & 32;
```

When other codes, such as 5, are used, then the evaluation is more complicated because c_type[c] & 5 evaluates to true because c equals 4 or c equals 1 as well as c equals 5. Hence the right hand side of the equation is

```
(c_type[c] & 1) & ((c_type[c] & 4)>2)
```

which is considerably more complicated. The point of this example is that program efficiency is best when the codes are based on the values represented by the single bits in an integer.

If the program allows for several character types, You can define them as in

Table 8.2.

Table 8.2
Special Character #define Codes

define	code	meaning
#define	UP 1	/* 00000001 upper case */
#define	LO 2	/* 00000010 lower case */
#define	NUM 4	/* 00000100 numerical */
#define	SPC 8	/* 00001000 space bar */
#define	PUNC 16	/* 00010000 punctuation */
#define	CTRL 32	/* 00100000 control */
#define	OPER 64	/* 01000000 operators */
#define	BRKT 128	/* 10000000 brackets */

Note that you are using only 1 bit per code value. To see if a character is punctuation, you need only to perform a bitwise AND with the code value. If it returns true, the character is of that type.

```
#define is_a_punctuation_mark(ch) = c_type[ch] & PUNCT
```

This definition depends, of course, on the `c_type[]` array containing the proper code values. The character translation array is defined as **static short** `c_type[]`.

```
static short c_type[] =   {
        0,32,32,32,32,32,32,32,32,32,      /*  0 - 9   */
        32,32,32,32,32,32,32,32,32,32,     /*  10-19   */
        32,32,32,32,32,32,32,32,32,32,     /*  20-29   */
        32,32,8,16,16,0,0,0,0,16,          /*  30-39   */
        128,128,64,64,16,64,16,64,4,4,     /*  40-49   */
        4,4,4,4,4,4,4,4,16,16,             /*  50-59   */
        64,64,64,16,0,1,1,1,1,1,           /*  60-69   */
        1,1,1,1,1,1,1,1,1,1,               /*  70-79   */
        1,1,1,1,1,1,1,1,1,1,               /*  80-89   */
        1,128,0,128,64,0,0,2,2,2,          /*  90-99   */
        2,2,2,2,2,2,2,2,2,2,               /*  100-109  */
        2,2,2,2,2,2,2,2,2,2,               /*  110-119  */
        2,2,2,128,0,128,64,0  };           /*  120-127  */
```

All the punctuation marks have a 16 in the corresponding array element. For example, the question mark, ASCII value 63, is represented by a 16 in `c_type[63]`.

Defining Macros using this translation array

With this translation array, you can now **define** any number of macros. For example, to see if a character is a numeral, write

```
#define is_a_numeral(c) ( (c_type[c] & NUM )
```

Any character that corresponds to 4 in the translation array (and that is only the numerals) returns true for this macro. This translation array together with the definitions made earlier allow you to create the macros in Table 8.3.

Table 8.3
Character-Translation Array Macros

macro	definition
#define isupper(c)	((c_type[c]) & UP)
#define islower(c)	((c_type[c]) & LO)
#define isnum(c)	((c_type[c]) & NUM)
#define isalpha(c)	((c_type[c]) & (UP | LO))
#define isalnum(c)	((c_type[c]) & (UP | LO | NUM))
#define isblank(c)	((c_type[c]) & SPC)
#define ispunct(c)	((c_type[c]) & PUNC)
#define iscontrl(c)	((c_type[c]) & CTRL)
#define isoper(c)	((c_type[c]) & OPER)
#define isbrackt(c)	((c_type[c]) & BRKT)

Now a program can use these macros to examine characters in an efficient manner. For example, a parser program that must examine each character in a string and determine its type could use these macros. It would execute much more quickly than a program that examines sets of values with function calls that use multiple comparisons. These particular macros usually appear in the header file ctype.h. Print the file ctype.h for your system and see how it compares to these definitions.

Two Dimensional Arrays

A two-dimensional array can be declared as

```
int a[][];
```

which indicates to the compiler that the array has two dimensions. For example, a ten row by two column array is

```
int a[10][2];
```

and the elements can be manipulated with standard syntax:

```
a[i][j] = 2 * j;
```

The elements could be read in by using a simple loop:

```
for(i=0; i < 10; i++)
  for(j=0;j<2;j++)
  scanf("%d \n",&a[i][j]);
```

An **extern** or **static** two-dimensional array can be initialized in a manner similar to a one-dimensional array.

```
int a[2][3] ={1,2,4,5,7,9};
```

The first row, a[0][0] and a[0][1] contains 1 and 2, respectively. Each row fills up before the elements in the next row, that is, two-dimensional arrays are stored in row major fashion.

Look at some examples of initializing **static** two- dimensional arrays. To see the flexibility allowed in array initialization consider this matrix:

$$\begin{bmatrix} 1 & 3 & 5 \\ 2 & 4 & 6 \\ 3 & 5 & 7 \\ 0 & 0 & 0 \end{bmatrix}$$

One method of initialization is

```
int y[4][3] =   {
                { 1, 3, 5 },
                { 2, 4, 6 },
                { 3, 5, 7 },
                };
```

Another method of initialization is

```
int y[4][3] =   {
  1, 3, 5, 2, 4, 6, 3, 5, 7
  };
```

In yet another method

```
int y[4][3] =  {        yields
                        { 1 },1 0 0
                        { 2 },2 0 0
                        { 3 },3 0 0
                        { 4 } 4 0 0
                        };
```

The maxim to remember when using any of these methods is that any uninitialized element is set to 0. Also, the arrays must be of storage class **static**. The ANSI standard permits initialization of **auto** arrays.

Arrays larger than two dimensions can be declared in a similar manner. The command

```
static float x[][][];
```

creates a **static** array of type **float** of three dimensions. Another way to think of multidimensional arrays is as arrays of arrays. Actually, that is how **C** treats them. For example, a 10-row by 4-column array can be thought of as an array of 10 arrays of dimension 4. A three-dimensional array is an array of arrays of arrays.

Array elements can be manipulated-much the same as any data object. For example, we have used arrays in several programs using such statements as

```
if(x[j] < x[i]) swap(x[i],x[j]);
```

and

```
for(i=0; i < n; i++)
  printf("%d ",x[i]);
```

Matrix multiplication provides an example of using an array. the two matrices, a and b,are of size 4 by 3 and 3 by 2.

$$\overset{a}{\begin{bmatrix} 2 & 3 & 4 \\ 5 & 5 & 3 \\ 8 & 2 & 4 \\ 2 & 5 & 9 \end{bmatrix}} \overset{b}{\begin{bmatrix} 5 & 4 \\ 6 & 3 \\ 7 & 2 \end{bmatrix}}$$

The resulting product array of size 4 by 2. The elements are

$$\begin{bmatrix} 2x5 + 3x6 + 4x7 & 2x4 + 3x3 + 4x2 \\ 5x5 + 5x6 + 3x7 & 5x4 + 5x3 + 5x2 \\ 8x5 + 2x6 + 4x7 & 8x4 + 2x4 + 4x2 \\ 2x5 + 5x6 + 9x7 & 2x4 + 5x3 + 9x2 \end{bmatrix}$$

which gives a matrix

$$\begin{bmatrix} 56 & 25 \\ 76 & 45 \\ 80 & 48 \\ 103 & 40 \end{bmatrix}$$

The algorithm to perform the multiplication is

```
for each row of matrix a
  Multiply each element in the row by
  the corresponding element in the
  corresponding column of matrix b.
  Place the sum of the products in the
  new element identified by the row
  of matrix a and the column of matrix a.
```

The program segment to perform the multiplication is shown in Listing 8.2.

Listing 8.2

Matrix Multiplication

```
for(i=0;i<m;i++)
  for(j=0;j<n;j++)
    {  c[i][j] = 0;
       for(k=0;k<p;k++)
         c[i][j] += a[i][k]*b[k][j];
    }
```

End of Listing

In Listing 8.2, i is the row counter up to m rows and j is the column counter up to n columns. The k is the element counter equal to the number of columns in matrix a and the number of rows in matrix b (both must equal p). The resulting matrix, c, has the dimensions m byn.

Arrays in **C** can be treated like arrays in other languages. There are several other ways to work with arrays in **C**. Some may seem cryptic at first and some are more efficient than others. First you must know more about pointers.

Pointers

A pointer is a data object that contains the address of another object. There are two important operators: the address operator & and the indirection operator *. Both are unary operators.

The address operator returns the address of a variable. The address is stored in a pointer.

```
int n = 5;           /*  declare an integer  */
int *ptr;            /*  declare a pointer variable  */
  ptr = &n;          /*  assign the address of n to ptr  */
```

In the preceding sequence the variable n has the value 5. The pointer variable ptr is declared as a pointer, and the address of n is assigned to the pointer variable.

You can use the indirection operator to refer to the value held in the address that is pointed to by ptr.

```
m = *ptr;
```

assigns m the value of the address pointed to by ptr, m is equal to 5. You have encountered these two operators before in the swap function:

```
void swap(m,n)
int *m,*n;
{  int temp;
   temp = *m;        /*  1  */
   *m = *n;          /*  2  */
   *n = temp;
}
```

The function accepts as arguments, the addresses of the two variables to be interchanged. The arguments must then be declared as pointers because they contain addresses. The variable `temp` is a normal integer. In line 1 the literal translation assigns the contents of the address pointed to by `m` to the variable `temp`. Line 2 causes the contents of the variable pointed to by `n` to become the contents of the variable pointed to by `m`.

Pointers can be confusing. This example is not a real program, but illustrates what is going on when pointers, the address operator, and the indirection operator are used. Consider the following declarations:

```
int m,n,i;
int *a,*b,*c;
```

A simplified model of memory usage with arbitrary addresses follows.

variable name in **main**()	address
m	ffea
n	ffe8
a	ffe6
b	ffe4
c	ffe2

All variables, **ints**, and pointers to **ints** have storage space reserved and a valid address, but none has been initialized. Suppose you make the following assignments:

```
m = 3;
a = &m;
n = *a;
b = &a;  /*  ok as an example, but not generally done  */
c= a;
```

As a result of the assignments, the memory locations contain values.

variable name in **main**()	address	value
m	ffea	3
n	ffe8	3
a	ffe6	ffea
b	ffe4	ffe6
c	ffe2	ffea

The pointer a contains the address of `m (ffea)`. The variable `n` is assigned the value stored in the address stored in `a`. Thus `n` is assigned the value of memory location `ffea` so `n` becomes 3. The pointer `b` is assigned the address of a that is, `b` contains `ffe6`. Finally, the pointer `c` is assigned the valued stored in `a`, or `ffea`.

Now write a function to use the variables within the function.

```
f1(&m,n);   /*  pass address of m and value of n  */

            f1(x,y)
            int *x,y;
            {
              *x = 2*y;  /* value stored in address stored
                            in x becomes 2 times y ..  6 */
              y = 2 * y; /*  y is doubled ..becomes 6  */
            }
```

The memory results are

variable name		address	value
f1()	main()		
	m	ffea	6
	n	ffe8	3
	a	ffe6	ffea
	b	ffe4	ffe6
	c	ffe2	ffea
x	ffde	ffea	
y	ffe0	3 then 6 then 12	

Because x is passed as a pointer, it contains the address of m. As a result x acts much like a. You could have made the function call by passing a instead of the address of m:

```
f1(a,n);
```

The variable y is passed as a value and is a typical local variable known only inside the function.

Pointers and Arrays

An array name is, in actuality, very much like a pointer but not exactly the same. For the array a, a is the address of the first element, a[0]; hence, you have a choice of how to declare a. The first is **int** a[], the declaration we have been using so far. The second is **int** *a, which is a pointer. Because a[0] is an address and *a is also an address, the two forms of the declaration are nearly equivalent. The difference is that the pointer is a variable and can appear on the left side of an assignment operator, that is, it is an lvalue. The array name is a constant and cannot appear on the left side of an assignment operator. In other respects the pointer version and the array version are the same.

Consider the declaration of the array a and the pointer ptr.

```
int a[], *ptr;
```

The pointer could be assigned the address of a[0]

```
ptr = &a[0];
```

but this syntax would not be in the accepted style. You could simply assign the pointer the value of a

```
ptr = a;
```

This code is cleaner and accomplishes the same result. The assignment works because the following equality is true

```
a == &a[0]
```

Pointers can be used in the declaration of arrays. For example, the array declaration

```
char a[];
```

could have been

```
char *a;
```

An array of pointers can be declared as

```
char *a[];
```

which means that a is an array whose elements are pointers. The use of pointers or arrays together with the explicit dimensioning or the omission of dimensioning can create confusion. Figure 8.1 presents a simplified model of what goes on in memory.

```
address          memory location          symbolic
                 values                   name

  1              T                        a[0]
  2              i  o                     b[0]
  3              m  k  T                  c[0]
  4              \0 l  e                  c[1]
  5                 a  n                  c[2]
  6                 h  n  C               d[0]
  7                 o  e  a               d[1]
  8                 m  s  l               d[2]
  9                 a  s  i               d[3]
 10                 \0 e  f
                       \0 \0

                 pointer
                 values

 50                 1                     a
 51                 2                     b
 52                 3                     c
 53                 6                     d
 54                 3                     c   in f1()
```

Figure 8.1: *Simplified Model of Memory Pointer Values*

Consider a program with **main**() and 1 function, `f1()`. The **main** program contains the the declarations:

```
char *a;
char b[];
char c[3];
char d[4];
```

The function `f1()` contains the declaration

```
char *c;
```

The declarations result in the allocation of addresses 50 through 54. Each contains an address (a pointer) that refers to the location of the actual string. The strings are stored in the addresses 1 through 10. The exact contents of address 1 through 10 depends, in part, on which value was stored last. For example, if the values of `a`, `b`, `c`, and `d` are:

```
a == Tim\0
b == Oklahoma\0
c == Tennessee\0
d == Calif\0
```

Then one may or may not be sure of the value of any one of these. For example, If `a` is assigned the string `"Tim"` then the addresses 1 through 4 contain `T,I,M,` and \0. However, if `b` is assigned the value of `"Oklahoma"`, then `a[1]` through `a[3]` will change. In fact, the string terminator will also be lost.

The values of address 50 may change. The values of addresses 51 thru 53 can not. `a` is a pointer variable and its value can change. The identifers `b`, `c`, and `d` are constants so their values remain intact. For example, if `a` is incremented then the contents of address 50 is modified. Consquently, the beginning address of `a` is lost and not recoverable. Since `b` is a constant, it may not be incremented.

It is good practice to follow some simple guidelines when declaring and using arrays.

1. When you wish to reserve space for strings and you do not want to overwrite or lose the space, declare the string as an array and use explicit dimensioning.
2. When copying strings, make sure the destination string has been declared and dimensioned so that there is enough room in the destination to hold the copy.
3. When one wishes to remember the starting position of a string, use an array as opposed to a pointer. Otherwise, use a temporary character pointer to store the beginning address of the string.
4. When working with copies of strings such as when the copy is a local variable in a function to which a string has been passed, use a pointer. This simplifies the code since the space for the character array has already been allocated in the calling function.
5. Pay close attention to the order of program statements so that your program does not unintentionally modify the contents of an array. Be wary of side effects when a string has been passed to an array.

Pointer Arithmetic

Pointers are variables. They are not integers, but they can usually be displayed as unsigned integers. (Be careful: A system may store a pointer some other way so make no assumptions. Pointers can be incremented and decremented; added and subtracted. For example, ptr++ causes the pointer to be incremented, but not by 1. one. Suppose n is an integer and the system stores integers in two bytes. Further suppose the address of n is 17500. The integer n would occupy bytes 17500 and 17501. The code

```
int n, *p;
n = 12;
p = &n;
p++;
printf("%u\n",p);
```

displays 17502. The pointer p is originally assigned the value 17500. The incrementation, p++, increments the number of bytes of the storage class for the particular machine. If the system used four bytes to store an integer, then p++ would have resulted in p being equal to 17504.

The general rule about pointer arithmetic is that

> **An arithmetic operation on a pointer performs the operation in bytes of the appropriate storage class.**

The **float** pointer *fp when incremented on a system that uses 4 bytes to store a floating-point value, adds 4 to the address stored in fp.

Remember that pointers must be initialized before use. The code segment that follows looks fine but it is actually incorrect because the pointer fp has been declared but not initialized.

```
float *fp;
fp++;
```

The preceding is an error typical of beginning **C** programmers. The result is unpredictable. A correct version is

```
float *fp;
static float x[] =   {3.15, 4.5 , 7.91, 9.34   };
fp = x;
fp++;
```

As you have seen there are several equalities in array indexing. Given an array x of type **float** and a pointer fp, the following equalities hold true:

```
float x[], *fp;
/*  assume x has been initialized  */
fp = &x[0];
fp + 5 == &x[5];
++fp == &x[1];
fp--;
*fp == x[0];
*(fp) == x[];
*(fp + 5) == x[5];
*(fp + 5) == x[0 + 5];
*(fp + 5) == x + 5;
```

These equalities underscore some equivalents in **C** syntax. A function with an array argument can have either of the following:

```
dothis(a)          /*  1  */

dothis(&a[0])          /*  2  */
```

Both declarations work, but programmers usually only use number 1. Within the function the array argument can be declared either as

```
dothis(a)
int a[];
{
```

or

```
dothis(a)
int *a;
{
```

The declaration **int** a[]; declares **a** to be a constant pointer to an array of **int**. The declaration *a declares **a** to be a variable pointer to an **int** and is the preferred method.

There are several operations that can be performed on a pointer. You can find the pointer's address, for example.

```
int n, *p1,*p2;

p1 = &n;
p2 = &p1;
```

The second pointer can be declared as a pointer to a pointer

```
int **p2
```

but does not have to be so declared. In another operation the pointer can be incremented by the number of bytes used for the data objects' storage class.

```
ptr++;  /*  move to the next variable address  */
```

A third operation applies the indirection operator *.

```
*ptr1 = 400;    /*  assign 400 to variable pointed to  */

*ptr2 = 2 + (*ptr1);
        /* assign 2 plus the value of the variable
        pointed to by pointer 1 to the variable
        pointed to by pointer 2*/
```

You can also find the address of a pointer.

```
ptr2 = &ptr1;
```

A fifth operation takes the difference of two pointers.

```
int *pa,*pb
pa=&x[0];
pb=pa;
while((*pa = getchar()) != '\n') pa++;
size = pa-pb;
```

The preceding pointer subtraction results in size containing the number of bytes of the array x.

Pointers and Multidimensional Arrays

A pointer to an array contains the address of the first element. In a one-dimensional array, the first element is `&a[0]`. In a two-dimensional array, it is `&a[0][0]`. Given the example,

```
int a[][];
int *pa2;

pa2 = a;  /*  same as pa2 = &a[0][0]  */
```

The question is: what does `pa2+1` point to? To answer, recall that a two dimensional array is stored by rows. The next element is `a[0][1]`, so

```
pa2+1 == &a[0][1]
```

You need to know how many elements are in each row to know precisely where **pa2** is pointing. For example, if **x** is a 10 row by 12 coumn array of type **float**, the 13th element is the first element of row 2.

```
float x[10][12];
float *pa2;
...
pa2 = &x[0][0];
/*  the following equalities are true  */
pa2+2 == &x[0][2]
pa2 + 10 == &x[0][10]
pa2 + 12 == &x[1][0]
```

The 13th element of **x** is the first element of the second row. Because the counting starts at 0 or the 13th element is `x[1][0]`.

You may not always be sure of the number of columns. Furthermore, you may want to increment from one row to the next. Under these circumstances, there is another way to access the first element of each column. Recall that **x** is another name for the address of `x[0][0]` and that `x` can be assigned to `pa2` (for example, `pa2 = x;`). As a result the notation `x[0]` refers to `x[0][0]` and `x[1]` refers to `x[1][0]`. In other words when one subscript is omitted, the second subscript is assumed to be 0. Hence,

```
x[3] refers to x[3][0]
x[5] refers to x[5][0]
x[10]refers to x[10][0]
```

Because the second subscript is assumed to be 0, it is possible to treat a row of a two-dimensional array as a one-dimensional array. Suppose you have a quicksort (Listing 6.21.) in your library. It has as its header line

```
quick(x,left,right)
```

where `x` is a one-dimensional array. You can pass one row of a two-dimensional array as

```
quick(x[3],l,r);
```

where `x[3]` is a pointer to the first element in the third row (a one-dimensional array).

When the number of rows is an undetermined amount, the declaration could be

```
int n[][10]
```

which is an array of 10 columns and an unspecified number of rows.

Arrays as Strings

A string is a character array terminated by the null character. To specify an array of strings where the number of characters plus the null is indeterminate, you must declare an array of pointers to type **char**.

```
char *name[];
```

The preceding declaration says that name is an array of pointers. Each pointer contains the address of the first element in the array (that is, the name).

```
name[0] = "First string in the array"
name[5] = "Sixth string in the array"
```

This is a little easier to understand when you recall that a single string can be declared

```
char *name;
```

and that name can be assigned in this manner:

```
char *name = "First mi Last";
```

In the array of this example, the subscript refers to the row, so `name[5]` is the address of the first element in row 5.

The subscripts can be manipulated and pointer arithmetic performed. Consider this example:

```
char *name[], *person;
/*  assume the following assignments are allowed */
/* by your compiler  */
name[0] = "Mildred";
name[1] = "Lucille";
name[2] = "Gertrude"

/*  now make a pointer assignment  */
person = name[0];    /*  makes person same as name[0] */
person++;            /*  increment pointer  */
  /*  person now has the address such that  */
  /*  *person == 'i'  */
```

The **index** can be incremented by writing

```
for(i=0;i < 3; i++)
  printf("%s \n",name[i]);
```

The output is the three strings:

```
Mildred
Lucille
Gertrude
```

The **index** `i` refers to the `i`th element of the array. The array elements are pointers to strings, so the `i`th string is each of the three strings respectively.

Since `name` is an array of pointers, the pointers can also be incremented. The loop can be rewritten as

```
for(i=0;i<3;i++)
  printf("%s \n",*name++);
```

or as a **while** loop:

```
while(i=0, i++ < 3)
  printf("%s \n",*name++);
```

Pointers and character arrays can be confusing to a beginning **C** programmer. With practice their use becomes understandable. A summary of their use follows.

char `s[]`	refers to character array or string
char `*s`	effectively the same thing as the **char**[]. The difference is `smfont that the array is a constant pointer,` but the pointer is a variable.
char `*s[]`	an array of pointers to strings

A special situation centers around functions which return a string. A string is really an array of characters. As an array, the name of the array or string is a pointer. When a pointer is passed to a function, the value of the string in the calling function may be modified by the function. No explicit return is required. The consequence of this situation is that there are two different ways for a function to return a string.

Consider the situation where a string, **s1**, is passed to a function. After some processing, a second string, **s2**, is passed back. The first method is to make **s1** and **s2** arguments in the function call as in the following code.

```
/*  calling or main routine  */
char s1[15], *s2;
...
/*  assume s1 exists  */
f(s1,s2);   comment call the string handling function
...

f(s1,s2)
char *s1,*s2;
{           /*  process s1 yielding s2  */
            return;   /*  empty return  */
}
```

A second method is to set the result of the function call to a pointer variable as shown here.

```
/* main routine  */
char s1[15] *s2;     /*  s2 must be a pointer variable */
                     /* because a constant may not be */
                     /* a lvalue.   */
s2 = f(s1);          /*  calling statement  */
...
char *f(s1)          /*  define function here  */
char *s1;
{
  char t[15];  /*  use an explicitly dimensioned  */
               /* string to ensure enough space  */
  /*  process s1 yielding t  */
  return(t);
}
```

These two methods both work. The first style is commonly used in the standard string handling functions. It suffers from the limitation that **s2** may not be bigger than **s1**. If it is bigger, then the memory addresses referred to by **s2** may be corrupted. The second method suffers from the need to make sure that the dimension of **t** is as large as the dimension of **s1**. The methods of doing so usually involve passing the string length to the function.

sscanf() and sprintf()

These two functions are special versions of **scanf** and **printf** that employ strings. The **sscanf**() function accepts input, not from the stdinput, but from an existing string. Similarly, **sprintf** writes formatted output to a string rather than to the standard output device. Both can be very useful in error checking and as vehicles for analyzing a string.

The **sscanf**() function is frequently used as a temporary storage location for input for the purpose of error checking. In general the form of **sscanf**() is

```
sscanf(s,"conversion string", variable list);
```

In this form **sscanf**() is very much like **scanf** except that the variable list is read from the string **s** instead of **stdin**. You could use this form to check input for validity before including it in a program.

Consider the coding of a menu choice. Say the user is expected to type a one or two-digit number. You could write

```
scanf("%d",&choice);
```

which assumes the user will type an integer. The problem is that the user might type a space or two before typing the digits, a letter instead of an integer, or add an extraneous character such as a period. To facilitate error checking, first accept the input as typed by writing

```
scanf("%s",s);
```

or

```
gets(s);
```

Then check to see if the string contains anything that is not a digit.

```
error = 0
  for(i=0;s[i] != '\0';i++)
  if(s[i] < '0'|| s[i] >9) error = 1;
```

The program logic can now check to see if the error condition is 1 (true) and if so, take some corrective action. If the input is fine it can be converted to an integer by the code

```
sscanf(s,"%d",&choice);
```

The function **sscanf**() can be used to read a number from the keyboard and perform a check on it's validity at the same time. The following code illustrates this idea. In it, `s` is a string read from the keyboard with **gets(s)**. Then leading blanks are stripped with loop:

```
while(s[i] ==' ' &&s[i])i++;
```

This loop terminates when a non-blank character other than the end of string character is encountered. At this point, `s[i]` is the first character in the string. The number is read from the string by using **sscanf**.

```
if(isdigit)s[i]) || (s[i] == '.')
  sscanf(&s[i],"%f",&um);
else
  puts("The input is not a number"),exit();
```

As the preceding shows, **sscanf** aids in the error checking aspects of data entry.

Also **sscanf**() is used to read formatted data stored in an array of strings. Arrays must have homogeneous data elements. If the data are placed in the array as strings, they can be pulled from the array one string at a time and then read using a **sscanf**() statement.

The **sprintf**() function is useful for assembling a string from different data types or from different variables. The string can then be used as a file name (Chapter 10),as a parameter passed to a function, as a way of creating an array of strings, or in any number of situations where a formatted string is appropriate. In general the form is:

```
sprintf(s,"conversion string",var list);
```

The contents of the variable list are written to the string s according to the format defined in the conversion string.

Consider the case where a disk drive letter or number is specified in a different part of the program then the filename.Suppose the disk drive (called the variable `dd`) is a and the filename (the variable `fn`) is `temp.doc`. The **sprintf**() command can be used to combine the two variables

```
sprintf(s,"%c%s",dd,fn)
```

Then the string s can be used as the complete file name. For example:

```
puts(s);
```

or

```
strcpy(fn,s);
```

The **sprintf**() function can be used to create an array of strings each of which is formatted. Consider the creation of an array of id numbers and names. The names are read from the keyboard, an id number is selected from an available list of numbers and a new array consisting of both names and numbers can be created from the two different inputs. The key statement would be:

```
sprintf(s[i],"%5d%s",id,name);
```

The two functions discussed here (**sscanf**() and **sprintf**()) can be very helpful. They are convenient means to build strings from nonstring components as well as for error checking.

Using An Array of Strings as Screen Messages

A practical use of an array of strings is to put out several lines of text on the screen. Many programs that display messages or directions use this approach. Suppose there are several help screens that are displayed at various times within a program. Let one of the screens be

```
You need to type two file names
when you run the program.  The
correct usage is
  Fcopy [-options] file1 file2
where file1 is the file to be copied
and file2 is the new file to be created.
```

```
The options are
  1 suppress line numbers
  2 suppress page numbers
```

The entire screen display can be placed in an array. If the array is called **usage** the declaration is

```
static char *usage[] = {
  "You need to type two file names",
  "when you run the program.  The",
  "correct usage is",
  "  Fcopy [-options] file1 file2",
  "where file1 is the file to be copied",
  "and file2 is the new file to be created.",
  "The options are",
  "  1 suppress line numbers",
  "  2 suppress page numbers",
  0
};
```

Notice the use of the **NULL** character, 0. It is used to signify the last string in the message. If all screens are the same, the calling program can use a loop counter to display all the lines. If the number of lines in a message varies, the **NULL** character (or empty string) signifies the end of the message array.

The array can now be displayed by a calling function. In this example, the function is `errhelp()`.

```
errhelp(strings)
char *strings[];
{
  char **lines;
  for( lines = strings; *lines; lines++)   /*  1  */
  printf("\t %s\n",*lines);
}
```

This function accepts the array of strings as its argument. A local variable, `lines`, is initialized to the first element of the original array. The local variable is incremented so that the pointer for the message is not modified (line 1). The loop continues until `*lines` evaluates to a **NULL** string. This function can be called via `errhelp(usage);`.

String Functions

Arrays and pointers to **char** arrays can be used to perform a number of string functions. Recall a string function from Chapter 6, the concatenation of two strings.

```
concat(s1,s2,s3)
char s1[],s2[],s3[];
{
  int n1,n2,n3,i,j;
  n1 = len(s1); n2 = len(s2);
  for(i = 0; i < n1;; i++)
    s3[i] = s1[i];
  for(j = 0; j < n2; j++)
    s3[i++] = s2[j];
  s3[i] = '\0';
}
```

This function uses character arrays as strings. The indices are incremented in a straightforward manner. An alternate version uses pointers and is shown in Listing 8.3.

Listing 8.3

String Concatenation via Pointers

```
concat(s1,s2,s3)
char *s2,*s2,*s3;
{
  while( *s1 != '\0') *s3++ = *s1++;
  while( *s2 != '\0') *s3++ = *s2++;
  *s3 = '\0';
}
```

End of Listing

The pointer version eliminates the need for the length function. The first **while** loop assigns the value pointed to by s1 to the address pointed to by s3 until the null character is encountered. Since *s3 is incremented after the last character in s1 was assigned to s3, the second **while** loop proceeds just as the first does. Finally, the null character is assigned to the current address pointed to by s3. Because *s3 was incremented on the last step of the second **while** loop no index values i and j are needed.

It is important to understand the statement

```
*s3++ = *s1++;
```

Because the indirection operator has a higher precedence than the incrementation operator, the preceding statement is equivalent to

```
*s3 = *s1;
s3++;
s1++;
```

although the form shown in Listing 8.3 is the accepted way of writing the statement.

Listing 8.4 shows how a string copy function can be written by using notation similar to that in Listing 8.3.

Listing 8.4

String Copy Function

```
scopy(s1,s2)
char *s1,*s2;
{  while(*s1++ = *s2++);
}
```

End of Listing

The **while** statement continues to assign the values from string two to string one until the condition inside the parentheses evaluates to 0 or false. When the null character of string 2 is encountered, it is assigned to `s1` and the value inside the parentheses is zero (false) and the loop terminates.

There is an important lesson to be learned from Listing 8.4: There are equivalent versions of pointer usage and array indices usage. Given this declaration of a string:

```
char s[];
```

the incrementation of the pointer and the array can take either of two forms.

```
*s++          or          s[i++].
```

Suppose you want to add the elements of an integer array.

```
for(i=0; i<n; total += x[i++]);
```

An equivalent form is

```
for(;*x != x[n]; total += *x++);
```

The latter version is more cryptic and is considered by many to be poor practice. Others think that the pointer version is more efficient and therefore worth the effort. This writer thinks that readability is of most importance and would prefer the array version.

String Length Revisited

Chapter 6 presented a string length function that used array indices. The code was

```
len(s)
char s[];
{
  int count = 0;
  while(s[count] != \0')
    count++;
  return(count);
}
```

The code can be rewritten with pointers.

```
len(s)
char *s;
{
  char *t;
  t = s;
  while( *t != '\0') t++;
  return(t - s);
}
```

The pointer method is considered more efficient and you should include it in your toolkit of useful functions.

ASCII to Numerical Conversions

A common programming practice is to accept data in one form (for example, as a character string) and then to make use of it in another form (for example as a numeric). Most **C** libraries contain a number of these conversion functions.

atoi(); Pronounced ASCII to integer converts a string to the equivalent integer. For example the string "-23" converts to the integer −23. It is used in this manner

```
static char s[] = "-23";
int n;
...
n = atoi(s);
```

atol(): This is an ASCII to long function which is very similar to **atoi**() except it returns a **long** integer.

atof(): This function is much like the previous two functions except that it converts a string to a **float** type real number.

itoa(): This function, pronounced "integer to ASCII", is the inverse of **atoi**(). It is called by writing

```
itoa(n,s);
```

and it converts an integer `n` into a string `s` terminated with \0.

Sorting an Array of Strings

You have seen a wide range of sort routines so far. They have all sorted simple arrays of integers in ascending order. However, programmers are frequently faced with the need to sort strings. If the strings are themselves elements of an array, you can proceed in a manner similar to the sort routines you saw in prior chapters. The difference is in how you make the comparison between array elements and in how array elements are interchanged.

Look again the quicksort in Chapter 6, Listing 6.21. Note that the function is called by the statement

```
quick(x,left,right)
```

where `x` is the array to be sorted, `left` is the index of the leftmost element in the partition and `right` is the index of the rightmost element in the partition. The calling sequence can be left alone, but the comparison and swap sections must be modified.

Comparing strings in **C** is done via a library function **strcmp**. This function compares two strings element by element until a difference is found. If the two strings are the same, it returns 0. If the first string is lexicagraphically, greater than the second string, a positive number (usually 1) is returned. If the second string is greater a negative value (usually −1) is returned. It is called by the statement

```
strcmp(s1,s2);
```

where `s1` and `s2` are pointers to strings.

A companion function, **strncmp**, compares two strings to `n` places. It is called by the statement

```
strncmp(s1,s2,n);
```

Older compilers do not require any special header files to accompany the use of string functions. Many newer compilers, UNIX compilers, and ANSI standard compilers require that `string.h` be included at the top of any file using string funcitons.

The comparison statements in quick sort are

```
while(x[i] <= pivot && i < right)) i++;
while(x[j] >= pivot && j>left) j--;
```

If`x[i]` and `pivot` are strings, then the statements should read

```
while(strcmp(x[i],pivot)<= 0 && i < right)) i++;
while(strcmp(x[j],pivot)>= 0 && j>left) j--;
```

The swap statements also need to be changed. The basic difference is that a straight string assignment cannot be made. Instead, you need to copy the strings with the **strcpy**() function. Its general form is

```
strcpy(dest,source);
```

where `dest` is the destination string and `source` is the original string. The destination is on the left to imitate the way an assignment statement works.

The quicksort routine uses string copy in lieu of element assignments in lines 1, 4, and 5.

```
/*  1  */   {  pivot = x[left];

/*  4  */   {t = x[i];x[i] = x[j]; x[j] = t; }

/*  5  */   t = x[left]; x[left] = x[j]; x[j] = t;
```

These lines need to be changed to

```
strcpy(pivot,x[left]);

strcpy(t,x[i]);strcpy(x[i],x[j]);strcpy(xj],t);

strcpy(t,x[left]);strcpy(x[left],x[j]);strcpy(x[j],t);
```

The data objects that are strings instead of integers also need to be changed. The resulting program is shown in Listing 8.5.

Listing 8.5

Sorting an Array of Strings

```
/*  x is declared as char *x[N]; */
/* and is assumed to be initialized.   */
left = 0; right = N-1;
quick(x,left,right)
char *x[];
int left,right;
{
int i,j;
char pivot[20],t[20];
if(right > left)
  { strcpy(pivot,x[left]);
     i = left + 1;
     j = right;
     do
     {
       while(strcmp(x[i],pivot)<= 0 && i < right)) i++;
       while(strcmp(x[j],pivot)>= 0 && j>left) j--;
       if(i<j)
         strcpy(t,x[i]),strcpy(x[i],x[j]),
                 strcpy(xj],t);
       while( i < j);
       strcpy(t,x[left]),strcpy(x[left],x[j]),strcpy(x[j],t);
       }
     }
     if( j > left + 1) quick(x,left,j-1);
     if(j < right - 1) quick(x,j+1,right);
return;
}
```

End of Listing

This example illustrates how a basic algorithm such as the quicksort can be modified to handle different data types. The string functions, **strcmp** and **strcpy** were used to manipulate the data objects in the array to be sorted. These are useful functions to go with **strcat** (concatenation) and **strlen** (length).

Pointers to Functions

In some programming situations, you may wish to include a choice of functions. For example, if a sort routine is comparing two data objects, one function may compare integer data types, and another may compare strings. The calling program uses a pointer to the appropriate function as an argument in the calling statement. To declare a pointer to a function that returns an **int**, write

```
int (*f1) ();
```

This declaration says that `f1` is a pointer to a function that returns **int**. If the function returned nothing, the declaration would have been

```
void (*f1) ();
```

The pointer is to the function. The data type specifier indicates what data type is returned by the function to be called.

This declaration is not to be confused with

```
int *f1();
```

which means that `f1` is a function (not a pointer) that returns a pointer to type **int**. The two declarations produce very different results

Consider a sort routine (called `sort`) that is general in nature and works with a variety of data types. Its arguments are an array, `x`, a swap function, `swap`, and a comparison function `cmp`. Each is actually a pointer.

```
void sort( x,n, swap, cmp)
char *x[];
int n;
int (*swap) (), (*cmp)();
{
```

The array to be sorted is called `x` and is an array of pointers to strings. The size of the array is `n`. The identifiers `swap` and `cmp` are pointers to functions that return integers. There may be several swap functions and several corresponding compare functions. The calling program must contain the logic to call the sort routine with the proper pointer value

One swap function might swap strings of variable length, another might swap fixed-length strings, and another might swap single characters. Each function has its own name. The swap function can be assigned the address of a function by using the address operator.

```
swap = &str_swap();
```

The address operator is not really needed, however. The preceding command can be replaced by

```
swap = str_swap;
```

which is the accepted practice.

Another common declaration is to declare a pointer to a function which returns a pointer as shown here.

```
int *(*f)();
```

Its use is similar to declaring a pointer to a function as in

```
int *f();
```

The difference is that the first of these two functions returns an **int** while the other returns a pointer to an **int**.

Finally, pointers may be cast. In subsequent chapters you will see the need for this capability. For now, an example is appropriate. The following shows how an integer pointer is cast to a character pointer.

```
int *n;
char *cp;
...
cp = (* char)n;
```

The syntax (* **char**) is a cast to a character pointer.

The **C** language is a pointer oriented language. The pointer practices discussed here are only some of many. You will continue to learn about pointers as you investigate additional topics.

ANSI Standard: volatile Type Modifier

Applications that are hardware dependent frequently declare a pointer to a memory address such as a communications port. The value in that memory location may be changed by something other than the program itself. For example:

```
unsigned *port_stat;
...
while(*port_stat == 1)
  ;
/*  loop to wait until the port is not busy  */
```

Some optimizing compilers have trouble with the preceding code. They might assume that the contents of the port status cannot change in the **while** loop and execute it only once. To avoid this, declare the machine or hardware memory location pointers as **volatile**.

```
volatile unsigned *port_stat;
```

As a general rule, use the type modifier **volatile** whenever an object can change in ways that are not recognizable by the compiler.

Summary

Arrays in **C** are declared as **int** `x[10]`. The preceding declares an array of 10 integers. However, the array name is actually a pointer to the first member of the array. The equivalence `a == &a[0]` holds true. An array can be declared without explicit dimensioning such as **float** `b[]`. Finally, an array can be declared as a pointer as in **char** `*s`.

Each of the various methods work because they are ways of declaring pointers. An array declared with square brackets is a constant pointer. An array declared as a pointer is a variable.

AS with other data types, only **static** arrays can be initialized when declared. Automatic arrays must be initialized in the body of the code.

Two dimensional arrays are declared as in **int** `x[20][4]` which provides for a 20 by 4 array of ints. When refering to an array with subscripts, the usual row-major convention applies as in `a[i][j]`. When the second subscript is ommitted, the first subscript refers to the first element of the row. For example, `b[3]` refers to `b[3][0]`.

Pointers are closely related to arrays. The difference between **char** `s[]` and **char** `*s` is that the square brackets declare a constant while the asterisk declares a variable. When you want to specifically provide space for an array's elements, use a constant such as **int** `x[20]`. When working with function copies or subsets of existing arrays, use a variable (pointer)(declaration.

Strings can be thought of as character arrays in which the last element is the **NULL** character, \0. A wide range of string functions are available in **C**. String concatenation, string length, and string copy are examples from prior chapters. There are several string to numeric conversions: **atoi**(), **atol**(), atof(), and **itoa**() are examples. They provide for convienent means of creating a new data object from one of a different type.

The functions **sscanf**() and **sprintf**() are similar to **scanf**() and **printf**() with the difference that the two new functions read or write to strings. For example **sscanf**(s,conversion string, item list) reads from **s** instead of **stdin**. The function **sscanf**() is useful in input error checking. The function **sprintf**() is useful in assembling strings from non-character data.

The operator **sizeof** works with arrays. When applied to an array name it returns the number of bytes in the entire array. For example, if the array is **int** `x[10]` then the result of **sizeof**`(x)` returns 20. When applied to a pointer declaration such as **char** `*s`, **sizeof**`(s)` returns 2, the size of the pointer.

Pointers can be used with function declaration and function calls. The declaration **int** `*x();` creates a function that returns a pointer to an **int**. The declaration **int** `(*x)()` creates a pointer to a function that returns an **int**.

EXERCISES

UNDERSTANDINGS

1. Explain the difference between an array name and a variable defined as a pointer.
2. What does **sizeof** return when applied to an array name?
3. The expression `p + q`, where `p` and `q` are pointers is valid. What is wrong with `p*q`?

USAGE

4. Explain what each of these declares:
   a. **char** `X[10][10];`
   b. **int** `**p;`
   c. **char** `*a;`
   d. **float**`*x[5][3];`
   e. **char** `(*a) [5];`
   f. **char** `**a;`
   g. **int** `*n[10];`
   h. **float** `(*val) ();`
5. Which is wrong, a or b? Why?

```
int n[];
int *m;
n[0] = 12;
n = m;  /* a */
m = n;  /* b */
```

6. Use an example to explain what this function does.

```
void cout(s)
char *s;
{
  while(*s) putchar(*p++);
}
```

7. Consider the following program segment. Explain how the expression in the **if** statement is evaluated.

```
int (*pcomp)();


if( (*pcomp)(ptemp, pa[j]) < 1)
```

APPLICATIONS

8. Write a program using **sscanf**() and other commands that accepts a string from the keyboard and checks to see if it is a signed number (either real or integer) including a possible sign. If the input is not as desired, the user is told that the input is incorrect the program gives the user another opportunity.
9. Write a function `getword()` that returns a pointer to a string taken from **stdin**. The input word is terminated by either a space or by the return (Enter) key.
10. Rewrite the string length function using pointers, but implement with a **for** loop instead of a **while** loop.
11. Rewrite the `bin_ser` (binary search) routine from Chapter 2 using pointers instead of an array with indices.
12. Write a function, `getarray(x,n)`, that reads `n` integers into array `x` from the keyboard.
13. Consider two arrays of size `n` and type **double**. Write a function to calculate the Pearson-product moment correlation coefficient. If one array is called `x` and the other `y`, then the correlation coefficient is

$$r = \frac{n\sum(xy) - \sum(x)\sum(y)}{\sqrt{((n\sum(x^2) - (\sum(x))^2)(n\sum(y^2) - (\sum(y))^2))}}$$

Write the function two ways. First, use arrays and increment array indexes. Second, use pointers to arrays and increment the pointers.

14. Write a program That implements the code illustrated in the discussion of pointers and variable values on page 000 and prints out the addresses and the values of the memory locations used.
15. Rewrite the Shell sort, Listing 8.1, to sort an array of strings.
16. Rewrite the quicksort for an array of strings so that pointers to array members are swapped instead of using **strcpy** to swap the actual strings.
17. Write a program that calculates grade averages for a class of up to 20 students. Each student's grades are entered using −9999 as a sentinel to end input.

9

Structures, Unions and Dynamic Memory Allocation

Advanced programs need sophisticated ways of representing data because the problems in them involve related items that must be tied together. The data items may be heterogeneous. For example, a structure may define a data item to represent an employee. The program must contain the employee's name, address, phone number, id number and other similar information. A structure is a definition that places all the separate data parts under one label, i.e., employee.

A structure is an aggregate data type much like a record in Pascal. The structure is a systematic collection of elements of different data types (including pointers). Structures have an advantage over arrays, whose elements must be homogeneous.

Functions are the building blocks of **C** programs. Functions operate on data. Structures are used extensively to organize data so that the program and its functions can easily manipulate the data.

Structures provide sophisticated ways of representing data. Structures can have items or fields of any valid data type including arrays and other structures. Structures can become global variables, defined in header files, and used in other ways to provide access and control of data. This chapter explains their use.

This chapter also contains a section about the use of dynamic memory allocation that is the allocation of memory only when needed. In sophisticated programs, a program needs to carefully control the amount of memory set aside for different data objects. Dynamic memory allocation is frequently used with structures and user-defined data objects.

Declaring a Structure

In general the form of the structure is

```
<storage-class> struct tag-id {
                       data object1;
                       data object2;
                       ...
                       };
```

The storage class is optional. The keyword **struct** and the braces are required. The tag is usually used, but there are situations in which it is not required. The data objects are any valid **C** data objects such as **short int** n; or **char** *[];. The data objects inside the braces are called the template. Once the structure has been declared, it may be used.

Consider the simple example of a student's course schedule.

```
struct s_sked {
  long int s_id;
  int courses[6];
  };
```

The student's id number is stored as a **long int**. A **long** is used because the number may be the same as a social security number. (This discussion temporarily avoids any error checking.) The id number for each course is stored in a six element array. If the student is taking fewer than 6 courses, creating a six element array is probably a waste of storage space, but you will address that issue a little later.

Given that s_sked has been defined, a variable may be declared that is of that type.

```
struct s_sked my_sked;
```

This statement says that my_sked is a data object of the type s_sked. Additional variables may be declared of the same type.

```
struct s_sked fall_sked,spg_sked;
```

Operations on Structures

A structure may be initialized (provided it is **external** or **static**) as in the following example:

```
static struct s_sked my_sked = {234564321,542,348,239,541}
```

The second element in the structure is a six element array. Since only four values are provided, the other two will be initialized to zero.

The only operation allowed on a structure itself is the address operator, &. You can create a pointer to a structure and assign the address to the pointer. Unlike the K&R standard, The ANSI standard permits direct structure assignment and passing a structure as an argument. Many newer compilers support this feature.

```
struct my_sked, *sp;

sp = &my_sked;
```

Pointers to structures are subject to the typical pointer arithmetic and manipulation techniques. So, although there is little you can do with the structure name, pointers to structures open up all sorts of possibilities.

Access to structure members is gained through the period operator (.) or structure member operator (->). The element my_sked.s_id refers to the student id or first member of the structure. It may be assigned, added, changed, or otherwise operated on as any other integer might be. The statement

```
id = my_sked.s_id;
```

is an example of assigning the student id found in the structure my_sked to the program variable id. Similarly, the statement,

```
course2 = my_sked.courses[1];
```

assigns the second element of **courses** to the variable **course2**.

The number of courses a student is taking can be found by incrementing through the **courses** element.

```
n = i = 0;
while(my_sked.courses[i++] != 0 &&(i < 6)) n++;
```

Because my_sked is **static**, any course[i] not set to a value is 0. The loop checks to see if the course is 0 and increments the index i. An additional check to see if i has exceeded the limit of 6 is included to prevent going past the end of the array. If n is the number of courses, n is incremented for each course that is not 0.

The tag part of a structure is used to provide an identifier in a subsequent declaration statement. If the template is only going to be used once in declaration statements, the structure definition and variable declaration statements can be combined.

```
struct  {
          long int s_id;
          int courses[6];
        } my_sked, fall_sked;
```

Notice that the tag is missing. In this situation it is optional. You would include it if this particular variable were being declared and others might be declared later.

```
struct  s_sked  {
          long int_id;
          int courses[6];
        } my_sked;
...
struct s_sked fall_sked,spg_sked;
```

You have already learned that structures can be initialized provided they are **external** or **static**. Suppose you provide a header file called defs.h, that includes this structure declaration:

```
external static dimens {
                  int width;
                  int height;
                  int length;
                  };
```

A file might include the statements

```
#include "defs.h"
...
volumn()
{struct dimens box;
```

This example says that dimens is **static**, but box is declared inside the function volumn. As a result, box is **auto** and cannot be initialized. To initialize box in the function, box would have to be **static** as it is in the fragment that follows.

```
volumn()
{
static struct dimens box = {12,15,6};
```

In the previous case, the tag (dimens) was static, but the variable box was not. In this latest version, box is static and can be initialized.

Structures can be data objects in another structure provided they have been defined. Consider the structure date which appears as a member of employee.

```
struct date {
        char month[4];
        int day;
        int year;
        };

struct employee {
        char lname[20];
        char mi;
        char fname[20];
        struct date birthday;
        };
```

If a variable emp is declared as

```
struct employee emp;
```

The year of emp's birthday can be accessed by using the member operator.

```
age = thisyear - emp.birthday.year;
```

The member operator associates left to right so this example works. If two variables, thismon and thisyear, are integers containing the current month and year, then a person's age in years depends on whether his or her birth month has occurred. The correct code would be

```
if(thismon >= emp.birthday.month)
  age = thisyear - emp.birthday.year;
else age = thisyear - emp.birthday.year - 1;
```

A similar result can be obtained with the conditional operator, but the statement may be a bit long and unwieldy. To use the conditional operator and also avoid writing the same expression twice, you can rewrite the code as

```
age = thisyear - emp.birthday.year;
age = thismon >= emp.birthday.month ? age : age-1;
```

Arrays of Structures

Once a structure has been declared, an array of those structures may be declared.

```
static struct player  {
                char name[MAX];
                int at_bats;
                int hits;
                float bat_avg;
                };

static struct player team[NO_PLYRS];
```

The variable `team` is an array of structures, each of which is a `player`. Individual members can be referenced via the array index.

```
team[i].bat_avg = (float) team[i].hits / team[i].at_bats;
```

The `i`th player can be referenced just as the `i`th element of any array can be referenced. Arrays of structures behave like any other arrays. Reading in the game stats for baseball `team` is an example of reading in any array of structures.

```
for(i =0;i < NO.PLYRS; i++)
scanf("%s %d %d",
 team[i].name,&team[i].at_bats,&team[i].hits);
```

Add the statement that calculates the individual player's batting average to the loop to fill the third member of the structure on the fly.

```
for(i =0;i < NO.PLYRS; i++)  {
scanf("%s %d %d",team[i].name,&team[i].at_bats,&team[i].hits);
team[i].bat_avg = (float) team[i].hits / team[i].at_bats;
}
```

If this code is too hard to read, the individual members can be read on separate lines:

```
for(i =0;i < NO.PLYRS; i++)  {
  scanf("%s",team[i].name);
  scanf("%d",&team[i].at_bats);
  scanf("%d",&team[i].hits);
  team[i].bat_avg =
    (float) team[i].hits / team[i].at_bats;
  }
```

Structures can be ungainly items. Pointers can be quite helpful in working with structures.

Pointers and Structures

Structure names are constants. Unlike array names, which are themselves pointer constants, structure names cannot be passed to functions. However, a pointer to a structure can be passed as an argument to a function. Thinking of a team as an array of structures should help you understand that the array is a pointer. If the input code is a function the array can be passed

```
get_stats(team)
struct player team[];
{
```

or declared as a pointer

```
get_stats(team)
struct player *team;
{
```

However if an individual player is declared to be of type `player`, the array can not be passed to a function. The following code, for example, is incorrect:

```
struct player individ;

/*  incorrect  */
dothis(individ)
struct player individ;
{
```

You could however be declared the array as a pointer.

```
struct player *ind;

dothis(ind)
struct player *ind;
{
```

A pointer can be passed as an argument to a function, but a structure cannot. A pointer to a structure is like other pointers: it can be incremented, its address taken, and used as a variable. Using pointers with structures requires a notation like this:

```
total += (*ind).hits;
```

The preceding notation adds the number of hits found in the structure pointed to by `ind` to the old value of `total`. An equivalent notation is

```
total += ind->hits;
```

The pointer symbol, `->`, is used in place of the indirection operator and the member operator.

The following two statements are equivalent:

```
(*ind).hits;
ind->hits;
```

But these two are not the same:

```
*ind.hits;
(*ind).hits;
```

The parentheses are required because of the order of operations. The member operator has a higher precedence than the pointer operator. The pointer operator, `->`, has a higher precedence than the increment operator, `++`. Thus, the statement

```
++ind -> hits;
```

increments `hits`, not `ind`. Because the pointer operator has a higher precedence, the object that `ind` points to is referenced and then incremented. In the following two statements:

```
total += ++ind -> hits;  /*  1  */
total += ind++ -> hits;  /*  2  */
```

statement 1 increments `hits` and then `total` is increased. In statement 2, `hits` is added to `total` and then the pointer `ind` is incremented, not `hits`. This is because in statement 1, the following parentheses are implied:

```
++(ind -> hits)
```

In statement 2 the `++` is bound to `ind` by the implied parentheses

```
(ind++) -> hits
```

The last example means that the increment operator is applied to `ind` after accessing the member `hits`. If the intent is to access `hits` and then increment `hits`, the notation is

```
ind -> hits++
```

Another point of clarification is in order for the notation

```
*ind -> hits
```

which is the same as

```
*(ind ->hits)
```

The notation means to fetch whatever is pointed to by `hits`. Therefore, to use `*ind -> hits`, `hits` must also be a pointer. If `hits` is a pointer, then

```
*ind++ -> hits;
```

first access whatever is pointed to by `hits` and then increments `ind`. The last statement is much like

```
*ptr++
```

which as you saw earlier accesses whatever is pointed to by `ptr` and then increments `ptr`.

Does all this seem confusing? It should because it is. Working with structures and pointers to structures takes practice. The next few chapters will provide the practice.

Nested Structures

A structure can have another structure as a member. Any structure appearing in the template must be declared "above" the current template. That is, "forward" declarations are not allowed. Consider the example of creating statistical information for baseball players. The first structure could be the player's name.

```
struct names {
        char last[20];
        char first[15];
        };
```

The next structure template uses the **name** structure in the template.

```
struct player {
        struct names name;
        int number;
        char pos[2];
        };
```

The structure **names** contains a player's first and last name. In the structure for a player, the singular **name** is declared to be a structure of type **names**. The **player** structure can now be used in a statistical structure.

```
struct stats {
        struct player indiv;
        int at_bats;
        int hits;
        float bat_avg;
        };
```

These structures are now available to be used with variable names.

```
struct player roster[NPLYRS];  /*  array of players  */
struct stats game;             /*  stats 1 player  */
                               /*  for one game  */
struct stats season;           /*  stats 1 player  */
                               /*  for whole season  */
struct t_stats[NPLYRS + 1];    /*  array of stats with */
                               /* room for team totals  */
```

The first structure declares **roster** to be an array of structures, each of which is a **player**. The second structure declares **game** to be a **stats** type structure. The structure **season** is the same thing, but it contains the stats for an entire season.

One player's game stats can be assigned in the following manner:

```
game.player.name.first = "Tim";
game.player.name.last = "Grady";
game.player.number = 7;
game.player.position = "ss";
game.at_bats = 4;
game.hits = 2;
game.bat_avg = (float) game.hits / game.at_bats;
```

The first two lines are nested three deep. The third and fourth lines use members from two structures (**game** and **player**). The last three lines use only members from the **game** structure that are simple data types (**int** and **float**).

The efficiency of this collection of structures can be improved by the use of pointers. Suppose a **roster** is an array of pointers to **player** structures.

```
struct player *roster[];
```

An individual player can now be accessed via pointer.

```
roster -> name.first;
```

The preceding means that **roster** points to an individual player. A loop to run through the entire team can be incremented with a pointer instead of an index. For example:

```
while(*roster++ -> name.number != 7);
roster--;
```

searchs through the roster's numbers until it finds a match with 7. If the team stats are also declared as a pointer,

```
struct stats *team[NPLYRS];
```

the player's stats can now be accessed in the same loop.

```
while(*roster -> name.number != 7) {roster++; team++;}
```

If you now wish to display an individual's average, the statements are:

```
printf("%s %s",*roster->name.first,*roster->name.last);
printf("'s batting avg is %f\n",*team->bat_avg);
```

Since **roster** and **team** are both pointers and both were incremented together in the loop, then both point to the same player.

Pointers as Structure Members

A template may contain any valid data object, including a pointer. For example, the structure names from above can have the standard string representation as a pointer to a **char** array.

```
struct names  {
        char *last;
        char *first;
        };
```

In addition, a member can be a pointer to a structure. We can rewrite the stats structure by using a pointer to the player structure.

```
struct stats  {
        struct player *indiv;
        int at_bats;
        int hits;
        float bat_avg;
        };
```

The variable **indiv** is now a pointer to a player. A team can be defined as an array of pointers to a stats structure:

```
struct stats *team[NPLAYERS];
```

The **team** variable can now access more than just the player information. It can reference a player via the stats type structure.

```
team -> player -> name.first
```

In the preceding code team points to a particular player, which points to the first name. Used in this way, pointers can make the program more efficient.

Structures and Functions

Older compilers compilers did not allow structures to be passed to a function. They required that a pointer to a structure be passed as the argument. Consider the structure:

```
struct names  {
        char *first;
        char *last;
        }  coach, umpire;
```

A function call that expects player as the argument gets

```
struct names *sp;
sp = &coach;
prnt_it(sp)
struct names *sp;
{& printf("%s ", sp-> first);
printf("%s \n",sp -> last);
}
```

The pointer sp is passed as the function argument. Of course, individual structure members can be passed as function arguments as in the code that follows.

```
float average(player.hits,player.at_bats)
int hits,ab;
{  float avg;
   avg = (float) hits / ab;
   return(avg);
}
```

Self-Referential Structures

A structure may contain a pointer to itself as one of the members. It may not contain a full declaration of a structure of the same type.

```
struct item  {
        char name[10];
        int age;
        struct item *next;
        }
```

This type of structure is useful in constructing linked lists and related data types. These concepts will be discussed in detail in Chapter 12.

The proposed ANSI standard will permit entire structures to be passed as function arguments. It will also permit direct assignment between structures such as

```
struct player dh, team[NPLYERS];
...
read in team data
...
dh = team(i);
```

The standard will also permit returning an entire structure as a result of a function call.

```
struct player do_avg(indiv)  /*  pass a structure  */
struct player indiv;
{  indiv.bat_avg = (float) indiv.hits / indiv.at_bat;
   return(indiv);  /*  return a structure  */
}
```

A third change is that structures may be assigned across an equals sign just as simple data types are permitted to do.

Many current generation compilers incorporate these features. When the ANSI standard is adopted, all will.

Structures and typedef

The operator **typedef**, introduced in Chapter 3, has been used repeatedly in this text. It is used to create synonyms for data types including storage class. For example, a **float** type may be referred to as a `real` after defining it as

typedef float real;

Everything between the word **typedef** and the word `real` is a synonym for the word real.

Since structure definitions can be long, it is sometimes convenient to use the keyword **struct** to provide a synonym. In an earlier example, a function was declared as

```
struct player doavg(indiv)
```

If **typedef** is used

```
typedef struct player PLAYER;
```

the function can be declared as

```
PLAYER doavg(indiv)
```

thus making the declaration more readable.

Some other simplifications can occur. A TEAM can be defined as

```
typedef struct stats *team[] TEAM;
```

and used to declare variables of this type:

```
TEAM home visitor;
```

Now both home and visitor are considered arrays of pointers to structures of type `stats`.

A complex number can be defined as a structure by using the **typedef**.

```
struct complex {
        float real;
        float imag;
        };

typedef struct complex COMPLEX;

COMPLEX ab, cd;
```

The variables ab and cd are both be structures of the complex type. The preceding definition can be rewritten as

```
typedef struct complex {
                float real;
                float imag;
                } COMPLEX;
```

As you can see **typedef** helps make a program portable and readable.

The scope of a **typedef** depends on where it is declared. If declared inside a function, the scope is local to the function. If declared outside a function, it is global to any function declared after it in the file. If included in a header file, the **typedef** is global to any file that includes it.

Bit Fields

C can perform low-level operations such as bit shifting and address manipulation. One of the basic tools in these operations is the bit field structure. This structure sets up a word or byte as a structure so that each bit can be accessed. You might want such access when checking flags in the operating system or controlling external devices.

A field is a set of adjacent bits within an integer (**int**). The number of bits in each field is specified by using a colon followed by the number of bits. Consider the case of the equipment flag in the IBM PC. The flag is a 16-bit word that contains information about the type of equipment in the system. A structure to represent the flag could be

```
struct equip {
        unsigned no_prntrs: 2;
        unsigned ser_ptr  : 1;
        unsigned game_por : 1;
        unsigned no_rs232 : 3;
        unsigned dma_on   : 1;
        unsigned no_disk  : 2;
        unsigned vid_mode : 2;
        unsigned pl_ram   : 2;
        unsigned dummy    : 1;
        unsigned ipl_dsk  : 1;
        } e_flag;
```

The first two bits contain information on the number of printers installed on the system. The second field, (third bit) tells whether a serial printer is present or not. The third field indicates whether a game port is present. The number of RS-232C cards present is indicated in the fourth field. You can determine if a dma chip is present with the fifth field. The number of disk drives in a system is contained in the sixth field. Several video modes are possible; the current video mode is identified in the seventh field. The number of bytes of planar ram on board is found in the next field. The dummy field is just a place holder. The last field is 1 if the ipl disk is installed.

A flag like this is set when the user turns the computer on. Some flags can be changed. For example, the video mode is contained in a 2-bit field called `vid_mode`. The values possible are

```
00        not used
01        40 by 25 black &white on color card
10        80 by 25 black &white on color card
11        80 by 25 black &white on mono card
```

You can use this flag to determine if the computer is using a color card or a monochrome card. The fields behave like unsigned integers as this code shows:

```
if(e_flag.vid_mode == 3) mode = BW;
else mode = COLOR;
```

In earlier chapters BW and COLOR would have been defined as 0 and 1 respectively. One would have to gain access to the equipment flag in the computer's memory through an assembly language interface (which is discussed in a later chapter). Another way to gain access is to get the address of the equipment flag and assign that address to a pointer. The pointer can then be passed to a function that masks off the bits and makes the assignments to the structure.

There are a number of considerations to keep in mind when using bit fields. One is that some computers keep the bits in order from left to right (high to low order) but other computers are just the opposite. You must be familiar with the characteristics of the machine in use. When writing a program that must be portable, this is extremely important.

It is permissible to create a bit field structure longer than one **int**. However, any one field cannot overlap the **int** boundary. Unnamed fields are used for padding. For example:

```
struct flag {
        unsigned :12;
        unsigned va21
        unsigned val2
        unsigned val3
        };
```

This creates 12 leading bits that are not used. It is usually good for program maintenance to name the padded field. The first field is

```
unsigned padding : 12;
```

The intent of the first field is now made clear. For portability, use a variable in the field length. Instead of 12, which assumes a 16-bit **int**, assign the field width to a variable calculated from **sizeof(int)**.

```
pad_field = (sizeof(int))* 8 - 4;
...
unsigned padding :  pad_field;
```

A 16- bit **int** now yields a padding field width of 12. A 32-bit **int** results in a padding field width of 28.

Unions

C structures do not permit variant fields as Pascal does. The union gives **C** a similar capability, however. A **union** is a variable that may take on different data types in different situations. In general the form of the **union** is

```
union tag_name  {
        int membr_one;
        float membr_two;
        char membr_tre;
        };
```

The **union** has the appearance of a structure. But the difference is that the value of a **union** variable is only one of the members. The storage used for a **union** is large enough to hold the largest member in the member list. Once defined, a **union** variable can be declared in this way:

```
union in_value  {
        char one_ch;
        int two_ch;
        }  answer;
```

Additional unions can be declared like this

```
union in_value response;
```

The members of a **union** can be manipulated in much the same way that a structure is manipulated.

```
n = answer.two_ch;              /*  assign member to n  */
if(response.one_ch == 'a' ) newmenu();
                                /*  use member in an expression  */
pu = &answer;                   /*  take address of union  */
```

It is the programmer's responsibility to attend to an important point. The last data object (member) stored in the **union** is the only data object stored in it. The programmer must keep up with the last member and type stored. The **union** only holds a value for one data type. If a new assignment is made, the previous value is forgotten.

```
answer.one_ch = 'A'; /*  use first member  */

answer.two_ch = 27;  /*  erase first */
                     /* assignment and use */
                     /* second member.   */
```

Although pointers to unions may be used just like pointers to structures, the unions themselves may not be passed as function arguments, used in assignment statements, or returned by a function. A variable may be a pointer to a **union** just as a pointer can point to a structure.

```
union in_value *choice;
```

The members can be referenced by using the pointer operator.

```
item = choice -> one_ch;
```

A **union** can be a member of a structure, thus acting something like the variant field in a Pascal record. The **union** can, however, appear as any member of the structure, not just the last one.

```
struct   {
        int id_no;
        char ch;
        union pass  {
               int integer;
               char character;
               float real;
               }
        int q;
        }  *code;
```

The members are accessed as with a structure.

```
code -> pass.integer = 57;
```

A **union** can have any valid data type as a member, including another **union** or a structure. A **union** can contain a pointer to a **union** of the same type. Like structures, unions can be self- referential.

Case Study: Unions and Cipher Programs

The fact that one set of memory locations can contain values that appear under different aliases can be exploited by a coding, or encryption, program. The idea is to store a string of characters in a **union**. The union's two possible members are two arrays. The first array is a one-dimensional array, say of length 20. The second array is two-dimensional, with the number of rows and the number of columns as two factors of the dimension of the first array, 4 and 5 for example.

```
a1[20]
&
a2[5][4]
```

A string is entered in the array. The second member of the **union** is used to create an array that is put out into another string, one column at a time. For example:

```
string1 = "Now is the time Tim"
```

is stored in a **union** as

```
static union  {
  char a1[20];
  char a2[5][4];
  }  key;
```

If **string1** is copied into **key.a1**, then **key.a1** holds the same characters as **string1**. Using **puts(key.a1)** will display

```
Now is the time Tim
```

The other member of the union is **key.a2**. It looks like this

```
Now
is t
he t
ime
Tim\0
```

If **key.a2** is copied into **string2** one column at a time

```
k = 0;
for(j=0;j<4;j++)
  for(i=0;i<5;i++)
    string(k++) = key.a2[i][j];
string[k] = '\0';
```

then **string2** looks like this:

```
NihiTosemiw em tt \0
```

Clearly the two strings

```
Now is the time Tim
```

and

```
NihiTosemiw em tt
```

bear little resemblance to each other. The second string can be decoded by simply reversing the procedure. Listing 9.1 shows the use of a **union** in the cipher problem.

Listing 9.1

Cipher Program

```
/*        program to illustrate the use of a union as a
          cipher translation technique
*/
#include <stdio.h>
#define   BLANK '\040'
#define   LEN 20
#define   ROW 5
#define   COL 4
#define   LASTCH LEN-1
#define   EOS '\0'

union  {
          char a1[LEN];
          char a2[ROW][COL];
          } key;
void encode(),decode(),init_key(), message();

main()
{
  int i,j,k;
  char *s1,*s2;
  init_key();   /*  set union to all blanks  */
  printf("Type in a string \n");
  gets(s1);
  s1[LASTCH]= EOS;
  message(s1); /*  put message into the union  */
  printf("the string is now \n"); puts(s1);
  printf("and the union is \n"); puts(key.a1);

  encode(s2);   /*  create coded string  */
  printf("the second string is now \n"); puts(s2);
  printf("and the union is \n"); puts(key.a1);

  decode(s2); /*  decode string two  */
  printf("now print the union again \n");
          puts(key.a1);
  printf("end of program \n\n");
  exit();

}
```

```
void init_key()
{  int i;
   /*  initialize the first union member  */
   for(i=0;i<LASTCH;i++) key.a1[i] = BLANK;
   key.a1[LASTCH] = EOS;
   return;
}
void message(s1)
char *s1;
{  int i;
   printf("The string is copied into the union\n");
     for(i=0;i<LASTCH;i++)
       if( s1[i] != EOS )
         key.a1[i] = s1[i];
       else break;    /*  quit for loop  */
   return;
}
void encode(s)
char *s;
{  int i,j,k;
   printf("\n\nBegin transposition process.\n");
   k = 0;
   for(j=0;j<COL;j++)
     for(i=0;i<ROW;i++)
       s[k++] = key.a2[i][j];
   s[LASTCH] = EOS;
   return;
}
      void decode(s)
      char *s;
      {
        int i,j,k;
        /*  put the coded string in the union  */
          k=0;
          for(j=0;j<COL;j++)
            for(i=0;i<ROW;i++)
              key.a2[i][j] = s[k++];
          key.a1[LASTCH] = EOS;
          return;
      }
```

End of Listing

Memory Management

C provides for dynamic memory allocation. Some objects, such as **static** arrays initialized in code, **auto** variables in a function, and values created by recursive calls, are allocated memory space by **C**. Other variables, such as pointers to buffers do not have memory set aside for their use. The programmer must request the system make memory available from the heap as needed. There are several **C** functions related to memory allocation and management.

One memory allocation function is **malloc**(). It finds a block of contiguous memory and reserves it for use. In general the form of **malloc**() is

```
buf_ptr = malloc(num_bytes);
```

The **malloc**() function returns a pointer to an area of memory the size of num_bytes. If the function does not work, it returns 0 which is not a valid pointer value. Suppose you needed 1k of memory. To provide it, you write

```
unsigned int amount = 1024;
char *buf_ptr;
char *malloc();  /*  or externchar *malloc()  */

buf_ptr = malloc(amount);
```

The buffer pointer, `buf_ptr`, now points to the first address in a 1k block of memory. The program can now use the memory as it wishes.

The amount, or `num_bytes` argument, for **malloc**() is always in bytes. If you are storing another data type, use **sizeof** to determine the number of bytes for that data type. Then multiply the result of **sizeof** by the number of items for which you wish to make room. Since **malloc**() always returns a pointer to a **char** type, you may need to cast the pointer to the proper type. The following example allocates memory for 100 **float**-type objects.

```
char *malloc();
float *fp;
fp = (float *) malloc( ((sizeof) float)* 100);
```

Now `fp` is a pointer to the first memory location that contains the first of 100 **float** objects. To return the allocated memory to the heap use the **free**(pointer) function.

The **free**(pointer) function frees up the reserved memory space. It unallocates the memory that **malloc**() reserved. The pointer must contain the address returned by **malloc**(). Normally, memory is freed in reverse order from its allocation. If the **free**() function works correctly, it returns 0. If an error occurs, it returns −1. It is good practice to always check the operation of the **free**() function and trap any errors that occur.

An example of the use of **malloc**() and **free**() is shown in Listing 9.2.

Listing 9.2

Memory Allocation and Deallocation

```
/*  example  */
unsigned int amount = 1024;
char *buf_ptr;
char *malloc();
/*  allocate memory  */
buf_ptr = malloc(amount);    /*  pointer to mem area  */
/*  program process goes here  */
/*  unallocate the memory  */
if( free(buf_ptr) == -1)
  /*  print error message here  */;
else
  /*  free worked ok so go on with program  */
```

End of Listing

Memory allocation is often used with input and output buffers when the amount of memory needed is not known in advance. Consider the case of a text editor. The size of the text file is simply not known before the program begins. You might allocate a buffer region of a certain size and then enlarge it if needed. The example in Listing 9.3 shows how you can start with a small amount of memory and enlarge it if needed.

Listing 9.3

Enlarging Allocated Memory

```
#include <stdio.h>
#define  SIZE 2048
#define  EXIT 005   /*  control E stops the data entry  */
char *malloc();     /*  declare memory allocator  */
char *start;        /*  point to beginning of mem space  */
char *end;          /*  point to end of mem space  */
char *cur_pos;      /*  point to current position  */
char *last;         /*  point to last character typed  */
int index = 0;      /*  number of regions used  */
char *next_blk[];   /*  pointer to another region  */
int num_blks;       /*  number of blocks of mem used  */
int instruct();     /*  provide user directions  */
```

```
start = malloc(SIZE);  /*  first region  */
/*  make sure malloc worked */
if(start == 0)  {  puts("out of memory!");
        exit();  }
end = start + SIZE -1;  /*  last mem loc  */
cur_pos = start;        /*  current position  */
next_blk[index++] = start;  /*  first mem block  */

instruct();          /*  call routine to provide instructions  */
while( (*cur_pos = getchar()) != EXIT)
{  /*  cur pos is new character  */

   /*  echo character to the screen  */
   putchar(*cur_pos);
   /*  check to see if this block is full  */
   if(end - cur_pos) == 0)
   /*  get some more memory  */
   {  if((next_blk[index] = malloc(SIZE)) == 0)
        {  puts(" Out of memory.");break;   }

        /*  move pointers  */
        cur_pos = next_blk[index++];
        end = cur_pos + SIZE -1;
   }  /*  end of out of mem this block check  */
   ++cur_pos;  /*  increment pointer  */
}  /*  end of while loop  */
last = cur_pos - 1;  /*  last char in this area  */
num_blks = index - 1;/*  number of blocks used  */

/* continue processing  */
```

End of Listing

A seen in Listing 9.3 the technique of enlarging memory makes heavy use of pointers. Notice that the memory region in use does not have a name. If you were to make it an array, what would you do when the array filled up?

The character that is typed in is not assigned to a **char** variable such as ch. You might have expected to see

```
ch = getchar();
```

If ch had been used then another assignment would have to be made to *cur_pos. Our program simply makes the assignment directly without the need for ch.

The-out-of memory check is done by comparing the values of end and cur_pos. When they are the same, cur-pos has reached the end of the allocated storage and a call is made to **malloc**() for more memory. If there is no memory available, the program drops out of the read loop (**while**) with a **break** statement. If **malloc**() is successful, the cur_pos pointer is moved to the first address of the new block of storage. The first address of each new block is stored in next_blk[]. Since the memory areas returned by **malloc**() do not have to be in contiguous blocks, you must keep track of each starting address by using `next_blk[]`.

The text stored in the memory can be printed to any file with a simple loop. Listing 9.4. shows how to display the text on the screen.

Listing 9.4

Displaying Contents of Memory Region

```
/*  write the text to the screen   */

/*  loop thru each memory region   */
for(index = 0; index <= num_blks;index++)
{  cur_pos = next_blk[index];  /*  first char */
   end = cur_pos + SIZE - 1;   /*  reset pointer   */
     /*  loop thru the current region char by char   */
   while( (end-cur_pos) > 0)
                                   {  putchar(*cur_pos);
                                      ++cur_pos;
                                   }
}  /*  end for loop   */
```

End of Listing

Another way to make more memory available is through the function **realloc()**. This function changes the size of the previously allocated memory. If the original allocation was done with

```
buf_ptr = malloc(size);
```

the rellocation might be

```
buf_ptr = realloc(buf_ptr,newsize);
```

The function returns a pointer to a new address of memory which begins the newly allocated storage. The new memory may or may not begin at the same place as the old block of storage. If there is not enough memory available in the same contiguous block that the previously allocated memory, the contents are moved to an entirely new area. This can be dangerous if you are creating certain types of data structures which depend on loop counters. The **realloc**() function can make an area of memory larger or smaller. It returns 0 if unsuccessful.

alloc(): Some systems provide the function **alloc**(). It works like **malloc**() with the exception that all the bytes allocated are initialized to 0. Check your system's documentation to see if **alloc**() is available.

When the allocated memory is going to be used for a data object that is not a simple data type (such as **char** or **int**), then **calloc**() is used. This function, like **malloc**(), returns a pointer to a character. In general its form is

```
pointer = calloc( n, sizeof(object))
```

where `pointer` refers to the desired data type and `n` is the number of objects of that type. The operator **sizeof** is used to provide a portable program and to calculate the number of bytes each object requires.

Suppose the goal is to allocate space for a structure like this one:

```
structure person   {
            char name[20];
            char address[25];
            int age;
            long int id;
            };
```

A pointer to a structure of this type is declared as

```
struct person *per_ptr;
```

Storage for 10 **persons** is allocated with the expression

```
calloc(10, sizeof(person))
```

Regardless of the number of bytes used to store **person** on your system, this expression will work. It does, however, return a pointer to a character and the pointer in this case is for a **person** type structure. It is necessary to cast the returned pointer so it is of the correct type.

```
per_ptr = (struct person *) calloc(10,sizeof(person));
```

The necessary statements to begin a program that includes these examples are shown in Listing 9.5.

Listing 9.5

Allocating Space for a Structure

```
#include <stdio.h>
structure person   {
            char name[20];
            char address[25];
            int age;
            long int id;
            };
struct person *per_ptr;
char *calloc();           /*  must be declared  */
int n = 10;
per_ptr = (struct person *) calloc(n,sizeof(person));
```

End of Listing

The stdio.h library contains a definition of BUFSIZ that can be used with the memory management functions. This symbolic constant is set to some value such as 512 or 1024, and can then be used in a statement.

```
ptr = malloc(10 * BUFSIZE);
```

Since BUFSIZE is defined in stdio.h, the preceding statement is portable. Look at your version of stdio.h to find out what BUFSIZ is set to and be aware that on some systems BUFSIZ is _BUFSIZ.

Allocating as Much Memory as Possible

There are times when one might want to make a good deal of memory available to a program. For example, a communications program or a print formatter may be more efficient if a buffer is very large. The general idea is to allocate a memory area that is near to or greater than that which is likely to ever be available. If that allocation fails, decrement the number of bytes by some reasonable amount such as 256 bytes or 512 bytes. Then try to allocate the memory again. Using a loop, repeat the process until the allocation succeeds. Listing 9.6 illustrates this idea.

Listing 9.6

Allocating as Much Memory as Possible

```
int num_byts = 65024;          /*  sys dependent  */
char *buff, *malloc();
int min_buff = 1024;           /*  min usable size  */

/*  loop to find as much memory as possible  */
for( ; ; num_byts -= 512;)     /*  loop decrements by 512  */
  { if( num_byts < min_buff )
     { puts("Not enough memory available.");
       exit();
     }
     buff = malloc(num_byts);     /*  try for mem space  */
     if(buff != 0)                /*  found some  */
       break;                     /*  break off the search  */
  } /*  end of for loop  */
```

End of Listing

One problem is that this method gobbles up nearly all free memory and that can have a disastrous effect on a program. To deallocate some memory for stack growth and other heap uses, the last **if** statement can be changed to:

```
if(buff != 0)
{  free(buff);             /*  deallocate the memory  */
   num_byts -= 2048;       /*  shrink size of buffer  */
   buff = malloc(num_byts);    /*  allocate new buffer  */
   break;                  /*  now break off the search  */
}
```

The preceding code immediately frees up the newly acquired memory and then shrinks the size of the request. The number 2048 is arbitrary. It might well be something like 512 or 1024. The code makes the memory allocation again and it will surely work since the previous request for a large amount worked just before this **if** statement. As a precaution, add an error check to the second **malloc()** call

A Discussion of a Memory Management Example

Consider the case of a simple text editor. There is no way to know in advance how much memory will be needed. The text, newlines, carriage returns, white space, and special markers are all placed in an area of memory. Pointers keep track of the first location, the current location, the last location that contains a character of some kind, and the last available memory location. When all this area is used up, more memory is allocated. A pointer is used to point to the next block of memory. The blocks of memory do not need to be contiguous because pointers are used to go from one block to the next.

There are some questions to answer. First, how large should you make each block of memory? Assuming the screen is an 80 by 24 region and that at least two lines are used for messages and indicators (such as row number, line number, and the like), there are 22 lines for text. Most lines of text are 60 or less characters. One screen is 60 by 22 or 1320 characters. One printed page is approximately 55 by 60 or two screens worth. The disk probably stores a file in 512-byte sectors. Since 2048 is 4 x 512 and also a little more than 1.5 screens of text, choose 2048 as the amount of memory to be allocated at one time. Another programmer could choose a different amount. In reality, a memory of 2048 bytes will hold more than two screens of text because newlines are stored as just another character, but are displayed by moving the cursor to the next line.

Another question is what do you do when memory is exhausted? The user of the editor doesn't want the program to just stop. We need a cushion of some kind. There are several solutions. One is to begin by allocating two blocks of memory. When the first is full, allocate a third block and then begin using the second block. This process continues until the request for memory fails. The nth or last block is still available for the user. A warning message is displayed and the user is told to save the current contents to disk to avoid a problem. When the last buffer is half full, the editing process is stopped and the last half of the last block is deallocated. The user still has 1024 bytes available in memory and they may be needed by the stack when the save option is called. This technique lets the user be human; most people try to type just a little more after the warning and before saving the file.

The memory allocation can be hidden (abstracted) by encapsulating it in a function called `get_mem()`. The low-on- memory warning is placed in a function called `low_mem()`. The program is set up by creating the pointers to the various places.

Style Tips

Take care not to let your use of **malloc**() run rampant without thought. If you are tempted to use only dynamic memory allocation and avoid fixed allocation such as arrays, you may waste memory. Many machines insist that allocated memory blocks fall on fixed blocks. Some machines store memory block sizes in a hidden field. These practices can waste as much as 20 percent of the free space in a program. When a simple array will do, do not compound your debugging problems with a potentially wasteful **malloc**() call.

When a program requires only a few copies of a given structure, use a fixed array. The improved program efficency will make up for the small amount of wasted space.

Study the typical execution situation. When you arrive at a typical number of allocated blocks, arrange to allocate a number of blocks or areas of memory all at once and then discard (**free**) them all at once. Alternately, allocate the blocks as needed, but **free** them all at once. You can also create an array of pointers to blocks of memory. Allocate all the blocks of memory and store the pointers in the array. As blocks of memory are needed, bump the array index. To free the whole collection of blocks for reuse, move the array index to the top (beginning) of the array.

The last method can be modified when the various blocks of memory have short lifetimes. Create a **static** array and as blocks are allocated using **malloc**(), instead of freeing the block, place the pointer in the array. When another block is needed, get it from the array as long as a block is available via the array. This improves efficiency by avoiding calls to **malloc**() and making the **free** procedure much simpler.

In complicated programs, where there are repeated calls to **malloc**() (or **calloc**() for user-defined data structures) it is good practice to place the **malloc**() function inside another function such as `getmem()` or `m_alloc()`. Then, if changes to the **malloc**() calls need to be made because of changes in the user- defined data structures, only one function needs to be changed. You do not need to run all over the program looking for calls to **malloc**() and changing them. This practice is analogous to defining constants at the top of a program.

There are many more examples of using dynamic memory allocation techniques. Experience and practice can lead a programmer to skill with these techniques. Throughout the remainder of this text, memory allocation will be a commonly used concept.

Summary

A structure is an aggregate data type composed of other data objects. For example, the structure for a library book could be

```
struct book   {
        char title[20];
        char author[20];
        char num[15];
        int copy;
        };
```

Additional books can be declared by writing

```
struct book checked,ordered;
```

The individual members of a structure can be accessed via the member operator, `checked.copy = 2;` a pointer can be established that references a structure.

When initialized, the individual members are referenced via the operator `->`.

A **union** is a data structure that can hold data objects of different types and storage requirements. Only one data type can be used at a time.

Given a **union** of a **float** object `x` and an **int** `n`, if the **float** object is used, then the **int** object is not active . However, if one makes an assignment to the **int** object, then the **float** object is not being used. Both data objects, `x` and `n`, occupy the same storage space.

Structures and unions can have other structures or unions as their members. If you want to have a structure of the same type as a member, it must be declared as a pointer.

EXERCISES

UNDERSTANDINGS

1. How many data items can be stored in a union at one time?
2. Is the structure "tag" required? Give an example of a structure with no tag.
3. Pascal has something called a variant record, which is a field in a record that can take on different type definitions when needed. How is this done in **C**?
4. Name some of the distinguishing differences between arrays and structures.
5. Explain the meaning of the term template.
6. What is meant by a self-referential structure?

USAGE

7. Explain when to use the period (.) operator and the arrow (`->`) operator.
8. In order to initialize the elements of a structure when it is declared, what must be the storage class?
9. Create a **typedef** that describes the structure employee as it appears in the early section of this chapter. The **typedef** results in a `EMP` data type.
10. Write a declaration of a function returning a pointer to a structure of type `book`.
11. What is the difference between these two?

    a. `(*thig).item = 10;`
    b. `thig->item = 10;`

12. What gets incremented in each of these?

    a. `++(thig) -> item;`
    b. `++thig -> item;`
    c. `(thig++) ->item;`
    d. `thig -> item++;`

APPLICATIONS

13. Create a structure to represent an inventory item in a car- parts store. The item needs an item number, name, description, price, location code, and in-stock code.

14. Create a function that copies a structure of the type in #13 to another structure of the same type.
15. Write a quicksort function for structures of the type in #13 where the sort key is the part number. The structures are stored in an array of size N.
16. Write a function that encrypts a 7-character password so that the encrypted password never begins with the same character as the unencrypted password.
17. Create a function to translate a rational number (i.e., fraction) into a decimal number stored in string form. Use only integer arithmetic. [hint: create the string with **sprintf**.] The algorithm should be much like the long division algorithm. The rational number should be stored as a structure.

e.g.
```
typedef rational {
        long int numer;
        long int denom;
} RATNUM;
```

Pass pointers and a string to the function

```
rtos(t,b,s);
```

where t is the numerator, b is the denom, and s is the string.

e.g.

```
     19.333
3)   58              19 = 58/3
     3
     28            1000 = (58 % 3) * 1000
     27
      1 000         333 = 1000/3
```

18. Write a program that chains menus together. Each menu is called by a display_men() function which has as its argument a pointer to the desired menu. Each menu is an array of strings. The main menu should make sense based on the previous menu. One should be able to go backward through the previous menu(s). Do not write the code to execute items listed on any of the menus. Write a stub routine(s) to illustrate that the correct feature was found.
19. Write a function free_spc() which returns the number of free bytes available in the system (e.g., the heap).

10

Files

A file is a complex data type that is stored external to main memory, usually on disk or tape. Files are created in several ways: with editors or word processors, by programs, or from other files with the assistance of a program. Like arrays and structures, a file must be declared and defined by the program. Unlike arrays and structures (which are stored in main memory during the life of the program), files are stored on external media. A program may read or write to a file. **C** provides special commands for file operations.

Most **C** files can be thought of as a list of characters that include newlines, spaces, tabs, letters, numerals, punctuation marks, and control characters. The list terminates with an end-of-file (**EOF**) marker. **EOF** is usually -1 on a Unix system; other operating systems use a different marker.

All input studied thus far has been from the standard input device (**stdin**) and the output has been sent to the standard output device (**stdout**). Input has been a stream of characters (a text file) and output has been a stream of characters (another text file). There has been no need to indicate that you wanted to use these default files. When other files are needed, however, they must be specified.

Accessing a File

Input and output functions are not part of **C** itself; they are part of a library. The library goes by different names depending on the system. Under Unix the compiler automatically looks in the library for the functions. On micros the user must specify which libraries are to be incorporated at link time. The header file contains macros and definitions needed by the i/o functions. When using i/o routines, you must always include the file `stdio.h` (**#include** `<stdio.h>`). There are exceptions to the rule (such as using **printf** without including `stdio.h`), but it is good practice to always include `stdio.h`.

One of the definitions contained in `stdio.h` is for a structure called **FILE**. It is a constant and so is written with uppercase letters. (Some implementations use a structure, others use **typedef** and a structure.) **File** is used like a data type. Its presence in `stdio.h` makes it global in scope. A file is declared using the **FILE** type and the **fopen**() function. Suppose you want to open a file to serve as the output file. You could write

```
FILE *fopen() *fptr;                  /*  1  */
fptr = fopen("results.dat","w");      /*  2  */
```

Line 1 is a declaration statement, and **fopen**() and `fptr` are pointers to a structure of type **FILE**. In other words, **fopen**() and `fptr` are of data type **FILE**.

Line 2 actually opens the file and makes the logical connection between the filename (`results.dat`) and the file pointer (`fptr`). The file pointer is used to refer to the file. The name of the file is used by the operating system. Hence, a connection between the system name (`results.dat`) and the program name (`fptr`) is made by the file-open statement. To break this connection and put the file away, one uses a file-close statement.

```
fclose(fptr);
```

This statement performs some necessary housekeeping chores on the output buffers and disconnects the system name from the program name. Notice that the argument for **fclose** is `fptr`, not `results.dat`.

Most newer systems provide the declaration in `stdio.h`, but older **C** implementations require that the ***fopen()** pointer be declared in the application program. Hence, the earlier statement could have been:

```
FILE *fptr;
```

Check your `stdio.h` file to see what your system requires. If it does not **include** a declaration of **fopen**(), it is good practice to declare it in your own stddefs.h file. A portable program can be modified by either adding or deleting one line of the definitions header file, and not the actual code.

In general the form of the file open command is

```
fptr = fopen(filename,mode)
```

where `fptr` is a pointer to a type **FILE**, filename is the system name of the file and is a character string, and mode is the type of operation to be performed. The mode can be one of three types and is represented as follows:

- `"w"` means to write to the file. If the filename exists, it is deleted and a new file opened.
- `"r"` means to read from a file. If the file does not exist, an error is returned, that is, **NULL** is returned as the value of **fopen**().
- `"a"` means to append a file. New data are added to the end of the file.

Error Checking: The **fopen**() function returns **NULL** if there was an error while trying to open a file. A programmer can take advantage of this to make sure a file open command is successful. For example:

```
if( (fptr = fopen("results","w")) != NULL)
  { perform file read steps  }
else
  { print an error message }
```

If the file-open command is successful, the program proceeds as intended. If it fails, an error message is printed. There are many possible reasons for the error. The disk-drive door might be open, the disk could be full, the filename may be too long, the file may be in another directory, and so on. (A sophisticated error trap can keep a program from crashing because of human error.)

The file close function, **fclose**(), also returns a value that can be used with error traps. the function returns 0 if the close operation is successful; otherwise, it returns −1. It is good practice to check for a successful close operation because portions of a file can be lost if it is not closed properly.

If the file name is declared as a pointer, the quotation marks can be eliminated.

```
#include <stdio.h>
FILE *infile, *outfile;
static char *testdat ="test.dat";
static char *results = "results.dat"

if( (infile = fopen(testdat,"r")) != NULL)
  { ... }

if( (outfile = fopen(results,"w")) != NULL)
  { statements  }

fclose(infile); fclose(outfile);
```

Using pointers to character arrays is the most common method of specifying file names. It is easier to read and provides for more efficient operation than other methods. It is much like declaring constants at the top of a program: When you need to change a file name, you need to change it only in the declaration section.

Simple File Operations

The function **getchar**() returns a character from the standard input device (**stdin**) and is defined in `stdio.h` as

```
#define getchar() getc(stdin)
```

The function to return a single character from a file is **getc**(`filepointer`). It, **getchar**(), is simply the **getc**() function applied to the **stdin** file pointer. Table 10.1 lists several other file operations with counterparts in simple i/o.

Table 10.1
File I/O Functions

file i/o function	simple i/o function
getc(fptr)	**getchar**()
putc(ch,fptr)	**putchar**(ch)
fprintf(fptr,"cs",list)	fprint("cs",list)
fscanf(fptr,"cs",*list)	**fscanf**("cs",*list)
fgets(sptr,len,fptr)	**gets**(sptr)
fputs(sptr,fptr)	**puts**(sptr)
fgetc(fptr)	**getchar**()
fputc(ch,fptr)	**putchar**(ch)

Both **getc**() and **putc**() are direct counterparts of their simple i/o cousins. The **getc**() function has already been mentioned; **putc**() writes a single character to the output stream. The resilts of **getc**() are nearly identical to those of **fgetc**()

and the results of **putc**() and **fputc**() are also almost the same. The difference is that **getc**() and **putc**() are macros while **fgetc**() and **fputc**() are true functions.

Formatted input and output are provided via the file versions of **printf**() and **scanf**(). Both **fprintf**() and **fscanf**() work exactly like their nonfile counterparts with the exception of the file pointer. The input and output are performed on a file, not the standard input and output devices.

Two cases in Table 10.1 do not correspond exactly to the simple i/o counterparts. The **fgets**() function returns a string not longer than `len` (length) from the file; the simple **gets**() function does not require the `len` argument. As a result, \0 is appended to the string. The **fputs**() function does write a string (including the null terminator) to the file, but it does not write a newline character as do some versions of **puts**().

Listing 10.1 illustrates how a file can be typed in at the keyboard and then copied to a disk file on the default directory.

Listing 10.1

Create a File from Keyboard

```
#include <stdio.h>
main()
{ FILE *ofp;    /*  declared output file pointer  */
  static char newstuff[] = "newstuff.dat";
  int ch;
  if( (ofp = fopen( newstuff, "w") != NULL)
    {
    while( (ch = getchar()) != EOF )
      fputc(ch,ofp);  /*  echo to output  */
      fclose(ofp);
    }
  else
      printf(" error in file open.\n");
}
```

End of Listing

The file pointer, or stream, is `ofp` (output file pointer). The external file name is `newstuff.dat`. The if statement makes sure that the file open statement is successful. The while statement reads a character and then echoes it to the file. Finally, the file is closed. The external file now exists on the disk. `Newstuff.dat` can be found in the users directory. It may be copied to the screen or printer. It may even be used as input for Listing 10.2 which reads a file and echoes it to the standard output device. Note that the file was closed with no error checking. What should have been done?

Listing 10.2

File Read Program

```
#include <stdio.h>
main()
{  FILE *ifp;
   static char newstuff[] = "newstuff.dat";
   int ch;
   if((ifp = fopen(newstuff,"r")) != NULL)
     {
     while( (ch = getc(ifp)) != EOF)
       putchar(ch);
       fclose(ifp);
     }
   else
     printf("error in opening file.");
}
```

End of Listing

Listing 10.2 is much like 10.1. The differences are that the **fopen**() statement mode has been changed from "w" to "r" so that the file can be read instead of written to. The **while** statements have also changed. The statement that read from the keyboard was

```
while( (ch = getchar()) != EOF )
  fputc(ch,ofp);    /*  echo to output  */
```

The **getchar**() function reads from the keyboard; the **fputc**() function writes to the stream. The opposite is true in Listing 10.2.

```
while( (ch = getc(ifp)) != EOF)
  putchar(ch);
```

Listing 10.2 reads the character from the file by using **getc**() and writes it to the screen by using **putchar**().

Notice that no effort is made to pick off newline or other special characters. Any newline characters are simply copied to the stream. When written to the screen, they have an effect. As far as the file is concerned, they are just like any other character.

Suppose you want to read each character from one file and write it to another. Listing 10.3 shows how to write the program.

Listing 10.3

File Copy Program

```
#include <stdio.h>
main()
{ FILE *ifp,*ofp;
   static char oldfile[] = "tim.dat;
   static char newfile[] = "grady.dat";
   int ch;
   if((ifp = fopen(oldfile,"r")) != NULL)
     { if((ofp = fopen(newfile,"w")) != NULL)
         { while( (ch = fgetc(ifp)) != EOF)
              fputc(ch,ofp);
              fclose(ofp); fclose(ifp);
         }
     else
         printf("error in opening output file.");
     }
   else
     printf("error in opening input file.");
}
```

End of Listing

Listing 10.3 illustrates the simplest file i/o commands but is not too useful. It only works for the two files tim.dat and grady.dat. A better version that accepts the file names on the command line will be shown in a later section. As it is, Listing 10.3 is stuck with the file names that are hard coded into the main program.

The next example, Listing 10.4, is useful and shows a code segment that reads data from file `addres.dat` into available memory. The code is from an address label printing program and it allocates storage for the addresses as needed. You can review the use of **malloc**() as you study Listing 10.4.

Listing 10.4

File Read and Memory Allocation

```
FILE *fp;
struct addr   {
  char name[24];
  char addr1[24];
  char addr2[24];
  char csz[24];
  struct addr *next;
  struct addr *prior;
  } list_entry;
```

```
void load()
{
register int t,size;
struct addr *info, *temp;
char *p, *m;
/*  open file  */
if((fp=fopen("address.dat","r"))==0)
  {  printf("file open error"); exit();   }
/*  file load process  */
size = sizeof(list_entry);
start = malloc(size);
if(!start)
  {  printf("Out of memory\n"); return;  }
info = start;
p = info;
while((*p++ = getc(fp)) != EOF)
{     for(t=0;t<size-1);++t)
          *p++ = getc(fp);    /*  read one byte  */
      info ->next = malloc(size);
      if(!info -> next)
          {  printf("out of memory\n"); return;  }
      info->prior = temp;
      temp = info;
      info = info -> next;
      p = info;
}
free(temp->next);
temp->next = 0;
last = temp;
start->prior = 0;
fclose(fp);
}
```

End of Listing

The function `load()` shown in Listing 10.4 opens a file (`addr.dat`) for read. After the appropriate error checking, each record is read one byte at a time. The memory management function **malloc** is called for each new record. Once the file has been entirely read into memory, the pointers are set to the needed values and the function terminates. Another function may be written to print each record on a printer that contains blank labels.

The next example uses command line arguments to copy two files. Listing 10.5 uses command line arguments and is invoked with this line

```
fcopy file1 file2
```

Listing 10.5

File Copy Utility

```
main(argc,argv)
int argc;
char *argv[];
{
/*  declaration section  */
char source[30],dest[30],ch;
int n,i;
FILE *fds,*fdd;
/*  check for correct number of arguments  */
if(argc != 3)
  { printf(" Need two file names.\007\n");
    exit();
  }
/*  make sure file names are not the same  */
if(strcmp(argv[1],argv[2]) == 0)
  { printf(" Can not copy to itself.\007 \n");
    exit();
}
/*  copy arguments to file names to use o,d code  */
strcpy(source,argv[1]);   /*  copy arg[1] to source  */
strcpy(dest,argv[2]);   /*  copy arg[2] to dest  */
/*  program now continues as before  */
/*  except for the input of file names section  */
if((fds = fopen(source,"r"))!= NULL)
{ if((fdd = fopen(dest,"w")) != NULL)
    { while(( ch = fgetc(fds)) != EOF)
        fputc(ch,fdd);
      fclose(fdd);fclose(fds);
    }
  else
    printf("Error in opening %s.",dest);
}
else
  printf("Error in opening %s.",source);
```

End of Listing

This program is usually available as a utility on any computer system. It's importance is in understanding how files are copied. With this understanding you can write other file copy utilities that filter or manipulate the file contents on the way by.

The Printer as a File

In Chapter 2, you looked at ways to send output to the printer (MS-DOS) or a print file (Unix). The next utility is a generalized method of doing the same thing.

The example in Chapter 2 used the `print.h` header file shown in Listing 10.6.

Listing 10.6

print.h

```
/*  header file to be included with
/*  programs that write to the lineprinter
#define PRINT fprintf
#define PUTCHAR fputc
FILE *PRN;
static char stdlst[] = "prn";  /*  system dependent  */
open_prn()
{  if((PRN = fopen(stdlst,"w")) != NULL)
          ;         /*  no statement  */
   else printf("Error--- printer not ready.\n");
}
clos_prn()
{  fclose(PRN);  }
```

End of Listing

The command **FILE** specifies *PRN which is a pointer to a file. In the command PRINT PRN is the file specified. The header file is not really necessary if you realize that **FILE** type and external file name are required. This header file hides the necessary commands for writing to a file so that the programmer, without knowing how files work, can send output to the printer.

The earlier example (Listing 2.4) can be rewritten as shown in Listing 10.7.

Listing 10.7

Write to Printer as a file

```
/*  Sample program where printer is output file  */
#include <stdio.h>
FILE *printer
static char stdlst[] = "prn"

main()
{  int n =5;
   char ch = 'G';
   float x = 12.375;

   /*  print to the screen  */
   putchar(ch); putchar('\n');
   printf(" This is a normal output line.\n");
   /*  print to the line printer  */
   if((printer = fopen(stdlst,"w")) == NULL)
     printf("Error --- printer not ready.\n");
   else
     {  fprintf(printer,"Sample line of text.\n");
        fputc(ch,printer); fputc('\n',printer);
        fclose(printer);
     }
}
```

End of Listing

Listing 10.7 makes use of standard file i/o. The internal file name is printer. The external file name is prn. **C** treats the printer as any other file with the exception that you may not use the "r" or "a" modes in the **fopen**() statement. Other file commands may be used with the printer.

The display of a file on the printer provided by some implementations of modern languages on a PC are inadequate. The DOS utility type is very simple with few options. The print utility is sometimes acceptable, but it lacks versatility. The routines discussed here allow you to include line numbers, file name labels, and number the pages. It also skips the page perforations.

Logically speaking, the printer is a file, so the problem is similar to a file copy routine. Listing 10.8 shows the necessary code.

Listing 10.8

Printing Files with Options

```
/************************************************
 *                                              *
 * Program:   prt                               *
 *                                              *
 * Task/function: print several files           *
 *            with line numbers and             *
 *            page breaks.                      *
 *                                              *
 * Programmer:Tim Grady                         *
 *                                              *
 * Located in:prt.c                             *
 *                                              *
 * Called by: prt [-lnp] file1 file2 file3...   *
 *            note:  flags are case insensitive *
 ***********************************************/
/* The file names are typed at the command line.
   The program puts page numbers at the bottom of the page
   and places the file name in the upper right hand corner
   A command line switch option allows you to suppress
   the line numbers, the title, and the page numbers.
     l is the option to suppress line numbers
     p is the option to suppress page numbers
     n is the option to suppress name of the file
   The options may appear in any order.  The following are
   all valid:
     prt file.c
     prt -l file.c
     prt -n file.c
     prt -p file.c
     prt -ln file.c
     prt -pnl file.c
     prt -pl file.c
     prt -lnp file.c
```

```
#include <stdio.h>
#include "ctype.h"
#include "math.h"
/*  global variables  */
#define PG_NO_LINE 62
        /*  this is the line on which the page */
        /* number is printed  */
#define NO_LINES 54 /*  The number of lines of text  */
                   /* on a single page.   */
FILE *ifp,*ofp;     /*  ifp is current file  */
                   /*  ofp is output file  */
static char printer[] = "PRN";
         /* PRN is MSDOS name for the printer
            this version has a printer dependent
            feature in that both a lf and cr must
            be sent to cause a newline at the
            printer.  Other implementations may
            only require a lf i.e.  \n
            On a Unix system, it creates a
            file called PRN which may be
            printed with lp.  */
struct options
        {  short int line_nos;
           short int page_nos;
           short int title;
  };

main(argc,argv)
int argc;
char *argv[];
{
  void tabs();                    /*  tab t spaces  */
  void bottom();                  /*  bottom of pg  */
  void set_ops();                 /*  sets options  */
  char *oldfile,curfile[20];
  struct options flags;           /*  flag values  */
  char *choices;                  /*  option string  */
  int ch;                         /*  individual chars  */
  float n;                        /*  line numbers  */
  int i;                          /*  loop counter  */
  int pg;                         /*  page number  */
  int t;                          /*  tab spaces  */

  /*  initialize flag values  */
    flags.line_nos = 1;
    flags.page_nos = 1;
    flags.title = 1;
```

```
  /*  check to see if command line switches are set  */
  if(argv[1][0] == '-')
    {
      strcpy(choices,argv[1]);
      set_ops(&flags,choices);  /* set flag values */
      i = 2;  /* use second command line parameter
                                   as first file*/
    }
  else
    i = 1;  /* first parameteris first file */
/*  check to see if any files are in the list  */
  if(argc == i)
    { printf("\t No file names found.\n");
      printf("\t The command line should be:\n");
      printf("\t\t pr5 [-options] filename filename \n");
      exit();
    }
if((ofp =fopen(printer,"w")) != NULL)
{ /*  printer file successfully opened  */
  for(;i<argc;i++)
       /*  loop thru the files print each one  */
  {
    strcpy(oldfile,argv[i]);
    strcpy(curfile,argv[i]);
    if((ifp = fopen(oldfile,"r")) != NULL)
      /*  file successfully opened  */
    {
      printf("Printing %s \n",oldfile);
      /*  top of main loop  */
      pg = 1;  /*  initialize page number  */
      n = 1.0;   /*  initialize line number  */
      /*  go to new page for top of file  */
      fprintf(ofp,"\n\f\r\n\r\n\r");
      tabs(50);
      if(flags.title)
                                 fputs(curfile,ofp);
      fprintf(ofp,"\n\r\n\r\n\r\n\r");
      if(flags.line_nos)
       fprintf(ofp,"%4.0f ",n);  /*  print line no.1  */
```

```
          while((ch = getc(ifp)) != EOF)
         { if(ch != '\n')  /*  watch for end of line  */
             fputc(ch,ofp);  /*  copy character  */
           else   /*  put in line number  */
             {  fputc(ch,ofp);  /*  echo new line  */
                n++;  /*  bump line number  */
                if((int)n % NO_LINES == 0)
                  {  fprintf(ofp,"\n\r\n\r");
                     tabs(30);
                     if(flags.page_nos)
                       fprintf(ofp,"%d\n\r ",pg);
                     else
                       fprintf(ofp,"\n\r");
                     pg++;

                     /*  next line skips paper perfs  */
                     fprintf(ofp,"\n\f\r\n\r\n\r\n\r\n\r");
                  }

                /*  then print new line number  */
                if(flags.line_nos)
                  fprintf(ofp,"%4.0f ",n);

                } /*  end of else  */
           } /*  end of while  */
           if(flags.page_nos)
             bottom( (int)n, pg);
                /*  place page number at bottom  */
           fclose(ifp);   /*  close current file  */
       } /*  end of main loop  */

       else  /*  get here because file did not open  */
             printf("Could not open file %s.\n",oldfile);

    } /*  end of for loop  */
  } /*  end of printer file open if statement  */
    else /*  get here if printer was not ready  */
      printf("Can not open printer\n");
  fflush(ofp);
  fclose(ofp);   /*  close the printer  */
}/*  end of main routine  */

void tabs(t)
int t;                  /*  skip t spaces  */
{
  int i;
  for(i=1;i<t;i++)
    fprintf(ofp," ");
}
```

```
void bottom(n,pg)
int n,pg;           /*  go to bottom of page */
                    /* to print pg no.   */
{
  int i;
  for(i=1;i< (PG_NO_LINE-(n % NO_LINES)-4);i++)
    fprintf(ofp,"\n\r");
  tabs(30);
  fprintf(ofp,"%d\n\r",pg);
}
/* This function sets flags in a structure to false if
     they are included on the command line.
     choice l or L is used to suppress line nos.
     choice p or P is used to suppress page numbers
     choice n or N is used to suppress the file name
*/

void set_ops(flags,choices)
struct options *flags;
char *choices;
{
  int i,n;
  /*  find out the length of the string  */
  n = strlen(choices);
  i = 1;   /*  start at the second char in choices  */
  while(i<n)
    {  switch(choices[i])
       {  case 'l':
          case 'L':flags ->line_nos = 0;
                   printf("Line numbers suppressed.\n");
                   break;
          case 'p':
          case 'P':flags ->page_nos = 0;
                   printf("Page numbers suppressed.\n");
                   break;
          case 'n':
          case 'N':flags ->title = 0;
                   printf(file name suppressed.\n");
                   break;
          default: break;
       }
       i++;  /* repeat for next option in the list.  */
    }
}
```

End of Listing

Listing 10.8 contains internal documentation that speaks for itself. One of the important functions it includes evaluates the options that appear on the command line. Study this program as an example of using command line arguments with option flags.

The next listing deals with the problem of breaking a big file into several smaller ones. The big file, called **pastools** consists of many Pascal procedures. Each procedure is preceded by a header line. All the header lines have the same format: They begin with a **-h-** followed by the directory information and then the function file name. The program finds the leading **-h-** and then picks off the directory and file information. An appropriate file open command is made, the contents of that file are copied into the new file, and then the file is closed. This process is repeated over and over again until the end of file is used.

Listing 10.9

Extracting Modules from a Larger File

```
/*****************************************************
 *                                                   *
 * Program:       unpack          file:  unpack.c    *
 *                                                   *
 * Task/function: pull all of the functions          *
 *                out of the pascal_tools            *
 *                file.  All functions begin         *
 *                with -h- followed by dir           *
 *                information.                       *
 *                Manual pages follow the            *
 *                functions.                         *
 *                                                   *
 * Programmer:    Tim Grady and Dave Hein            *
 *                                                   *
 * input file:    pastools                           *
 *                                                   *
 * output files:  see file called pastools.top       *
 *                files defined in                   *
 *                SOFTWARE TOOLS IN PASCAL, by       *
 *                Kernighan and Plauger.             *
****************************************************/
```

```
/*  global definitions  */
#include <stdio.h>
#define LF 0x0a
#define SPACE 0x20
#define BACKSLASH 0x5c          /*  \ */
#define SLASH 0x2f              /*  /  */
#define DASH 0x2d               /*  -  */

FILE *infile, *outfile;

char datafile[]="pastool";
char output[25];
```

```
main()
{
char ch,prev1,prev2;
                        /* earlier characters  */
int i;

  /*   open the original file  */
  printf("opening pastool file \n");
  if((infile = fopen(datafile,"r")) == NULL)
    {
      printf("error in opening file \n");
      exit();
    }
  while((ch = getc(infile)) != EOF)
              /*  process till eof  */
    {
      /*   grab the file name from pastools  */
      printf("starting after new file name \n");
      while( (ch = getc(infile)) != SPACE);
        output[0]='d';output[1]=':';output[2]=BACKSLASH;
          /*  file names start with d:\ */
        for(i=3;(output[i]=getc(infile)) != SPACE;i++)
          /*  and continue with string from file  */
          if(output[i] == SLASH)output[i]=BACKSLASH;
            /*  change / known to be in string to \ */
          output[i]='\0';
          /*  change last space to null - c string end  */
          while((ch=getc(infile)) != LF);
```

```
        /*  ***  open current output file   ***  */

        printf("opening %s \n",output);
        if((outfile = fopen(output,"w"))==NULL)
                /*  attempt to open file  */
          {
            printf("unable to open file %s \n",output);
            exit();
          }
        else
          /*  send char by char to output file  */

          {
            printf("beginning to copy file\n");
              /*  copy chars to new file until  */
            prev2 = getc(infile);
            prev1 = getc(infile);

            while(( (ch = getc(infile)) != 'h')
                            || (prev1 != DASH)
                            || (prev2 != LF))
            {
              if(ch == EOF) exit();
                putc(prev2,outfile);
              prev2 = prev1;
              prev1 = ch;
            }
            putc(prev2,outfile);
            fclose(outfile);
            printf("file %s closed \n",output);
          } /*  end of else  */
      } /*  end of while not eof  */
  }/*  end of main  */
```

End of Listing

Listing 10.9 illustrates many of the common features of file handling programs. The file open statements are all couched in error traps. Character translations take place (SLASH is changed to BACKSLASH) and id strings are parsed. These same techniques can be applied to other file bursting programs.

Formatted File I/O

A text file is just a list of characters terminating in an end-of-file marker. Sometimes there is a need to treat the file as having a particular format. You may want to treat the file as an array of columns, for example. Each column is spaced or formatted with certain constraints. In other words, treat the file as if it were a structure of well-defined fields. Consider the set of data that follow. The **fprintf**() and **fscanf**() allow you to treat the file in this manner:

Tom Andrews	3456 Oak Ln	236 9475
Missy Baker	423a Artsy St	453 1284
Sam Cool	14 Hale St	236 3421
Vicky Hahn	1831 Geary Blvd	236 7649
Trey Morton	156 Vine Ave	453 5623

The names occupy the first 15 positions. The addresses occupy the next 15 places, and the phone numbers the next 8. A single line of data can be read in from this file (called `black.bok`) using a **fscanf**() call

```
FILE *fp;
char *fname = "black.bok";
char name[15], add[15], ph[8];
...
if(( fp = fopen(fname,"r")) != NULL)
  { while( fp != EOF) {
      fscanf(fp,"%15s %15s %8c",name,add,ph);
      printf("%s %s %s \n",name,add,ph);
  }
}
fclose(fp);
else
  printf(" Error in opening file.\n");
```

The three fields are read by using the **fscanf**() command and three fields in the conversion specifier.

Some additional names can be added to this file by using the **fprintf**() function.

```
/* read another record  */
scanf("%*s\n",name);
scanf("%*s\n",add);
scanf("%*s\n"ph);
/*  open file for appending  */
if( (fp = fopen(fname,"a")) != NULL)
  fprintf(fp,"%15s %15s %15s",name,add,ph);
  fclose(fp);
```

A file that consists of data in the format

```
number name '\n'
```

also provides an example of reading formatted data. Each line contains an integer and a string followed by a newline character. The lines can be read by writing

```
scanf(filepointer,"%d %s %c",&number,name,&ch);
```

and echoed to the screen by writing

```
printf("%d %s %c",number,name,ch);
```

Error Checking

The **fscanf**() function returns the number of arguments successfully read. If an error occurs, the function returns −1. A prudent programmer checks the result to make sure all the arguments were matched with data.

```
errcnt = fscanf(fp,"%d %f", &n,&x);
if(argcnt == -1) printf(" Error in reading file.\n");
```

A better error trap verifies the exact number of arguments.

```
if(argcnt != 2) printf("Error in reading file.\n");
```

When counting arguments with strings, the length of the string is the number of arguments returned by the string alone.

The **fprintf**() function returns −1 if an error occurs; otherwise, it returns 0. You can check its operation in a manner similar to the **printf**() function.

The **ferror**() function is used to find out the error number that has occurred. Not all **C** compilers implement this function, but most do. Its form is

```
err_num = ferror(fptr);
```

where `err_num` is an integer variable declared to hold the number of the error. The argument `fptr` is a valid file pointer to an open file. The function returns the number of the error that has occurred. If no error has occurred, the function returns 0.

The example that follows shows how **ferror**() is used.

```
if(ferror(fptr)) printf("Error no.  is %d\n",ferror(fptr));
```

The preceding code is equivalent to

```
err_num = ferror(fptr);
if(err_num) printf("Error no.  is %d\n",err_num);
```

The **ferror**() is used in error traps in conjunction with other functions. For example, if the **fopen**() statement fails, it returns −1. The error can then be passed to an error- processing function.

```
if( (fptr = fopen(fname,"w")) != NULL)
  { errnum= ferror(fptr);
    errors(errnum);
  }
```

The user-defined function `errors()` would be set up to accept a number as its argument and then display the appropriate message to the user. This approach is usually better than simply terminating the program. For example, suppose the printer is turned off, or a disk-drive door is open, or a disk is write-protected. Each of these conditions produces an error that the function `errors()` could deal with by pointing out the error to the user. The user fixes the condition and the original function is recalled.

The function `errors()` might need to know what function produced the error. A pointer to the function can be passed to the `errors()` routine so that the appropriate function can be called after the `errors()` subroutine has finished.

The **ferror**() function retains its value until reset. Once an error has been dealt with, the **ferror**() function needs to be reset using **clearerr**(). This function is not available on all systems but is available if **ferror**() is available. The **clearerr**() function is

```
clearerr(fptr);
```

It sets the value of **ferror**(`fptr`) to 0. It should be used as soon as an error has been dealt with so that the **ferror**() function returns valid results the next time it is used.

Using the Buffer

Stream-oriented input and output means that a stream or collection, of characters is read into a buffer or memory area, and then the program grabs the data byte by byte from the buffer. Conversely, any output is first stored in the buffer and then the buffer, contents are "flushed", or copied, from the buffer to the disk file. This happens when either the buffer is full or the file is closed.

Functions That Act on the Buffer

Fflush(): The buffer contents can be copied to the file at any time by using the **fflush**() command. Normally, the contents are flushed automatically upon closing a file or when the buffer is full. The **fflush**() command is

```
fflush(fp);
```

The file remains open after this operation. It is used as a safeguard against the accidental loss of data that occurs after a program crash or abnormal program termination. When a program terminates normally, all files are closed. When a file is closed, the buffer is automatically flushed. The function returns 0 if the operation is successful.

Exit(): A program can be terminated at any time by calling the **exit**() function. One purpose is to flush all buffers from open files this action ensures no loss of data. The **exit**() function may have a number as its argument. For example, **exit**(0) is used to indicate a normal termination. If the number is non-zero, the **exit** is not considered normal. The numbers are different for different systems. The number corresponds to an error code. Check your system manual for the valid codes.

_exit(): A companion function to **exit**() is **_exit**(). The difference is that **exit**() flushes all buffers and closes the files, but **_exit**() simply terminates the program without closing the files. Applications programmers usually do not use **_exit**. It is used by systems programmers to **exit** with the files open and then to perform emergency maintenance on them.

User-Defined Buffers

Stream i/o as discussed so far has been restricted to ASCII files. If you want to use buffered i/o with binary files, you must **define** buffer and two additional commands: **fread**() and **fwrite**(). The commands are used to access the file.

fread(): This function is used to copy an array of items from the input stream It general form is

```
fread(buffer, length, num_items, fptr);
```

where buffer is a pointer to the array that will hold the data, length is the number of bytes in each item, num_items is the number of data items (of size length) to be read, and fptr is the pointer to the open file. The buffer is a pointer to a character array. It is usually defined as follows.

```
char *buffer;
```

Suppose the data file contained items that had 200 bytes each. To read two of these items, you could write

```
length = 200:
num_items = 2;
fread(buffer,length,num_items, fptr);
```

The **fread**() function leaves the in-file pointer at the byte immediately following the last byte read. If an eof is encountered, only the bytes prior to the eof are read in. The function returns the number of items read or 0 if an error occurred.

Suppose you want to use **fread**() to read a collection of codes and prices in this format:

code	price
34527	12.45
32454	34.67

Each code occupies five so they can be declared as a 5-byte field. The longest price is five characters long with one a decimal point. The length of an item is the sum of the lengths of the two fields, or 10 bytes long. If a typical disk sector holds 512 bytes, then 51 of the items can be read at one time. The declarations are

```
FILE *fp
static char *fn ="price.dat";
char *buffer;
int len,num_itms;

len = 10; num_itms = 51;
```

The file-open statement is

```
fp = fopen(fn,"r");
```

The file read statement is

```
fread(buffer,len,num_itms,fp);
```

Assuming no errors occur, the buffer contains 51 sets of 10 characters, which are available to the program for use. Additional code must be written to incorporate the contents of the buffer into the program. It is, of course, appropriate to encase the file open and file read statements in conditional expressions:

```
if( (fp = fopen(fn,"r") != NULL)
  if( (fread(buffer,len,num_itms,fp)) != num_itms)
    /*  error occurred  */
  else
    /*  process the data  */
else
  /*  error in opening file  */
```

Because **fread**() should return the number of items read, the conditional read provides an error-checking mechanism. It also allows the programmer to use buffered input and to define the buffer defined as needed. The **fread**() also allows you to read, append, or transmit binary files.

fwrite(): This function is the complement to **fread**(). Its form is:

```
fwrite(buffer,length,num_items,fptr)
```

which is just like the **fread**() statement. The two functions can be used together to copy a file from one place to another. One use is as ameans to list a file on the line printer. The pseudocode for the program is

```
define input and output buffers

open source file
open printer as a file

while not end of file
  read one buffer full from source file
  copy input buffer to output buffer
  write output buffer to printer
```

Low Level I/O Functions: Unbuffered I/O

So far, only buffered file i/o has been examined. The operating system brings part of the file into a buffer, where characters are handed to or from the program one at a time. A file is a stream of characters. Unbuffered file i/o allows you to specify the file elements to be read or written directly. Since these operations are very close to the machine operation, they are called low-level functions. High-level functions studied so far are restricted to ASCII type files. Low-level functions may be used with either ASCII files or binary files.

Table 10.3
File Descriptors

file descriptor	device (file)
0	keyboard (**stdin**)
1	screen (**stdout**)
2	error list (**stderr**)

A file is then referred to by its file descriptor.

Low level file operations use the `open()` function , perform manipulations, and then `close()` the file. The typical form of the `open()` function is

```
file_descriptor = open(file-name,mode);
```

where file_descriptor is the integer mentioned earlier. The file-name is a pointer to the external filename, and the mode is a short integer used to specify read, write, or read and write modes.

Table 10.4
File Modes

mode	meaning
0	read only
1	write only
2	read and write

Several rules apply to modes. If mode 0 (read) is used, then the file must already exist. If a file is opened in the write mode, then the contents of a file with the same name are erased and a new one created. If the file name does not exist, it cannot be opened. To use a new file in the write mode, it must first be created with the `creat()` function. A file opened in mode (read and write) does not erase the existing contents.

The `open()` function returns −1 if the file opening statement is unsuccessful. Hence a programmer can use an **if** statement with low level file operations, much like we did with a high level file operation.

```
if( (fd = open(fname,1) != -1)
  /* file is open and available */
else
  /* error message */
```

Any file that is opened must be closed with the `close()` function.

```
close(file_descriptor).
```

An empty file can be created by the `creat()` function:

```
creat(file_name,proc_mode);
```

In the preceding code `file_name` is a pointer to a file name and `proc_mode` is the protection mode. The protection mode is the same as the Unix protection mode, on other operating systems it may vary. For example, Aztec **C** on the IBM-PC ignores the `proc_mode`. If compatibility with a Unix system is needed, the `proc_mode` should be octal 666. The Unix protection modes are coded into three digits. Each digit refers to a type of user: owner, group, or world. The protection digits are summarized in Table 10.5.

Table 10.5
File Permission Codes

protection digit	meaning — permission
6	read/write permission
5	read and execute
4	read permission
2	write permission
1	execute permission
0	no access

The file creation statement that follows allows the owner read/write permission, the group read and execute permission, and the world execute permission., and everyone else read permission.

```
creat(fname,651);
```

Once opened for read access, the file contents are accessed via the `read()` function. In general the form is

```
read(fd,in_buffer,num_bytes);
```

where `fd` is the file descriptor, `in_buffer` is the character array set up to accept characters from the file, and `num_bytes` is the number of bytes or characters to be read. Be careful not to try to read past the end of the file. The `read()` functions returns a -1 if the read attempt is unsuccessful.

Listing 10.10 to reads a file called `test.dat` to illustrate the use of `read()`.

Listing 10.10

Low level File Read

```
          /*  example of use of read function  */
          int fd1,num_bytes = 400,buf_size = 512,n,i;
          char in_buf[buf_size];
          static char *fn = "test.dat";
/*  1  */ if( (fd1 = open(fn,0) == -1)
            puts("Error-can not open file.");
          else
/*  2  */   while( (n =read(fd1,in_buf,num_bytes)) != 0)
              for(i=0;i < n;i++)  {
                putchar(in_buf[i]);
                if(i % 80 = 0) putchar('\n');
              }
          close(fd1);   /*  close the file  */
```

End of Listing

Line 1 contains an `open()` command. The program file descriptor (`fd1`) is logically connected to the external file name (`test.dat`) via the pointer `*fn`. The `open()`

statement is performed conditionally. If an error occurs, a simple error message is displayed. Line 2 reads the file 400 bytes at a time. It might seem strange that the buffer size is 512 but the number of bytes read on each pass is 400. The reason why lies in how the media are used by the operating system. If one sector is 512 bytes, the system i/o handles disk i/o more efficiently if it is done in such a manner. This does waste some space on the disk, however. The data are echoed to the screen in lines of 80 characters. At the end of 80 characters, a linefeed is used to send the cursor to the next line. The file doesn't need to have the newlines imbedded within it for the screen output to be successful.

The low-level file write function is simply `write()`. It is the complement of the `read()` function. Its typical form is:

```
write(fd,out-buffer,num_bytes);
```

where `fd` is the file descriptor, `out_buffer` is the name of the character array holding the data to be written to the file, and `num_bytes` is the number of bytes to be written. The `write()` function returns −1 if an error occurs. In use it is much like the `read()` function. The example in Listing 10.11 reads lines from the keyboard, stores the line in the output buffer, and writes the buffer contents to a file.

Listing 10.11

Low-Level File Write

```
          /*  example of use of write function  */
   int fd1,num_bytes,buf_size =512,i;
   char out_buf[buf_size];
   static char *fn = "test.dat";

/*  1  */ if( (creat(fn,666) = -1)
             puts("Error - can not create file.");
          else
/*  2  */ if( (fd1 = open(fn,1) == -1)
             puts("Error-can not open file.");
          else  {
/*  a  */    do   /*  execute this loop at least once  */
             {
             /*  read a line from keyboard  */
/*  3  */    for(i = 0; (out_buff[i] = getchar()) != '\n')';i++)
               ;
             num_bytes = i;
/*  4  */    out_buff[i] = '\0';
             /*  write line to file  */
/*  5  */    write(fd1,out_buff,num_bytes);
             }
/*  b  */ while(num_bytes > 0);
          close(fd1);
   }
```

Line 1 conditionally creates the file. If the file already exists, its contents are erased. The protection mode is strictly arbitrary. If the `creat()` function is successful, line 2 conditionally opens the file in the write mode. If the `open()` is successful, the do-while loop (from a to b) performs two operations: it reads a line from the keyboard, and writes the line to the file. Line 3 reads characters until a newline character is encountered. Line 4 appends a null character to the end of the string, and line 5 actually writes the contents of `out_buff` to the file. Finally, the file is closed when the loop terminates.

This program segment has no prompt to the user. It should! Neither does it provide the directions for ending the input sequence. You simply press Return at the beginning of a line to end the loop.

Listing 10.12 uses both `read()` and `write()` to copy a file. The file i/o commands are low level.

Listing 10.12

Low-Level File-Copy Utility

```
#include <stdio.h>
#include <ctype.h>
#define BUFFSIZE 512
#define READ   0
#define WRITE   1

main()

  {
  char source[12],*dest[12];  /*  file names  */
  int fds,fdd;                /*  file descriptors  */
  int n,i;                    /*  num bytes to r/w  */
  char bufr[BUFFSIZE];

  /*  get names of files  */
  printf("Type name of source file and press return.\n");
    i = 0;
    while( (source[i++] = getchar() ) != '\n');
    source[i] = NULL;

  printf("Type name of destination file and press return.\n");
  i = 0;
```

```
while( (dest[i++] = getchar() ) != '\n') ;
dest[i] = NULL;

/* open files */
if( (fds = open(source,0) == -1)
  {
    printf("Error -- can not open %s\n",source);
    exit(0);
  }
else
  if( (fdd = creat(dest,0644)) == -1)
    {
      printf("Error -- can not open %s\n",dest);
      exit(0);
    }
  else /* both files open with valid names */
  /* copy files one buffer full at a time */
  while( (n = read(fds,bufr,BUFFSIZE) ) > 0)
    if(write(fds,bufr,n) != n)
      printf("Error in writing to %s\n",dest);

printf("Copy complete.\n");
}/* end main */
```

End of Listing

Random Access File Operations

Fseek(): A file is normally read in a sequential manner. The file pointer is positioned at the next byte to be read or written. The **fseek**() function allows one to access any byte in the file directly. The typical form of **fseek** is

```
long fseek(filepointer, offset, refvalue);
```

The element filepointer refers to the file in use. The element `offset` is the number of bytes from the reference point to which the pointer is to be moved; `offset` must be a **long** value. The `refvalue` is a number telling the reference point from which offset is added. The possible values are

```
0  count from the beginning of the file
1  count from the current position
2  count from the last byte in the file.
```

For example, to read the 5th byte (character) in a file, you would move to it with

```
offset = 5;
fseek(fp,(long)offset,0);
```

To read each character in a file use a loop to increment offset until **EOF** is located.

```
while( (fseek(fp,(long)offset++,0) == 0)
{  getc(ch);
   putchar(ch);
}
```

The preceding is not an example of good programming, but it does illustrate how each byte can be accessed via the **fseek** command. You could have used a **getc**(ch) command in a loop to perform the same task.

A more realistic example reads a record by using the **fseek**() command. Recall the earlier example in which a record consisted of a name (15 characters), an address (15 characters) and a telephone number (8 characters). A record consists of a total of 38 characters. The first record begins at offset = 0. The second record begins at offset = 38. To read the fourth record, write

```
offset = 0;
reclen = 38;
recnum = 4;
fseek(fp,offset + recnum*reclen,0);
```

Any record number can be read with this or some variation of this command. Do not read past the end of the file. One should include error-checking code to prevent reading past the end of file.

Suppose the number of records is not known. A function to find the number of records is shown in Listing 10.13.

Listing 10.13

Find Number of Records in a File

```
                no_recs(fp,fname,reclen)
                FILE *fp; char *fname
                long int reclen;
                {  int recnum;
                   if( (fp = fopen(fname,"r") != NULL)
/*  1  */          {  fseek(fp,-reclen,2);  /*  goto first byte */
                                            /* of last record   */
/*  2  */             recnum = ftell(fp)/reclen;
                      fclose(fp);
                      return(recnum);
                   }
                   else printf("Error in opening file.\n");
                }
```

End of Listing

Line 1 uses the option 2 to indicate that the byte to be located is referenced from the end of the file. It positions the file element pointer 38 bytes in front of the **EOF** position. Some systems automatically append two or four characters to the end of every file. In those cases, the middle argument `-(reclen + 2)` or `-(reclen`

+ 4) ensures that the special characters are skipped over and not considered part of the last record. Line 2 uses a new function **ftell**(fp). This function tells the byte number relative to the beginning of the file. The statement

```
recnum = ftell(fp) / reclen;
```

divides the position by the record length which yields the record number. This assumes that the first record is the zeroth record. If the first record is referred to as record number 1, then the statement is

```
recnum = (ftell(fp) / reclen) + 1;
```

Additional statements can be added to prevent running past the end of file.

The calling program can assign the number of records in a file to a variable by the statement

```
numrecs = no_rec(fp,fname,reclen);
```

The code that follows reads the records conditionally.

```
if(recnum <= numrecs) fseek(fp,recnum*reclen,0);
else printf("Attempt to read past end of file.\n");
```

Error traps and functions that aid in preventing errors are well worth the time and effort spent developing them. Always include such code.

Rewind(): This function repositions the file pointer to the first character in the file:

```
rewind(fptr);
```

In **rewind**(), fptr is a valid pointer to an open file. It does not return a value. A programmer can create this function with the command

```
fseek(fptr,0L,0);
```

which positions the file pointer to the first byte in the file. The **fseek**() function returns a value that can be used in error checking.

feof(): This function returns non-zero if the end of file has been read from the input stream. This handy function is not available on all systems. It is used to check if the end of file has been read; thus it prevents an attempt to read past the end of file. In general its form is:

```
feof(fptr);
```

where fptr is a valid pointer to an open file. A program segment that uses this function is

```
while(/*  loop to read a file  */)
  { ...
    if(feof(ptr)) break;
```

The **if** statement is ignored unless the end of file is reached. At that time the loop is terminated.

Random Access and Low level File Operations

Low-level file operations **include** opening a file for both read and write. This allows one to create random-access files. The open command is

open`(fd,2);`

which means that the file is open for both read and write access. Individual records may be accessed in a manner very similar to that of the **fseek**() command. The low level counterpart is called **lseek()**. It is used to move the "next byte to be read" pointer to any place in the file. In general its form is

lseek`(fd, offset, ref_point)`

where `fd` is the file descriptor, `offset` is the number of bytes away from the reference point the position pointer is to be moved, and `ref_point` is the starting position for the function. The possible reference points are:

```
0   -  start at first byte in file,
1   -  start at current position in the file
3   -  start at the last position in the file.
```

The function returns a 0 if the function call was successful and a negative value if it fails. As in the **fseek**() function, `offset` must be a **long int**.

The **lseek()** function is very much like **fseek**(). The first, **lseek()**, is low level and unbuffered. It can be used with ASCIII files and binary files. The second, **fseek**(), is high level and features buffered i/o on a stream. It can only be used with ASCII (or EBCDIC) files. The compiler takes care of the details of a particular hardware configuration.

stdio.h and Files

The header file `stdio.h` contains definitions important to file operations. One of these is `BUFSIZ`, which can be used in place of the buffsize defined in a program. Using `BUFSIZ` ensures that you are making the most efficient use of the storage media on your system, and makes the program portable.

Another symbolic constant defined in `stdio.h` is `MAXSTREAM`, which indicates the maximum number of files you can have open at one time. It also helps make your program portable.

ANSI Standard and File Operations

The proposed ANSI standard affects file operations. As it is now defined it eliminates low level file operations. Although it hardly seems likely that compiler manufacturers will go along with this. The ANSI standard does enhance the **fopen**() modes and include many of the Unix 7 features. The ANSI standard includes a new function **freopen**(), which has the form

freopen`(filename,mode,file_pointer)`

The object **freopen** is a pointer to a **FILE** type. If not declared in `stdio.h`, you must declare it in the program or program header. This function closes the open stream pointed to by `file_pointer` and reopens it pointing to another name (filename). **freopen**() function returns a pointer to a type **FILE**. Its most common use is in the redirection of **stdin**, **stdout**, or **stderr**.

The modes for **fopen**() **include** "r", "w", and "a" as before. They also include:

```
"r+"  open for update (read and write)
"w+"  truncate or create for update
"a+"  append plus open or create for
      update beginning at eof
```

The "+" features allows easier use of random-access files because a file item pointer can be moved by using **fseek**(). Then the contents can be either read or written to. If two processes open the same file for append+, either may write to the file without fear of destroying the information written by the other file.

Summary

Files are supported with a wide range of standard file-support functions. Some are i/o, others are **open()** and **close()** with error checking, and others support positioning of file pointers.

C supports both high-level and low-level file operations. These permit the programmer to use techniques similar to other high-level languages, or to work at the hardware level with input and output.

The i/o operations include character read and write, formatted read and write of simple data types, and macros for reading characters. The typical file used in **C** is a collection of characters, not an array of records as in many languages. This characteristic of **C** permits simple file copy and manipulation programs.

There are a range of functions to support random access file operations. You can position the file pointer at any record in a record type file and read or write to records in a file. There are functions for rewinding, file positioning, and position reporting. **C** has excellent file-operation commands and utilities.

EXERCISES

UNDERSTANDINGS

1. What is the nature of a typical **C** file? How can you think of it conceptually?
2. What is the usage of the keyword **FILE**? Where is it defined?
3. Explain the difference between stream and buffered i/o.
4. What is the difference between file pointers and file descriptors?
5. What is **EOF** and why is it important?
6. Under what conditions is a file closed automatically instead of by the **fclose**() function.
7. Explain the difference between the **append** mode and the **write** mode.

USAGE

8. What does **fopen**() return? **fclose**()?

9. What is the error indicator when a file open command fails?
10. What is the relationship between **getchar**() and **getc**()?
11. Explain the normal use of file descriptors 0,1, and 2.
12. How can a **rewind**() which puts the file position pointer at the top of the file be implemented?

APPLICATIONS

13. Rewrite the program from listing 5.1 so that the depreciation schedule is written to a disk file instead of to the **stdout**.
14. Write a program that copies a file from one disk to another using the **fread**() and **fwrite**() functions. The program prompts the user to type in the file names.
15. Write a program that creates another copy of an ASCII file but with the addition of line numbers at the beginning of each line. The new file should add `n` in front of the filename.
16. Write a program to remove the line numbers created by the previous program.
17. Write a program to add `CR` to each line of a text file so that a printer that requires both `CR` and `LF` works properly.
18. Write a program that converts all lowercase letters in a file to uppercase and writes the result back to a file.
19. Write a general error trap routine for disk and printer file operations. The program uses **ferror**() to return the error number and then process the error. It should tell the user the nature of the problem and restart the previous function after the user presses a key.
20. Write a function that returns the size of a file in bytes.
21. Write a program to list a file on the printer. It must leave a top and bottom margin of 6 lines each. The file name must appear in the bottom left-hand section of each page. The page number must be printed in the bottom center of each page.
22. Write a program that creates output to a file. The program prompts the user for the destination: screen, disk, or printer. The choice uses a pointer to a file that performs the selected output.
23. Rewrite the `ck_name` routine so that it includes a check of valid disk names, directories, and subdirectories.
24. Using the `cipher` routine from Listing 9.1 to write a password encryption routine. Store the encrypted password in a file. Write a program that asks for the password (7 - character) and then checks to see if the password is correct.
25. Write a program that reads a data file containing a series of 4 line addresses and prints mailing labels. Each label is capable of holding 6 lines and 24 characters.
26. Create the functions `do_open(filename, mode)` and `do_close(fp)` which perform the open and close file functions including error checking. If an error

occurs, the do_open function reports the error and **exits**(), otherwise it returns a pointer to the file. Another program can then use these functions to open or close a file with error checking while keeping the code clean and understandable.

27. Write a function called do_name() that accepts as input a drive letter(optional), subdirectory (optional), and filename. The function uses **sprintf** (see Chapter 8) to assemble the three components into a string that is returned by the function as a complete filename. The function is called by:

```
fn = do_name(dd,dir,name);
```

where the data types are

```
char *fn;
char dd;
char *dir;
char *name;
```

28. LISP programmers know that the language uses many, many parentheses. A common error is to have a mismatch in the number of parentheses. For example, a typical expression is

```
->(match'(a?x c ?y) '(a b ?z d e))
((((*var* y) d) ((*var* z) c) ((*var* x) b)))
```

Write a program that looks through a LISP source file and finds the line number in which the mismatch occurs. Use the following program as test data.

```
(DEFUN M-EXPAND-AUX (I L)
        (COND ((NULL L) NIL)
                (T (APPEND (M-EXPAND-AUX (CAAR L) (CADAR L))
                        (M-EXPAND (CDR L))))))

(DEFUN M-EXPAND-AUX (I L)
        (COND ((NULL L NIL)
                (T (CONS (LIST I (CAAR L) (CADAR L))
                        (M-EXPAND (CDR L )))))

(DEFUN M-ALTER-SUB (E L)
        (COND ((NULL (CDR L)) L)
                (T (M-ALTER-SUB CAR L)
                        (M-ALTER-AUX (CDR L))))))
```

29. Write a function get_rec() which reads a **struct** into memory and returns a pointer to the first char in the structure.

30. Write a program dump.c which prints multiple files to the line printer. It differs from prt.c by (1) options list appears as the last entry on the command line, (2) the options list begins with a / instead of a -, (3) all options are normally off, and the date and time are printed on the top line. To turn an option on, it must be included in the command line argument.

11

Hardware-Dependent Operations

C was originally designed to write operating system software to control computer operations and reduce the need for coding in assembly language. In this chapter you will look at several ideas related to control of the inner workings of the computer. Clearly, when working this close to the hardware, much of the code is nonportable; however, the goal is to make the code as portable as possible. The two operating systems referred to here are Unix Version 5 and MS-DOS 2.X or 3.X. Some assembler routines are needed to connect **C** code to the inner workings of IBM PCs and MS-DOS. The Unix connection is made via system- dependent libraries such as curses. In most cases both IBM-PC (MS-DOS) and Unix versions are presented.

This chapter describes keyboard routines and video output routines. Although **C** provides standard i/o routines, program performance and modern applications packages require additional i/o functions. This chapter introduces these i/o concepts. You will also examine how **C** interfaces to user or non-DOS devices through ports. All these additional functions are system dependent to some degree. If your hardware environment is not discussed here, the techniques can be modified to work on your system.

Keyboard Routines

The standard input routines **getchar**() and **scanf**() are useful functions and you have made use of them throughout. Other routines, such as `getdec()` and `getnum()`, have been added to input integers and reals, respectively. These input routines, are not particularly fast and are, of course, buffered, that is, you must press the Return, or Enter key, before input data are made available to the program. At times you need unbuffered input. Many modern applications, such as word processors, require that each key be available to the program as soon as it is pressed. You will learn about some unbuffered input routines in this chapter. Frequently, a process is continued until a key has been pressed. The process is interrupted, and then the program looks at the keyboard to see which key it was. In this chapter you will also learn how to make the program aware that a key has been pressed.

The functions that serve these purposes are:

1. `key_pressed()`	Returns true if a key has been pressed.
2. `inkey()`	Fetches one character from the keyboard, but does not echo it to the screen. It is unbuffered and does not require the user to press Return.
3. `empty_key_buf()`	Clears all characters from the keyboard buffer.

You have already read about the need for the first two functions. The third is needed because, since the return key is not used to flush the keyboard buffer, one may need to flush the buffer to be sure the buffer is empty at some point in a program.

Before you can write these functions, you must understand how MS-DOS handles the same functions on an IBM PC or compatible and be able to connect **C** to DOS with a minimum of assembly language.

In itself MS-DOS is a topic that warrants several books. For the present purposes, you need to know that MS-DOS uses a variety of interrupts to provide machine-level services. Most of these services are disk-related. **C** provides most of what you need in the way of file i/o, and so disk DOS calls are not discussed here. MS-DOS also provides keyboard services via interrupt 21h which is accessed via assembly language. Interupt 21h accepts functions to perform a variety of i/o routines. In other words, a program provides a function number to interrupt 21h and DOS performs the needed service. The problem for the **C** programmer is to gain access to int 21h.

Using assembly language

C provides a simple interface to assembly language via the directives **#asm** and **#endasm**. The directives surround a series of assembly-language statements in this manner:

```
#asm
  /*  assembly language statements  */
#endasm
  /*  the # must be in column 1  */
```

The compiler provides all the support needed by the particular assembler to translate the code into a working program. Many programmers prefer to write their assembly language code in separate files and then link in the object code. In the case of MS-DOS there are several competing assemblers that require different "magic words" surrounding the actual code. The **#asm**- **#endasm** technique is considerably more portable than the separate file technique, but you will look at both methods here.

The 8088 and 8086 processors uses several registers for program control, variable passing, returning results, and controlling the stack. You can not learn all the details here, but you must understand the most inportant concepts.

There are four general purpose registers: AX, BX, CX, and DX. Each is a 2-byte register. The two halves of each register may be accessed as `ah`,`al`,`bh`,`bl`,`ch`,`cl`,`dh`, and `dl`. Parameters are passed to functions via addresses (pointers) in these registers. Results are returned via the AX register. The stack pointer, SP, is accessed relative to the base pointer, BP. Consequently, most assembly language routines that are called from **C** begin by pushing BP onto the stack. Prior to returning to the calling program, the routines pop BP back off the stack. Any parameters passed to a function are found relative to BP. For example, the first parameter is located at address BP + 4, the second at BP + 6, and so on. Many routines also preserve the AX through DX registers by pushing them onto the stack upon entry into the routine and restoring them prior to leaving the routine. When the assembly language code is placed inline, that is, placed between **#asm** and **#endasm** statements these housekeeping chores are done for you.

You need a connection between **C** and DOS to pass the value (number) of the DOS function via interrupt 21h. The assembler code shown in Listing 11.1 provides this link.

Listing 11.1

Passing The Value of DOS Function via int 21h

```
push  bp             ; preserve bp
mov   bp,sp          ; use stack pointer as bp
mov   ah,[bp + 4]    ;place function number
                     ;in ah
mov   dx,[bp + 6]    ;grab second parameter
int   21h            ;call DOS interupt
pop   bp             ;restore bp
ret                  ; exit function and return to
                     ;calling routine
```

End of Listing

Interrupt 21h needs two parameters. The upper half of AX carries the function number. DX contains any other value needed by the interrupt. The result is returned in AX. A short summary of some of the possible calls is listed in Table 11.1

Table 11.1
DOS Interrupt 21h Functions

ah value =function #	dx (dh or dl) =parameter al	description	returns
1	-	get char from keyboard	contains character
2	dl = character	display char on screen	
6	0xff	see if a key has been hit	true if key has been pressed
7	-	get character from keyboard do not display it	al contains character
0xb		check keyboard status	al contains 0xff if a key has been struck; 0 otherwise.
0x0c		clears keyboard buffer	

There are several other functions besides the six listed here. You will learn about them later.

Many compilers provide access to int 21h with a built-in library function called `dos()` or `bdos()`. If your compiler does not provide these system-dependent functions, you need one. The discussion that follows uses `dos()`.

If you want to write `dos()` as an assembly language program and then link in the resulting object file, there are several ways you can do it. Listing 11.2 shows one method that works works with the Aztec (tm) compiler.

Listing 11.2

dos.asm Function as a File

```
/* ;*********************************************** */
/* ;**                                           ** */
/* ;**  file:  dos.asm                           ** */
/* ;**                                           ** */
/* ;**  contains 8086 assembly language routine  ** */
/* ;**        to allow c programs to call standard ** */
/* ;**        dos functions.                     ** */
/* ;**                                           ** */
/* ;*********************************************** */
;implements dos function calls via int 21h
;.
;written for AZTEC assembler as.exe
;
;called by dos(function_number,dx_value)
;returns value of al register
                                    ;***********************
                                    ;intel/masm version    *
                                    ;***********************
                                    ;pgroup group  prog
codeseg segment byte public         ;prog  segment byte public 'BYTE'
                                    ;              assume cs:pgroup
                public  dos_        ;              public dos
dos_    proc    near                ;dos   proc    near
                push    bp
                mov     bp,sp
                mov     ah,[bp + 4]
                mov     dx,[bp + 6]
                int     21h
                mov     ah,0
                pop     bp
                ret
dos_    endp                        ;dos   endp
codeseg ends                        ;prog  ends
        end
```

End of Listing

The comments on the right in Listing 11.2 indicate how you would have to modify the code to work with MASM or ASM provided by Microsoft. Different assemblers may require other modifications. One of the best methods is to place the code inline (Listing 11.3) so that the specifics of different assemblers.

Listing 11.3

Inline Assembly Language Function

```
unsigned int dos(ax,dx)
unsigned int ax,dx;
{
#asm
  mov  ah,[bp + 4]
  mov  dx,[bp + 6]
  int  21h
  mov  ah,0
#endasm
}
```

End of Listing

Your compiler will add the necessary overhead and magic words to make the routine work.

You can now make use of this function in a program. Some other functions, written entirely in **C**, can be added. The first simply checks to see if a key has been pressed.

```
int key_pressed()
{
  dx = 0xff;
  al = dos(0x06,dx);
  if( al == 0) return 0;
  else return(1);
}
```

The next accepts a character from the keyboard but does not echo it to the screen.

```
int inkey()
{
  return( dos(0x07));
}
```

The third function flushes the keyboard buffer.

```
int empty_key_buf()
{
  dos(0x0c);
}
```

The first function uses two global variables, `dx` and `al`. It is good practice to define all the necessary variables in a header called `dos.h` as shown in Listing 11.4.

Listing 11.4

dos.h Header File

```
/* ************************************************ */
/*          dos.h
          header file for dos related programs
*/
extern int dos();
int al,dx;
extern inkey(),
  key_pressed(),
  empty_key_buf(),

/* ************************************************ */
```

End of Listing

The assembly language program, `dos()`, is declared as an external function. The keyboard functions are also declared as external. This means that a file containing these functions has been compiled and will be linked in as needed. The header `dos.h` is placed at the top of any program or file that uses these functions. You may place the dos() function in the same file as the keyboard functions if the inline version is used.

MS-DOS provides a few other routines not already available in **C**. One tells how many disk drives are present in the system. Another selects a drive as the logged drive. A third returns the number of the current drive. All three are useful to the **C** programmer using a PC. Each of these functions makes use of the `dos()` function you already have in place. The int 21h function numbers are

`0x19`	return number of current disk drive
`0x0e`	return the number of drives
`0x0e,drive`	select drive

The three **C** functions are shown in Listing 11.5.

Listing 11.5

Disk Information Utility Functions

```
/* cur_disk() returns the value of the current disk drive
              A is 0
              B is 1
              C is 2 etc
*/
int cur_disk()
{
  return(dos(0x19));
}
/* ************************************************ */
/*   num_drives(); returns the number of drives    */
int num_drives()
{
  dx = cur_disk();  /*  place current disk # in dx  */
  return(dos(0x0e,dx));
}
/* ************************************************ */
/* set_drive(dx) logs on to drive d
                  returns -1 if drive number is out of
                                      range.  0-4
************************************************/
int set_drive(dx)
int dx;
{
  al = num_drives();    /*  need for error checking  */
  if(dx < 0 || dx > (al-1) ) return(-1); /* must be valid
                                            drive number */
  else dos(0x0e,dx);  /*  set logged on drive  */
  return;
}
```

End of Listing

A file containing all six MS-DOS related functions can be defined and compiled. The header file should be expanded to declare the three new external functions. Any program that used only one of these functions needs to **include** the header file shown in Listing 11.6.

Listing 11.6

Revised dos.h Header File

```
/*          dos.h

            header file for doscall.c programs
*/
extern int dos();
int  al,dx;
extern inkey(),
     key_pressed(),
     empty_key_buf(),
     cur_disk(),
     set_drive(),
     num_drives();
```

End of Listing

These routines make minimal use of assembly language. Most of the code is **C** and portable between compilers. They work only under MS-DOS, however, so you need to learn some equivalent Unix functions.

You cannot use the `dos()` function with Unix, but then you do not need to. The disk select, current disk, and number of disks are not relevant on most Unix systems. The three keyboard routines can be created as **C** library functions. You will see how this is done on a Unix system later.

MS-DOS: Accessing BIOS Keyboard Routines

The MS-DOS int 21h is a software interrupt. It is made available from the software of MS-DOS and is not part of the hardware. The `dos()` routine shown earlier uses this software interrupt rather than interfacing directly with the software in ROM. The ROM BIOS program is firmware. In contrast to the DOS routines, which are loaded at boot time, BIOS is part of the computer. Consequently, DOS calls are likely to be more portable and easier to upgrade with newer versions of DOS. However, some programs need to access the routines in BIOS directly. For example, the keys that represent special, or extended characters such as pgdn or alt-home do not translate to normal ASCII characters. The MS-DOS functions used earlier can work as well as BIOS calls for accessing these characters, but many programmers prefer to use BIOS calls. Suppose you need to rewrite keyboard routines to make use of BIOS int 16h, the keyboard interupt.

When a key is pressed, a 2-byte code is placed in the keyboard buffer. The two interrupts (BIOS int 16h and DOS int 21h) both access this buffer. If a regular character is in the buffer, the high byte is 0 and the low byte is a value in the range 1—255. If an extended character is in the buffer, the low byte is 0 and the high byte is in the range 1—255.

The int 21h function 6 reads 1 byte at a time. So, if the byte value is 0, the dos() call is performed again to read the second byte. The BIOS int 16h returns an exact copy of the keyboard buffer (2-bytes) into ax. Consequently, the two routines are very different.

An assembly language routine to process keyboard functions is shown in Listing 11.7. The two functions `keyhit()` and `keyrd()` are equivalent to `dos()` functions `key_pressed()` and `inkey()`. A **C** function is needed to read extended keys as well as normal ACII value keys.

Listing 11.7

Keyboard BIOS Assembly Language Function

```
;& keyboard.asm
;
;assembly language routine to call int 16h of BIOS
;
;keyhit();  returns TRUE if a character is ready in buffer
;keyrd() ;  returns character in al
;shift();   returns shift status in al
;           codes correspond to bits in kb_flag in BIOS eq
;             80h ...insert on
;             40h ...caps lock toggled
;             20h ...num lock toggled
;             10h ...scroll lock toggled
;              8h ...alt key pressed
;              4h ...ctrl-shift pressed
;              2h ...left shift pressed
;              1h ...right shift pressed
;
; assembled with AZTEC assembler as.exe
;
codeseg   segment   byte public
          public    keyhit_,keyrd_,shift_
;
keyhit_   proc      near
          mov       ah,1   ; code to see if a key pressed
          int       16h
          jz        nokey  ; if zero then no key pressed
          mov       ax,1   ; code meaning char is present
          ret
nokey:    mov       ax,0   ; code meaning no char present
          ret
keyhit_   endp
;
;
```

```
keyrd_  proc   near
        mov    ah,0    ; code to read next character
        int 16h
        ret
keyrd_  endp
;
;
shift_  proc   near
        mov    ah,2    ; code to check shift status
        int    16h
        ret
shift_  endp
;
codeseg ends
        end
```

End of Listing

You could also write a **C** program to place the appropriate assembly language code inline. This would improve the portability between compilers.

These assembly language routines are not enough to correctly interpret the special keys, however. A short program to return these key values is needed. A preliminary version of such code is shown in Listing 11.8. A you study it, notice how the function first checks to see if a key has been pressed. If so, then it reads the character and checks to see if the character (located in the low-order byte) is 0. If not, then the character is not an extended character. If the low order byte is binary zero, then the actual character (now called a scan code) is in the high- order byte. The ch is set to this byte which is the scan code for a special (extended) character.

Listing 11.8

Unbuffered Key Read Function

```
unsigned read_key()
{
  unsigned ch;

  while(!keyhit());
    ch = keyrd();
    if( (ch &0xff) == 0)
      ch = ch >> 8;
    return(ch);
}
```

End of Listing

The problem with this function is that, although it returns the appropriate scan code for the special keys, the calling program does not know whether the key is a special key or a normal key. The IBM PC has 256 possible normal characters and another 256 possible scan codes for special characters. this routine returns values between 0 and 255. Any given value, such as 75, can either be a normal character (K) or a special character (Left Arrow). There are several ways to deal with this. One is to add 256 to the returned code whenever the key is part of the extended character set. Another is to make use of a series of definitions and two possible character translation arrays. (Character-translation arrays were discussed in chapter 8). The first maps all the normal keys, and the second maps the extended keys. Each array makes use of a series of **#define** statements that set up the characters' values. For simplicity, only the first 128 characters are defined in the statements that follow.

```
#define ESC    0x1b   /* These are normal ascii chars */
#define BELL   0x07
#define BS     0x08
#define TAB    0x09
#define LF     0x0a
#define FF     0x0c
#define CR     0x0d
#define XON    0x11
#define XOFF   0x13
#define CTRL_C 0x03
#define DEL    0x7f
#define EOF    0x1a
#define SPACE  0x20

#define F1     0x13b  /* function keys */
#define F2     0x13c
#define F3     0x13d
#define F4     0x13e
#define F5     0x13f
#define F6     0x140
#define F7     0x141
#define F8     0x142
#define F9     0x143
#define F10    0x144

#define S_F1   0x154  /* shift Functions keys */
#define S_F2   0x155
#define S_F3   0x156
#define S_F4   0x157
#define S_F5   0x158
#define S_F6   0x159
#define S_F7   0x15a
#define S_F8   0x15b
#define S_F9   0x15c
#define S_F10  0x15d
```

```
#define  A_F1   0x168   /*  Alt Functions keys  */
#define  A_F2   0x169
#define  A_F3   0x16a
#define  A_F4   0x16b
#define  A_F5   0x16c
#define  A_F6   0x16d
#define  A_F7   0x16e
#define  A_F8   0x16f
#define  A_F9   0x170
#define  A_F10  0x171
```

```
#define  F1   0x15e   /*  Ctrl Functions keys  */
#define  F2   0x15f
#define  F3   0x160
#define  F4   0x161
#define  F5   0x162
#define  F6   0x163
#define  F7   0x164
#define  F8   0x165
#define  F9   0x166
#define  F10  0x167
```

```
#define  LFARW    0x14b   /*  left arrow  */
#define  RTARW    0x14d   /*  right arrow  */
#define  UPARW    0x148
#define  DNARW    0x150
#define  HOME     0x147
#define  END      0x14f
#define  PGUP     0x149
#define  PGDN     0x151
#define  BACKTAB  0x10f
```

```
#define  END   0x175   /*  Control END  */
#define  HOME  0x177   /*  right arrow  */
#define  INS   0x152   /*  INS key  */
#define  DEL   0x153   /*  DEL key  */
```

```
unsigned keys[] = {
        0,01,02,CTRL_,4,5,6,BELL,BS,TAB,
        LF,11,FF,CR,14,15,16,XON,18,XOFF,
        20,21,22,23,24,25,EOF,ESC,28,29,
        30,31,SPACE,33,34,35,36,37,38,39,
        40,41,42,43,44,45,46,47,48,49,
        50,51,52,53,54,55,56,57,58,59,
        60,61,62,63,64,65,66,67,68,69,
        70,71,72,73,74,75,76,77,78,79,
        80,81,82,83,84,85,86,87,88,89,
        90,91,92,93,94,95,96,97,98,99,
        100,101,102,103,104,105,106,107,108,109,
        110,111,112,113,114,115,116,117,118,119,
        120,121,122,123,124,125,126,DEL   };
unsigned ext_keys[] = {
    0,01,02,03,4,5,6,7,8,9,
    10,11,12,13,14,BACKTAB,16,17,18,19,
    20,21,22,23,24,25,26,27,28,29,
    30,31,SPACE,33,34,35,36,37,38,39,
    40,41,42,43,44,45,46,47,48,49,
    50,51,52,53,54,55,56,57,58,F1,
    F2,F3,F4,F5,F6,F7,F8,F9,F10,69,
    70,HOME,UPARW,PGUP,74,LFARW,76,RTARW,78,END,
    DNARW,PGDN,INS,DEL,S_F1,S_F2,S_F3,S_F4,S_F5,S_F6,
    S_F7,S_F8,S_69,S_F10,_F1,_F2,_F3,_F4,_F5,_F6,
    _F7,_F8,_F9.C_F10.A_F1.A_F2.A_F3.A_F4.A_F5,A_F6,
    A_F7,A_F8,A_F9,A_F10,114,115,116,_END,118,_HOME,
    120,121,122,123,124,125,126,127  };
```

These two arrays in the preceding segment , `ext_keys[]` and `keys[]`, allow you to keep the two character sets separate because the special keys are mapped to unique values. The `read_key()` function must be modified to use the arrays. Listing 11.9 shows the result of the modification.

Listing 11.9

Improved KeyRead Function

```
unsigned read_key()
{
unsigned ch;    /*  character to be returned  */

while(!keyhit);    /*  wait for a key to be pressed  */
  ch = keyrd();    /*  grab char form kb buffer  */
  if( (ch= keyrd() &0xff) == '\0
    ch = ext_keys[ch >> 8];
                                        /* map to extended
                                        key array */
  else
    ch = keys[ch && 0xff];
                                        /*  map to keys[] array  */
  return(ch);
}
```

End of Listing

A new header file will have to be created to take advantage of these definitions. The ingredients of the needed header follow.

```
/*  keyboard.h  */
extern keyhit(),keyrd(),shift();
/*  You then add the new definitions  */
/*  and declare the translation arrays  */
unsigned ax,al;
/*  Then you must add in the new version  */
/* of key_read()  */
```

Any file that uses `key_read()` and the definitions must include the command

```
#include "keyboard.h"
```

and must link in the assembly program `keyboard.asm` (object code version).

The program could have added 256 (100h) to each of the extended character (scan) codes within the `read_key()` program. The code would have read

```
ch = (ch >> 8) | 0x100;  /*  add 100h to scan code  */
else
  ch &= 0xff;              /*  use only the low order byte  */
return(ch);
```

The limitation of this approach is that every character must have 100h added to it. Sometimes it is advantageous to map a character to a different value. For example, if you want to make the DEL key work just like the BACKSPACE key, then the entry in the `ext_keys[]` array that corresponds to the DEL key is BS (for BACKSPACE). Some programs such as word processors want some of the special keys to perform a task similar to that of control keys in the normal character set. For example, if you want ctrl- a, ctrl-A, and ctrl-left_arrow to all mean word left within the program, then all three entries, two in the `keys[]` array and one in the `ext_keys[]` array, are set to the same value. The value could be defined in advance as

```
#define WORDLEFT 0x173
```

The corresponding elements of the translation arrays would read WORDLEFT.

Careful use of translation arrays gives you control over the keyboard that you do not have if the scan codes are treated in a simplistic manner. The values of the keys are translated into constants, which can then be used in the application program as needed.

Accessing Ports: Computer programs need to "talk" to other devices through ports. These programs are highly system dependent. On an IBM PC the ports are accessed through DOS and BIOS calls. You have studied have an assembly language routine, `dos()`, that provides a connection between **C** code and int 21h of MS-DOS. Now you need to add code to do the actual talking. In other words, we need another assembly language routine to connect the **C** code to the BIOS communications port routines.

The MS-DOS int 21h functions to read and write from the async port are 3 and 4 respectively. These functions are probably too simplistic, to be practical in everyday use, but they do work when the program performs a straight-forward task such as reading a stream of characters from the comm device or sending output to the port.

Recall that the function number is passed to the `dos()` function as the first parameter. The second parameter, if present, is the character to be sent. The two functions are

```
void char_out(ch)
char ch;
{
  dos(4,ch);
}

void char char_in()
{
  return( dos(3) );
}
```

Neither of these two functions provides the support that a program might need, such as XON, or XOFF, and no provisions are made for checking a port's status. To create a more sophisticated program, use BIOS routines. This requires another assembly language program, which is shown in Listing 11.10.

Listing 11.10

Assembly Language Function for int 14h

```
;  comm.asm
;
;  program to access the communications port of PC
;  via bios interupt 14h.
;
;  called as comm(ax,dx);
;           ah contains the function call 0-3
;           al contains the bit pattern for function
;            call parameter
;           dx contains the port number (0 or 1)
;
;  returns  ax
;
;assembled with AZTEC assembler as.exe
;
codeseg      segment   byte public
   public    comm_
comm_        proc      near
             push      bp
             mov       bp,sp
             mov       ax,[bp+4]  ;f() value in ah
             mov       dx,[bp+6]  ;port number
             int       14h
             pop       bp
             ret
comm_        endp
codeseg      ends
             end
```

End of Listing

Listing 11.11 provides the link between **C** code and the BIOS routines. The assembly language code is kept to a minimum, and as before it can be placed inline if desired. Listing 11.11 shows the new header file that you need.

Listing 11.11

Header File for Comm Port Programs

```
/*  header file for communications port programs  */
extern comm();   /*  assembly language program to
                     invoke int 14h */
#define COMM1 0
#define COMM2 1
unsigned ax,dx,ah,al,dh,dl;
unsigned short  port = COMM1,
                baud = 2,
                parity = 3,
                stopbit = 1,
                databit = 7;   /*  default settings  */
unsigned short line_status, modem_status;
```

End of Listing

You can now write a series of routines to take advantage of the BIOS code. The first is a port initialization program.

Port Initialization: An IBM PC or compatible normally supports two communications ports, COMM1 and COMM2. Both can be initialized to a combination of settings. The register `ah` is set to 0 and the register `al` contains a bit pattern representative of the desired initialization. The initialization codes are shown in

Table 11.2.

Table 11.2
Comm Port Initialization Values

bits	parameter	bit values		meaning
		binary	decimal	
7–5	baud rate	000	0	baud = 110
		001	1	150
		010	2	300
		011	3	600
		100	4	1200
		101	5	2400
		110	6	4800
		111	7	9600
4–3	parity	00	0	no parity
		01	1	odd
		10	2	none
		11	3	even
2	stop bits	0	0	1 stop bit
		1	1	2 stop bits
1–0	data bits	10	2	7 data bits
		11	3	8 data bits

You need a function to place the value into the `al` and then to combine the `al` and `ah` values to create `ax`. The `make_ax()` function does this as the code that follows shows.

```
unsigned make_ax();
{
  ax = (ah << 8) | al;
}
```

You can set the various values by assigning the baud, parity, stop bits, and data bits, and then calling `init_port()` as Listing 11.12 shows.

Listing 11.12

Comm Port Initialization Function

```
void init_port()
{
  al = (baud << 5) | (parity << 3)
                   | (stopbit << 2)
                   | databits;

  ah = 0;
  make_ax;
  comm(ax,port);   /*  call bios routine  */
}
```

This is an important function because every port should be initialized before it is written to.

Sending Characters out a Port: To send a character out of the port, you could, of course, use the dos() version mentioned earlier. Since you have already created the BIOS assembly language routine, however, it is convenient to stick with the current routines and header file. Listing 11.13 shows how to use the existing elements to send characters out from a port.

Listing 11.13

Sending Characters Out a Comm Port

```
unsigned short send_char(c)
char c;
{
  unsigned short error;
  al = c;
  ah = 1;           /*  code to send a character  */
  make_ax();
  ax = comm(ax,port);      /* port is global and must be set
                       prior to calling this program  */
  error = ax & 0x8000;     /*  set error to bit 7 of ah   */
                    /* if error is 1, then char
                       was not transmitted.  If
                       error is zero then char
                       was transferred ok.*/
  line_status = ax >> 8; /* line status contains the
                       ah bit patterns for the
                        line status bits*/
          /* bit meaning if bit set
              7  time out
              6  trans shift register empty
              5  trans hold regs empty
              4  break detect
              3  framing error
              2  parity error
              1  overrun error
              0  data ready
          */
  return(error);
}
```

End of Listing

In addition to sending a character out the desired port, Listing 11.13 provides additional information about the status of the line that the calling program can use in an error-checking routine. Listing 11.13 returns either 0 (if the character is transmitted ok) or 1 (if the character is not transmitted), which the calling program can use as part of its own logic.

Reading a Character In From a Port: Calling `comm()` with a value of 2 in **ah** causes a character to be read in that port. This routine also returns the line status with the difference that if bit 7 of the line-status byte is set, it indicates that data set ready was not received. If the line status byte is 0, no error was encountered. Now consider Listing 11.14, a routine that receives characters from a port. This routine, like the **send_char** routine, uses port as a global variable. You may wish to pass the port as an argument in both routines.

Listing 11.14

Receiving Characters From Comm Port

```
unsigned short recv_char()
{
  unsigned short ch;
  ah = 2;   /* code for receiving a char  */
  al = 0;   /* place holder  */
  make_ax();
  ax = comm(ax,port);    /* call bios routine  */
  line_status = ax >> 8; /* grab ah  */
  ch = ax &0xff;         /* char is in al  */
  return(ch);
}
```

End of Listing

Checking Port Status: The final function in this collection of communications port routines, checks the port and modem status. Listing 11.15 presents the function `ck_status()`.

Listing 11.15

Check Comm Port Status

```
void ck_status(line,modem)
unsigned short *line,*modem;
{
        ax = 0x0300;    /*  code to check status  */
        ax = comm(ax,port);
        *line = ax >> 8; /*  line status byte  */
        *modem = ax &0xff;      /*  modem status byte  */
                /*  line status byte is as it was
                    in the send_char() function.
                     modem status byte is:
                     bit  meaning if bit set
                      7 received line sig detect
                      6 ring indicator
                      5 data set ready
                      4 clear to send
                      3 delta recv line sig detect
                      2 trail'g edge ring detector
                      1 delta data set ready
                      0 delta clear to send
                */
}
```

End of Listing

The function `ck_status()` uses two pointers ,so it would be called with the statement

```
ck_status(&line_status,&modem_status);
```

As in earlier functions, the `port`, `ax`, `ah`, and `al` are global variables.

The functions described thus far in this chapter can now be used to write device control, modem programs, terminal-emulation packages, and similar programs. All but one short function are in **C**. The header file supplies a collection of global variables. The header and these functions can be combined into one large header file or the functions can be placed in a library file. The library technique is preferred because a header should contain declarations and definitions but a library houses functions. If all these functions are in a library, then the header file in Listing 11.16 must be included with any file that calls them.

Listing 11.16

Comm Port Header File

```
extern comm();    /* assembly language program to
                     invoke int 14h */
extern send_char(),recv_char(),init_port(),ck_status(),
       make_ax();
#define COMM1 0
#define COMM2 1
unsigned ax,dx,ah,al,dh,dl;
unsigned short port = COMM1,
               baud = 2,
               parity = 3,
               stopbit = 1,
               databit = 7;  /*  default settings  */
unsigned short line_status, modem_status;
```

End of Listing

The assembly language function in Listing 11.17 may be called by **C** programs. There are several that you want to be able to use. As in earlier examples, you need a header file to provide constants and definitions to be used by video routines. The header file simplifies references to color and monochrome screens, foreground and background colors, and character attributes such as reverse video and blinking. Listing 11.18 shows the header file.

Video I/O and Screen Management

Video i/o is system dependent because the hardware differences are significant. This section looks at both IBM PC and Unix screen management.

The IBM PC and MS-DOS provide extensive video routines. You need another assembly language function, `video.asm`, to provide the connection between **C** programs and the system BIOS. Listing 11.17 shows this function.

Listing 11.17

Assembly Language Function for Video Interrupt

```
; program          video.asm bios call of function = 10h
;                  vid(pax,pbx,pcx,pdx);
;                  unsigned *pax,*pbx,*pcx,*pdx
;                    /*  pointers to the register values  */
; returns          pax,pbx,pcx,pdx...register values
; assembled with AZTEC assembler as.exe
  codeseg segment byte public
          public  vid_
  vid_    proc    near
          push    bp
          mov     bp,sp
          mov     ax,[bp + 4]
          mov     bx,[bp + 6]
          mov     cx,[bp + 8]
          mov     dx,[bp + 10]
          int     10h
          pop     bp
          ret
  vid_    endp
  codeseg ends
          end
```

Listing 11.18

BIOS Video Header File

```
/*   header file for calls to bios_video()
     which supports the C module bios_video.c */
extern int vid();  /*  assembly lang for int 10h  */
      #define  UNDERLINE  1
      #define  NO_UNDRLN  0
      #define  NORMAL     7
      #define  REVERSE    0x70
      #define  HI_INTENS  0X08
      #define  LO_INTENS  0
      #define  BLINK      0x80
      #define  NO_BLINK   0
      #define    BW4025   0
      #define    BW8025   2
      #define    COLOR40  1
      #define    COLOR80  3
      #define    MONO     2
```

```
#define WHITE  7
#define BLACK  0

#define TRUE   1
#define FALSE  0

#define FORWARD    TRUE
#define BACKWARD   FALSE
#define MAXROWS24


static   unsigned         ax,bx,cx,dx;
static   unsigned short   al,ah,bl,bh,cl,ch,dl,dh,fore,back;

unsigned short blink ,intensity ,color = 7,underline;


/* these functions are listed as part of the header file, but
   will be moved later to a library of video routines.*/
unsigned whole(rl,rh)
unsigned short rl,rh;
{
   unsigned rx;
   rx = (rh << 8) | (0xff & rl);
   return(rx);
}


/*  function to create foreground attribute   */
unsigned fore_attr(intensity,color,underline)
unsigned short intensity,color,underline;
{
  unsigned short t;
  switch (color)
  {  case 7:
     case 0:
     case 2:
     case 3:
     case 4:
     case 1:
     case 5:
     case 6:  break;
     default:  color = WHITE;break;
  }
  if(underline) underline = 1;
     /*  make sure underline is 1 or 0  */

     t = (intensity | (color & underline));
     return(t);
  }
```

```
/*  function to create background attribute  */
unsigned short back_attr(blink,color)
unsigned short blink,color;
{
  unsigned short t;
  switch (color)
  {  case 7:
     case 0:
     case 2:
     case 3:
     case 4:
     case 1:
     case 5:
     case 6:  break;
     default:  color = BLACK;break;
  }
  if(blink) blink = 1;   /*  make sure blink is 1 or 0  */

  t = blink | color;
  return(t);
}
unsigned int attrib_byte(fore,back)
unsigned short fore,back;
{
  unsigned short t;
  t = (back & 0x0f) << 4;
  t |= fore;
  return(t);
}
```

End of Listing

The file `video.h` contains some surprises, such as a built-in function to create foreground and background bytes. This function is useful if you need to know how a character is stored in memory. The BIOS video i/o routines display a character as 2 bytes. The first byte is the actual character and the second byte contains the two attributes foreground and background. The background attribute is a 4-bit value that occupies the 4 most significant bits of the low order-byte. The foreground attribute is also a four bit value and it occupies the 4 least significant bits of the attribute byte. Each of the attribute values, foreground and background, is a combination of a flag (1 bit) and color (3 bits). All of these items are assembled into one 16-bit value that is passed to the BIOS int 10h. The result is a character with attributes that is displayed.

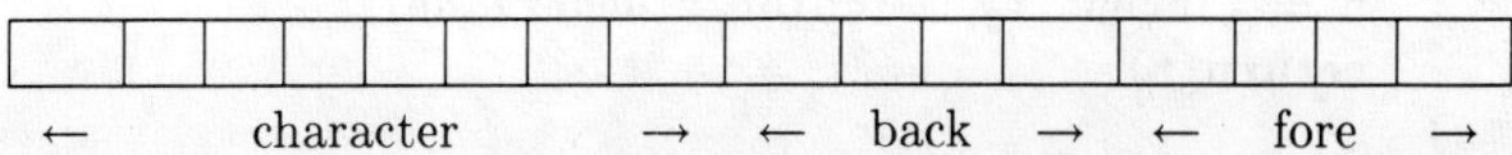

attribute byte - monochrome

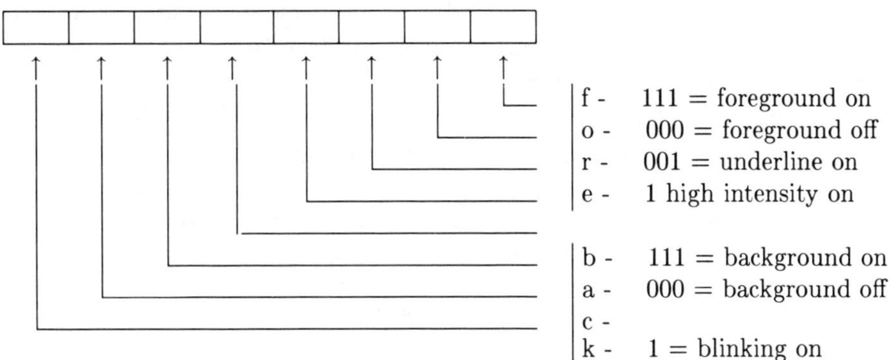

attribute byte - color

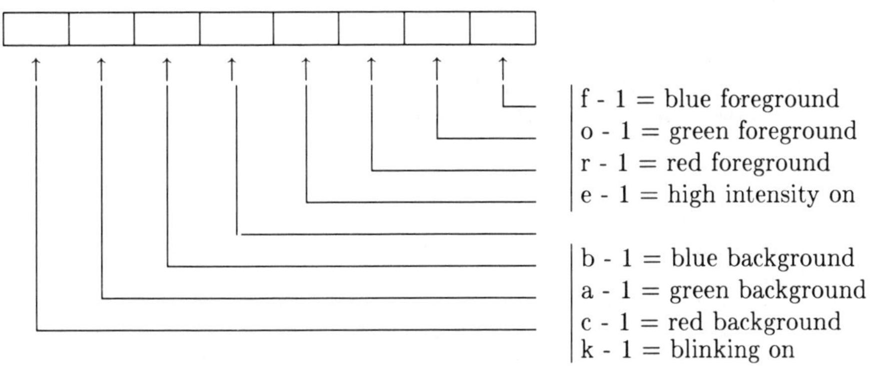

The color and monochrome bytes are similar. One difference is that the color foreground byte does not allow underlining. In fact, if bit 0 is 1, then the foreground color is blue. Many applications programs such as word processors, show true underlining on a monochrome screen but show blue on a color machine.

Two of the functions in the header file, `fore_attr()`,and `back_attr()`, are designed to easily build the foreground and background values. To use `fore_attr()`, the calling program assigns values to `intensity`, `color`, and `underline`, then it calls the function. Similarly, the calling program assigns values to `blink` and `color` before calling `back_attr()`. The two values, foreground and background, are then assembled into one byte by calling `attrib_byte()`. This function returns one byte, which contains both attributes in the proper bit representation. Another function, `whole()`, combines the character and the attribute bytes into one 16-bit word. That word is passed to the video output system via `video()`, the assembly language routine.

A Library of Video Routines: You can now build a library of video routines which can be called by the user's application program. The library functions are declared as external in the file `video.h`. This section discusses some members of this library.

The first function sets the video mode. The possible modes are listed in the file `video.h`. For this function to set the mode to color with a 80 by 25 screen, the calling program must contain the statement.

```
set_v_mode(COLOR80);
```

The function to set the mode to color is shown in Listing 11.19.

Listing 11.19

Video Mode Set Program

```
/*  function to set the video mode  */
void set_v_mode(n)
int n;
{
  ah = 0;           /*  0 is code for set mode  */
  switch (n)        /*  make sure n has valid value  */
  {  case BW4025:
     case BW8025:
     case COLOR40:
     case COLOR80:  break;
     default:  n = BW8025;break;
  }
  al = n;
  ax = whole(al,ah);
  vid(&ax);   /*  assembly language call  */
}
```

End of Listing

Programs frequently need to place the cursor in some particular screen location. When the row and column are the x,y coordinates of the cursor on the screen a function to position the cursor is shown in Listing 11.20.

Listing 11.20

Set Cursor Position Function

```
/*  function to set cursor position  */

void set_cur_pos(row,col)
int row,col;
{
  ah = 2;    /*  code for this function  */
  al = 0;
  ax = whole(al,ah);
  dh = row;
  dl = col;
  bx = 0;    /*  force page to zero  */
  cx = 0;    /*  dummy value so that dx can be passed  */
  dx = whole(dl,dh);
  vid(&ax,&bx,&cx,&dx);  /*  recall that these are global */
                         /* variables  */
}
```

The converse of the cursor-positioning function is a function to read the character at the cursor position. The function in Listing 11.21 returns the row and column numbers via two pointers passed to the function.

Listing 11.21

Read Cursor Position Function

```
/*  function to read cursor position  */

void get_cur_pos(row,col)
int *row,*col;
{
  /*  upon return dh and dl contain row and col  */
  ah = 3;
  al = 0;
  ax = whole(al,ah);
  bx = 0;
  cx = 0;
  dx = 0;
  vid(&ax,&bx,&cx,&dx);
  *row = dx >> 8;
  *col = dx &0xff;
}
```

End of Listing

The function shown in Listing 11.22 writes one character with attributes at the current cursor position. This function can be used in conjunction with a keyboard-reading program to echo only those characters that are not special (such as the editing keys of a word processor. The program must first establish the foreground and background values and then call this function.

```
fore = fore_attr(LO_INTENS,WHITE,NO_UNDRLN);
back = back_attr(NO_BLINK,BLACK);

attrib_putc(ch,fore,back);
```

Listing 11.22

Write a Character With Attributes

```
/*          function to write one character     */
/*          with attributes to screen at cursor pos */

void attrib_putc(ch,foreground,background)
int ch;
unsigned short foreground,background;
{
  ah = 9;
  al = ch;
  ax = whole(al,ah);
  bh = 0;  /*  force page to be zero   */
  bl = attrib_byte(foreground,background);
  bx = whole(bl,bh);
  cx = 1;  /*  character count forced to zero   */
  vid(&ax,&bx,&cx);
}
```

End of Listing

The function itself assembles the entire word made up of the foreground and background attributes plus the character to be displayed. A related function displays a function at the current cursor position without attributes and is called by the statement `tty_putc(ch);` and is shown in Listing 11.23.

Listing 11.23

Write a Character without Attributes

```
/*          function to write one character    */
/*          without attributes to screen at cursor pos */
void tty_putc(ch)
int ch;
{
  ah = 10;
  al = ch;
  ax = whole(al,ah);

  bh = 0;     /*  force page to be zero   */
  bl = WHITE;/*  force character color   */
  bx = whole(bl,bh);

  cx = 1;     /*  character count forced to zero   */

  vid(&ax,&bx,&cx);
}
```

End of Listing

Another output function writes a string to the screen with attributes. Like routines that write the character with attributes, the foreground and background values must be established prior to calling the function.

```
fore = fore_attr(HI_INTENS,BLACK,NO_UNDRLN);
back = back_attr(NO_BLINK,WHITE);

attrib_puts(s,fore,back);
```

Listing 11.24 shows function that builds the character with attributes word and determines the string length.

Listing 11.24

Write String With Attributes

```
/* ******************************************** */
/* function to write a string                   */
/* with attributes to screen at cursor pos      */
/*                                              */
void attrib_puts(s,foreground,background)
char *s;
unsigned short foreground,background;

{
  int length;
  length = strlen(s);

  ah = 9;
  al = ch;
  ax = whole(al,ah);

  bh = 0;  /*  force page to be zero  */
  bl = attrib_byte(foreground,background);
  bx = whole(bl,bh);

  cx = length;  /*  number of characters to print  */

  vid(&ax,&bx,&cx);
}
```

End of Listing

You are now ready to scroll the screen up or down and to clear the screen. The IBM PC allows you to treat the screen as a window and to treat subsets of the screen as screens, or windows, in their own right. A screen is defined by x,y coordinates of the upper left hand corner and the lower right hand corner. A full screen has 0,0 as the upper left and 24,79 as the lower right hand corner. Suppose you want to define two structures that contain needed data about a subscreen, page and `full_screen`. The two structures are shown in Listing 11.25.

Listing 11.25

Defining Windows

```
/*  the following definition is identical to  */
/*  the definition of a window  */
typedef char boolean;
typedef struct  { /*  define window type  */
        int x;
        int y;
        int wx;     /*  x,y position in window  */
        int wy;
        int num_rows;
        int num_cols;
        int cur_row;
        int cur_col;
        boolean cursor;  /*  true if cursor on, */
                   /* false otherwise  */
        struct  {
                unsigned short attribute;
                char *item;
                }  row_item[MAXROWS];
        }  page;

/*  initialize a data item full_screen so that scroll */
/*  functions can be used with page structure */
/*  if smaller pages (windows) are not defined  */

page full_screen =  {
       0,0,0,0,         /*  upper left hand corner  */
       24,80,           /*  set screen size  */
       0,0,             /*  set cursor position  */
       TRUE,            /*  turn cursor on  */
       { NORMAL,' ' }  /*  set attribute  */
  };
```

End of Listing

A function to clear the screen must identify the page to be cleared. Listing 11.26 shows function `cls()` which uses the `full_screen` definition as a global variable. It also uses a function called `pg_scroll`, which scrolls a window of any size up or down. The clear-screen function is called by

```
cls();
```

Listing 11.26

Clear Screen Function

```
void cls()
{
*  page *pp;   /*  pointer to page structure  */
   pp = & full_screen;   /*  select full screen  */
   pg_scroll(pp,MAXROWS,FORWARD);  /*  call scroll function  */
}
```

End of Listing

The last video library function to be presented here is Listing 11.27, which scrolls a window of any size up or down. The calling program must first identify the active page (pointer to a page structure) decide how many lines to scroll the window, and which direction to scroll. The statements that accomplish these tasks are

```
page *current_page,*pp;
...
/*  set current_page values  */
pp = current page;
lines = 2;                    /*  number of lines to scroll  */
direction = FORWARD;
pg_scroll(pp,n,direction);   /*  call scroll function  */
```

Listing 11.27

Scroll Active page

```
/*                  function to scroll active page                    */

void pg_scroll(ppage,n,direction)
page *ppage;          /*  pointer to a page data type  */
int n,direction;
{
  ah = direction ?  6 :  7;    /*  FORWARD is TRUE  */
                               /*  BACKWARD is FALSE  */

  if( n >= ppage->num_rows) al = 0;   /*  blank out window  */
  else al = n;                        /*  scroll n lines  */
  ax = whole(al,ah);
```

```
bh = 0x20;      /*  set blank as fill attribute  */
                bx = bh << 8;

                /*  set upper left of window  */
                ch = ppage->x; /*  set row  */
                cl = ppage->y; /*  set col  */
                cx = whole(cl,ch);

                /*  set lower right corner of window  */
                dh = ppage->x + ppage->num_rows;
                dl = ppage->y + ppage->num_cols;
                dx = whole(dl,dh);

                vid(&ax,&bx,&cx,&dx);
}
```

End of Listing

You now have a very useful video library that can provide sophisticated video output using windows, colors, and character and string attributes.

You can assemble the library into one file in the following fashion:

```
#include "video.h"
/*  typedef for page structure  */
/*  declaration of full screen  */
extern vid();   /*  assembly language routine  */
/*definitions for these functions
        whole();
        fore_attr();
        back_attr();
        attrib_byte();
        set_v_mode();
        set_cur_pos();
        get_cur_pos();
        pg_scroll();
        attrib_putc();
        tty_putc();
        attrib_puts();
        cls();
*/
```

After you assemble the library, the header file that you need is similar to the header file you used in Listing 11.18. The differences are the addition of the external function declarations and the omission of functions in the header file itself. The code that follows incorporates the changes.

```
/*  header file as shown in listing 11.18  */
extern set_v_mode(),  /*  video i/o library  */
       set_cur_pos(),
       get_cur_pos(),
       pg_scroll(),
       attrib_putc(),
       tty_putc(),
       attrib_puts(),
       cls();
extern page,full_screen;  /*  windows  */
```

Unix and Video I/O: All the functions in the preceding section have been for IBM PCs and compatibles. There are some corresponding Unix functions available through the curses library. Unix System V and the Berkeley versions include this library. A calling program must include `curses.h` which provides the definitions and declarations needed by these functions.

Any calling program must first call `initscr()` and end the section that uses these functions with `endwin()`. The other function statements are bracketed between these two function calls. The Unix library refers to what you have been calling `full_screen` as `stdscr`.

Table 11.3 illustrates the equivalences between the IBM PC video library functions and the Unix curses functions.

Table 11.3
Video Library Functions

Unix function	IBM PC video library
`clear()`	`cls()`
`addch(ch)`	`tty_putc(ch)`

`addstr(s)`	`attrib_puts(s)`
	`back = BLACK,NOBLINK`
	`fore = WHITE,LO_INTENS,NO_UNRLN`

`move(y,x)`	`set_cur_pos(row,col)`
`getyx(pp,y,x)`	`get_cur_pos(&row,&col)` `pp == full_screen`
`refresh()`	`set_v_mode(BW8025)` `pp = full_screen`
`scroll(win)`	`pg_scroll(pp,1,FORWARD)` `pp` points to current page
`attrset(attrs)`	/* no equivalent function */ `attrs` are attributes which are terminal dependent and available via the `/ usr/lib/terminfo directory`

The structure used for a window is available in `curses.h` and should be listed on your printer so that you can understand it well enough to make assignments to window structures. The Unix programmer's reference manual has a section on curses. It is extensive and you should study it to grasp its importance.

Using curses and unbuffered keyboard input: Many programs must read a character from the keyboard, and not echo it automatically; the logic of the program must determine what happens. For example, editors and word processors accept characters and echo them if appropriate. There is usually a good deal of processing that goes on between the time the key is pressed and the time it is displayed on the screen. If a special key such as ESC is pressed, its value is not echoed, but it causes the program to perform a special task, such as changing modes or displaying a help menu.

Unix and curses require that `curses.h` be included in a file that makes calls to the curses library. The library must be linked with the `-lcurses` option. For example, the compile line might read

```
cc test.c -lcurses
```

To switch from the normal buffered keyboard routines with automatic echo, the program must contain three function calls: `initscr();`, `cbreak();`, and `noecho();`. At this point the program can read a single key and assign the result to `ch` with the statement

```
ch = getch();
```

To send the character to the screen, you might choose the `wprintw()` function, which is like using printf() to a window.

```
wprintw(stdscr,"%c",ch);
```

The screen does not scroll as it is presently. To enable scrolling, the program must say

```
scrollok(stdscr,1);
```

The program can switch (and must switch before exiting) to a normal terminal mode with the command

```
endwin();
```

Listing 10.29 illustrates the use of these commands and provides the "feel" of the vi editor on Unix systems. The program has two modes: insert and command. To switch from command mode to insert mode, the user presses `i`; to switch from insert mode to command mode, the user presses ESC. When the program is in the insert mode, it simply echoes the characters as they are typed. When it is in the command mode, it recognizes only certain keys: `x,d,u,/,s,q`, and :. In this example these keys invoke a message telling what key was pressed. The `q` causes the program to stop.

Listing 11.29

Unix Keyboard Interpreter

```
/*  Program:     Keyboard interpreter
**
**  Programmer: Ken McReynolds
**              Kathy Stewart
*********************************************************/
#include <stdio.h>
#include <curses.h>

#define  ESC 27
#define  EX 120
#define  DEE 100
#define  YOU 117
#define  COLON 58
#define  ESS 115
#define  SLASH 47
#define  EYE 105
#define  INVALID 0
#define  QUIT 81
#define  LF 10
#define  BELL 7

/* *** SET UP TRANSLATION ARRAY **** */
short c_type[] =   {
  0,0,0,0,0,0,0,0,0,0,           /*  0 - 9  */
  LF,0,0,0,0,0,0,0,0,0,          /*  10 - 19  */
  0,0,0,0,0,0,0,ESC,0,0,         /*  20 - 29  */
  0,0,0,0,0,0,0,0,0,0,           /*  30 - 39  */
  0,0,0,0,0,0,0,SLASH,0,0,       /*  40 - 49  */
  0,0,0,0,0,0,0,0,COLON,0,       /*  50 - 59  */
  0,0,0,0,0,0,0,0,0,0,           /*  60 - 69  */
  0,0,0,0,0,0,0,0,0,0,           /*  70 - 79  */
  0,QUIT,0,0,0,0,0,0,0,0,        /*  80 - 89  */
  0,0,0,0,0,0,0,0,0,0,           /*  90 - 99  */
  DEE,0,0,0,0,EYE,0,0,0,0,       /*  100 -109  */
  0,0,0,0,0,ESS,0,YOU,0,0,       /*  110 - 119  */
  EX,0,0,0,0,0,0,0  }            /*  120 - 127  */
```

```
main()
{
 int ch;

 initscr(); noecho();
 cbreak();  /* Unix curses functions
              needed inhibit echo
              and enable unbuffered
              keyboard input*/
 scrollok(stdscr,1); /*  enable scroll feature  */

 wprintw(stdscr,
   "To exit, press <Q> while in command mode \n");

 ch = EYE;  /*  initial state is insert mode  */
 /*  loop until q key is pressed  */

 do
 {
 switch(ch)
  { case EYE  : wprintw(stdscr," INSERT MODE ");
                wprintw(stdscr," press ESC to exit INSERT \n");
                while( (ch = getch() != ESC)
                  addch(ch);
                wprintw(stdscr, " COMMAND MODE \n\n");
                break;
    case EX   : wprintw(stdscr," char delete key pressed \n");
                break;
    case DEE  : wprintw(stdscr," delete flag key pressed \n");
                break;
    case YOU  : wprintw(stdscr," undo key pressed \n");
                break;
    case ESS  : wprintw(stdscr," substitute key pressed \n");
                break;
    case SLASH  : wprintw(stdscr," pattern matching key
                        pressed \n");
                break;
    case 0    : addch(BELL);  /*  invalid key pressed  */
                break;
    default   : break;
    }
 }while( (ch = c_type[getch()]) != QUIT);

 endwin();    /*  terminate curses windowing  */

}/*  end of program  */
```

End of Listing

This example is, of course, not an editor, but it illustrates how the keys can be interpreted and echoed to the screen or not echoed to the screen as needed.

Summary

This chapter contains examples of functions and programs that deal with control of computer operations, mostly input and output. **C** is a portable language; however, many hardware limitations require nonportable functions to process keyboard and video data.

The IBM PC and compatible machines always include the standard i/o functions of the **C** standard library. Unbuffered keyboard routines and special key codes are not always included. To provide these elements requires two things: assembly language code to link the **C** functions to the operating-system keyboard routines and functions to interpret the special scan codes of the PC. This chapter presents and discusses functions to support unbuffered keyboard input routines.

Many applications programs make use of communications ports. This chapter presents functions to support such communications on a IBM PC and provides the necessary assembly language links.

One of the most hardware-dependent areas of programming is video output. This chapter presents a wide range of functions to directly control the video output of an IBM PC. Unix has the header `curses.h` and accompanying functions to support windows and direct video control.

The topics of this chapter are frequently used in modern programs, such as text editors, telecommuncations programs, and spreadsheets.

EXERCISES

UNDERSTANDINGS

1. Explain the difference between buffered and unbuffered input.
2. Some compilers have a function called `getch()` and a corresponding function `ungetch()`. If your compiler has these two functions, find out what they do and how they work.

APPLICATIONS

3. Write **C** functions that place the PC assembly language programs from Listings 11.9 and 11.10 as inline code instead of separate assembly language programs.
4. Add to the code of Listing 11.28. Add an array that stores one page of text and saves it in a file on request. Add support for the four arrow keys and a save command.
5. Create a function to put a menu in a window on the screen. (Unix users should employ the curses lib).
6. Write a debug program that displays the register values in a window.
7. Write an interactive program that displays all the scan codes for special characters that appear on the keyboard. If you use an IBM PC include alt-A to alt-Z keys.
8. Write a program that echos lines of characters to the screen... unless the ESC key is pressed. At that point, called the command mode, special keys are recognized. These keys each result in a special message appearing on the screen. The keys and their messages are

   `x` character delete key pressed
   `d` delete flag key pressed
   `u` undo key pressed
   `:` command line key pressed
   `s` substitute key pressed
   `/` pattern matching key pressed

   When in the command mode, if the `i` is pressed, the program goes back to to echoing characters until the ESC key is pressed again. Use a character translation array. This program should use a character translation array as discussed in the lecture notes. It also uses unbuffered keyboard input...via a function called `ungetch()`. See the instructor about unbuffered input.
9. Write a function `prt_rdy()` which returns a 1 or 0 depending on whether the printer is ready to receive output.

PROJECTS

10. Write a modem file transfer program. It should transfer a file between a Unix machine and a PC.

11. Create a video game using unbuffered input. Select keys to control the operations of the good-guys. For each player write a **struct** of your own design. For example:

```
struct guy  {
        int x,y;    /*  coordinates  */
        int direction;
        int vel;    /*  speed  */
        };
```

Write functions to display, move, and erase the "things" and to perform related tasks. Keep score in a window.

12. Create a turtle graphics system. The turtle is represented by a special character such as a triangle. The system is interactive and has two modes: edit and interactive. The commands the system recognizes are: `home`(move turtle to center of screen), `showturtle` (makes the turtle visible), `hideturtle`, `clearscreen`, `forward(n)` (moves turtle in same direction as head n spaces (`backward(n)`, `right(n)` (rotate turtle's heading right n degrees), left(n), `repeat n (command list)` (causes the commands which follow to be repeated n times), `pendown` (causes a line to be drawn in the path of turtle movement) and `penup`. The edit mode simply provides for the editing of a procedure. All procedures are stored in memory. In the interactive mode invoking a procedure name should cause its execution. All procedures must be global and recursion is allowed. The following commands should draw a flower:

```
clearscreen
home
pendown
repeat 36( right 10 repeat 4(forward 50 right 90) )
```

The contents of the workspace should be saveable and retrievable.

12

Data Structures

Data structures are fundamental to computer programming in any language. As programmers work on algorithm development and problem analyses, they make crucial decisions about data structures. A data structure is a representation of the data in the program; the choice of a data structure influences how the rest of the program is constructed. This chapter is a survey, not an exhaustive study of data structures.

The topics discussed in this chapter are frequently the subject of entire texts. By necessity, only fundamental concepts and examples are presented. The basics of stacks, queues, linked lists, **double** linked lists, and trees are presented along with a discussion of how they can be implemented in **C**. These structures, when coupled with pointers and memory allocation, are at the heart of the power of **C**. Case studies serve as the vehicle for studying how data structures are implemented in **C**.

Stacks: A First Look

A stack is a buffer in which data items are retrieved in the reverse order from which they are placed in the buffer. A stack can be thought of as a stack of plates or dishes. A collection of clean plates are stacked up. The first plate winds up on the bottom of the stack and the last plate placed on the stack is the top. In computer programs data items are placed on the top of the stack and retrieved from the top. When an item is placed on the stack it is said to be "pushed" on the stack. When an item is retrieved, it is said to be "popped" off the stack. Since the last item placed on the stack is the first off, a stack is also known as a Last-In-First-Out (LIFO) structure.

A rudimentary stack can be created as an array. In the examples that follow, the stack items are integers but they can just as well be floats, structs, unions, or any other valid data type. The stack is declared as an array, and then items can be pushed and popped as needed. Listing 12.1 illustrates this idea.

Listing 12.1

Stack as an Array

```
#define MAXX 20
int stack[MAXX];

static top = 0;           /*  top is the index of top */
                          /* position on the stack   */

void push(n)
int n;
{
  if( top >= MAXX )          /*  stack full   */
    printf(" Stack overflow.  \n");
  else
    stack[top++] = n;
}

int pop()
{
  if( --top < 0)
    {  printf(" Stack underflow \n");
       return(-1);
    }
  else
    return( stack[top] );
}
```

End of Listing

These routines have limitations. One is that the stack is a fixed size. In some applications a fixed stack size is ok. In others it presents an arbitrary limit. Another limitation is that the error code for `pop()` is -1. Therefore, -1 cannot be a legitimate data value. The programmer may need to change the error code for other applications.

Listing 12.2 presents a version of a stack that is faster than Listing 12.1 because it uses pointers to a region of memory. The size of the region is arbitrary. Despite the advantage of being faster than the array version ,but Listing 12.2 still suffers from an arbitrary upper limit.

Listing 12.2

Stack that uses Pointers

```
#define REGION 64
int *sp;          /*  stack pointer  */

int *top,*bottom;/*  top and bottom of stack  */

int get_mem()
{
  sp = (int *) malloc( (sizeof(int)) * REGION);
          /*  allocate memory space  */
  if(sp == 0)
    return(-1);          /*  error in memory allocation  */
}

void init_stack()
{
  bottom = sp;  /*  set bottom of stack to sp  */
  top = bottom + (sizeof(int) * REGION) - sizeof(int);
}

void push(n)
int n;
{
  sp++;
  if( sp > top >) /*  stack full  */
    printf(" Stack overflow.  \n");
  else
    *sp = n;
}

int pop()
{
  int n;
  if( sp == bottom )  /*  stack empty  */
    {  printf(" Stack underflow \n");
       return(-1);
    }
  else
    {  n = *sp;
       sp--;
       return(n);
    }
}
```

End of Listing

The functions in Listing 12.2 support a stack that, by using pointers, is fast and easy to use. A program that uses these routines begins with

```
main()
{
  get_mem();
  init_stack();
}
```

A most familiar use of a stack is in the construction of a RPN calculator. The operands are pushed on the stack, an operator is applied to the top two members of the stack, and the result is pushed back on the stack. Much of the code is concerned with error checking that is, in making sure the stack is not empty or treating an empty stack as the operand 0. Two functions are needed to clear an entry (to pop the last operand off the stack and discarding it) and clear the stack. The stack can be cleared by moving the stack pointer to the bottom of the stack. The calculator program is an exercise at the end of this chapter.

Queues: A First Look

A queue is a First-In-First-Out (FIFO) structure. The first item in is the the first item out. In a sense a queue is like a line at a ticket counter. The first person in the line is the first person served. The word queue means line. Buffered data is always a queue. The data are put in a buffer until the program can process them. Each data item is pulled out of the queue in the same order it was placed into the queue.

The simplest method of implementing a queue is with an array, as Listing 12.3 shows.

Listing 12.3

Queue as an Array

```
#define MAXX 20
int queue[MAXX]

static back = MAXX;      /* front and back of queue are  */
static front =MAXX;      /* both at the same place  */
                         /* so the queue is empty  */

int putq(n)
int n;
{
  if( back < 0 )
    printf(" Queue full or used up \n");
  else
    queue[back--] = n;
}
```

```
int getq()
{
  if( front == back)
    { printf(" queue is empty \n");
      return(-);
    }
  else
      return(queue[front--]);
}
```

End of Listing

The operation of this queue is illustrated by Figure 12.1. The initial state of the queue is that the front and back are in the same place.

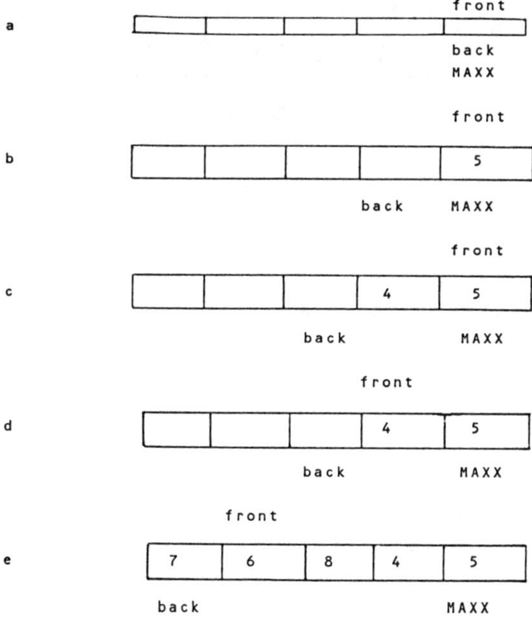

Figure 12.1: *A Queue as an Array*

Figure 12.1 shows some of the problems with a simple array queue: There are only so many places in the queue. The front of the queue moves to the left. Even though (case e.) there are available spots in the queue to the right of the front, no values can be placed in the queue. The solution to this problem is to allow the back of the queue to wrap around to the `MAXX` position.

Circular Queue

A circular queue is not a circle, but simply a queue in which the back is allowed to wrap around to the original position. Figure 12.2 represents a circular queue.

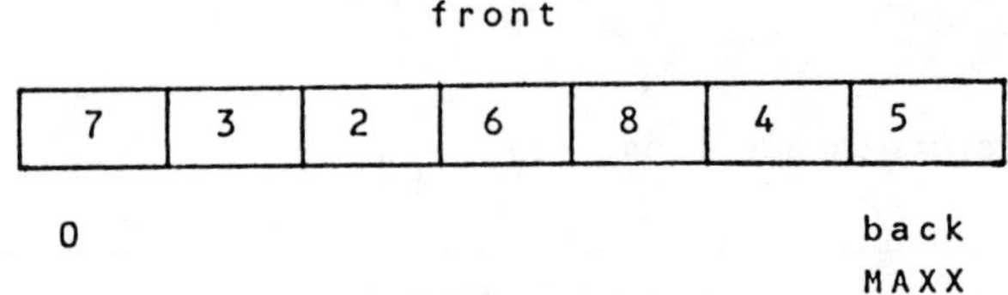

Figure 12.2: *Circular Queue*

The function that places a value in the queue is concerned with overwriting the front of the queue, not with running out of room at the low end of the array. This function is shown in listing 12.4.

Listing 12.4

put_queue function

```
int putq(n)
int n;
{
  if (back == front)
    printf("Queue is full \n");
  else
    queue[back--] = n;
  if( back < 0 ) back = MAXX  /*  recycle position */
                              /* of back  */

}
```

End of Listing

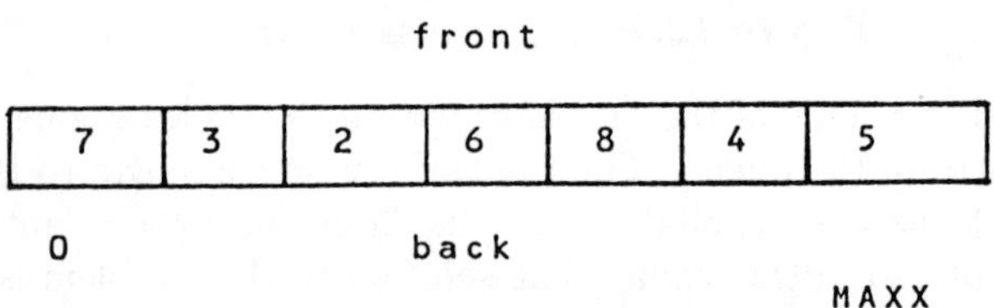

Figure 12.3: *Full Circular Queue*

Figure 12.3 also indicates a problem with the `getq()` function. When the queue is empty, `front` and `back` are at the same position (`MAXX`) (see Figure 12.2) and no values can be retrieved. When back has wrapped around and front and back are at the same position, then the queue is not empty. One solution is to create an empty flag which is used to see if a value can be retrieved. It is also advantageous to place `front` one position ahead of `back`. Listing 12.5 reflects this addition.

Listing 12.5

get queue item function

```
front = MAXX + 1;
static char empty = 1;    /*  original value  */
int getq()
{  int n;
   if( (empty)
   {  printf(" queue is empty \n");
      return(-1);
   }
   else
      {
        if(front == 0) front = MAXX + 1;
        n = queue[--front];
        if( (front - 1) == back ) empty = 1;
        return(n);
      }
```

End of Listing

The function to put a value in the queue must set the empty flag to false when an item is put in the queue as shown in Listing 12.6.

A circular queue is better than a simple array queue in most cases. When the program is simple and there is no chance of running out of room in the queue, then the linear method is faster. In most cases a circular queue is more efficient. An analysis of the particular application yields a reasonable value for `MAXX`.

Listing 12.6

put_queue function - revised

```
int putq(n)
int n;
{
  if (back == front)
    printf("Queue is full \n");
  else
    {  queue[back--] = n;
       empty = 0;
       if( back < 0 ) back = MAXX;  /*  recycle position */
                                    /* of back  */
    }
}
```

Linked Lists

Stacks and Queues as implemented with arrays require a fixed amount of memory and are limited by the memory size. Their simplicity makes them useful in straightforward applications. They are easy to understand and maintain, but they are not as flexible as the next structure you will studt. When the number of data items (particularly complicated data types such as structures) is unknown the situation calls for a linked list.

A linked list is like a chain of data items connected by pointers. As figure 12.4 shows, each data item contains a pointer to the address of the next item.

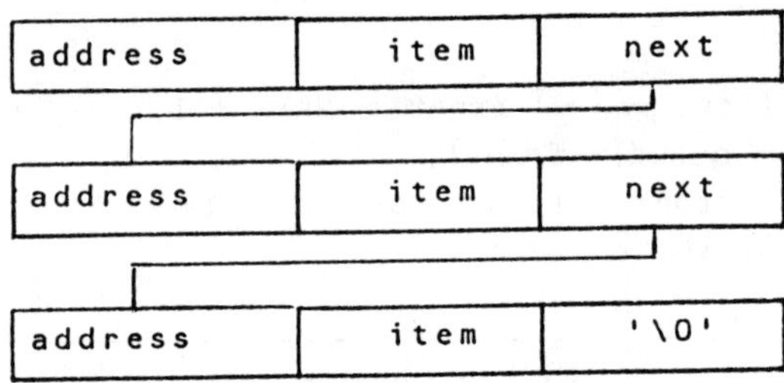

Figure 12.4: *Linked Lists*

Unlike arrays a linked list can be stored in non-contiguous memory. Space can be allocated as needed, and the upper limit is the available memory in the computer. The linked list is declared as a structure.

```
struct data_info   {
        char name[20];
      int age;
      struct data_info *next;
};
```

The structure contains two data fields: **name** and **age**. The third member of the list is a pointer to another structure of the same type. A program can now declare members of the linked list.

```
struct data_info *first;
```

Pointers declare the data object but do not reserve memory space. A call to **calloc**() reserves the space.

```
first = calloc(1, sizeof(data_info);
```

The list member is initialized as follows:

```
first->name = "Tommy Smith";  /* assuming ANSI
                                 standard and string
                                 initialization
                                 allowed.  */
first->age = 22;
first->next = 0;              /* A zero value means
                                 that this is the last
                                 item in the list */
```

Linked lists are usually thought to have a first (head) member and sometimes a last (tail) member. The head and tail are assigned at the beginning of the program.

```
static struct data_info *head = first,*tail = first;
```

The result is the linked list shown in Figure 12.5 that contains one item and a pointer to the head of the list as well as a pointer to the tail of the list.

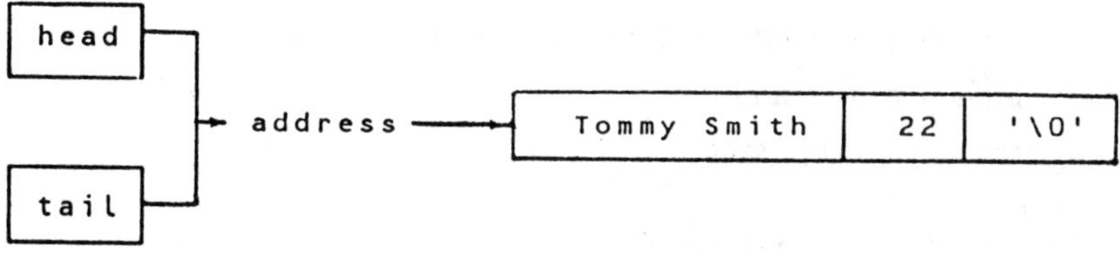

Figure 12.5: *Linked List with a head and tail*

You do not have to give names to the rest of the members in the list because each points to the next. For example, to add a list member at the end, you need only to allocate the needed memory and see that last points to the new member. The previous last must now point to the new last. Figure 12.6 shows how the process works.

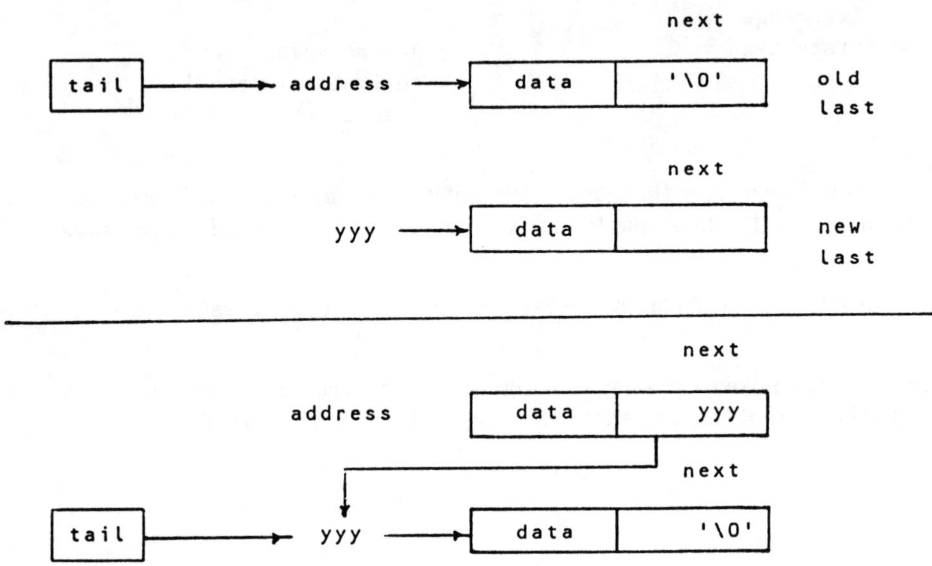

Figure 12.6: *Assigning new members to a list*

The code to implement this addition is

```
struct data_info *new;
...
new = calloc(1, sizeof(struct data_info) );
tail->next = new;
new->next = 0;
tail = new;
```

A reasonable amount of data abstraction can be achieved by placing the **calloc**() inside a function and placing the call to `get_mem()` inside the function **ap-pend**(). Listing 12.8 shows the resulting code.

Listing 12.8

get_mem() function

```
struct data_info *getmem()
{
  struct data_info *p;
  p = calloc(1, sizeof(struct data_info) );
  return(p);
}

void append()
{
  struct data_info *new;
  new = getmem();
  tail->next = new;
  new->next = 0;
  tail = new;
}
```

End of Listing

The function `getmem()` returns a pointer to a structure. Anytime another structure is needed, the only call is to `append()` which creates a pointer to a new structure via a call to `getmem()` and then reposition the pointers to that tail points to the new last member in the list. The previous last member is set to point to the new last member.

You shall need two additional functions: one to insert a member into the list (see figure 12.7) and one to delete a member from the list (figure 12.8). The code to implement the `insert` function is shown in Listing 12.9. The code to implement the `delete` function is shown in Listing 12.10.

Listing 12.9

linked list insert function

```
/* code to determine old1's value
   must already exist */

void insert(old1,new)
struct data_info *old1, *new;
{
  if(old1 == tail) append(new);
  else
    {  new->next = old1->next;
       old1->next = new;
    }
}
```

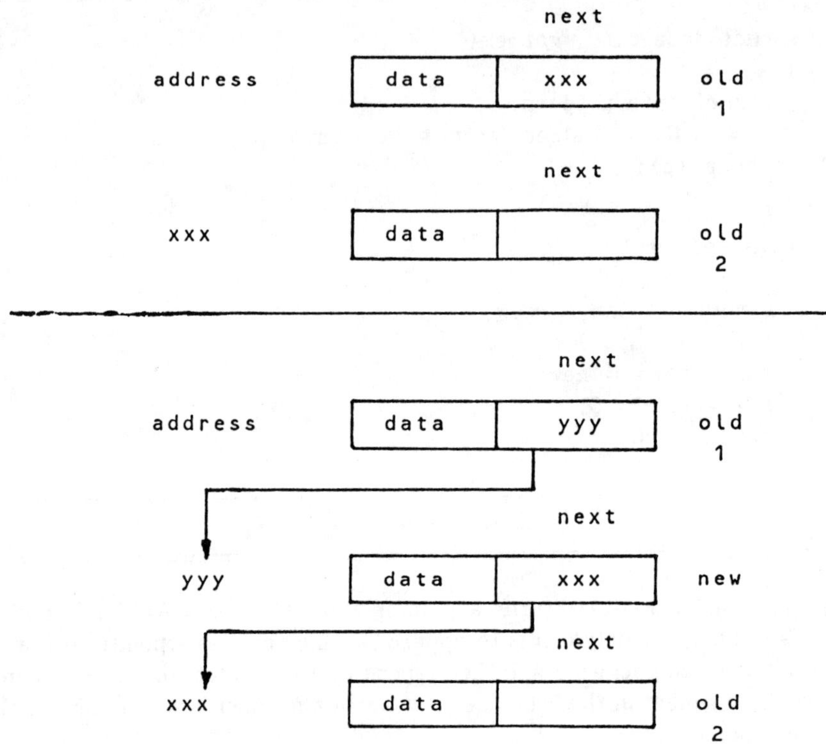

Figure 12.7: *Adding and Deleting Members from the List*

The code needs to know only what member of the list is to precede the new member of the list. If the old member is already the last one in the list, then the existing function (`append()`) is called with an assignment of `new`.

Listing 12.10

Linked List delete function

```
void delete(old1,old2)
struct data_info*old1,old2;
{
  if(old2 == head)
    head = old2->next;    /*  simply move head   */
  else
    old1->next = old2->next;
  relmem(old2);    /*  function to free up memory  */
}
```

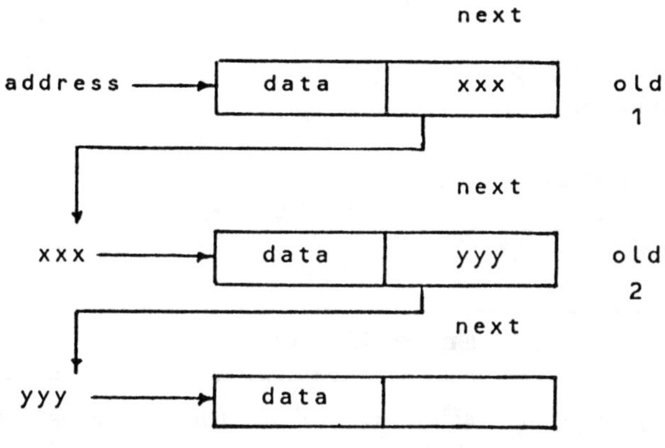

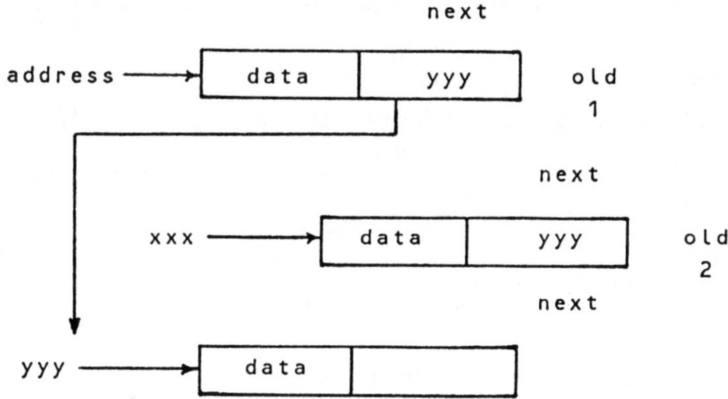

Figure 12.8: *The* append() *function*

As in the `insert()` function, the values of `old1` and `old2` must already be known when `delete()` is called. The best way to find these values is to run through the list looking for a particular data item by using a linear search. The search must retain pointers to the structure to be deleted (`old2`) and the previous structure (`old1`). Should the item to be deleted be the first member of the linked list, the only task is to redirect head to point to what was the second element in the list.

The `delete()` function makes a call to `relmem()` which is a function to free the memory no longer needed. The `relmem()` function, which is shown in Listing 12.11, is another abstraction technique to hide the details of the **free**() function from `relmem()`. It can also be called from other places in a program.

Listing 12.11

rel_mem function

```
short int relmem(p)
struct data_info *p;
{
  return(free(p));
    /*  returns 0 if free worked ok, */
    /* else returns -1  */
}
```

End of Listing

When the `relmem()` function is called, the value returned can be used for error checking within the calling program.

One problem with the `insert()` function is that you cannot insert an item in front of the list. A way to do this is to make the first argument in the function equal to 0.

```
insert(0,new);
```

Then the program can check for 0 inside the function as Listing 12.12 shows.

Listing 12.12

Revised insert function - linked list

```
void insert(old1,new)
struct data_info *old1, *new;
{
  if(old1 == tail) append(new);
  else
    if(old1 == 0)
    q{  new->next = head->next;
        head = new;
     }
    else
     {  new->next = old1->next;
        old1->next = new;
     }
}
```

End of Listing

One other task needs to be done to make a linked list work: The program must search through the list for a particular member of the list. If the name is the key field, and a value called `person` has been initialized with the value (in this case, the name) to be found, then the `search()` function is as shown in Listing 12.13.

Listing 12.13

The Function to Search a linked list

```
struct data_info *search(person)
char person[20];
{
  struct data_info *p;
  p = head;
  while( !p )
    {  if(strcmp(p->name,person) == 0)
          break;
       p = p->next;
    }
  return(p);          /* return 0 if item not found */
}
```

End of Listing

Stacks as Linked Lists

The stack examples you have seen so far were limited by the arbitrary size limitations of the arrays. If you use a linked list, then you are limited only by the amount of available free memory. The `push()` and `pop()` functions become `append()` and `delete()` functions. If the last list element is considered the top of the stack, then you only add to the list and as always delete the last element (LIFO). Figure 12.9 illustrates how the procedure works.

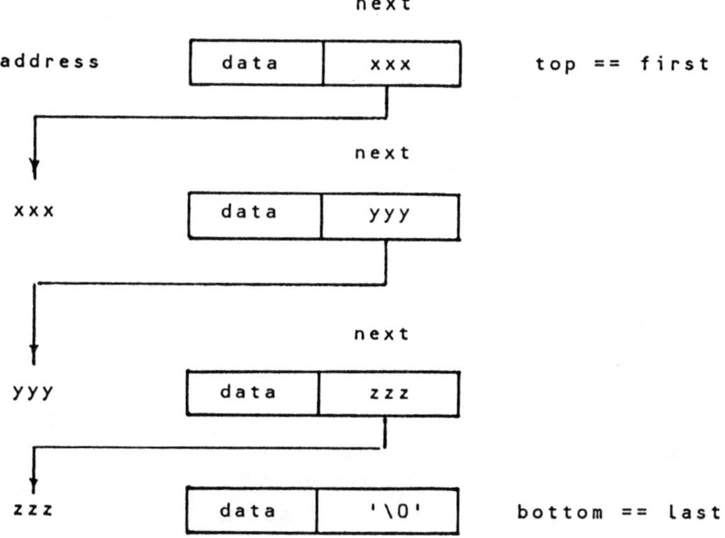

Figure 12.9: *A Stack as a Linked List*

The stack, containing **float** numbers, is declared as

```
struct stack  {
        float item;
        struct stack *next;
      };
```

and `top` and `bottom` are declared as

```
static struct stack *top, *bottom;
```

Then one stack element is allocated and the pointers are initialized.

```
top = getmem();
bottom = top;
top->next = 0;            /*  nothing below top  */
static char empty=1;      /*  stack is empty  */

/*  function to allocate memory for stack element  */
struct stack *getmem()
{
  struct stack *p;
  p = calloc(1, sizeof(struct stack) );
  return(p);
}
```

For simplicity, consider the stack empty when `top` and `bottom` are the same. Actually, could put a value in the top, but it would complicate the error checking for an empty stack.

Listing 12.14 shows the `push()` function, which acts as if it were inserting a value at the front of the list.

Listing 12.14

stack push() function

```
void push(x)
float x;
{
  struct stack *new;
  new = getmem();              /*  allocate space  */
  if(new = 0)                  /*  no memory left  */
    printf("Out of memory \n");
  else   /*  continue  */
  {
    new->next = top;       /*  new top points to old top  */
    top = new;             /*  bump top of stack  */
    top->item = x;         /*  assign x to data position  */
    empty = 0;             /*  stack not empty  */
  }
}
```

Listing 12.15 shows the pop() function, which is similar to the delete() function.

Listing 12.15

stack pop function

```
float pop()
{
struct stack *temp;
float x;

if(empty)
  { printf(" Stack empty \n");
    x = 0.0;
  }
  else
    { temp = top;          /*  save pointer to top  */
      x = top->item;       /*  grab value  */
      top = top->next;     /*  move top down  */
      relmem(temp);        /*  free up memory  */
      if(top == bottom) empty = 1;
    }
  return(x);
}
```

End of Listing

The pop() function uses the relmem() function to free the memory that is no longer needed as Listing 12.16 shows.

Listing 12.16

memory release function

```
/*  function to release memory not needed  */
short int relmem(p)
struct stack *p;
{
  return(free(p));
           /*  returns 0 if free worked ok, */
           /* else returns -1  */
}
```

End of Listing

Using typedef with Linked Lists

The last few functions all include repeated declarations of

```
struct stack *pointer;
```

or

```
struct data_info *pointer.
```

Using **typedef** in these situations can help in two ways: the programs are easier to read and they are more portable. The declaration

```
typedef struct stack    {
                float x;
                struct stack *next;
}ITEM;
```

allows you to declare variables of type ITEM.

```
void push(x)
float x;
{
  ITEM *new;
  new = getmem();    /*  allocate space   */
  if(new = 0)        /*  no memory left   */
    printf("Out of memory \n");
  else               /*  continue  */
...
```

Using **typedef** also allows you to simply some of the functions. For example:

```
/*  function to allocate memory for stack element  */
struct stack *getmem()
{
  struct stack *p;
  p = calloc(1, sizeof(struct stack) );
  return(p);
}
```

becomes

```
/*  function to allocate memory for stack element  */
ITEM *getmem()
{
  ITEM *p;
  p = calloc(1, sizeof(ITEM) );
  return(p);
}
```

These same functions can be used in other programs by using different structure definitions. If the **typedef** statement is changed, the other functions work without modification. The only exception to this rule is when an individual data type **float**, for example appears in the function. Another **typedef** solves this problem.

```
typedef float DATATYPE;
```

A a result, a function such as **push()**, which specifies the data type, can be changed as follows.

```
/*  old version  */
void push(x)
float x;
{

/*  new version  */
void push(x)
DATATYPE x;
{
```

With these two new typedefs, the same functions can be used with any of the simple data types. The changes are made only to the **typedef** statements.

Two-Way Linked Lists

Clearly, there are instances where you want to be able to traverse the list in either direction. A two-way linked list has two pointer elements: one pointing to the next element and another pointing to the previous element. Figure 12.10 illustrates the concept of a two-way or double-linked list.

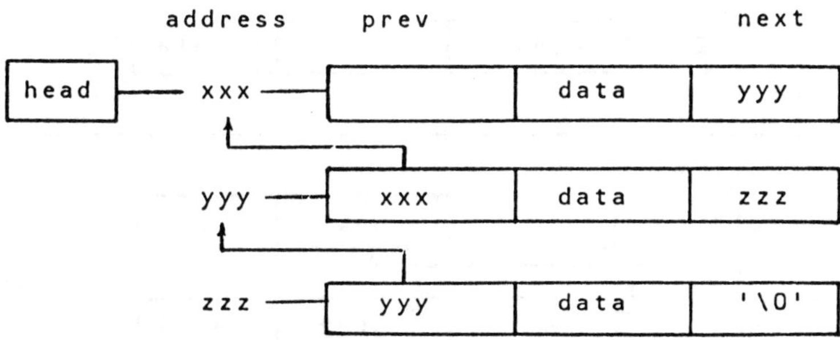

Figure 12.10: *A Two-way Linked List*

The two-way linked list has a head and the last element points to nothing (**value** == 0). The initialization of a double linked list is similar to that of a single linked list.

```
typedef float itemtype;
typedef struct dllist   {
                itemtype x;
                struct dllist *next;
                struct dllist *prev;
              }  ITEM;
ITEM head;
ITEM *init()        /*  create head  */
{
  head = getmem();
  head->prev=0;
}

/*  getmem() and relmem() are the same as before  */
```

The insert and delete functions are illustrated in figures 12.11 and 12.12. The code to implement the functions is shown in Listing 12.17.

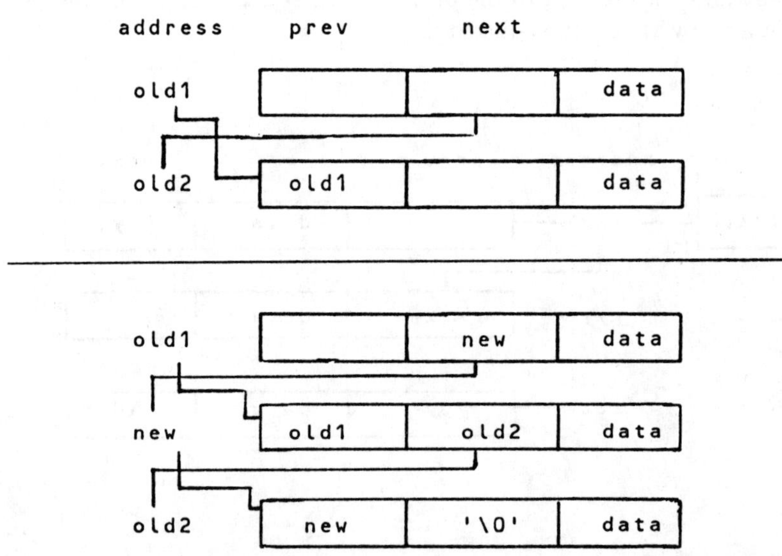

Figure 12.11: *Inserting an item in a two-way linked list*

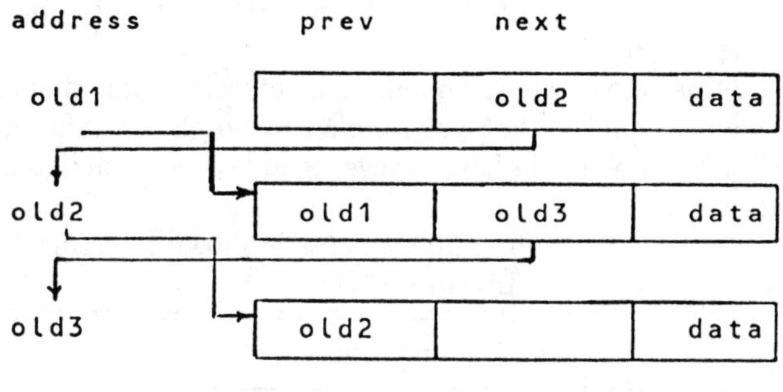

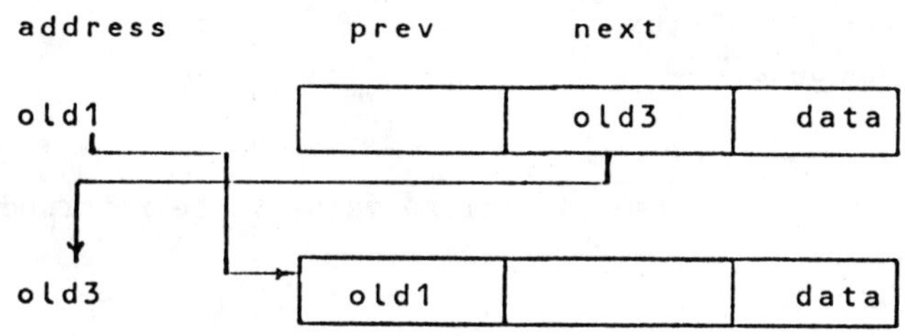

Figure 12.12: *Deleting an item from a two-way linked list*

Listing 12.17

Double Linked Lists insert & delete

```
void insert(old1,new)
ITEM *old1,*new;
{
qnew->next = old1->next;
 new->prev = old1;
 old1->next = new;
 new->next->prev = new;
}

void delete(old2)
ITEM *old2;
{
 old2->prev->next = old2->next;
 old2->next->prev = old2->prev;
 relmem(old2);
}
```

Circular Queue as two way linked list: A circular queue was implemented as an array earlier in this chapter. Like the stack, the circular queue is limited by some arbitrary size. A two-way linked list can improve on the performance of the queue. The queue still has a size limit, but if reached the limit can be increased so that the queue does not get full.

The way to do this is to create the queue elements with a function and establish the number of queue members that you think will do the job the first time the function is called. If the queue fills up, however, call the function again so that the queue is doubled in size.

The function to allocate the first 20 elements is shown in listing 12.18.

Listing 12.18

make_queue function

```
#define Q_NUM 20
ITEM *first, *last;
int makequeue()
{
  ITEM *temp;
  int r;          /*  initialize value to be returned  */
  r = 0;
  register i;
  first = getmem();  /*  preserve pointer to 1st item  */
  temp = first;
  for(i = 1; i < Q_NUM; ++i)
    {
      if( (temp->next = getmem()) != 0)
        { temp->next->prev = temp;
          temp = temp->next;
        }
      else
        { r = -1;  /*  error in memory allocation  */
          break;
        }
    }
  last = temp;
  return(r);
}
```

End of Listing

Listing 12.18 creates Q_NUM items that all point to the next and previous elements. None has any data in the data sections. The first time this function is called, the front and back of the queue are initialized to the first element.

```
ITEM *front, *back;
...
if(makequeue() != -1)           /* successful creation
                                   of q elements */
{  front = back = first;        /* position queue
                                   pointers
   last->next = front;          /* have last item
                                   in queue point to
                                   first element */
first->prev = last;             /* first elem refers
                                   to last elem
}
```

When **makequeue()** is called the next time(s), the front and back pointers do not necessarily point to the front of the queue. The new queue is inserted right after the current front element in the queue. Then front points to the new first element and the new last element points to **back**. The queue expansion is illustrated in Figure 12.13.

```
/*  assume makequeue() has just been called  */
back->prev = last;
front->next = first;
last->next = back;
first->prev = front;
```

The **makequeue()** function is called when the queue is full, that is, when the front catches up to the back. The time to call **makequeue()** is when an item has been inserted at the front of the queue and the front is pointing to the back. Assume that a function called **putq()** places a new item in the queue and then moves the pointer to front.

```
putq(x)
{
  ...
  front->x = x;
  front = front->next;
  ...
}
```

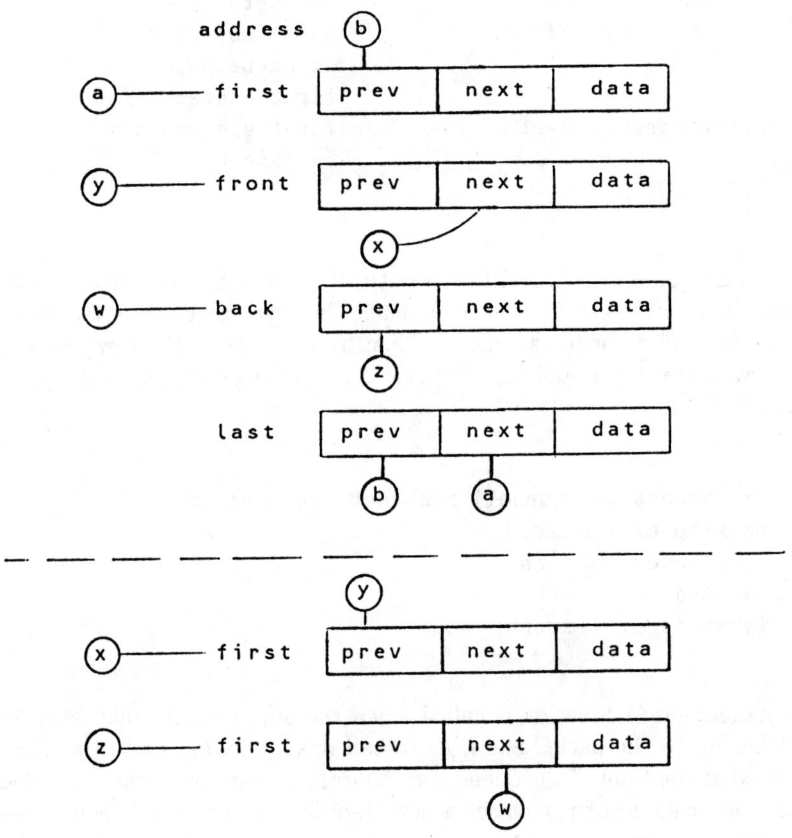

Figure 12.13: *Circular Queue Expansion*

To make use of `makequeue()`, `putq()` is modified by inserting the necessary statements to increase the size of the queue when necessary. Listing 12.19 shows the code to do this.

Listing 12.19

Increasing queue Size

```
front->x = x;
if(front->next == back)
  if(makequeue() != -1)
    {
      back->prev = last;
      front->next = first;
      last->next = back;
      first->prev = front;
    }
front = front->next;
```

End of Listing

By implementing a circular queue as a two-way linked list with a method to expand the list allows you to make the queue a reasonable size rather than big enough to handle the worst case. If you look at the routines carefully, you will see that they could have been implemented with single, or one-way, linked lists. The advantage of the two-way method is that it allows you to put an item back in the queue. Many programs use a look-ahead technique that examines the next item in the queue, and if it meets certain criteria, puts the item back in the queue. An item is always picked off the back of the queue. If the item needs to be put back, the pointers for the back item need to be restored.

```
void putback();
{
  back = back->prev;
  empty = 0;
}
```

Binary Trees

Binary trees (trees with two branches) are an extension of the linked-list idea, in which the elements are stored in a non sequential fashion. The list's elements are maintained in a sorted fashion. A binary tree looks like an upside down tree. The top element is the root and the rest of the tree builds from the root as Figure 12.14 shows.

The nodes of a tree point to two other nodes: a left node and a right node. Trees are subject to a variety of naming conventions. Sometimes all nodes after the root are called branches or children. A node with no branches is called a leaf. For simplicity, call all the nodes subtrees. Since the original node (root) is a tree, all the others are called subtrees. When a process is performed on a tree, it is common practice to apply the process to the left node and then to the right node. This is a recursive notion in that if you start at the root and apply a process, it is recursively applied to the subtrees until the nodes are empty, that is, until the pointers have the a value of 0).

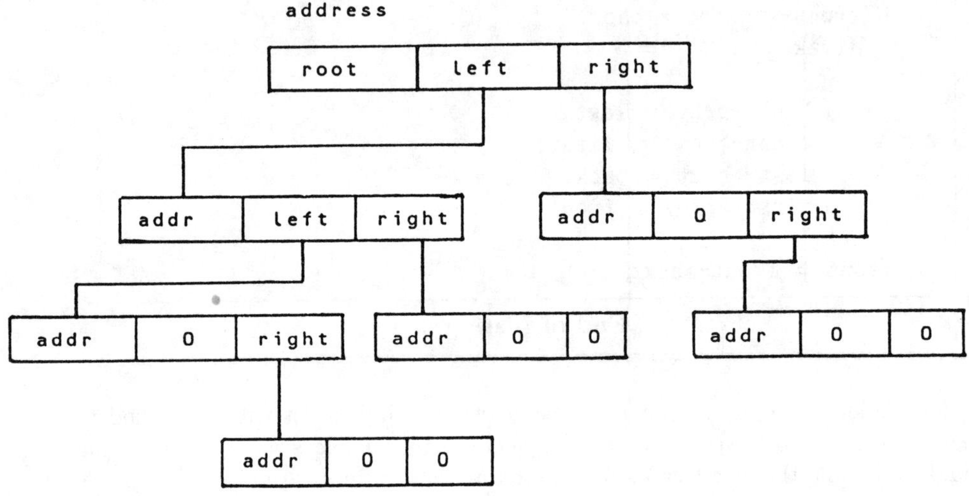

Figure 12.14: *A Model of a Binary Tree*

The advantage of a binary tree is that the items can be placed in the tree in a sorted manner. Then the processes of inserting a node, deleting a node, searching for a node, and retrieving information can be accomplished in a more efficient manner than with linear linked lists. Speed and efficiency are accomplished at the expense of more complicated code.

A sorted tree can be illustrated by a simplified example as shown in figure 12.15:

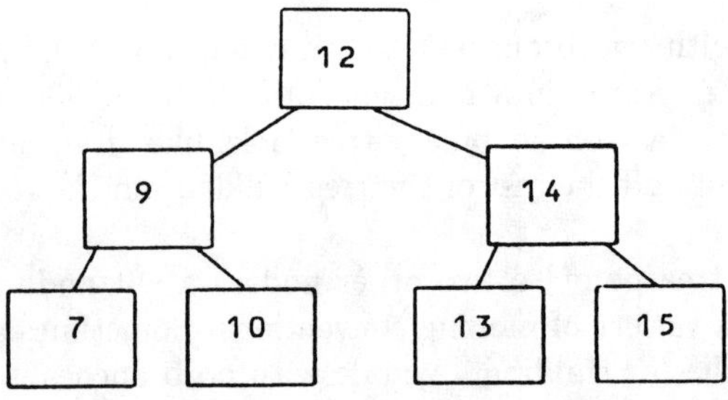

Figure 12.15: *A Simplified Tree Structure*

Each left node contains a number less than the value in its parent node. Each right node is greater than its parent node.

To make the tree structure practical you need methods of dealing with equal values, empty nodes, inserting nodes, deleting nodes, finding data, and so on. The first task you face is that of creating the original node. Listing 12.21 shows how to initialize a binary tree. As you study it, remember that a tree is a special case of linked lists; therefore, each node on a tree is a structure.

Listing 12.21

Binary Tree Initialization

```
typedef float itemtype;

typedef struct node  {
          itemtype x;
          struct node *left;
          struct node *right;
          }TREE;
TREE root;

TREE *init()           /*  create root   */
{
  root = getnode();
  root->left = 0;
  root->right = 0;
}
```

End of Listing

The functions to allocate memory, `getnode()`, and release memory, `relnode()`, are functionally equivalent to `getmem()` and `relmem()`, two functions that you have already studied Listing 12.22 shows how `getnode()` and `relnode()` are used.

Listing 12.22

Allocating and Deallocating Memory for trees

```
/*  function to allocate memory for tree branch   */

TREE *getnode()
{
  TREE *p;
  p = calloc(1, sizeof(TREE) );
  return(p);
  }
```

```
/*  function to release memory not needed  */

short int relnode(p)
TREE *p;
{
  return(free(p));

  /*  returns 0 if free worked ok, */
  /* else returns -1  */

}
```

End of Listing

A subtree can be created by declaring it, calling **getnode()** to allocate the memory, and then assigning the proper values to the pointers and data item(s).

```
{
  TREE *subtree;
  TREE *current;
  ...
  current = root;
  subtree = getnode();
  ...
}
```

A branch can be inserted in the tree with the function shown in Listing 12.23.

Listing 12.23

Binary tree insert function

```
void insert(prev,new)
TREE *prev,*new;
{
  if(new->x <= prev->x)
    {
    new->left = prev->left;
    prev->left = new;
    }
  else
    {
    new->right = prev->right;
    prev->right = new;
    {
}
```

End of Listing

Either the left node or right node is updated depending on the relationship between the data items in the new branch and the existing branch. The binary tree `insert()` function is an extension of the insert function for a single linked list. The `delete()` function is similar to the `delete()` function shown earlier for the single linked list.

The real difficulty is in looking through, or traversing the tree. There are three standard ways to traverse a tree: preorder, inorder, and postorder.

PreOrder Tree Traversal

When random data are placed in a binary tree, the tree is balanced (for the most part), and can be searched in order. That is, the relative size of the data items allows you to look through the tree in the order of the data until the desired node is found. The search starts at the root and goes left if a left node is available. The search then is performed on the right node; the sequence is to look in the left nodes first and the right nodes second. Since the subtrees are of the same structure as the root, the search continues recursively until the item is found. For a tree with `n` levels, the maximum number of comparisons is `n`. A tree with five levels might contain 31 data items yet require at most five comparisons to locate any item in the tree. Listing 12.24 shows how the traversal works.

Listing 12.24

Pre-order tree traversal

```
TREE *node;
node =root;

void search(node,n)
TREE *node;
itemtype n;
{
  if(p)
  {  if( n == node->n) return;    /*  found data   */
     search(node->left,n);
     search(node->right,n);
  }
  else printf(" item not found \n" );
}
```

End of Listing

In-Order Traversal

An in-order traversal is accomplished by looking for or processing data in the order in which it is normally listed by going to the smallest element, processing the data, and then going to the next item. This is accomplished by first traversing the tree to the lowest-order data item. The three steps in a recursive procedure are to search left, process the data, and then search right. Listing 12.25 shows how the traversal works.

Listing 12.25

In-Order Tree Traversal

```
void search(node,n)
TREE *node;
itemtype n;
{
  if(p)
    {  search(node->left,n);
       if( n == node->n) return;  /*  found data  */
       search(node->right,n);
    }
  else printf(" item not found \n" );
}
```

End of Listing

The function in Listing 12.25 is recursive. It is originally called by using root as the node and the data to be found as n. The search begins with the left node, performs the comparison, and then continues the search with the right node. If the tree had only one node, one left branch, and one right branch, the function would go to the left branch, perform the operation, and then go to the right branch. Since the left- branch data is smaller than the right-branch data, this is an in- order traversal. Recursion is used to traverse all the branches of the tree.

Post-Order Traversal

To examine all the nodes of a tree beginning with the bottom elements, (from the bottom up to the root), you can use a postorder algorithm. Listing 12.26 shows how the algorithm is implemented.

Listing 12.26

Post-Order tree traversal

```
void search(node,n)
TREE *node;
itemtype n;
{
  if(p)
    {  search(node->left,n);
       search(node->right,n);
       if( n == node->n) return;    /*  found data   */
    }
  else printf(" item not found \n" );
}
```

End of Listing

This method of tree traversal is useful for creating a RPN calculator, deleting selected items from the tree, and other back-to-front methods.

Printing A Binary Tree

A tree is a handy structure for holding and searching for data that is sorted. Frequently, a program needs to print the contents of the tree. An in-order tree traversal does job in an efficient manner as Listing 12.27 shows.

Listing 12.27

Printing a Binary Tree

```
TREE *node;
node = root;

void print_tree(node)
TREE *node;
{
  if(node)
    {  print_tree(node->left);
       printf("%f \n",node->x);
       print_tree(node->right);
    }
}
```

Summary

Data structures are important in any programming language. In **C** they form the basis for most programs. You have looked at stacks, queues, circular queues, linked lists, stacks and queues as linked lists, double linked lists, and trees. Each has numerous applications.

Stacks can be represented as arrays or as linked lists. Simple applications use arrays; a sophisticated application, involving memory-allocation techniques might use a linked list.

Many modern applications, such as word processors and telecommunications packages, use queues; most use circular queues. A queue was represented as either an array or a linked list. Queues can grow in size when the application needs flexibility.

Stacks, queues, linked lists, and combinations of these data structures require a collection of functions. You have studied functions that initialize the structure, append items to the end, insert items, delete items, and search for items. You have also studied special cases, such as `push()` and `pop()` which are special cases of generic insert and delete functions. A a programmer you need to be able to adapt these functions to specific applications.

Binary trees provide special linked lists for representing sorted data. Items can be placed in the lists, removed from them searched for, and operated on in a more efficient manner than linear linked lists. The tree traversal methods preorder, inorder, and postorder are alternatives when you need to process all or part of the data in a tree. Tree-traversal methods are usually recursive. Iterative methods are harder to write and harder to understand.

EXERCISES

UNDERSTANDINGS

1. Define each of these terms:
   a. stack
   b. queue
   c. circular queue
2. Compare the advantages and disadvantages of implementing a stack as an array with implementing a stack as a linked list.
3. What is a tree node?
4. What makes a tree a binary tree?
5. Give a natural language description of the terms push and pop.
6. Why are keyboard buffers frequently implemented as circular queues?

USAGE

7. Explain the purpose and operation of the function `l_alloc()` as follows:

```
typedef struct node  {
          struct node *next;
          struct node *prev;
          int lineno;
          char *line;
          }  NODE;

NODE *l_alloc(n)
int n;
{
  NODE *new,*temp;

  new = (NODE *) malloc(n * sizeof(NODE));

  if(new != null)
  {  for(temp = new; 1+temp-new < n; temp = temp->next)
        temp->next = temp+1;
  temp->next = (NODE *)NILL;
  }

  return (new);
}
```

APPLICATIONS

8. Write a program that uses a stack to simulate a RPN calculator.

9. Write a program that uses a binary tree and postorder traversal to simulate a RPN calculator.

10. Create a binary tree consisting of peoples' names. Use the inorder traversal method to print the contents of the tree on the video screen.

11. Write a program that stores names and phone numbers as records or nodes of a tree. The tree is traversed so that the following works:

    ! clears the display and starts over. When a letter is pressed, the first name and phone number that begins with that letter is displayed. If return is pressed, the second name that begins with that letter is displayed. If a second letter is pressed, the first name that begins with these two letters is displayed, and so on. If no match, display the last item displayed.

12. Rewrite **`getmem()`** and **`relmem()`** as macros.

13. Create a series of functions that implements a queue as a single linked list.

14. Write a function that searches for a particular item that is a member of a double linked list.

15. Write a program that (1) creates a binary tree of items that are a part number plus a part name and are inorder by part number, (2) saves the tree on disk, (3) reads the tree from disk into memory, and, (4) prints the tree on the printer (PC) or print file (Unix).

16. Write a program to exam a source code file. Create a table of unique identifiers and a list of the line numbers at which they appear.

17. Write a program to parse a Pascal statement according to the following BNF rules. The program should use a tree to divide the statement into its constituent parts.

BNF rules (subset of entire Pascal Syntax)

```
     statement ::= unlabeled-stmt |
                   label:unlabeled-stmt
 unlabeled-stmt::= simple statement |
                   structured-stmt
   simple-stmt ::= assignment-stmt |
                   procedure-stmt |
                   goto-stmt
structured-stmt ::= compound-stmt |
                   conditional-stmt |
                   repetitive-stmt |
                   with-stmt
 compound-stmt ::= BEGIN statement {;statement} END
conditional-stmt ::= if-stmt | case-stmt
       if-stmt ::= IF expression THEN statement
                   IF expression THEN statement
                   ELSE statement
assignment-stmt ::= identifier := expression
    expression ::= simple exp |
                   simple exp relop simple exp
         relop ::= =|<>|< |<=|>= |> |IN
    simple exp ::= [+|-] term| simple exp addop term
         addop ::= +|-| OR
          term ::= factor | term mulop factor
         mulop ::= *| /| DIV |MOD |AND
        factor ::= identifier | number | (expression) |
                   function designator | set |
                   NOT factor
```

For example, a successful parse for the expression

`TAX := TAX + INC;` follows.

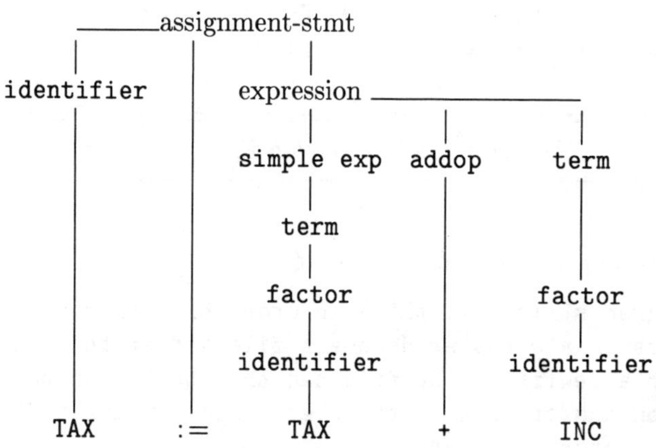

13

Filters, Sorts and Searching

A preponderance of programs are filters. The program receives input data, performs some modifications or transformations, and outputs the filtered data. This chapter illustrates the filtering concept with a practical example. The second topic, sorts, has already been mentioned several times in earlier chapters. The earlier examples of Shell sort, selection-and- exchange sort, Shell-Metzner sort, and quicksort are internal sorts. They sort data stored entirely in the computer's memory. This chapter presents external sorts such as the merge sort and also shows some complicated sorts that can be used with aggregate data types.

This chapter extends the concepts of internal searching to external data searching and to hashing techniques. The topics and concepts presented here add to the programmer's tools as the programming problems become more difficult.

In the microcomputer environment, word processor files are commonplace. One word processor, Wordstar, creates files that contain a number of control characters for such things as tabs, spaces, Returns, etc. When using Wordstar files for other things (such as input to compilers, or data for other programs). The control characters frequently impede successful use of the file. A utility to strip the file of these special control characters is shown in Listing 13.1.

Listing 13.1

Wordstar File Conversion Program

```
/*
    Authors = Tim Grady and Dave Hein

    This program strips all the high order bits from the
    characters in a wordstar document file and writes the
    result to a newfile.  The file can then be listed on
    the screen and/or transferred over a modem using a 7
    data bit protocol.
```

```
The program is executed by typing
  fcopy file1.doc file2.doc
where file1.doc is the original file and file2 is the
destination file.

*/

#include <stdio.h>
FILE *fp1,*fp2;
static char source[30],dest[30];

main(argc,argv)
int argc;
char *argv[];
{
int ch;          /*  The character read in and either */
                 /* filtered out or passed on.   */

/*  check to see if there are two parameters  */
if(argc < 3)
  {
    printf(" Two file names required.  \n\n");
    printf(" e.g.  fcopy oldfile.doc newfile.doc \n");
    exit();
    /*  program is terminated  */
    }

/*  copy filenames from command line into strings  */
strcpy(source,argv[1]);
strcpy(dest,argv[2]);

/*  open both files  */
if( (fp1 = fopen(source,"r")) == NULL)
  {
    printf("\n cannot open %s \n",source);
    exit();

    }
if( (fp2 = fopen(dest,"w")) == NULL)
  {
    printf("\n cannot open %s char92n",dest);
    exit();
    } /*  files are open  */
```

```
while ((ch=fgetc(fp1)) != EOF)
  {
    /*  shave off upper bit marking word end  */

    if (ch > 128) ch -= 128;
      /*  all ws chars >128 brought down  */
      /*  an alternative is to AND each character with  */
      /*   127 (1111111 base 2) */
      /*     ch &= 127; */
      /*  Another alternative is to see is the  */
      /* character an ascii value and if not */
      /*  then to AND it with 127.   */
/*  handle cases of phantom space and forced space  */
switch ( ch )
  {
  case 0x06 :             /*  phantom space => 0x20  */
  case 0x0F : ch = 0x20;/*  forced space => 0x20  */
              break;
  default :   break;
  }

/*  filter acceptable and unacceptable characters  */

/*some ok characters to pass:
  0x08 = backspace                   h
  0x09 = tab                         i
  0x0a = line feed                   j
  0x0c = form feed                   l
  0x0d = carriage return             m
*

/*  swallow other chars or transfer them to output file  */
if ( ch==0x01 ||          /*  a normal pitch  */
                          ch==0x02 || /*  b bold  */
                          ch==0x03 || /*  c print pause  */
                          ch==0x04 || /*  d double */
                          ch==0x05 || /*  e user defined  */
                          ch==0x07 || /*  g rubout  */
                          ch==0x0b || /*  k hdr /footer  */
                          ch==0x0e || /*  n alt pitch  */
                          ch==0x10 || /*  p not used  */
ch==0x11 ||               /*  q user defined  */
                          ch==0x12 || /*  r user defined  */
                          ch==0x13 || /*  s underline  */
                          ch==0x14 || /*  t re-strike  */
                          ch==0x15 || /*  u not used  */
                          ch==0x16 || /*  v subscripts  */
```

```
    ch==0x17 || /*  w user defined   */
    ch==0x18 || /*  x strike-out   */
    ch==0x19 || /*  y ribbon color   */
    ch==0x1a )  /*  z not used   */
    {;          /*  do nothing with these   */
    }
  else
    fputc(ch,fp2)/*  write to output file   */
  } /*  close both files   */
fclose(fp1);
fclose(fp2);
}   /*  end of main   */
```

End of Listing

This Wordstar file-conversion utility contains examples of key programming ideas. The program checks to see if the correct number of command line arguments have been passed to the program. It provides error checking when opening the files. The exact characters to be filtered are documented with comments, and the logic of the program is documented internally. The difference between this and any other filtering program is simply which characters are to be deleted or changed.

Another program of this type might add carriage returns to a printer file when a printer requires them. Others include utilities that transfer files between Unix machines and MS-DOS machines, and either add or remove a CR to each line. They also change the **EOF** marker to that which is appropriate for the target machine. Some programs translate data files created by one application so that they may be used by a different application. Filter programs are common and should be part of a programmer's toolbox.

Sorting

Computer sorting techniques are important to many applications. Some of the simple sorts, (for example, selection-and-exchange, insertion, Shell, and quick) work well with internally stored data. External sorts are used when the data files are too big to fit in memory. These routines bring portions of the data into internal memory, make the necessary comparisons, and then write the results back out to the external files. The actions that follow review some of the ideas from earlier chapters, embellish the internal sorting techniques, and look at some external sorting techniques.

Internal Sorting

The sort process always involves three important aspects. The first is the nature of the data to be sorted. Second, the comparison routine must be applicable to the data structure under consideration. Finally, the swap, or exchange, routine must also be compatible with the data structure. If you adopt a basic method of internal sorting such as the quicksort, then the three factors that dominate programming considerations are data type, comparison function, and swap function.

When the data type is simple, (**int**, **char**, **float**, or some modification of these), and the data elements are stored in an array, the problems are simple. It is helpful to review how the quicksort applies to sorting an array of integers. Look again at listing 6.21 to review how it works. works.

The quicksort is generally regarded as a very fast internal sort. The data type in Listing 6.21 is an array of integers (line 1). The comparison is a straight comparison of data elements identified by their respective subscripts (line 2) and the swap is executed in place (line 3) rather than in an expensive function call. This is the simplest possible sorting situation. To use an array of different data objects, as long as they are a simple data type you need only to modify line 1. However, if the data type becomes complex, then the comparison and swap routines must also change.

Sorting an Array of Strings: Sorting a complex data type requires similar logic, yet it is different in the three ways mentioned earlier. Clearly, the data array can be declared as **char** `*x[N]`; which is an array of N strings. Consequently, the comparison steps must change to employ the **strcmp**() function from the **C** library. Recall that the **strcmp** function returns −1,0,or 1 depending on the lexical order of the two strings being compared. For example:

```
if(strcmp(s1,s1) <= 0) /*  action  */
```

Finally, the swap routine must move the entire string by using the **strcpy**() function.

```
strcpy(dest,source);
```

And, of course, since **strcpy**() does not provide any error checking, the dest string must be large enough to hold the source string. This can result in a terrible mess if a larger string is copied into a place where a shorter string had been. Any contiguous string might be overrun. The solution is to create a second array of pointers to the strings and then to sort the pointers while leaving the strings alone.

Sorting via an Array of Pointers: An effective step toward generalizing a sort and speeding up the swap routine whenever a complicated data structure is being used is to create a corresponding array of pointers. Then the pointers are swapped, not the actual data structures. Prior to the sort you need to create and fill the array of pointers.

```
char *strgptrs[N];    /*  array of pointers to strings  */
...
for(i=0;i<N;i++)
  strgptrs[i] = &x[i];
```

Now the function can be modified to eliminate the string copy, or **strcpy**(), function calls. Instead, the pointers are reversed.

```
char *t;
...
t=strgptrs[i];strgptrs[i]=strgptrs[j];strgptrs[j]=t;
...
t=strgptrs[left];strgptrs[left]=strgptrs[j];strgptrs[j]=t;
```

The comparison routine must be modified to use the array of pointers rather than the strings.

```
      while(strcmp(strgptrs[i],pivot) <= 0 && i < right)) i++;
      while(strcmp(strgptrs[j],pivot) >= 0 && j>left) j--;
```

These changes can be put into a quicksort for strings, as shown in Listing 13.2.

Listing 13.2

Quicksort of Array of Strings

```
quick(x,left,right)
char *x[];
int left,right;
{
  char t[81],pivot[81];
  int i,j;
  if(right > left)
   { strcpy(pivot,x[left]);
     i = left + 1;
     j = right;
     do
     {
      while(strcmp(strgptrs[i],pivot) <= 0 && i < right) i++;
      while(strcmp(strgptrs[j],pivot) >= 0 && j>left) j--;
      if(i<j)
        {
          t=strgptrs[i];strgptrs[i]=strg[trs[j];strgptrs[j]=t;
        i++;j--;
        }
     }while( i < j);  /*  end of do-while  */
      t=strgptrs[left];
      strgptrs[left]=strgptrs[j];
      strgptrs[j]=t;
     }
   if( j > left + 1) quick(x,left,j-1);
   if(j < right - 1) quick(x,j+1,right);
return;
}
```

End of Listing

The logic of this quicksort is the same as that of the original quicksort function. The differences are the declaration of the data type, the comparisons, and the swap techniques.

The swap routine is always a source of concern in sort functions. When the data object is simple, that is, where it is integral or real, the swap can be just like the swap that follows. However, it is generally considered good practice to put the swap in a separate function.

```
void swap_cp(x,y)
char *x,*y;
{
  char *t;
  t = x;
  x = y;
  y = t;
}
```

Similar functions can be written for other data types, such as **float**. A sort for different data types can be written by calling the correct swap routine.

The comparison routines can also be written as separate functions. When the data type is simple, the comparison function is written in terms of the pointers. For example, when sorting integers by using an array of pointers, the comparison function can be

```
int int_comp(x,y)
int *x,*y;
{
  return(*x - *y);
}
```

Like the string compare routine, this one returns a negative, 0, or positive value, depending on the order of the two values being compared. Similar functions can be written for other simple data types.

Generalized Versions of the Quick sort: The logic of the quicksort is fixed. The routine changes when the the data type being sorted changes. One way to deal with this is to call the sort by passing pointers to the appropriate data types and the appropriate swap and comparison routines. For example, the declaration

```
static void (*swap)();
```

means that you are declaring a pointer to a function that returns nothing. A similar declaration for the comparison function can be

```
static int (*compare)();
```

which is a pointer to a function that returns an **int**.

There are two ways to handle the problem. One is to initialize the pointers outside the function call and then call the function as before.

```
compare = comp1;
```

In this case `comp1` is an external function which is appropriate because the data being sorted and compared is a **static** variable. The second way is to pass the compare function to the sort function as a pointer.

```
quick( datapointer, first, last, comp_function pointer);
```

Suppose the data are floats in the array `x` and the compare function is called `comp()`. The function call could be

```
void quick(x,first, last, comp)
float *x[];
int first,last;
int (*comp)();
{

  /*  the comp function can be used  */
  if( (*comp) (*x[i],*x[j]) <= 0)  /*  action  */
```

The comparison function must have previously been declared and the pointer initialized.

```
external float int_comp();  /* declare an external
                               function to compare
                               floats.
                               Note:  this might be
                               encapsulated in a
                               header file */

int (*comp)();              /* declare pointer to
                               comparison function */

comp = int_comp;            /* initialize pointer */
```

Now the pointer can be passed to a function as shown earlier.

The swap function problem can be handled in a similar fashion.

```
external float_swap();

void (*swap)();   /*  declare a pointer to a function  */

swap = float_swap;/*  initialize the pointer  */
```

You can write a generalized quicksort that assumes that pointers to the data are being passed to the routine and that pointers to the crucial functions, `compare()` and `swap()`, are also passed.

```
void quick(a,l,r,comp,swap)
char *a[];
int l,r;
int (*comp)();
void (*swap)();
{
```

The array a is an array of pointers to characters. This will usually suffice even if the data to be sorted are not characters; the pointers are what will be sorted. The comparison and swap functions must, of course, be initialized before the function is called. The complete function is shown in Listing 13.3.

Listing 13.3

Generalized quicksort function

```
void quick(a,l,r,comp,swap)
char *a[];
int l,r;
int (*comp)();
void (*swap)();
{
  int i,j;
  char *pivot;

  if(r > l)
  {  pivot = a[l];
     i = l + 1;
     j = r;
     do
     {
       while((*comp)(a[i],pivot) <= 0 && i < r)) i++;
       while((*comp)(a[j],pivot) >= 0 && j>l) j--;
       if(i<j)
         (*swap)(a[i],a[j]);
     }
     while( i < j);
       (*swap)(a[l],a[j]);
  }

  if( j > l + 1) quick(x,l,j-1,comp,swap);
  if(j < r - 1) quick(x,j+1,r,comp,swap);
return;
}
```

End of Listing

Unix systems usually contain a quicksort function called **qsort**(). It is called by the command:

```
qsort(a,na,width,comp)
```

where

```
char a[];
int na;
int width; q/*  size of an element in bytes  */
int comp;   /*  compare function  */
```

When a system provides such a function, there is, of course, no reason to roll your own.

Sorting Pointers to Structures: Many if not most advanced applications use structures as their principal data type. However, sorting structures involves moving entire structures when the data items are to be swapped as is usually done in sort programs. A better technique than sorting the actual structures is creating an array of pointers to the structures and then swapping the pointers, not the structures. This technique is much like the technique of sorting an array of strings. The difference is that a structure contains a key field. The comparison and swap routines, as always, are different.

Consider a structure and an array of those structures.

```
struct item
  {  char name[20];
     char info[15];
     int id;
  };

struct item x[N];
```

An array of pointers acts as an index to the array.

```
struct item *sp[N];
```

You need the two familiar functions `compare()` and `swap()`. The `compare()` function needs a key field. In this case assume the id field is the key.

```
int s_comp(sp1,sp2)
struct item *sp1,*sp2;
{
  return( (sp1->id > sp2->id ?  1 :  -1) );
}
```

The `swap()` function is

```
void s_swap(sp1,sp2)
struct item *sp1,*sp2;
{
  struct item *t;
  t = sp1;
  sp1 = sp2;
  sp2 = t;
}
```

The comparison function is for integers. If the key field is not an integer, then a different comparison is needed. If, for example, the key is `name`, then the heart of the function is be

```
return( strcmp(sp1->name,sp2->name) );
```

As with the general case for the quicksort, a collection of compare functions should be written and a pointer to the right one used in the sort program.

The use of a key complicates matters. The comparison function can be generalized by passing a pointer to the key in the call to the compare function.

```
int s_comp(sp1,sp2,key)
struct item *sp1,*sp2;
char *key;
{
  return( strcmp(sp1->*key,sp2->*key) );
}
```

The key is treated as a string because virtually any field can be compared for lexical order. The user must, of course, initialize the key pointer before calling the function. Some programmers use **strncmp**() instead of **strcmp**() and assign a fairly small value to n. This speeds the comparison when the key field is large.

The final problem is sorting multiple keys. Knowing the number of keys and their order is important. Multikey sorts, or radix sorts, are performed in the reverse order of their precedence. The keys can be stored in an array and the sort performed repeatedly in a loop.

```
char *sortkeys[];
nk = 3;    /*  the number of keys can be  */
           /* determined in a variety of ways  */

for(i = 0;i <nk;i++)    /*  load up key array  */
  { printf("Type the %d the key name \n");
    gets(sortkeys[i];
  }

for(i = nk-1; i > 0; --i)    /*  loop nk times  */
  { key = sortkeys[i];    /*  choose key  */
    switch key
      { /* choose the proper compare and
           swap pointers depending on the
           data type of the key */
      }
    sort(x,left,right,comp,swap);   /*  call sort  */
}
```

Completing the program to sort structures is a matter of completing the structure equivalents to the data declarations and applying the generalized quicksort algorithm. It is left as an exercise.

External Sorting

When the data to be sorted do not fit in memory, then an external sort is employed. These programs bring only portions of the data into the computer's memory during the comparison and swap portions. Two different external sorts are presented here. The first, a merge sort, works well with sequential files. The second, a file version of quicksort, works well with random- access files.

Merge Sort: One of the most common external sorts is the merge sort. It is fairly easy to implement and debug. To create a merge sort, place the items into one of two other files, depending on the items relative order. Assuming that you want to place the items in ascending order, you place any item that is less than the previous item in temporary file 1. If the item is greater than the previous item, it is placed in temporary file 2. The two files are then merged back together by comparing the two leftmost (or least ordered) items in the two lists. The smaller of the two is placed in the original file. A pointer is advanced in the file from which the item was copied, so that two more items can be compared. This process is repeated until the original file is reassembled in an ordered form. The entire process is repeated until all the original items are placed into one temporary file. The original file is then in order. Figure 13.1 illustrates this algorithm.

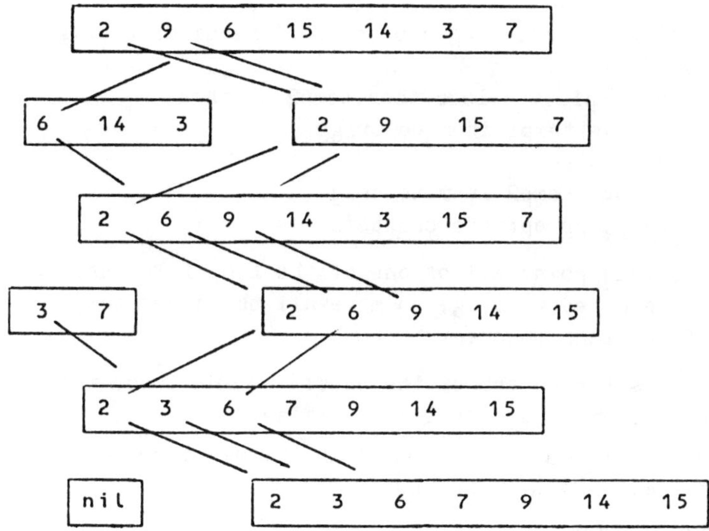

Figure 13.1: *Merge Sort*

The algorithm can also be illustrated with psuedocode. Consider the following definitions:

int `i` is the counter for original file.
`j` and `k` are counters for temporary files.
`l` and `m` are the lengths of the temporary files.

files **`orig,temp1,temp2`**

The psuedocode that represents a merge sort is

```
while not done    /*  done is established when temp file 1 */
                  /* is empty after phase 1  */

set counter of temp1 to 0 and of temp2 to 1
assign first item from orig file to be first item of temp2
loop from 2nd item in orig file to last item
  if current item > prev item then assign it to temp2
  otherwise assign it to temp1
  increment appropriate counter in temp1 or temp2

assign l and m the lengths of temp1 and temp2
assign done = true if temp1 is empty

if not done, then begin process of rebuilding orig file
  while j <= l or k <= m
    if temp1.j is less then temp2.k, then
      move temp1 item to orig
    otherwise,
      move temp2 item to orig
    bump appropriate counters

  at this point all of one of the temp files has
  been moved to orig, so move all the other temp
  file items to orig.

this is the bottom of the outside while loop, which is
repeated if the done flag is false.
```

Consider a case of a file that consists of records. These records consist of a name, an id code, and a dollar amount.

sample record

```
M. Tim Grady\0 2456 65.29\n
```

The newline character delimits the record. The first element of the item is a string, the second is a 4-digit integer code, and the third is a 5-digit floating-point number. A file consists of a collection of these records. Each record can be read by using the **fscanf**() function.

```
fscanf("%s%5d%5.2f",name,&n,&x);
```

A record can be defined as a structure. For example:

```
typedef struct  {
  char *name;
  int code;
  float cost;
} RECORD;
```

Now the program can use pointers to data items of type RECORD.

The program to perform a merge sort on a file of this type is shown in Listing 13.4.

Listing 13.4

Merge Sort

```
#include <stdio.h>

FILE *original,*t1,*t2;

typedef boolean char;
boolean done = 0;
typedef struct   {
          char *name;
          int code;
          float cost;
  } RECORD;
RECORD *x,*y,*z,*prev;

main()
{
  int i,j,k,;            /* record counters */

  while(!done)           /* main loop of program */
    {
      k=1;j=0;            /* t2 will have at least 1 item */

      /* open original file */
      if( (original = fopen("testdata","r")) == NULL)
        { printf("Cannot open data file.\n");
          exit();
        }

      /* open both temp files */
      if( (t1 = fopen("temp1","w")) == NULL)
        { printf("Cannot open work file no. 1 \n");
        exit();
      }
      if( (t2 = fopen("temp2","w")) == NULL)
        { printf("Cannot open work file no. 2 \n");
        exit();
      }
```

```
 /*  now all three files are open  */
read_rec(original,prev);   /*  get first item  */
write_rec(t2,prev);        /*  put first rec in t2  */
comment loop thru the rest of the file
while( (read_rec(original,x)) != EOF)
  {
    if( x->code <= prev->code )
      {  write_rec(t1,x);
         j++;
      }

    else
      {  write_rec(t2,x);
         k++;
      }
    prev = x;
  } /*  end of while read_rec loop  */

fclose(original); fclose(t1); fclose(t2);

if(j == 0) done = 1;
  /*  if no items in t1, then done is true  */

if(!done)
{
/*  this section reassembles the two lists  */

/*  open all three files  */
if( (t1 = fopen("temp1","r")) == NULL)
  { printf("Cannot open work file no.  1 \n");
    exit();
  }
if( (t2 = fopen("temp2","r")) == NULL)
  { printf("Cannot open work file no.  2 \n");
  exit();
}
if( (original = fopen("testdata","w")) == NULL)
  { printf("Cannot open data file.\n");
    exit();
  }

  read_rec(t1,y);
  read_rec(t2,z);
```

```
      while(j &&k)  /*  wkile one file has elements  */
        {
          if( y->code < z->code)
            {
              write_rec(original,y);
              j--;
              if(j) read_rec(t1,y);
            }
          else
            {
              write_rec(original,z);
              k--;
              if(k) read_rec(t2,z);
            }
        } /*  end of while j &&k loop  */
      while(j)  /*  first temp file unexhausted  */
        {
          read_rec(t1,y);
          write_rec(original,y);
          j--;
        }
      while(k)   /*  second temp file unexhausted  */
        {
          read_rec(t21,z);
          write_rec(original,z);
          k--;
        }
      fclose(original);fclose(t1);fclose(t2);
    }   /*  end of if not done section  */
}   /*  end of main while loop  */
/*  function to read one record from one file  */
int read_rec(fp,x)
FILE *fp;
RECORD *x;
  {
    return( fscanf(fp,"%s%5d%5.2f",
        x->name,&(x->code),&(x->cost)));
  }
```

```
/*  function to write one record to a file  */
int write_rec(fp,x);
FILE *fp;
RECORD *x;
  {
    return( fprintf(fp,"%s%5d%5.2f",
        x->name,x->code,x->cost));
  }
```

End of Listing

Sorting A Random Access File: The merge sort works well for sequential files. Each element (or record) of the file is compared to the adjacent element. When the file is a random- access file you are free to jump around in the file by using record numbers. In concepts the file is like an external array, as Figure 13.2 shows.

record number	file (array)
0	record data
2	record data
3	record data
4	record data
5	record data
.	
.	
.	
n	record data

Figure 13.2: *File as an Array*

The included elements are accessed via a pointer. Recall that some of the principles of working with random access files were discussed in Chapter 10. Because individual members are accessed directly and modified in place, the disk does not need to have room for a copy of the argument file nor does it need to have room for temporary files.

Thinking of the disk file as an array means that you can use the familiar internal sorts, but with modifications. Recall that the quicksort was called by

```
quick( A, l,r);
```

where `A` is the array and `l` and `r` are left and right indices of the array. Assuming that `fp` points to a file, then `disk_qs()` may be called by writing

```
disk_qs(fp,lrec,rrec);
```

In the preceding statement, `fp` is the file pointer, `lrec` is the left record and `rrec` is the right record. Clearly, the terms left and right in this context refer to conceptual, not physical, arrangements. The record names maintain a logical relationship to the quicksort of an array and the quicksort of a file.

To use a quicksort on a file, you must know how many records are in the file. If you know the numbers, simply declare numrecs in the file. You can also store the number in a special record (usually 0) in the file. If you do not know the number of records, you can calculate the number dynamically by the means in Listing 10.12. To perform the calculation, you must establish the initial values of `rrec`.

```
/*  assume record is defined as follows  */
struct item   {
  char name[20];
  int age;
  }record;
```

You also need a routine to position the file record pointer at the correct spot in the file. The **fseek**() routine serves this purpose. As Listing 13.5 shows, **fseek**() is wrapped in a `locate()` function.

Listing 13.5

Function to Locate ith record in random file: option 1

```
int locate(fp,i)
FILE fp;
long i;
{
  return (fseek(fp,(long)((i-1) * sizeof(record)),0));
}
          /*  record is a structure defined elsewhere  */
          /*  returns position or -1 if error exists  */
```

End of Listing

An alternative to this function is to pass the length or size of the record or structure to the function. This avoids the requirement that the variable name record exist in the calling program. Listing 13.6 shows this version.

Listing 13.6

Function to Locate ith record in random file: option 2

```
int locate(fp,i,rl)
FILE fp;
long i,rl;          /*  i is the record number */
                    /* rl is the record length  */
{
  return (fseek(fp,(long)((i-1) * rl),0));
}
          /*  returns position or -1 if error exists  */
```

End of Listing

Once positioned at a record you must supply a read it. Listing 13.7 shows a function that reads.

Listing 13.7

Function to Read a Record in Random File

```
int read_rec(fp,r)
FILE *fp;
struct record *r;          /*  r is pointer to structure  */
                           /* that is read  */
{
  return( fread(r,i,sizeof(record), fp) );
}
          /*  return 0 if an error occurs  */
```

End of Listing

Other quicksort support routines still needed are a routine to swap two records, a routine to compare key fields of two records, and a function to write a record. The swap routine is shown in listing 13.8.

Listing 13.8

Function to Swap Two records

```
swap_rec(fp,i,j)
FILE *fp;
long int i,j;
{
  struct record rec1,rec2;
  locate(fp,i);          /*  go to record i  */
  read_rec(fp,rec1);     /*  and read it  */
  locate(fp,j);          /*  go to jth record  */
  read_rec(fp,rec2);     /*  and read it  */
  write_rec(fp,rec1);    /*  replace i with j  */
  locate(fp,i);          /*  go to ith position  */
  write_rec(fp,rec2);    /*  write j in ith place  */
}
```

End of Listing

The swap function uses the two previous functions, `locate()` and `read_rec()`. It also contains a `write_rec()` function which is a complementary function to `read_rec()`. It is shown in Listing 13.9.

Listing 13.9

Function to write a single record

```
int write_rec(fp,i)
FILE *fp;
struct record *r;
{
  return( fwrite(r,1,sizeof(record),fp) );
}
  /*  return 0 if an error occurs  */
```

End of Listing

The function that compares two records (key fields) involves reading each record into a structure and then comparing the correct elements or members. If the key field is treated as a string, then the comparison is a simple call to the function **strcmp**(). Even if the **struct** member is not a string, this method eliminates the need to know the data type of the member. Of course, you could call an appropriate compare function based on the data type.

The pseudocode for the function that compares two records is:

use **sizeof** to find the number of bytes in key field

read member of record1 into s1

read member of record2 into s2

compare s1 and s2 using **strncmp**()

All these functions can be assembled into one program to sort a file. The implementation of the algorithm to sort a random-access disk file is shown in Listing 13.10.

Listing 13.10

Sorting Random Access Disk File

```
FILE *fp;
struct item  {
  /*  define the structure here  */
};
char sortfile[]="filename";
main()
{
  long int j;
  fp = fopen(sortfile,"r+");  /*  needs error check  */
  j = get_nrecs(fp) - 1;      /*  find number of records  */
  disk_qs(fp,(long)1,j,key);
  fclose)fp);
}
```

End of Listing

Listing 13.10 is deceptively simple. It calls a function `disk_qs()`, which in turn calls other functions as discussed earlier. Note the use of the `"r+"` option which is a way of opening an existing file for both reading and writing without erasing the existing file.

The quicksort routine, `disk_qs()`, sorts records in a disk file instead of elements in an array. Conceptually, the two sorts are identical. The code for the disk version is shown in Listing 13.11.

Listing 13.11

Quicksort Function for Disk Files

```
quick(fp,first_rec,last_rec,key)
FILE *fp;
long int first_rec,last_rec;
char *key;
{
  long int i,j;
  struct item *read_rec();
  char *pivot;
    if(last_rec > first_rec)
    {
      locate(fp,first_rec);
      pivot = read_rec(fp)->key;
      i = first_rec + 1;
      j = last_rec;
      do
      {
        locate(fp,i);
        while(strcmp((read_rec(fp)->key),pivot) <=0
                     && i < last_rec)
          locate(++i);

        locate(fp,j);
        while(strcmp((read_rec(fp)->key),pivot) >=0
                     &&j > first_rec)
          locate(--j);
        if(i<j) swap_rec(fp,i,j);
      }
      while( i < j);
      swap_rec(fp,first_rec,j);
  }

  if( j > first_rec+1 + 1)
    disk_qs(fp,first_rec,j-1,key);
  if(j < last_rec - 1)
    disk_qs(fp,j+1,last_rec,key);
return;
}
```

End of Listing

The calling sequence includes the file pointer, the number of the first and last record, and the key field. Prior to calling this function, you must determine the number of records in the file and what field is to be sorted. The comparison is performed by using a string compare function. Since the data type for any given field is not known in advance (at least in this general version), a string comparison is the best choice.

Searching

Retrieving data from some collection of data structures (searching) is important. This section focuses on three general types: sequential, binary, and hashing. The computer science literature abounds with studies of these and other search techniques. The purpose here is not to present an exhaustive review of all possible search techniques, but to illustrate how the main techniques can be implemented in **C**.

Sequential Searching

A search that looks through a list from the top to the bottom while checking each item for a match is a sequential, or linear, search. In search jargon the item to be matched is called a key. Given an array of size N, the search begins at array index 0 and ends either when a match is found or the end of the array is reached. A function to implement this technique is shown in Listing 13.12.

Listing 13.12

Sequential Search of an Array

```
int s_search(x,n,key)
int *x[];           /*  array to search  */
int n;              /*  size of the array  */
int key;            /*  the key to look for  */
{
                    int i;
                    for(i=0; t<n; ++i)
                      if(key == item[i])
                        return i;
                    return -1;  /*  return an invalid array */
                                /* index if no match found  */
}
```

End of Listing

This function is simple enough. It assumes an array of integers and a known array size. Another method is to place a flag as the last entry so that the array size does not have to be known in advance or passed to the function. A more general but slower version treats all integral data as character strings and compares them via **strcmp**().

Searching for a key in structures is similar, but it involves a more sophisticated data type definition as well as another method of indexing the array. The array of simple data types shown in Listing 13.12 has an index, the array subscript. When the data type is **struct**, an array of structures can be used. Since structures in non-ANSI **C** cannot be passed as function arguments, create an array of pointers to the structures rather than an array of structures.

memory	sp[]
struct item(1)	sp[0] points to item 1
struct item(2)	sp[1] points to item 2
struct item(3)	sp[2] points to item 3
struct item(4)	sp[3] points to item 4
struct item(5)	sp[4] points to item 5
struct item(6)	sp[5] points to item 6
struct item(7)	sp[6] points to item 7
struct item(8)	sp[7] points to item 8
...	
struct item(n)	sp[n-1] points to item n

The calling program must have defined the structures, created the memory space for each one, and loaded the array with the addresses of each. Assume the structure contains a key field called **zip**. Its value is 37043.

```
typedef struct item
        { ...
          int zip;
          ...
        }ITEM;
```

The array of pointers is

```
ITEM *x[];
```

The program then allocates the memory for the structure, places the pointer to the structure into the array, and fills the structure.

```
n = 0;          /*  initialize the number of structures  */
size = sizeof(ITEM);

x[n] = malloc(size);  /* allocate space for an item
                    and place the address in array
                    of pointers */
/*  code to fill up structure elements  */
/* e.g.,
     scanf("%d",x[n]->zip );
 */
n++;    /*  bump array counter  */
```

Once the structures exist and the array of pointers to them exists, you can perform a typical sequential search such as the search shown in Listing 13.13.

Listing 13.13

Sequential Search of an Array of Pointers

```
int s_search(x,n,key)
ITEM *x[];          /*  array of pointers to structures  */
int n;              /*  size of the array  */
int key;            /*  the key to look for  */
{
  int i;
  for(i=0; t<n; ++i)
    if(key == x[i]->zip)
      return i;
  return -1;    /* return an invalid array
                   index if no match found */
}
```

End of Listing

To understand how to search files in a sequential manner is simply extend the ideas you have already learned. Provisions need to be made to read the records and compare one field to the key. The **EOF** serves to limit the search instead of an end-of- array condition.

Sequential search methods, although simple in concept and easy to code, are slow if there are very many data points. When n is small, a sequential search may be the appropriate technique. When n is large, a faster method is needed.

Indexed Sequential Search

Even the simple array search uses an index, albeit the array subscript. If you can start the search by using an index that puts you in the neighborhood, however, the time needed to find a key in the list is reduced. Just s you use the tabs in your address book to speed your search for an address, the index helps the program get closer to the item you want. Once in the neighborhood, the search can proceed in a sequential manner. Clearly, the data must be in sorted form. Figure 13.3 helps explain this idea.

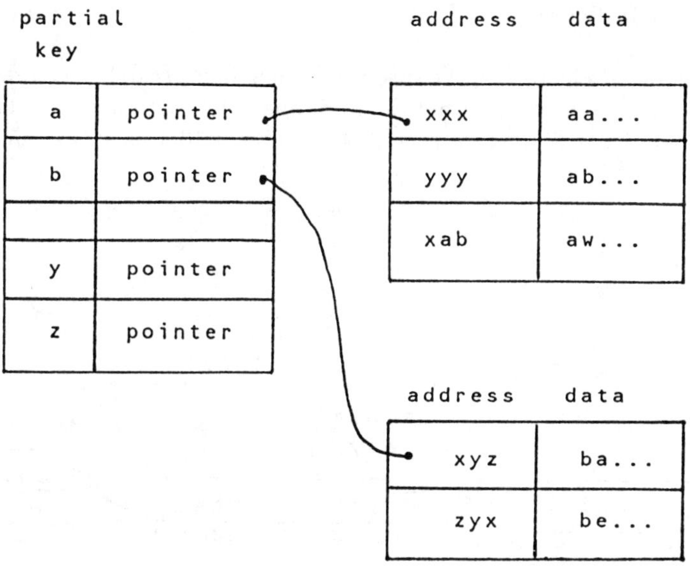

Figure 13.3: *Indexed Sequential Search*

The index contains a partial key in this case, one letter of the alphabet, and a pointer to the starting point of values that begin with this letter. It should also contain some information about the ending point of this section of the data. One way to define the index is

```
char *index[26];
```

The index as shown in Figure 13.3 is two dimensional. The index as declared in the preceding code has one dimension, that is, it is an array of pointers. The array subscripts (A...Z) can be mapped to the numbers 0—25 with the macro

```
#define ix(ch) ((ch) - 65);
```

or with some other simple way of converting the letter to an integer in the range 0—25. Then the value stored in the array can be referenced with the pointer expression

```
*index[ix(ch)]
```

Although this technique provides a simple solution to indexing alphabetically stored data, it does not contain a way to know where the section being pointed to ends. One solution is to calculate the number of items in one section by subtracting the pointers. Another is to use the pointer in the next position in the index as an end-of-section marker.

An alternate way to conduct a sequential search is with a linked list. This can be done as a straight search or as the second step in an indexed search.

Multilevel Indices

As the amount of data increases, the speed of a single-index search decreases because each section of data is searched from the beginning. A way to improve efficiency is to provide an additional index for each section. Figure 13.4 illustrates this idea.

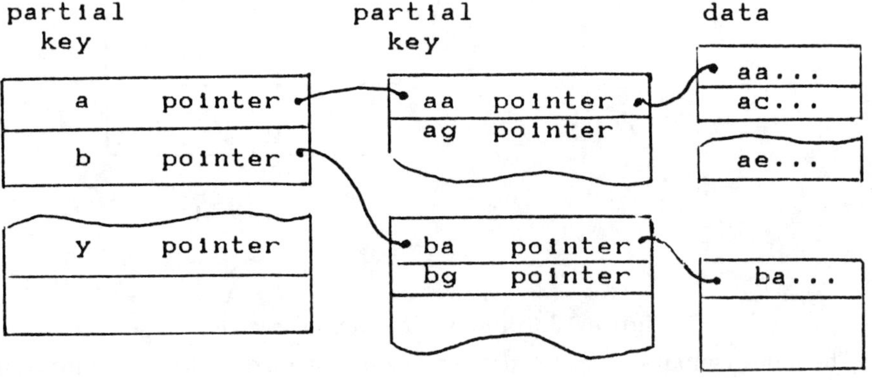

Figure 13.4: *Multi-level Indices*

The primary index is an array much like the index mentioned previously. The difference is that the pointers refer to another index. The secondary index is an array that contains another partial key and another pointer. Because the secondary index has as its elements two different data types, it is an array of structures. The actual data are stored as before.

Assuming that the data exist or are to be read into memory from some source, the data structures can be declared as

```
char *item[];          /*  data are an array of strings  */

typedef struct
  {
    char *skey;        /*  secondary key  */
    char *value;       /*  pointer to a data item  */
  } SEC_INDEX[4];      /*  array of these structures  */

SEC_INDEX *sec_index[26];

SEC_INDEX **pri_index[26]  /* an array of 26 pointers
                           to pointers which
                           are the sec_indices. */
```

This method also assumes that the data are in sorted order.

The indices must now be created. To do so, place the address of the first occurrence of AA or an A_ combination less than AG in the first member of the first secondary index.

```
sec_index[0]->SEC_INDEX[0].value = item[i];
```

The data value stored in item[i] must be located somehow. That part of the index-creation program left to you.

The other elements of the secondary index must also be created. For example, the secondary index that points to the first item greater than or equal to CG and less than CM is initialized as

```
sec_index[2]->SEC_INDEX[1].value = item[i];
```

where i is calculated by the program.

The primary index is created at the same time the first element of the secondary index is determined.

```
sec_index[0]->SEC_INDEX[0].value = item[i];
pri_index[0] = sec_index;
```

A search that uses multi-level keys first looks at the primary key to find the proper secondary index. The secondary index is searched for the secondary key, which is then used to locate the area of the data in which the key is to be found should it be there at all. Some of the same code used in single- level indexing can be used here.

```
#define ix(ch) ((ch) - 65);
...
sec_index = *pri_index[ix(ch)];
```

New code can be used to find the place where the search begins.

```
/*  find which of the 4 pointers to use  */
item = NULL;            /*  default value  */
for( i=0; i<4; i++)
  if(strncmp(key,sec_index->SEC_INDEX[i].skey,2) <= 0)
    item = sec_index->SEC_INDEX[i].value;
/*  if item is not equal to NULL, search can continue  */
/*  assume a pointer is also used to determine when to */
/* call off the search */
SEC_INDEX *lastp;

lastp = (*pri_index[ix(ch+1)])->SEC_INDEX[0].value;
```

The last code segment can be avoided if the secondary index structure, SEC_INDEX, is modified to include a field that points to the last data value in the data set. Once the starting and ending points in the data are determined, the search can be conducted in a normal sequential manner.

Binary Search

This procedure is a divide-and-conquer method applicable to sorted data items. The data can be in an array or a file. When the data are structures, a key field is used. The primary limitation of this algorithm is that the data must be in sorted order. Listing 13.14 incorporates the binary search algorithm.

Listing 13.14

binary search of an array

```
/*  N is number of array elements  */
/*  in x[N] and the array must contain a sorted list  */

int bin_ser(x,key)
int x[N];
int key;
{
  int left, right, mid, i;

  left = 0;
  right = N+1;

  while( right != left +1)
    {
      mid = (left + right)/2;
      if( x[mid] <= key)
        left = mid;
      else
        right = mid;
    }

  if( x[left] == key) return( left);
  else return(-1);    /*  not found  */
}
```

The binary search initially divides the array into two parts. If the key is in the left half, then the search area is limited to the left half; it is not, the right half is searched. The process is repeated until the partition is too small to search. At that point the leftmost element is the key or the key is not present in the list.

When applied to the list below where the key is 12 the search is as illustrated.

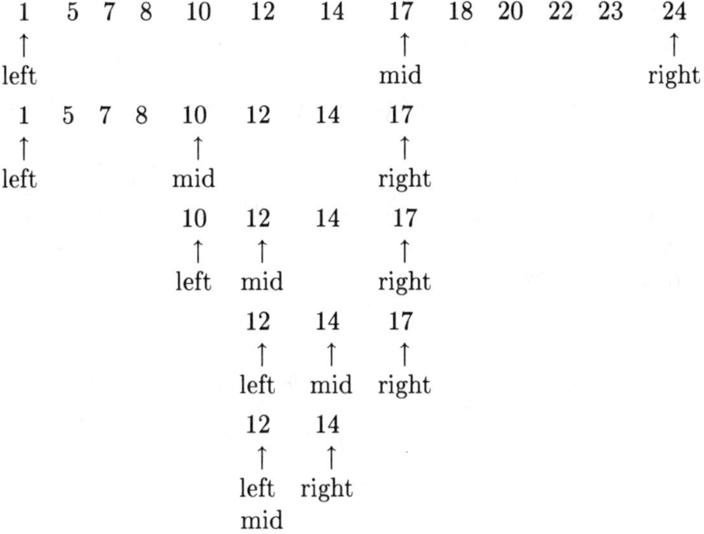

Hence `key` is found and is equal to `left`.

Search algorithms that include a sequence of comparisons can be time consuming. Is there a technique that does not depend on a series of comparisons? The next section shows that the answer is yes.

Hashing Functions

The goal of hashing is to speed up the search algorithm even when the data are not sorted. To do this you need a better index.

The simplest array has an index, even if it is only, the array subscript. A hashing (or hash) function is a sophisticated index that locates a key in a table. The table may be a simple array. but most of the time it is an embellished array. The table subscript or entry point, is calculated from the data itself. A function that generates a table index from the data value is called a hashing function.

The table is conceptually like an array, yet each entry can be a structure or the first entry in a chain of entries. The results of a hash function may also be a pointer to a memory address at which the structure is located. The hash function operates on the key value and generates a value between 0 and some upper bound. This value is then used as the address (for example, the array index or memory address) to locate a data value.

Suppose you want to store 100 integers, each with four digits. You need only 100 places to store the data. There is no need to reserve 10,000 memory locations because the largest 4- digit integer is 9999. In practice you usually reserve 125 percent of the expected storage locations. What you need is a mapping between the 4-digit numbers and the 125 memory locations. There are several possibilities, but one often selected is the method that takes the number modulo 125. In the general sense the array index is found by taking the key modulo arraysize. The hash function is really quite simple:

```
int i_hash(key)
int key;                    /*  value to search for  */
{
  return(key % 125 );     /*  a number between 0--124 */
}
```

For reasons that are beyond the scope of this book, the upper bound of this type of function should be a prime number. If it is 127, the calling program contains these statements:

```
#define SIZE 127

int x[SIZE];
```

Thus, x is an array that holds 127 possible values. Look at a few possible entries:

number (key)	array index = key%127
53	53
129	2
1187	44
964	75
5581	120

The hashing function creates an array index so that a sample of the array looks like this:

x

index	value
0	-
1	-
2	129
44	1187
53	53
120	5581

Everything is fine until two of the possible 10000 numbers hash to the same index. For example, 4362 modulo 127 is 44. When two keys hash to the same value, a collision is said to have occurred. There are several ways to deal with this problem.

A similar hashing function is available for use with strings. Suppose you want to search for a string (such as a name) in an array which is capable of holding 256 strings. The table is declared as

```
name *t[256];
```

The hashing function, shown here, is called with the statement

```
index = hash(s);
```

is the name you are searching for. The function call may also be shown as the array subscript as `t[hash(s)]`. The code for this hashing function is

```
int hash(s)
char *s;
{  return( ((unsigned)s) &0xFF);  }
```

The preceding code depends on the fact that **s** is a pointer, not acually the character string. Again, it is possible to find that two or more strings hash to the same index; that is, a collision occurs.

Probing

A straightforward solution to a collision is to start looking for an empty space in the array. To do this, you need some way of knowing if a location is empty or occupied. The easiest method of finding out is to initialize all locations to the same value, such as −1. Then, before placing a value in the array, you must check to see if the array's location is empty. If it is, put the value in that location. If not, begin a search for an empty spot. In a linear probe the algorithm simply proceeds from the current spot to the end of the array, to the top of the array, and back to the original spot. A code segment that specifies this type of probe is shown in Listing 13.15.

Listing 13.15

linear probe with hashing function

```
#define EMPTY -1
int full=0;
index = i_hash(key);
i = index;
while((x[i] != EMPTY) &&( !full) )
  {
    i = (i+1) % SIZE;
    if( i == index) full = 1;
  }
if( !full )
  x[i] = key;
else
  printf("data array is full\n");
```

End of Listing

Listing 13.15 begins at the hashing index as calculated by the function and looks at each location sequence to see if it is available. When the program finds an empty location, the search is over. A program that retrieves a key value performs a similar sequence.

Types of Hashing Functions

The modulus method of hashing works well enough. When the array size is small and the data are integers, one simple method is to take the nth digit, that is the first or middle value. This creates a one-digit index and, in some cases, is satisfactory. Another method is to folding the digits.

A folding algorithm takes some high-order digits and combines them with low-order digits to create an index. In other words, the high-order digits are folded onto the low-order digits. As an example, consider a collection of six-digit keys that are to be hashed into an array of size 101.

```
int i_hash(key)
long int key;
{
  return( (key/1000 + key%1000) % 101)
}
```

If the key is 548292, then the function would return

```
(548292/1000 + 548292%1000 )% 101
( 548 + 292 ) % 101
        840 % 101
          32
```

It is known that a folding algorithm produces a wider distribution of values across the allocated array.

When the data are characters instead of integers, the two algorithms modulus and folding can still be applied. One of the most common hashing functions used in other languages adds the ASCII values of the characters in the string, then applies the modulus operator to the total. For example:

```
int total;
char *key;
/*  accept a key value  */
n = strlen(key);
for(i = 0; i<= strnlen; i++)
  total+=key[i];
index = total % SIZE;
```

Applying this routine to the key of Milly and SIZE 29 yields

```
  (M+i+l+l+y) % 29
(77+105+108+108+121) % 29
  519 % 29
    26
```

Another method uses the **atol**() function supplied with most **C** libraries.

The folding hash function when applied to character strings depends on combining the bit patterns of the characters. Consider a four character key that is to be mapped into an index of 0–63. The algorithm treats each of the four characters separately. The first and fourth are exclusively ORed as are the second and third characters. The two results are XORed and then ANDed with 63. This is the main statement:

```
index = ((key[0] ^key[3]) ^(key[1] ^key[2])) | 63;
```

When applied to the key value of **ACER**, **index** equals

```
(( 82 ^ 65 )          ^          (69 ^ 67)          | 63
 (   19               ^            6  )             | 63
                     21                             | 63
                                                   21
```

These and other hashing functions can be applied to other data types, such as **float**. The concept is the same: find a function that produces an index to a table so that the item can be retrieved directly.

When the data structure is abstract, that is, a **struct**, then one field in the record must be a key field. An appropriate hashing function is then applied to the key field. Again the hashing concepts remain the same.

Collision Resolution

The central difficulty with hashing functions is what to do when two keys hash to the same index. Earlier in this chapter you looked at a simple probing technique. As the number of data points increases, this technique slows down. It also tends to cluster around certain values.

Other linear probing techniques include (1) setting aside an overflow area as either a new table or an extra N locations at the end of the hash table and (2) performing a probe for an empty location in a more sophisticated manner. A quadratic probe,for example begins by looking in a different area of the table. The new index is found by adding the square of a loop control variable (modulo `tablesize`) to the first index.

All probing techniques can tend to cause clusters. To avoid this, you might have to employ other clash-avoidance schemes.

Rehashing is one such scheme. Since hashing works well, why not hash the key again? Even if two different keys yield the same index by using one function, there is no reason why they should with a different function. A common practice is to have three or four hashing functions that are called in order as collisions occur. To use this procedure, you need to keep up with which hashing function is in use. If there are many collisions, this technique can be relatively slow and, of course, when all the rehash functions are used, a back up collision-resolution technique might still be needed.

Another technique of collision avoidance employs Fixed Size Buckets The number of clashes can be reduced by allowing several keys, all of which hash to the same index, to occupy that same address. To do this you must change the structure of the table so that each index is considered a bucket and each bucket has multiple slots. Figure 13.5 illustrates this idea.

index	key	slot1	key	slot2
0				
n	data	pointer		
21	ACER	27380		
82	MECH	27396	R	27408
max array				

Figure 13.5: *Buckets as Slots*

The array in Figure 13.5 is a two-dimensional array of records. This technique involves checking if the slot is empty. If not, then the slot counter is incremented to the next slot. Clearly, you must still provide for an overflow if all the slots in a bucket are used. This technique is faster than a linear probe, but the price for increased spped is wasted or unused, space in the array. What happens if you make each index the top of a linked list?

Making each bucket a linked list improves memory utilization. A normal hashing function is used to identify the bucket. Then a search of the linked list finds either a place to put a new entry or an existing entry. Since the linked-list search is linear, the search is slowed if the list is long. Figure 13.6 illustrates the idea of buckets as linked lists.

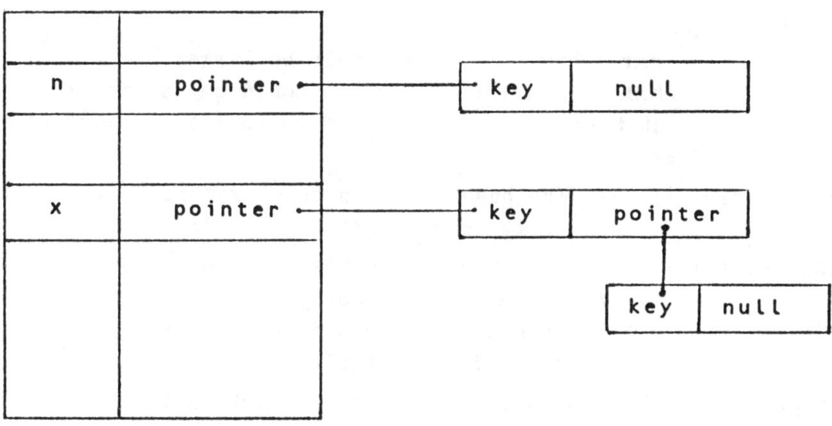

Figure 13.6: *Buckets as Linked Lists*

The use of hashing functions to quickly look up data can be best illustrated by an an example. Consider the horticulturist who wants a program to yield the common names of a plant in response to the scientific name. Listing 13.16 is such a program.

Listing 13.16

Hashing Function and Table Program

```
/*
      Title: Plant Cross Reference Program
    Purpose: Provides a simple way to look up the common
             name of a plant given the genus part of the
             scientific name of a plant.
    Comments:The data base in this example is small.  A large
             one is possible of course.  The limits will be
             from the amount of memory available in the
             computer.  All hash table programs suffer from
             this same limitation.
             Not all of the possible functions are listed
             here.  Those not shown could include:
               delete()   remove an item from table
               update()   change a value in the table
               save()     write table values to disk
*/
```

```
#include <stdio.h>
#define N 23    /*  The table size may also be calculated */
                /* dynamically  */
typedef struct
          {  char genus[10];   /*  could be larger  */
             char common[12]   /*  also could be larger  */
             int flag;         /*  used to indicate empty  */
          }ITEM;
ITEM *table[N];  /*  The hash table in this example is small  */
                 /*  as it is an example only  */
void inittbl();   /*  function to initialize the table */
                  /* to contain all empty codes  */
void filltbl();   /*  function to read data from file and */
                  /* place data in table */
int probe();      /*  function to find an empty address  */
int hash();       /*  hashing function to determine key  */
void tbl_entry(); /*  fills three fields in a table entry  */
int menu();       /*  function to display a menu  */
void find();      /*  look up a plant  */
int full = 0;     /*  table initialization variable  */

main()
{
                  int i,choice;
                  init_tbl();   /*  make all entries available  */
                  fill_tbl();   /*  make all table entries  */
                  while( choice = menu() )
                  /*  loop thru all the searches */
                  /* one wishes to make  */
                    {
                      if( (choice == 1)
                        {
                          printf("Type the genus name.\n ");
                          gets(s1);
                          find(s1);
                        }
                      else exit();
                    }
}
```

```
int menu()
{
  int choice,i;
  static *m_str[5] =  {
          "Plant Cross Reference Program",
          " ",
          "1.  Find a Plant",
          " ",
          "2.  Exit Program "  };
  choice = -1;
  while( (choice<1) || (choice >2) )
        {
          for(i=0;i<5;i++)
          puts(m_str[i]);
          printf)"\n\nType the number of your choice.  ");
          scanf("%d",choice);
          putchar('\n');
        }
  return(choice);
}
```

```
void inittbl()
{
 register i;
 int size;
 size = sizeof(ITEM);  /*  determine number of bytes in */
                       /* a record  */
 for(i=0;i<N;i++)
   {
     table[i] = malloc(size); /*  pointer to a record  */
     table[i]->flag = 0;      /*  set table entries to 0  */
   }
}
```

```
void filltbl()
{
  FILE *fp;
  register i;
  int n_items;
  char s1[10],s2[12],s3[10];
  printf("How many items are to be read?  \n");
  scanf("%d",n_items);
  if((fp = fopen("plants.dat","r")) == NULL)
    { printf"Cannot open file \n");
       exit();
    }
  else
    for( i=0;i < n_items; i++)
       {
         fscanf(fp,"%s%s",s1,s2);
         strcpy(s3,s1);
         n = hash(s3);
                 /*  use copy of s1 for hash */
                 /* purpose  */
         if(!table[n]->flag)
                 /*  see if occupied  */
           tbl_entry(n,s1,s2);
             /*  fill up record  */
             /*  pointed to by table */
             /*  and set occupied flag  */
         else
           {
             n = probe(n);  /*  find another spot  */
             if( n == -1)
               { printf("Table full \n");
                  exit();
               }
             else
               tbl_entry(n,s1,s2);
           }
       } /*  end of for loop  */
} /*  end of main function  */

void tbl_entry(n,s1,s2)
int n;
char s1[10],s[12];
{  strcpy(table[n]->genus,s1);
   strcpy(table[n]->common,s2);
   table[n]->flag = 1;
}
```

```
void find(key)
char key[10];
{
  register i,n;
  i = hash(key);
  if(!table[i]->flag)
    printf("This plant is not in list\n\n");
  else
    if( strcmp(table[i]->genus,key) == 0)
      printf("The common name for %s is %s\n\n"
        ,key,table[i]->common));
    else   /*  execute a linear probe  */
      {
        n=i+1;
        while( n != i)
      {
        if( table[n]->flag )
                /*  check only non-empty entries  */
          {  if( strcmp(table[n]->genus,key) == 0)
             printf("The common name for %s is %s\n\n"
                   ,key,table[n]->common));
          }
        n = (n++) % N;
      }
    } /*  end of second else  */
}
```

```
int probe(n)
int n;
{  register i;
   i = n;
   while((table[i]->flag) && ( !full) )
     {
       i = (i+1) % 23;
       if( i == n) full = 1;
     }
   if( !full )
     return( i);
   else
     return(-1);
```

```
int hash(s)
        /*  function uses only first 4 char for */
        /*  speed.  More characters can be used  */
char s[10];
{
  return(((key[0] ^ key[3]) ^ (key[1]^key[2])) || 23);
}
/* The following table illustrates the sample data
   for this program */
```

plant genus name	common name	hash value	index
Abies	Fir	1	1
Acer	Maple	15	15
Aesculus	Buckeye	6	6
Betula	Birch	15 clash	16
Carya	Hickory	18	18
Cercis	Redbud	9	9
Cornus	Dogwood	2	2
Cotinus	Smoke tree	3	3
Fagus	Beech	7	7
Ilex	Holly	10	10
Magnolia	Magnolia	14	14
Malus	Crabapple	7 clash	8
Picea	Spruce	11	11
Pinus	Pine	11 clash	12
Prunus	Cherry	11 clash	13
Quercus	Oak	5	5

There were four clashes, three of which were placed in the next possible index. One was placed two indices away.

End of Listing

Hashing Function Considerations

The goal of hashing tables and hash searching is to find a record directly, given a key value. It is a search technique that is appropriate for abstract data types that are frequently searched and frequently modified but have no sorting requirement.

The speed of hashing algorithms is usually achieved at the expense of memory space. Another disadvantage is that there is no easy way to determine the sorted order of records stored in the hashing table. If a table must be ordered and searched, use a binary search technique. If a table search based on key values is important, use a hashing table.

Hashing tables are used in many different applications. Compilers use hash functions to create and use identifiers in symbol tables. Modern dictionary and synonym programs use hashing tables to look up keywords and most frequently used words.

Summary

Filters are programs that accept data as program input, perform some processing and then output the modified data. Many computer programs are filters. The example in this chapter takes a word processor file that has special 8th-bit flags set for some characters. The program removes the special flags and outputs an ASCII-only file. Such a program is important when the filtered file is to be used as input to another program, such as a modem file-transfer program.

File filter programs frequently have standard modules. For example, the files must be opened and later closed. The file operations also should include necessary error checking.

Sorting programs are divided into two basic types: internal and external. In internal sorts all the data are in the computer's memory. These sorts involve making comparisons and interchanging (swapping() data elements until the data are in order. When the amount of data is small, a simple selection and exchange sort is suitable. If the data are already in partially sorted form, a shell or insertion sort may be appropriate. A fast, general-purpose sort based on the quicksort is a reliable compromise. The quicksort is fast and has few limitations.

A general-purpose sort needs to receive pointers to comparison and swap functions. These functions perform the comparison between two data structures and interchange two data elements as needed. Since the data to be sorted might be in any of several organizations, you may need to have several comparison and swap routines. Since data to be sorted are frequently stored as structures, using an array of pointers to the data elements is a sound method of creating a generalized sort. The array of pointers is passed to the function while the data are left alone. Finally, the sorted pointers are used to display or retrieve the data.

External sorts apply to either sequential files or to random files. A merge sort is a reliable method of sorting a sequential file. It requires disk or tape space for two temporary files. Only a couple of records are brought into memory at any one time. The merge sort is reliable and applicable to even very large external files.

A disk version of the quicksort may be applied to a random- access file. It does not require the use of temporary files. The external file can be thought of as an external array of structures (records). The quicksort needs to read and write records to the file, so the necessary disk i/o functions are needed. The logic of the quicksort is unchanged.

Searching is either sequential or random. Sequential searches look for an item in a sequential list; random searches code an ordered index to a table (hashing).

A sequential search for a key value simply starts at the beginning and looks through each data item until the key is found or the list is exhausted. It suffers from slowness when there are very many data points.

An indexed sequential search is a way of putting the search in the neighborhood of the key to be located. A sorted index is maintained in an array. The index points to a region of the data in which you can expect to find the key if it is to be found. Once in the correct region, the search continues in a sequential manner. A multilevel indexed sequential search is an index to the index. When there are very many data elements, a primary index points to a portion of a secondary index, which in turn points to a limited region of the data in which the key is to be found.

A way of speeding up a sequential search without reliance on indices is the binary search. It divides the data into two partitions, determines which partition contains the key, and then reduces the search to that partition. The process is repeated until the partition is of size 2. At that point the key has been located or it is not present. A binary search is a simple and fast way to find a key in sorted data. It also can be applied as the second phase in an indexed sequential search.

When the data are not in order but the application requires frequent searches for key values, a hashing function is a good choice. A hashing function manipulates the key so that an array (called a hash table) index, or address, is calculated. This allows you to locate a data element directly, without a sequence of comparisons. It is a very fast way to locate an item in an unordered list.

A hashing function should generate a distribution of data values evenly over the table. The number of entries in the table should be a prime number, and about 25 percent more table entry points than data elements should be provided. The process is to hash the key which results in a table entry point where you expect to find the desired data element. A problem arises when two or more keys hash to the same address. This is known as a hash collision.

Collision-resolution techniques include: (1) linear probing from the clash point to successive addresses until the key is found; (2) rehashing the key to a new address based on a different hash function; and (3) the use of buckets (table addresses), which head a linked list of keys that hash to that bucket. Using a linear probe works well when there are few data points. A bucket as a linked list is a good technique when there are many data values and maintaning a large, mostly unused array is a waste of memory.

Hashing functions are used in table searching applications, such as compilers, keyword searches, dictionaries, cross reference tables, and inventory indices. They provide one of the best ways to search unordered data.

EXERCISES

UNDERSTANDINGS

1. What is the fundamental difference between an internal sort and an external sort?
2. What are the reason for using an array of pointers to the actual data instead of sorting the data itself?
3. What is a comparison function? A swap function?
4. What is a filter program?
5. Why does not the library function **qsort**() not need a pointer to a swap function?
6. Explain the concept of a linear search on an array of names in alphabetical order. How is the search different if the names are not in alphabetical order?
7. Why does an indexed sequential search require that the data be in sorted order?
8. What would the advantage or disadvantage of an indexed sequential search be over a binary search when the data is an ordered array of 1000 names?
9. What is a hashing function?
10. What are two recommendations about the number of positions in a hashing table?
11. Recall the hashing function in the text that uses exclusive ORs to fold a four-character key resulting in a value in the range 0–63. The function uses a logical AND to ensure a value in the desired range. Listing 13.15 is similar except that the AND is replaced with a modulus operator (in this case % 23). Why are the two programs different?
12. Write the advantages and disadvantages of each of these hash collision resolution techniques:
    a. linear probe
    b. quadratic probe
    c. bucket with multiple slots
    d. rehashing
    e. buckets as linked lists
13. Under what conditions is a binary search probably better than a hashing function?

USAGE

14. Rewrite the hash function that folds six digit keys to one that folds four-digit keys by folding the two high-order bits onto the two low-order bits.
15. Rewrite the hash function that folds the four-character key into a single value between 0 and 63 to one that folds a six-character key to create an index between 0 and 127.

APPLICATIONS

16. Write a program that reads a file of names, places the names in alphabetic order and writes the file back to disk.
17. Create the file `sort.h` which contains the declarations for a set of external functions. Then create the file `sort.c`, which contains the comparison. and swap routines for different data types: **int**, **char**, **float**, **double**, and strings.
18. Write two functions: `xfopen()` and `xfclose()` which open and close two files. The functions perform the calls to **fopen**() and **fclose**(), perform the error checks and call the **exit**() routine if an error occurs. Then, any program wishing to open two files can simply call `xfopen(filename1,filename2)` without the confusion associated with the normal error checking in the calling program. Make `fp1` and `fp2` global (static) variables).
19. Write a generalized quicksort for structures that uses a single key.
20. The sort routines that use an array of pointers while leaving the actual data intact do not provide a method of printing the data in ordered form. Write a function that will print an array of N strings that has been sorted by using an array of pointers.
21. Write a program that creates an index to a file. The index file is analogous to the array of pointers in an array and contain the sorted record numbers of the file. The file itself should remain unchanged.
22. Modify the general-purpose quicksort routine to include a flag that indicates whether the array is to be sorted in ascending or descending order. The function should also include the code to sort in either order.
23. Using the data in the example in Listing 13.16, write a binary search program to perform the same results as that program.
24. Write a function for sorting street addresses. Sort first on street name, second on compass direction (No., So., etc), and third on street number. Then sort the following data:

    215 Mayflower Ave.
    6 Hale St.
    305 N. Broadway
    16 S. Broadwater
    128A Terry Ave.
    2310 Statler Ln.
    82 W. Main St.

25. Rewrite the probe function in Listing 13.15 to use a quadratic sequence.
26. Rewrite the program in Listing 13.15 to use buckets as linked lists to place and retrieve data elements.

PROJECTS

27. Create a file of 200 students. Each record contains a five digit id; last name; first name and middle initial; address; phone number; age; gender; emergency

contact by last name, first name, address, and phone number, hours completed; and grade-point average.

a. Write a program to sort the file and write the file back to the disk under the same name.
b. Create an index and store the index file.
c. Write an indexed sequential file access program that allows you to access a student record, display the record on the screen or printer, insert a student record, or delete a student record. These operations must result in a still valid index file and retain the sorted characteristics of the file.

28. Look up another 200 or more plants in a horticulture reference book. Create a file similar to the one in Listing 13.15. Write a program similar to the one in Listing 13.16 but with the following differences:

```
Add menu choices to:
        delete a plant,
        modify a plant name,
        add a plant to the file,
        look a plant up by its common name.
```

The program should use a hash function based on 10 characters (unless the name is less than 10 characters and uses a bucket as linked list method of collision resolution.

29. Simulate a grocery store check-out system. Provide a hash table capable of storing 1000 different items. The table allows for a product code, name, and unit price. The hash function should be based on the 8-digit product code. When a code is typed in (to simulate a wand reader), the screen should display the product name and price. Use a file to store a complete record of an individual's transactions as well as the total due. The store's inventory should be representative of real products and real prices. Use several hundred items as data.

Optionally, the program should deal with taxable versus non- taxable items and discounts based on quantity (for example, 3 for $1.00), 2 for 49 cents,and so on).

C++
Supplement

This supplement provides an overview to a new language, **C++** , which many feel will become the successor to **C** as the language of choice for applications programming. **C++** is a superset of **C** that retains the look and feel of **C** as well as its syntax and style while extending the language.

C++ was invented by Bjarne Stroustrup at the AT&T Computer Science Research Center of Bell laboratories. Stroustrup's book, *The C++ Computer Language* (Addison-Wesley, 1986) is the standard reference manual for the language. **C++** extends the **C** language by providing better user-defined data types, features for data abstraction, type checking, and expressans as modularity. It also provides mechanisms for the modern implementing concept of object-oriented programming.

C has its basis in systems programming. It was invented to reduce the time it takes to port low-level programs from one architecture to another. As a system-oriented language, it provides low-level features close the machine hardware. As a high-level language, **C** provides the control structures and modularity of procedural languages. **C++** contains improvements that aid the programmer such as inline functions, default argument values, and the overloading of function names. **C++** is an extension of **C**. It adds the notion of classes; a user-defined data type which represents a concept as opposed to an entity. The class is the central idea in **C++** .

Classes facilitate data abstraction and provide data integrity not possible in **C**. Classes almost guarantee initialization of variables, implicit type conversions, dynamic typing, generic functions, operator and function overloading, and user-controlled memory management.

Classes

A class is a user-defined data object together with its operators. It is more flexible and powerful than structures. Members of a class can be data types, such as in a structure, and they can also be functions. Several new terms and features pertain to classes. To understand the concept, consider this simple example:

```
class vector {
  float x;
  float y;
public:
  vector(float,float); // a function as a member
};
```

The preceding fragment defines `vector` as a class. Its syntactical style is similar to a structure with additions. The label public is part of the class definition. Those members found before the label public are considered private; those after are public.

```
/*  private part  */
  float x;
  float y;

/*  public part  */
  vector(float,float);  // a function as a member
```

A private member is accessible only by other members of the class. The public members of a class are accessible to functions and expressions outside the class.

C++ uses the **C** style of comments , `/*   ....   */`, and it also uses a comment that begins with `//`. The text between the double slash marks and the end of the line are considered a comment.

The public part of `vector` consists of exactly one item, a function. The function has the same name as the class, that is, `vector`. A function with the same name as the class is called a constructor. A constructor is a function used to create and initialize a variable of a particular class. It must, of course be defined.

```
vector::  vector(float a, float b)
{
  x = a;
  y = b;
}
```

The first line uses the symbol, `::` which is called a scope resolution operator. It is used to define functions which are members of a particular class. Hence, `vector` is a function belonging to class `vector`.

The definition of the constructor uses the `x` and `y` identifiers from the private part of the class. This is permitted because `vector()` is a member of the class.

A constructor is used to declare variables of type `vector` and to initialize them.

```
main()
{
...
vector velocity = vector(20.0, 10.0);
```

The data type is `vector`. The variable (data object) is called `velocity`, and `velocity` is initialized by calling the constructor `vector` with the arguments 20 and 10. The result is the creation of a variable of class `vector` that has the values 20 and 10.

One of the features of **C++** is that a variable may be declared at any time, not just at the top of a block. At the time a variable is declared, it may also be initialized via a constructor. In other words, C++ provides a means of initializing all variables regardless of storage class.

A class definition may also include definitions of the operations that may be performed on them. Suppose you want to add two vectors and assign the results to a third vector.

```
v3 = v1 + v2;
```

Under normal circumstances, this is not permitted because the + symbol does not apply to these data types. C++ permits the embellishment of an operator, which is called operator overloading, so the operator can apply to class objects.

Operator Overloading

Redefining an operator so that it applies to user-defined data objects is done within a class definition. Then operators +, - *, / = and so on may be used with a class, and when applied to a class data object, they perform differently than their original meaning. Consider adding the operator + to the vector class.

```
class vector {
        float x;
        float y;
public:
        vector(float,float);
        vector operator+(vector,vector);
};
```

The additional line declares an operator, +, which applies to two vectors. The modifier, vector, in front of the keyword operator declares the operator to be of type vector. It must also be defined, which is done outside the class definition.

```
vector operator +(vector a, vector b)
{
  return vector(a.x + b.x, a.y + b.y);
}
```

The operator is treated like a function but thought of as an operator. The definition is like that of a function, it returns a vector. The arguments are two vectors. The function calls the constructor `vector()`; therefore, the members `x` and `y` can be accessed. Notice that the dot operator is used in much the same way as it is with a **struct**. The arrow operator, ->, may also be used to access a class member. This usage is much the same as the use of with structures.

The overloaded operator can now be used in a program. For example:

```
main()
{
vector v1 = vector(10.0, 5.0);
vector v2(12.1, 2.4);     // same as above
vector v3;
v3 = v1 + v2;             // use of overloaded
                          // operator
/*  an equivalent statement would have been   */
v3 = v1 + v2;
```

An entity such as an operator may be an actual member of a class, as is the case in the preceding fragment. It may also be treated as a "friend" of a class. A friend has access to the private parts of a class without actually being part of the class. This results in an increase in efficiency due to improved overhead and data storage. Overloaded operators are good candidates for the modifier friend.

```
public:
  vector(float,float);
  friend vector operator+(vector,vector);
```

Class Functions

As you have seen, class members may be functions. A constructor is a special case in that it is declared to be of the same type (that is, the identifier is the same) as the class itself. Other functions may be declared within the class template. They may be defined either inside or outside the function.

Consider a function to print a vector's component values.

```
public:
  vector(float,float);
  friend vector operator+(vector,vector);
  void display();
};
```

The function display is defined by

```
void vector::display()
{
  printf("x is %7.2f, y is %7.2f \n",x,y);
}
```

An obvious question is what is the argument? The argument is optional. The function may have been defined as

```
void vector::display(vector a)
{
  printf("x is %7.2f, y is %7.2f \n",a.x,a.y);
}
```

The former, **void** `vector::display()` is preferred because the argument is assumed. The latter is easier to understand, however. The function may be called by writing

```
vector v1 = vector(10.1,5.0);
v1.display;      // call member function
                 // using first version
```

or it may have been called by

```
display(v1);     // call function with
                 // a vector argument
```

The function may be declared inside the template to avoid the necessity of an additional definition.

```
public:
  vector(float,float);
  friend vector operator+(vector,vector);
  void display()
     { printf("x is %7.2f, y is %7.2f \n",x,y);}
};
```

The results are the same as the earlier version which was declared outside the template, but this in line method is shorter. Putting the function definition inside the template and the definition elsewhere provides the programmer with needed information and hides the details of the definition.

Default Arguments: A truly useful feature of **C++** is the ability to provide default values for function arguments. This ability means that, if a function is called without the complete argument list, a default value is used. Consider this constructor.

```
vector::  vector(float a = 0.0, float b = 0.0)
{
  x = a;
  y= b;
}
```

When the constructor is used, the arguments may or may not be used.

```
main()
{
  vector v1 = vector(10.0,5.0);   // normal use
  vector v2(5.0);                 // only one argument
                                  // so default is
                                  // used for second
  vector v3;                      // use both default
                                  // arguments.
```

Default arguments used in a constructor function guarantee that any data object declared to be of type (class) `vector` will also be initialized. This is a major feature.

A second advantage of default arguments is that a function can be called with a variable number of arguments without error. Consider the class that defines a complex number.

```
class complex {
  double r,i;
public:
  complex(double real = 0.0, double imag = 0.0)
    { r = real;
      i = imag;  }
  friend complex operator +(complex,complex);
  void print();
};
```

Any use of the constructor complex() with or without arguments will always results in an initialization of the objects' elements. The programmer can make routine declarations such as

```
main()
{
  complex voltage;
```

which results in automatic initialization of the real and imaginary members of the object. The default values can be overridden when a value is supplied.

```
void f1(int n = 0, char * = " ");
...
f1(12);   // second value defaults to " "
```

A class variable may be declared and initialized in terms of another previously defined object, as the code shows:

```
main()
{
  complex v1 = complex(1.5,2.0);
  complex v2 = v1;
```

A function member of a class does not have to be a constructor. A vec_size() function can be a member.

```
public:
  vector(float,float);
  friend vector operator+(vector,vector);
  void display();
  double vec_size();    // argument assumed to
                        // be vector
};
```

The function vec_siz() is defined outside the template as

```
double vector::vec_siz();
{
  return sqrt(x*x + y*y);  // assume math.h
}                          // is present
```

Then the function can be used as this code shows:

```
main()
{
  vector impact = vector(12.2,15.0);
  float impac_siz;
  ...
  impac_siz = impact.vec_siz();  // use dot operator
```

Implicit Type Checking C++ has better type checking than **C** and also includes automatic type conversion. In **C** the function `f1()` expects a **double** argument.

```
double f1(x)
double x;
{
...
}
```

If used with an integer argument, an error may occur.

```
double y;
...
y = f1(4);
```

C++ implicitly adds the cast to **double**. The result is as if the code were written:

```
y = f1( (double) 4 );
```

Inline Functions: C++ provides in line functions that may be used in lieu of macros. The C preprocessor does not know C, so if parentheses are not very carefully used (and even when they are) a macro can introduce error when expressions are expanded. The inline function observes the same semantics as other functions, but the inline function is expanded in line. The result is the run time efficiency of a macro. Consider the function which raises a real to the second power, for example:

```
inline float pow2(float a) {return a*a);
```

The modifier inline is unique to **C++** . In **C** the macro could have been

```
#define pow2(a) (a*a)
```

But, when an expression is used in lieu of a number, the potential for error occurs.

```
/* in C, using the macro */
y = pow2(3*x+ 4);
```

expands to

```
y = (3*x +4*3*x +4); /* and if x is 5.0 */
y = 15 + 12*5.0+4;
y = 79;
```

The **C++** function expands properly and gives the correct answer.

Function Overloading

C++ provides a very powerful feature with function overloading. Functions of the same name but with different argument types can be used as if there was only one function. A programmer can use the function name with different argument types and still invoke the correct function.

Let the function **abs_val**() be defined for different data types.

```
overload abs_val;
...
int abs_val(int);
float abs_val(float);
```

Overloading is a very nice feature as it allows you to define (usually in a different file) several versions of the same function. The programmer can use the function name with a variety of arguments and be confident that data types will be compatible. Special cases that apply only to certain data types can be handled within the function definitions.

The vector Class

So far, you have used a simple version of `vector` as a class. C++ defines a more complete vector class (Stroustrup, page 28) and provides it as part of the language.

```
class vector {
  int * v;
  int sz;
public:
    vector(int);      // constructor
    ~vector();        // destructor
  int size() {return sz; }
  void set_size(int);
  int& operator[] (int); //reference operator &
  int& elem(int i) {return v[i]; }
};
```

This template includes a couple of items not mentioned so far. The destructor

```
~vector();
```

is a function that is to be called implicitly whenever a vector goes out of scope. It deletes the storage space allocated by the constructor so that when a vector goes out of scope, its memory space is reclaimed for potential reuse. Stroustrup defines it as

```
vector::  ~vector()
{
  delete v;    // delete is a C++ keyword
}
```

The second item in the vector template is a reference.

```
int& operator[] (int);
int& elem(int i) {return v[i];}
```

A reference acts as a name for an object. `A&` means a reference to A. A reference must be initialized and becomes an alternate for (in effect, a synonym for) the object with which it is initialized.

The first use of references is to pass the address of an object, not the object itself, to a function. This is a call by reference in the generic sense. A reference improves efficiency because a pointer is easier to pass than entire structures.

Derived Classes

The philosophy of C++ includes the notion of organizing a program around concepts, in other words, a class. The class enables you to create an object such as a sprite, icon, window, or graph, as a concept. The object (class) is then manipulated. For example, an icon is highlighted, moved around the screen, enlarged, modified, and so on. The notion of derived classes is one of a subclass; a class created from an existing class.

A class derivation is a way of building a new class(subclass) from another (base class). Through virtual functions, various types derived from the same base class can be uniformly handled as **if** each were of the base type. The base class may declare member functions that can be redefined with a variation of meaning for each derived class. For example, a base class of `icon` can have a function declaration for moving the icon. Subclasses for a collection of icons can all use the `move()` function in the same way.

Derived classes allow reuse of classes without modification or replication of existing code. The derived class inherits all the properties of the base class, and it also possesses the properties declared for it. Public members of the base class can be accessed as if they were members of the derived class.

Consider a class in a program that manipulates geometric objects. The base class is `shape`.

```
class shape {
  point center;  // assume point is defined
  color col;     // as is color
public:
  point position;
  ...
  virtual void rotate(int);    // virtual function
};
```

The virtual function allows the creation of a generic function. For any shape triangle, circle, or what have you, a rotate function is defined. However, when rotating a shape, the same function name, `rotate()`, is used. The keyword virtual makes the use of generic functions possible.

A subclass is defined in terms of the base class.

```
class triangle :  public shape {
public:
  ...
  void rotate(int)
  {  /*  function definition  */ }
};
```

The triangle is a class, but is derived from the shape class. The virtual functions such as `rotate()` are defined in this template. Now variables (data objects) of type triangle may be declared and initialized in a program.

A derived class constructor must initialize the base class part of the object as well as the derived class part. The derived class constructor calls the base class constructor.

The concept of derived classes is a powerful idea. If you are using windows as a concept in a program, a base class of window can be defined. Separate window types, each having all the properties of the base class, but each having distinct properties. One window could be strictly a display window, always appearing in the same place and used to present fixed text as information. Another could be a menu window used by the end user to make choices while running the program. Another could be an interactive window used to print and accept variable data. The list goes on. This example shows how object oriented programming makes **C++** a modern language indeed.

C++ shows off two new keywords: new and delete. They are used in lieu of

malloc() and **free**() and provide added flexibility.

The keyword new creates an object of the type specified and returns its address. If the type has a constructor, it is called to initialize the newly created object.

```
main()
{
  // node is a class
  node *np1;
  np1 = new node(s1);   // node() is a constructor
```

Since **np1** is a pointer, the arrow operator must be used to access a member function such as `display()`.

```
np1->display();
```

The keyword delete is used to free space allocated for a class object. By using new and delete together, a programmer can create objects whose lifetime is controlled directly. Stroustrup (pages 28—29) shows this with his vector class.

```
class vector {
  int * v;
  int sz;
public:
    vector(int);     // constructor
    ~vector();       // destructor
  int size() {return sz; }
  void set_size(int);
  int& operator[] (int);    //reference operator &
  int& elem(int i) {return v[i]; }
};

vector::vector(int s)
{
  if(s<=0) error("bad vector size");
  sz = s;
  v = new int[s];
}

vector::~vector()
{
  delete v;
}
```

The constructor is called when an object is declared to be of type `vector`. The destructor is called when a class object goes out of scope. All its space is reclaimed for potential reuse.

The keywords new and delete provide flexibility in controlling data objects life that is not available in **C**. It allows you to create an object that can be used after returning from the function in which it is created. Delete can be used to destroy them later.

A

Summary of Commands and Keywords

auto Automatic variable storage class modifier. For example **auto int**;

break Control of flow command.Causes termination of innermost **while**, **do-while**, **for** or **switch** statement. For example, **break**;

case See **switch**

char Character data type. For example, **char** ch;

continue Control of flow command. Terminates the current pass through the innermost **while**, **do-while**, or for loop but, continues with the next iteration of the loop. For example

```
for(..;..;..)
  { stmtn1;
    if(condition) continue;
  }
```

default See **switch**

double Data type declaring **double**-precision real number. For example, **double** x;

do-while Control structure. Loop is executed as long as the expression of the **while** statement is true. For example,

```
do
  {
    stmnt;
    stmnt;
  }
while(expression);
```

else See **if-else**

extern External storage class modifier. Causes variable (identifier) to be gloabal in scope and is defined elsewhere. For example, **extern** `randx();`

FILE **FILE** data type. For example, **FILE** *infile;

float Data type declaring single-precision real number.For example, **float** `x;`

for Control structure. Defines the parameters of a loop. Includes initialization of control variable, test condition, and incrementation and work statement(s) of the loop. For example,

```
for(initialization; test; incrementation)
  { statement;
    statement;
  }
```

goto Unconditional transfer of control to a label. For example, **goto** top;

if Conditional execution of a block of code. Following statement or block is executed only if expression is true (non-zero). For example,

```
        if(expresssion)
          statement;
or      if(expression)
          { stmnt1;
            stmnt2;
          }
```

if-else Control structure to execute one of two statements or blocks of statements. For example,

```
        if(expression)
          statement;
        else
          statement2;
or      if(expression)
          { stmnt1;
            stmnt2;
          }
        else
          { stmnt3;
            stmnt4;
          }
```

int Integer data type. For example, **int** i;

long Data type modifier. Causes normal variable to be twice its normal size. For example, **long int** i;

main() Defines the **main** function which is required in all programs. For example,

```
        main()
          { statements;
          }
or      main(argc,argv)
        int arg;
        char *argv[];
          { ...
          }
```

register Register data type. Variable is stored in a **register**. For example, **register** `i;`

return Function control statement to leave a function and return control to the calling function. Return also passes a value to the calling function. For example, **return**;
or **return**`();`
or **return**`(value);`

short Data type modifier for integrals. Causes data object to be half as big as an integer. For example, **short int** i;

sizeof Operator that returns the number of bytes to store a data object. For example, **sizeof**(x); or, **sizeof**(**int**);

static Storage class modifier. Causes data object to be persistent in life and global to the functions declared after it in the same file. If declared inside a function, local in in scope but persistent in life.

struct Aggregate data type specifier. Declares a complex data type consisting of members, not all of the same data type. For example,

```
struct [tag] {
        data type identifier;
        data type identifier;
        } [identifier];
```

switch Control structure to conditionally execute a block of code based on selected integral values. If the value in the **switch** expression is equal to a case value, the corresponding block of code is executed. For example,

```
switch (integral value)
  {
    case val1:  { stmnts;
                  break;
                }
    case val2:  { stmnts;
                  break;
                }
    default:    { stmnts;
                  break;
                }
  }
```

typedef Allows for the creation of synonyms for data storage classes. Every thing between the keyword **typedef** and the identifier, is a synonym for the identifier. For example,

```
typedef static long int integer;
```

union A single data object whose storage allocation is big enough to hold any one of the members in the **union** declaration. Only one member may be used at one time. For example,

```
union code {
        char x[20];
        char y[4][5];
  };
```

unsigned Data type modifier for integral types. Causes the data object to be stored without a sign bit. For example, **unsigned int** pointer;

The keywords that follow must begin in column 1 and the statement that they begin does not end with a semicolon.

#asm directive to indicate that the following statments are assembly language code. For example,

```
#asm
  /* assembly lang commands */
#endasm
```

#define Preprocessor keyword. Creates a symbolic constant or macro which is substituted in the code in the place of the substitution string. For example,

```
#define TRUE 1
```

or

```
#define even(x) ( (x) % 2? 0:1 )
```

#else Directive that is optional part of **#if**, **#ifdef**, **#ifndef** compiler directives. For example,

```
#if
  ...
  #else
  statements;
#endif
```

#endasm Terminating line of **#asm** directive.

#endif Terminating directive to accompany **#if**, **#ifdef**, or **#ifndef**

#if Compiler directive which permits conditional compilation if the corresponding expression is true.

```
#if DEBUG_ON
  statements;
#endif
```

#ifdef Compiler directive that permits conditional compilation if an identifier has been defined. For example,

```
#ifdef lpt1;
  printer = lpt1;
#else
  printer = prn;
#endif
```

#include Preprocessor directive to bring the contents of the specified file into the current file prior to compilation. For example,

```
#include <stdio.h>
  #include "mydefs.h"
```

#line assigns an arbitrary line number to the source line that follows.

#pragma an ANSI standard addtion that provides a mechanism to give compiler or implementation specific directions to a compiler.

#undef Compiler directive to specify that a particular identifier previously created with **#define** is no longer in existence. For example,

```
#undef MAXX
```

#ifndef Compiler directive that is the logical complement of **ifdef**. Permits conditional compilation if an identifier has not been defined. For example,

```
#ifndef EOLN
  static char EOLN = 10;
    #endif
```

Signifies token concatenation (ANSI standard) . Each **##** is removed and the tokens preceding and following the **##** are concatenated.

B

Predefined Structures Macros, and Constants

identifiers	*description*	*location*
BUFSIZ	contains number of bytes in a typical disk buffer for the system. Usually 512 or 1024.	stdio.h
__DATE__	value of date of translation of source file stored in string of type "mmm dd yyyy".	compiler
EDOM	integral constant that is assigned to errno when a domain error occurs.	math.h
EOF	end-of-file marker, usually −1.	stdio.h
ERANGE	integral constant assigned to errno when a range error occurs.	math.h
errorno	a global integral variable which is initally set to zero. Contains an error number when certain errors occur.	stdio.h (old) stddef.h (new)
FILE	structure defining the characteristics of an external data file. Usually a **typedef**.	stdio.h
__FILE__	name of the current source file.	compiler
getc(fp)	macro version of **fgetc**(). Reads a character from stream fp.	stdio.h
HUGE_VAL	positive **double** value of the largest real number possible. used as the returned value when a math overflow error occurs.	math.h
isalnum(c)	returns true if c is either a letter or a number.	ctype.h
isalpha(c)	returns true if c is a letter.	ctype.h

identifiers	*description*	*location*
iscntrl(c)	returns true if c is a control character.	ctype.h
isdigit(c)	returns true if c is a numeral.	ctype.h
isgraph(c)	returns true if c is a graphics character.	ctype.h
islower(c)	returns true if c is lowercase.	ctype.h
isprint(c)	returns true if c is a printable character.	ctype.h
ispunct(c)	returns true if c is a punctuation mark.	ctype.h
isspace(c)	returns true if c is the space bar.	ctype.h
isupper(c)	returns true if c is uppercase.	ctype.h
isxdigit(c)	returns true if c is a hexadecimal digit.	ctype.h
__LINE__	contains the current source line number.	compiler
NULL	a pointer value of 0. Indicates a file open failure or a invalid pointer value.	stdio.h(old) stddef.h(new)
putc(ch,fp)	macro version of **fputc**. Writes character ch to stream fp.	stdio.h
stdin	file pointer to the standard input device. Usually the keyboard. Value is usually 0.	stdio.h
stderr	file pointer to the standard error file. Usually 2.	stdio.h
stdout	file pointer to the standard output device. Usually 1.	stdio.h
SYS_OPEN	integral constant that contains the number of files that are guaranteed to be allowed to be opened simultaneously.	stdio.h
__TIME__	predefined string holding time of current translation in a string of the form "hh:mm:ss".	compiler
tolower(c)	converts c to lowercase.	ctype.h
toupper(c)	converts c to uppercase.	ctype.h

C

C Functions

function	description	*returns*	*error code*
abs(n)	calculates absolute value of real number.	absolute value	none
acos(x)	calculates arc cosine of number in range 0–π.	arc cosine	none
asin(x)	calculates the arc sine of number in range $0 - \pi/2$	arc sine	none
atan(x)	calculate arc tangent of number in range $-\pi/2$ $-\pi/2$	arc tangent of number if number > 1	0
atan2(x,y)	calulates arc tangent of two numbers.	arc tangent of x/y	none
atof(s)	convert ASCII string to **float** number.	**double** number	none
atoi(s)	convert ASCII string to integer equivalent.	integer	none
atol(s)	convert ASCII string to **long** integer equivalent.	**long** integer	none
calloc(n,size)	allocates and initializes bytes of memory for temporary storage.	pointer to a block of memory equal to n times size	**NULL**
ceil(x)	find the smallest integer that is greater than or equal to x.	**ceil** value	none
clearerr(fp)	clears any error for the file pointed to by fp.		none
cos(x)	calculate the cosine of number x.	cosine of x	none
cosh(x)	calculate the hyperbolic cosine of a number.	cosh of x	none
exit([n])	terminates program and closes all open files.	n/a	none

_exit([n])	terminates program without closing any open files.	n/a	none
function	*description*	*returns*	*error code*
exp(x)	calculates the exponential value of x.	e to x power	HUGE_VAL
fabs(x)	determines the absolute value of a real number.	absolute value	none
fclose(fp)	closes file pointed to by fp and releases fp to be used again.	0 if no error	−1
feof(fp)	check for end of file on stream fp.	non zero if eof else 0	
freopen (s,t,fp)	close file fp and reopen file s, using type (t) id.	pointer to file fp.	**NULL**
ferror(fp)	determines error status of stream fp.	non zero if error else 0.	
fflush(fp)	clears all data from stream fp.	0	non-zero
fgetc(fp)	read one character from fp.	character	−1 or neg
fgets(s,l,fp)	string of size l from stream fp.	string == s	0 if end of line
floor(x)	determine the largest integer less than or equal to the number indicated.	greatest integer val	none
fopen(f,m)	opens a file with the external name file f in the mode m	pointer to a type **FILE**	**NULL**
fprintf(fp,f,a)	print arguments (a) in the specified format to fp.	number bytes output	−1
fputc(ch,fp)	write a character to the file pointed to by fp.	0	−1
fputs(s,fp)	write a string to the file pointed to by fp.	0	−1
fread (b,s,n,fp)	reads info from file fp. Places data in buffer b Each data item is s bytes and n of them are read in.	n	0

function	description	*returns*	*error code*
free(ptr)	unallocates memory that has been reserved with **malloc** or **calloc**	0	−1
fscanf(fp,fmt,a)	reads args from stream fp according to conversion string fmt.	number of arguments read	−1 (**EOF**)
fseek(fp,o, code)	alters read/write position in disk file fp. offset (o) is a **long int** telling the number of bytes and code describes the point at which the offset begins (0,1,2).	current position	(**EOF**)
ftell(fp)	tells the current position in the file relative to the beginning.	current position	
fwrite(buf,s,n,fp)	write data to file fp from buffer buf. s is the number of bytes of each item and n is the number of data items to be written.	number of actually written.	0
get(s)	get a string from standard input	s	**NULL**
getenv(s)	get string associated with environment variable.	s	0
getchar()	read a char from buffer of **stdin** note: **getchar**() is a macro in stdio.h	pos integer of the character.	−1
index(s,ch)	same as **strchr**.		
itoa(n,s)	converts an integer into string of ASCII string terminated with\0.	s	none
log(x)	calculate natural logarithm of a number.	ln(x)	0
log10(x)	calculate common logarithm of number x.	**log**(x)	0
longjmp(e,v)	restores the environment saved by the last call of setjump with the corresponding env.	v	

function	*description*	*returns*	*error code*
malloc(n)	allocates n of bytes of memory.	pointer to first byte of reserved memory.	0
memchr(b,ch,n)	searches the first n bytes in memory area b for the character ch	ch	**NULL**
memcmp (b1,b2,n)	compares the first n bytes of memory area b1 to b2	−1,0,1 depending of lexicographical comparison.	
memcpy(d,s,n)	copies n bytes from memory area s to memory area dst.	pointer to d	
memset(b,ch,n)	sets the first n bytes in memory area b to ch	pointer to buf	
movmem(p,q,l)	copies l bytes from block of memory pointed to by p to that pointed to by q.		
pow(x,y)	raises x to the y value	x raised to y	0
printf(fmt,a)	writes args to standard output device according to conversion string fmt.	0	−1
putchar(ch)	writes character ch to the buffer of the standard output device. implemented as a macro in stdio.h	ch	−1
puts(s)	write a string to std output.	# of chars	**EOF**
qsort (p,n1,n2,f)	sorts elements of an array. n 1 is number of elems in array. n2 is width of each element, and f is name of comparison function.	sorted array pointed to by p.	none
rand()	random number generator.	psuedorandom integer in range 0 - 32767	none
realloc(p,s)	increases or decreases the size of a block of memory previously allocated and pointed to by p. s is the number of bytes.	p to first byte of new block of memory	0
rewind(fp)	reposition stream pointer to begining of file.		

function	description	*returns*	*error code*
rindex(s,ch)	same as **strchr**.		
scanf(fmt,a)	reads arg from buffer of standard input device according to the string fmt	number of arguments actually read	−1
setbuf(fp,buf)	defines the buffer to be used for the i/o stream fp	n /a	
setjmp(env)	saves its stack environment in env for later use by longjump.	0	
setmem(p,l,v)	sets the character value in each byte of the block of memory that begins at p and extends for l bytes.		
sin(x)	calculate the sine of a number.	**sin**(x)	none
sinh(x)	calculate the hyperbolic sine of x.	**sinh**(X)	HUGH_VAL
sprintf(s,f,a)	writes a to a string s in memory using the conversion string f.	number of characters including \0 placed in string	
sqrt(x)	calculates the square root of a real number.	square root of x	0
srand(seed)	random-number generator using a seed.	random integer in the range 0-32767	none
sscanf(s,f,a)	reads args (a) from string s in memory according to conversion string f.	number of items (a) read	−1
strchr(s,ch)	find the first position in string s in which ch appears.	integer of first occurrence	−1
strcat(s1,s2)	appends string s2 to the end of string s1.	n/a	none
strcmp(s1,s2)	compares two strings for equivalence.	−1 if or s1<s2 if s1 == s2 or 1 if s1 > s2	none

function	*description*	*returns*	*error code*
strcpy(s1,s2)	copies string s2 to string s1.	n/a	none
strcspn(s1,s2)	determines length of initial string segment made up of characters NOT in specified set.	length of seg	none

strlen(s)	determines the length of string s. characters in s, not including \0.	number of	none
strncat (s1,s2,n)	concatenate s2 to s1 to at most n positions.	s1	
strncmp (s1,s2,n)	compares first n positions of two strings.	−1 if s1 ! = s2	none
strncpy (s1,s2,n)	copy string s2 to string s1 up to n characters.	s1	
strpbrk(s1,s2)	search string for any one of a set of characters.	pointer to	character
strrchr(s,ch)	finds the last position in s in which ch appears.	integer representing index of last occurrence o character ch.	−1
strspn(s1,s2)	length of initial string segment made up of characters in a specified set.	length of span	
strtok(s1,s2)	finds a token separated by any of a set of characters.	pointer to substring.	
tan(x)	calculates the tangent of a real number.	**tan**(x)	
tanh(x)	calculate the hyperbolic tangent of a real number.	**tanh**(x)	
tmpfile()	creates temporary file. in update mode	file pointer	
tmpnam(s)	create temp file name s.	s	**NULL**
ungetc(ch,fp)	places ch back onto the input stream (buffered).	ch	−1 (**EOF**)
unlink(fp)	remove a directory entry which is the external name of the file pointed to by fp.	0	−1 (**EOF**)

D

Ansi C Standard Header Files

assert.h

This header provides diagnostic and debugging assistance

`assert`
`NDEBUG`

ctype.h

Character type identification (boolean) and translation

isalnum
isalpha
iscntrl
isdigit
isgraph
islower
isprint
ispunct
isspace
isupper
isxdigit
tolower
toupper

float.h

Float data type characteristics identifiers:

`This list is incomplete`

limits.h

Integer data type characteristics identifiers:

`This list is incomplete`

math.h

Declarations and definitions for mathematical functions

acos
`HUGE_VAL`

setjmp.h

Provides links to assembly-language far calls.

`jmp_buf`
longjmp
setjmp

signal.h

Provides operating system hooks for signal handling.

kill	signal
SIGABRT	SIGTERM
SIGFPE	SIG_DFL
SIGILL	SIG_ERR
SIGINT	SIG_ERR
SIGSEGV	SIG_IGN

stdarg.h

Provides for variable number of arguments for functions

va_arg	va_list
va_end	va_start

stddef.h

Miscellaneous constants and definitions

errno	ptrdiff_t
NULL	size_t

stdio.h

Definitons and macros supporting standard input and output

BUFSIZ	fread	remove	SYS_OPEN
clearerr	freopen	rename	tmpfile
EOF	fscanf	rewind	tmpnam
fclose	fseek	scanf	TMP_MAX
feof	ftell	SEEK_CUR	ungetc
ferror	fwrite	SEEK_END	vfprintf
fflush	getchar	SEEK_SET	vprintf
fgetc	getc	setbuf	vsprintf
fgets	gets	setvbuf	_IOFBF
FILE	L_tmpnam	sprintf	_IOLBF
fopen	perror	sscanf	_IONBF
fprintf	printf	stderr	
fputc	putchar	stdin	
fputs	putc	stdout	
	puts		

stdlib.h

Definitions to support functions found in the standard library.

abort	**malloc**
abs	onexit
atof	**rand**
atoi	realloc
atol	**srand**
calloc	strtod
exit	strtol
free	system
getenv	

string.h

Support for string handling functions.

memchr	strerror
memcmp	**strlen**
memcpy	**strncat**
memset	**strncmp**
strcat	strncpy
strchr	**strpbrk**
strcmp	**strrchr**
strcpy	**strspn**
strcspn	**strtok**

time.h

Miscellaneous clock and time function support.

asctime	difftime
CLK_TCK	gmtime
clock	localtime
clock_t	time
ctime	time_t
tm	

E

Portability Maxims

C is touted as a portable language; and except for severe machine dependenices such as PC-DOS screen i/o or the Macintosh interface, **C** is portable. The programmer can take steps which will aide in making a program portable. Some of these practices are cited here. Wherever possible, the programmer should build in portability through these practices. This appendix also deals, implicitly and explicitly, with programming style. Good style reduces debugging time, improves programming efficiency, and helps maintenance programmers.

Data Objects Storage Requirements

Clearly, different machines store data objects differently. On some machines, an **int** is 2 bytes; others use 4 bytes. The preprocessor can help mitigate these differences.

The preprocessor directives **#ifdef**, **#else**, and **#endif** can provide for definitions of the largest and smallest integers.

```
#ifdef IBMPC
  #define HI_INT 32767
  #define LO_INT (-32768)
#else
  #define HI_INT 2147483647
  #define LO_INT (-2147483648)
#endif
```

There may be other possibilities. In those cases a more complicated version may be written. Once these conditional definitions are made, the programmer is free to use HI_INT and LO_INT without worrying about the corretness of the values. If a change needs to be made to these few statements because the program is being compiled on a different computer, then the rest of the code does not need to be touched.

Unsigned integers are used to represent memory locations and to hold pointer values. Bitwise operations often depend on knowledge of size of the integer. A new data type, integer, can be defined to always be a 16-bit integer.

```
#ifdef IBMPC
  typedef unsigned int integer;
#else
  typedef unsigned short integer;
#endif
```

Now a program that must have a 16-bit unsigned integral value for bitwise manipulations is sure to do so. As with the previous example, You may need to add to this code to take care of the requirements of other systems.

Bitwise operations are dependent on the machine's word size. Some mask operations should take this in mind. For example, to set all the bits to 1, do not say

```
mask = oxffff;
```

because if an unsigned **int** is longer than 2 bytes, the leftmost bits will not be set to 1s. The correct method is

```
mask = ~0;
```

which sets all the bits to 1 regardless of the size of the **int**.

File Organization

Consistency in organizing files helps in debugging and maintenance. The following outline is a preferred method of organizing files.

```
/*  Title block explaining program purpose, author, */
/*  creation date, and modification log.   */

/*  preprocessor directives  */
  #include(s)
  #undefine(s)
  #define(s)
  #conditional(s)
  #if, #ifdef,
  #ifndef, #else, #endif

/*  external declarations  */
  extern variables
  extern functions

/*  local function  */
/*  comments describing function and its use  */
data-type function(args)
argument declarations
{ extern function declarations
  extern variable declarations
  local variable declarations

  c statements + /*  comments  */
}

/*  other local functions  */
```

A common header file to be included with all the program files that make up a program should be developed. It should have a name similar to the final program name. For example, if the program is called edit then the header file should be called edit.h. Do not place external variable definitions that allocate storage in header files. The common header file ensures that each file has the same set of definitons and macros for every file. This practice reduces the chances of inconsistent or conflicting definitions and aids the maintenance staff.

Place all the input, output, and memory management functions in separate files or libraries. These are the most system- dependent routines and should be kept together. When moving your code to a new machine, only those files will have to be rewritten and recompiled. In addition, keep all external variable definitions of a program in their own source file.

sizeof

Throughout the text, **sizeof** has been used to make a program portable. It is not without its limitations, however. For example, the preprocessor does not know **C**. Consequently, you can not say

```
#if sizeof(int) == 2
  typedef char boolean;
#else
  typedef unsigned short boolean;
#endif
```

The compiler recognizes **sizeof**, but the preprocessor does not.

Long variable Names

Many newer compilers allow very long variable names. Older ones allow a maximum of eight characters in an identifier. When moving a program with longer variable names to a machine and compiler that do not permit them, a set of defines can be created to create synonyms for the long names.

```
#define long_identifier newname
```

A header file with all the synonyms can be included in every file in the program. The existing code does not have to be modified.

Alignment Considerations

Some machines are permissive in their alignment requirements; others are not. As a general rule, it is best to declare the variables in decreasing order of alignment requirements. Some optimizing compilers do this anyway, but why depend on the compiler?

```
double x,y;
float t;
long ii;
unsigned reg;
int i,j,k;
short bool;
char ch;
```

The ordering also, in some cases, improves program efficiency by generating better stack usage. In no case will it hurt. The resulting program is portable and easier to maintain.

String Copy Functions

Many implementations of string copy routines use pointers to copy null-terminated strings. Two problems frequently arise. One happens when the destination string is declared as a character pointer (for example, **char** *s1. *s2). The library function, **strcpy**() does nt always work. It is best to declare the destination string as a character array (e.g., **char** s1[10]) which usually solves the problem. The second problem is when the null terminator is not found, the string copy function continues indefinitely. In these cases, the strncpy() function is one defense. It guarantees that the process will stop after n characters. If the string copy functions using pointers are used, it is good practice to

1. Verify that all strings terminate with a null character.
2. Before a string is copied, verify that the destination string is as big or bigger than the source string.
3. When a string is copied, the destination string is terminated with the null character.

Another method is to use the function **memcpy**(), which also specifies the length of the string.

Order of Evaluation

Do not write programs that depend on the order of evaluation of operands within expressions. Always use spacing, parentheses, or both to separate adjacent operators whenever the characters might have more than one interpretation. The statement

```
i = *p /* q;
```

should be

```
i = (*p)/ (*q);
```

because the symbols /* might be interpreted as the beginning of a comment. The statement

```
m = n+++p;
```

could be interpreted as

```
m = n + (++p);
```

or

```
m = (n++) + p;
```

Never use increment operators on a variable that appears twice in an expression. For example,

```
a = b++ (2*c + b++);
```

The order of evaluation of this expression is very implementation dependent. Calling functions twice within an expression is also a poor practice.

```
x = f1() + sin(y)* f1();
```

The order of evaluation of the terms of this expression is not guaranteed. Avoid such statements. Rewrite it as two statements.

Comparing Real Numbers

Many operations and math functions automatically convert **float** to **double** before performing the operation. For arithmetic comparisons, this is not true. Hence, in making arithmetic comparisons, if either operand is **float** or **double**, then cast the **float** to **double** before the test.

Float and or **double** values will only evaluate to equal if they are both exactly equal. it is good practice to allow a tolerance for making real number comparisons. For example, to compare two doubles, x and y, write

```
#define EPS 0.000001
...
if( (fabs(x-y) < EPS)    /*  consider this true if the */
                         /*  difference is very small  */
```

Comments in Preprocessor statements

Compilers differ in their interpretation of comments within **#define** statements. To avoid problems, place any comment in a **#define** after the substitution string and have at least one space between the substitution string and the comment.

Pointer Conversions

When converting pointers from one type to another, be careful. You can convert a pointer to an integral type that is large enough to hold the pointer. A pointer to a data object can be cast to a pointer to a smaller type and back again without problems. When converting a pointer of one type to a pointer of another type, an alignment problem can occur when the pointer is dereferenced. Use **malloc**() to return a **char** pointer to an area suitably aligned.

Character Sets

Many machines use the ASCII character set. However, do not write code that depends on the character set. For example, do not write statements such as

```
if( (ch > 64 && ch < 91) ...
```

rather, depend on the ctype.h header file macro

```
isupper(ch) ...
```

Similarly, do not use the difference between character values as a method of converting between uppercase and lowercase characters.

```
/*  wrong  */   ch += 32;
/*  right  */   tolower(ch)
```

Symbolic constants for characters should be written in their character form, not in their integer value. For example:

```
#define '0'  /*  right  */
#define 32   /*  wrong  */
```

F

ASCII Code Character Set

ASCII CODES

rightmost 4 bits	leftmost three bits digits 000	001	010	011	100	101	110	111
0000	NUL	DEL	space	0	@	P	‘	p
0001	SOH	DC1	!	1	A	Q	a	q
0010	STX	DC2	"	2	B	R	b	r
0011	ETX	DC3	#	3	C	S	c	s
0100	EOT	DC4	$	4	D	T	d	t
0101	ENQ	NAK	%	5	E	U	e	u
0110	ACK	SYN	&	6	F	V	f	v
0111	BEL	ETB	'	7	G	W	g	w
1000	BS	CAN	(	8	H	X	h	x
1001	HT	EM	)	9	I	Y	i	y
1010	LF	SUB	*	:	J	Z	j	z
1011	VT	ESC	+	;	K	[	k	{
1100	FF	FS	,	<	L	\	l	|
1101	CR	GS	-	=	M	]	m	}
1110	SO	RS	.	>	N	^	n	~
1111	SI	US	/	?	O	_	o	DEL

G

Operator Precedence

operator	associativity
() [] . ->	left to right
! ~ - (unary minus) ++ -- &(address) * (indirection) (type) cast operator **sizeof**	right to left
* (multiply) / % (modulus)	left to right
+ - (subtract)	left to right
<< >>	left to right
< <= > >=	left to right
== !=	left to right

<table>
<tr><th>operator</th><th>associativity</th></tr>
<tr><td>& (bitwise and)</td><td>left to right</td></tr>
<tr><td>^</td><td>left to right</td></tr>
<tr><td>|</td><td>left to right</td></tr>
<tr><td>&&</td><td>left to right</td></tr>
<tr><td>||</td><td>left to right</td></tr>
<tr><td>?:</td><td>right to left</td></tr>
<tr><td>=
*= /= %= += -=
<<= >>= &= ^= |=</td><td>right to left</td></tr>
<tr><td>, comma</td><td>left to right</td></tr>
</table>

INDEX